The Film Studies
Dictionary

The Film Studies Dictionary

Steve Blandford
Principal Lecturer in Theatre and Media Drama, University of Glamorgan, UK

Barry Keith Grant
Professor of Film and Popular Culture, Brock University, St Catharines, Canada

Jim Hillier
Head of Film and Drama, University of Reading, UK

A member of the Hodder Headline Group
LONDON

First published in Great Britain in 2001
This impression reprinted in 2004 by
Arnold, a member of the Hodder Headline Group,
338 Euston Road, London NW1 3BH

http://www.arnoldpublishers.com

Distributed in the United States of America by
Oxford University Press Inc.,
198 Madison Avenue, New York, NY 10016

© 2001 Steve Blandford, Barry Keith Grant and Jim Hillier

Whilst the information in this book is believed to be true and
accurate at the date of going to press, but neither the authors nor the publisher
can accept any legal responsibility for any errors or omissions

British Library Cataloguing in Publication Data
A catalogue record for this book is available from the British Library

Library of Congress Cataloging-in-Publication Data
A catalog record for this book is available from the Library of Congress

ISBN 0 340 74190 2 (hb)
ISBN 0 340 74191 0 (pb)

6 7 8 9 10

Production Editor: Lauren McAllister
Production Controller: Martin Kerans
Cover Design: Terry Griffiths

Typeset in 10 on 12 pt Minion by Cambrian Typesetters, Frimley, Surrey
Printed and bound in India by Replika Press Pvt. Ltd.

What do you think about this book? Or any other Arnold title?
Please send your comments to feedback.arnold@hodder.co.uk

Preface

At the start of a new century it would seem that reports of the death of the cinema were very much premature. After a brief struggle with television there now seems to be something close to a mutual dependency with the lines between the two media becoming increasingly blurred. In some form or another, and feeding markets which now go way beyond film theatres, it appears that the film industry is likely to remain central to our culture for some time to come. It is therefore against this background, one of growth and renewed energy, that we offer a new reference guide to the study of film.

We do this optimistically for a number of reasons. The most obvious is that people today are interested in films in numbers that would not have been thought possible at the end of the 1950s when cinema attendances plummeted, but more importantly people are also interested in understanding what they watch and in reading about films and the film industry in numbers that have increased dramatically in the last two decades. One need only consider the amount of space that general booksellers now devote to books about film, the number of bookstands that now appear in multiplexes and the proliferation of magazines devoted to various aspects of the cinema. Of more direct and specific relevance to this publication are the number of people who now take courses either in film itself or in media which includes a substantial element of film studies. These courses are offered at all levels in the post-compulsory education sectors of all the English-speaking countries at which this publication is aimed, and it is the authors' experience of teaching across these levels that has informed the content of the book.

With rare exceptions, people enter courses of study on film with a wide variety of prior experience of the subject. Unlike, say, English or History, there is a strong possibility that they have had very little previous formal education in the area, though they may well have acquired a great deal of informal film education. With this in mind, it seems that there is a strong need for an introductory reference work that provides signposts for the specialist film language that has grown up around both the film industry itself and the academic discipline of film studies.

The division implied in the last sentence is one of the hardest to cross. There is a highly specialist language, growing every day it seems, that surrounds film as a technology and an international industry. New ways of recording, manipulating and accessing moving images are proliferating at an astonishing rate and the patterns of international ownership and control of the film industry are constantly shifting. There are a number of authoritative guides around the specialist language of the industry and some of the best, notably Ira Konigsberg's *The Complete Film Dictionary*, also attempt to cover some of the territory of academic film studies. Yet the discipline of film studies has also produced a number of excellent guides which on the whole tend to avoid, or to treat rather slightly, the language of the industry.

This book, while in no sense claiming total inclusivity, attempts to balance both aesthetic and industrial technology guided by our perceptions of the needs of the range of contemporary students. Today's students of film, including those studying courses of which film is only a part, are likely to use a highly diverse range of sources during their studies: these might include academic work in film, media and cultural studies; magazines and journals that include interviews with directors, actors and technicians; the general press with its ever increasing film coverage; television profiles and interviews; and of course the Internet. This means that there is a clear need for a guide to a range of specialist language surrounding film that can span the powerful influence of philosophy and critical theory on academic film studies as well as the basic jargon of the cinematographer or film editor. Perhaps more importantly, such a guide should constantly attempt to show how the two halves of this division have important connections for anyone serious about a clearer understanding of film as an art, an entertainment, an industry and a mass medium in the contemporary social context.

Inevitably the selection of actual terms becomes a combination of pragmatism and the kind of loose principles outlined above. If a guide is to be truly accessible to a wide range of today's students it must be affordable, a consideration which places an immediate restriction on both the length of the book and the extent of its illustrations. The biggest problem to face is how to balance the comprehensiveness of the overall book with the depth of the individual entries. This inevitably brings us back to the needs of students of film resulting in a guide that has a wide range of technical entries, but a range that might reasonably be encountered by a student of film through research rather than by somebody working in a specialized sector of the film industry itself. At the same time the entries dealing with critical theory are amongst the more complex, though it is always made clear that these are starting points, and clear signposts to more complex accounts are always provided.

One of the keenest debates we had amongst ourselves was how to handle the question of national cinemas. It is very tempting to offer an entry on each major film-producing country, but quite early on it became clear that within the confines of this book it would be unwise, if not impossible. To begin with, it was extremely difficult to eliminate certain countries rather than others and to avoid some of the obvious traps such as a bias in favour of Western cinema. Finally we settled on the inclusion of key film movements, the titles of which sometimes include the name of a country (Italian neo-realism or French new wave), but decided against entries on national cinemas *per se* on the grounds that they would inevitably be superficial. There is, however, an entry on 'national cinema' which attempts to explore some of the fundamental problems in defining what that might mean for any one nation state in the light of recent thinking in, for example, the area of post-colonial theory.

Partly because of the pragmatic reasons outlined above there are no entries of any kind on individuals. Biographical dictionaries are both extremely attractive for the general reader and potentially useful when used with due caution. In a guide of this kind, that has to constantly signpost key elements of critical thought, such an approach is potentially highly misleading. Whilst there seems to be an all-powerful popular obsession with the mythology of the director as author, a guide such as this is less concerned with the contributions of particular people than with important trends and principles. However, the names of directors are provided for every film cited so that readers will have a sense of who was associated with what development historically. In a sense this does privilege the director's position in ways that may distort their real control over the film, but it is also intended to avoid any implication of uncomplicated authorship as in the form Scorcese's *Taxi Driver* or Hitchcock's *Rear Window*.

Unsurprisingly, we considered that careful cross-referencing would be a key feature for any user of a guide of this nature. Terms that have an entry of their own are printed in small capitals the first time they appear in another entry. We have kept the number of terms that simply direct the reader to another entry to an absolute minimum, even if this means providing just a brief definition with a number or cross-references. Where a usefully related term does not appear in an entry it is referred to at the end in the form 'See also . . .'.

Bibliographical references follow the Harvard system in providing the author's surname(s), the year of publication and, if particularly relevant, page numbers of key sections. If the bibliography includes two books by a single author in the same year they are referred to by an appended letter as in Balio (1976a). Bibliographical references appear either in the body of the entry where a point is being made either through direct quotation or direct reference to another's argument, or at the end of the entry in cases where it is considered that insufficient signposting towards further reading has been given.

Finally, it is worth emphasising that any sensible guide in this area will see itself not as a provider of neat definitions, or at least only rarely in its shortest and simplest entries. Much more of the time it is a summarizer of key debates and sometimes a contributor to them. To this end we not only provide signposts to further reading, but also encourage feedback from readers who are in disagreement with the way that we try to provide clear, but inevitably simplified, versions of the more complex ideas. We have set out to provide something that is of genuine use to students and teachers of film and it of the utmost importance to us to learn whether this has been the case.

Acknowledgements

The authors would like to thank the following for their help during the writing of *The Film Studies Dictionary*: at Arnold, Lesley Riddle, for commissioning the book and remaining patient and supportive throughout, and her colleagues Lauren McAllister and Martin Key; colleagues of Steve Blandford in the Department of Theatre and Media Drama at the University of Glamorgan, and Colin Gent for various kinds of computer wizardry, and colleagues of Jim Hillier in the Department of Film and Drama at the University of Reading; Dr. Will Webster, Dean of Humanities, Brock University; Fiona, Martha and Aaron Morey, Mitch Winfield, and Sam and Beth Blandford and Genevieve Habib and Gabrielle Grant for giving time and support when it was most needed; and all those friends and students who have inspired our continuing fascination in cinema.

16mm Introduced in 1923 as an amateur GAUGE and used widely for DOCUMEN-
TARY film-making after World War II, when it proved especially useful for combat
footage. Cheaper than 35MM film and used in lighter weight cameras, in the post-war
period 16mm became the major gauge for INDUSTRIAL FILMS, TELEVISION news and
documentary, particularly in conjunction with the development of FAST FILM STOCKS,
and lightweight cameras and transistorised SYNCHRONIZED SOUND technology, as well
as for EXPERIMENTAL and INDEPENDENT film-making (for example, in the pioneering
AVANT-GARDE films of Maya Deren and Stan Brakhage). See also SUPER 16MM.
Further reading: Cook & Bernink (1999), Winston (1996)

180° rule Also known as the imaginary line or axis of action – one of the rules,
or CONVENTIONS, of CONTINUITY EDITING. Under the rule, CAMERA positions for a
SCENE should remain on the same side of the ACTION – as if an imaginary line were
drawn behind it – so that in the edited scene, the CHARACTERS (and objects) retain
their spatial positions in the frame, which would be reversed on screen if the camera
was placed on the other side of the line. Breaking the rule by crossing the line is
considered likely to disorient the spectator. Like many of the rules of the continuity
system as they evolved in CLASSICAL HOLLYWOOD CINEMA, the 180° rule is part of a
system designed to make every effort to ensure that SPECTATORS are not confused. In
practice, the 180° rule can be broken without great disorientation, whether for deliberate effect (such as confusion or a DOCUMENTARY effect) or for complex group
scenes, or simply for flexibility in shooting (famously, the climactic pursuit in
Stagecoach, dir. John Ford, 1939, breaks the rule), or as a deliberate breaking of the
rule (as in Jean-Luc Godard's films). At the same time, the rule is firmly entrenched
and normally observed in MAINSTREAM FILM and TELEVISION.
Further reading: Bordwell & Thompson (1997)

30° rule One of the rules, or CONVENTIONS, of CONTINUITY EDITING, designed to
ensure that the SPECTATOR is not disoriented or reminded that the SEQUENCE of
SHOTS is anything other than natural or logical. Under the rule, CAMERA positions for
the second of two shots of the same subject must shift by at least 30° to avoid a JUMP
CUT – considered too obvious a reminder of the artifice of EDITING conventions. Like
the 180° RULE, the 30° rule is largely observed in MAINSTREAM film-making, though
the jump cut is now a more or less acceptable transgression.

35mm The standard film GAUGE for commercial film-making since it was introduced by Thomas Edison and Eastman Kodak in 1899. 65MM and 70MM have been
used for IMAGES of extra quality, but over time 35mm has been seen to strike a good
balance between cost and the ability to project a good quality image for projection.
See ANAMORPHIC LENS, ASPECT RATIO, WIDESCREEN.

3-D Motion picture process that creates the illusion of depth in the IMAGE, so that
there seem to be distinct planes of distance from the foreground to the background
of the SPACE within the FRAME. The process works by duplicating binocular vision
with two CAMERAS photographing the same PROFILMIC event from slightly different
ANGLES. By the end of the 19th century the effect had been achieved with still
pictures and widely available in the form of the stereoscope. A number of methods
have been employed to create the 3-D effect in film dating from the 1920s. The first

FEATURE shown in 3-D was *The Power of Love* (dir. Harry K. Fairoll, 1922), done in the anaglyphic process, which required viewing through special glasses. The process was not embraced by MAINSTREAM cinema, because of its poor picture quality and tendency to cause headaches. However, in the 1950s it was employed as one strategy for luring declining audiences back into theatres. A number of features in the early 1950s were SHOT and RELEASED in 3-D, including *Bwana Devil* (dir. Arch Oboler, 1952), *House of Wax* (dir. André de Toth, 1953), *It Came from Outer Space* (dir. Jack Arnold, 1953) and *Creature from the Black Lagoon* (dir. Arnold, 1954). Many 3-D movies were of poor quality, flimsy pretexts for exploiting the process's illusion of depth; as the novelty quickly wore off, PRODUCERS abandoned the process, and some films originally made in 3-D, such as *Dial M for Murder* (dir. Alfred Hitchcock, 1954) were released 'flat,' with regular EXHIBITION. Occasionally films are still made in 3-D, such as *Andy Warhol's Frankenstein* (dir. Paul Morrissey, 1974) and *Friday the 13th Part III* (dir. Steve Miner, 1982).
Further reading: Hayes (1989)

65mm   Release PRINTS in 70MM have normally been shot on 65mm negative stock – with the additional 5mm on the print available for SOUND TRACKS. In practice, 65mm is expensive to use and increasingly 70mm prints are BLOWN UP from 35mm negatives.

70mm   The widest GAUGE of film (other than IMAX), with twice the image area of 35MM and capable of producing very clear, bright IMAGES in PROJECTION, and therefore used for RELEASE PRINTS of expensive, PRESTIGE PICTURES. 70mm has been used either for 35mm NEGATIVES blown up to 70mm, or for making prints from 65MM negatives. The wide margins on 70mm prints allows space for the MAGNETIC SOUND tracks required for stereophonic SOUND.
Further reading: Belton (1992)

8mm   The narrowest GAUGE of FILM STOCK, also known as Standard 8mm. 8mm wide, with 80 FRAMES per foot and SPROCKET HOLES on both sides (though a magnetic strip could be added for SOUND), 8mm was used largely in amateur film-making and home movies (although also by some EXPERIMENTAL film-makers, like Stan Brakhage). 8mm was generally manufactured as 16MM film, then split down the middle during processing (hence sometimes known as double eight). Largely replaced by SUPER 8MM after 1966.
Further reading: Cook & Bernink (1999)

A

A certificate, AA certificate   RATING CERTIFICATES previously used by the BRITISH BOARD OF FILM CENSORS (BBFC). The A certificate (introduced in 1913, alongside the U or UNIVERSAL CERTIFICATE) indicated that a film was to be seen only by adults, over 18, though the introduction of the X CERTIFICATE in 1951 meant that the A certificate became more permissive. The AA certificate, introduced in 1970, indicated films that could be seen only by persons over 14, while A – for Advisory – indicated films that might contain material unsuitable for children (much as the present PG rating). These categories were abolished in 1982; the present British rating system is very similar to that operating in the US.

A feature (A film, A picture) Term used to designate a high budget film, destined for first run theatres and the top half of a DOUBLE BILL, as opposed to the B MOVIE, during most of the 1930s–1950s, when most film programmes included two films (plus other material: see SHORT FILM/SUBJECT). Although A features had higher budgets and PRODUCTION VALUES, they were not necessarily higher in achievement or quality than B MOVIES.

A list In post STUDIO SYSTEM HOLLYWOOD, where the AGENT and the PACKAGE dominate, at any given time there exists a clear ranking of STARS and DIRECTORS in terms of their desirability on a project. Since qualification for the the A list – which currently includes stars like Tom Cruise and directors such as Robert Zemickis – has all to do with track record and previous association with profitable films, the list is subject to constant revision over time.

Above-the-line costs The line divides costs involved in PRE-PRODUCTION and costs involved in the shooting/POST-PRODUCTION stages of a film's production. Above-the-line costs include fees for a PROPERTY (novel, play or original SCREEN-PLAY), SCREENWRITERS, PRODUCERS, DIRECTOR and ACTORS, agreed and contracted before shooting begins. See also BELOW-THE-LINE COSTS.

Absolute film A form of ABSTRACT FILM that is entirely non-representational. Viking Eggling, Hans Richter, Oskar Fischinger and Jordan Belson are among film-makers associated with this type of EXPERIMENTAL FILM. With IMAGES that seek to visualize such intangible concepts as shape and rhythm, absolute films are often considered a form of PURE CINEMA (Sitney, 1979). Many such films are structured like MUSIC: in *Begone Dull Care* (1949) Norman McLaren animates lines and shapes directly on the filmstrip to accompany a jazz piano SOUNDTRACK. See also AVANT-GARDE FILM.

Abstract film A form of EXPERIMENTAL FILM in which individual SHOTS have formal relationships rather than representational or narrative ones. Unlike ABSOLUTE FILMS, abstract films may employ representational IMAGES, but such qualities as composition, movement, and COLOUR provide the logic of EDITING and objects are less important for what they are than for their formal qualities. Man Ray's *Retour à la raison* (1923), for example, features barely recognizable images of nails and pins placed directly on the exposed filmstrip. CITY SYMPHONY films such as *Berlin: Symphony of a Great City* (dir. Walter Ruttman, 1927) also tend to play with formal qualities of image and editing in order to duplicate the rhythms of modern urban life. See also AVANT-GARDE FILM, PURE CINEMA.
Further reading: Curtis (1971), LeGrice (1977), Peterson (1994), Rees (1999)

Academy Awards Popularly referred to as the OSCARS – the annual awards given each March to film-makers and performers by the ACADEMY OF MOTION PICTURE ARTS AND SCIENCES, founded in 1927, when the first annual ceremony took place. Awards are made on the basis of votes cast by members of the Academy, themselves prominent

members of the American film establishment. The Academy's nominations for the most prominent award categories (Best Picture, Best Director, Best Actor/Actress) are widely reported and generally occasion renewed MARKETING campaigns for the films.

Academy leader See LEADER

Academy of Motion Picture Arts and Sciences Founded in Los Angeles in 1927, its most public function is the annual awarding of the ACADEMY AWARDS or OSCARS. Arguably more important is its setting of 'Academy Standards', which govern technical aspects of film-making (such as ASPECT RATIO) and distribution throughout the industry.

Academy ratio See ASPECT RATIO

ACE American Cinema Editors, the honorary professional body for film and television EDITORS in the US; members include the initials A.C.E. after their names in a film's CREDITS.

Acetate (base) The light sensitive EMULSION which registers images onto film needs a transparent, strong, flexible base material. Originally, this was made from cellulose NITRATE, which was so highly combustible and unstable over time that many early films have been lost forever due to fire or decay. Cellulose nitrate was replaced in 1951 by cellulose acetate (or triacetate) – SAFETY FILM. Polyester, stronger and longer lasting, is often used today.

Acting The act of pretending to be another in a film, taking on a role, has reflected the history of cinema itself in the evolution of its practices, especially its relationship to critical concepts of REALISM and NATURALISM. For most cinemagoers the performer is still central to their experience of films and ACTORS' performances are judged on loosely defined notions of believability, whereas theorists since Sergei Eisenstein and Bertolt Brecht have argued for different ways of viewing performance. As Macdonald (in Hill & Church Gibson, 1998) points out, film acting has also been the subject of debates on the extent to which film actors can control the effects their screen presence produces. The KULESHOV EXPERIMENT drew attention to the way in which EDITING (and other techniques) was the real producer of meaning in a performance, making it possible, some argue, to make even inadequate performers 'look good' by purely technical means.

The most revered North American actors (particularly since World War II) have been associated with the realism exemplified by Lee Strasberg's ACTORS STUDIO, the METHOD and performers like Marlon Brando, Robert De Niro, Al Pacino and Meryl Streep, but even within the boundaries of a broad realist-naturalist tradition, performances in the the films of, say, Ken Loach, and in the CZECH NEW WAVE and ITALIAN NEO-REALIST traditions, reach extraordinary levels in their attempts to entirely submerge the performer within the role. See also ACTOR, STAR, STAR SYSTEM.
Further reading: Naremore (1988)

Action (1) The instruction given by the DIRECTOR on the SET to begin a TAKE. (2) Those events that occur on the SCREEN – that is, the movement of the subject(s) within the CAMERA'S field of vision. (3) The general PLOT or narrative of a film.

Action film, action-adventure film Loosely, any movie with fast-paced narrative featuring a lot of VIOLENCE and physical ACTION such as chases, fights, stunts, crashes and explosions, and where action dominates over dialogue and CHAR-ACTER, as in *Speed* (dir. Jan De Bont, 1994) and *The Rock* (dir. Michael Bay, 1996). The term is also sometimes used to refer collectively to those GENRES that tend to have action, such as the CRIME FILM, GANGSTER FILM, MARTIAL ARTS FILM, SPY FILM, SWASHBUCKLER and the WAR FILM, to distinguish them from more domestically oriented genres such as ROMANTIC COMEDY, MELODRAMA, and the WOMAN'S FILM, although since the 1970s and the BLOCKBUSTER success of such movies as *Raiders of the Lost Ark* (dir. Steven Spielberg, 1981) and its two SEQUELS, the action or action-adventure film has developed into a distinct genre.

In the 1970s a number of films by young American DIRECTORS, notably John Carpenter (*Assault on Precinct 13*, 1976) and Walter Hill (*The Driver*, 1978; *The Warriors*, 1979), emphasised the kinetic potential of cinema and awareness of the traditions of the classic action and ADVENTURE FILMS, particularly those of Howard Hawks. At the same time, directors from other countries were making action films revealing the influence of American genre movies. The Australian *Mad Max* (1979) and its two sequels, *The Road Warrior* (1981) and *Mad Max Beyond Thunderdome* (1985), all directed by George Miller and featuring the future American STAR Mel Gibson, invoked the ROAD MOVIE with its elaborate car chase SEQUENCES. Action movies were the speciality of Hong Kong cinema, and both John Woo (*A Better Tomorrow*, 1986; *Hard Boiled*, 1992) and Jackie Chan have successfully integrated into HOLLYWOOD.

Douglas Fairbanks was the first action STAR, in such movies as *The Mark of Zorro* (dir. Fred Niblo, 1920) and *The Black Pirate* (dir. Albert Parker, 1922), followed in the 1930s and 1940s by Errol Flynn in *Captain Blood* (dir. Michael Curtiz, 1935) and *The Adventures of Robin Hood* (dir. Curtiz, 1940), and later by Tyrone Power in the REMAKE of *The Mark of Zorro* (dir. Rouben Mamoulian, 1940) and *The Black Swan* (dir. Henry King, 1942). While action heroes such as Victor Mature and Burt Lancaster were known for their broad, muscular physiques, since *Rocky* (dir. John G. Avildsen, 1976), the criterion for action stars seems more on anatomy than acting, with contemporary action stars such as Stallone, Jean-Claude Van Damme, Steven Seagal, Chuck Norris and Bruce Willis offering impressive bodies for visual display and as the site of ordeals they must undergo in order to defeat the villain(s). The perfect embodiment of this EXCESS of physicality is former bodybuilder Arnold Schwarzenegger, in such films as *The Running Man* (dir. Paul Michael Glazer, 1987), *Predator* (dir. John McTiernan, 1987) and of course, *The Terminator* (dir. James Cameron, 1984), in which he plays an emotionless robot.

Both Tasker (1993) and Jeffords (1994) have discussed the hyerbolic MASCULINITY in these films as an expression of American IDEOLOGY regarding politics and gender, reasserting male power and privilege during and after the Reagan administration. To what extent female action heroes such as Sigourney Weaver in *Alien* (dir. Ridley Scott, 1979) and its sequels, Linda Hamilton in *Terminator 2: Judgment Day* (dir. Cameron, 1991) and Geena Davis in *The Long Kiss Goodnight* (dir. Renny Harlin, 1996) are progressive representations of women in the action film or merely contained within a masculine sensibility, has been a matter of considerable debate.

Further reading: Cook & Bernink (1999), Holmlund in Cohan & Hark (1993), Willis (1998)

Actor The term actor has raised particular questions for film, primarily because of the STAR SYSTEM. The actor in MAINSTREAM CINEMA is rarely a simple performer of a role, but rather a complex set of meanings produced from a range of sources (Dyer, 1979): the actor as TEXT in turn interacts with the meanings generated by a specific role within a specific film. There have been radically different traditions and approaches to the idea of the screen actor and perceptions of the status of screen acting have changed several times. Many early films did not use professionals actors, believing actors were simply there to be photographed, like the rest of the MISE-EN-SCÈNE. Actors also suffered from the low cultural status of film, with screen acting always compared unfavourably to that in the theatre. Only in the late SILENT era was there any substantial erosion of this view.

The dominant Western serious acting tradition comes largely from Konstantin Stanislavski's ideas on training for the theatre and revisions of his methods such as THE METHOD adopted by THE ACTORS STUDIO in the 1940s and 1950s, whose inheritance has been highly influential on screen actors since. Apart from its espousal of a technique heavily dependant on interior emotional recall, The Actors Studio encouraged a view of actors as active agents in the creation of film, a partial challenge to an AUTEURIST view that relegates the actor to the status of a DIRECTOR'S puppet. The actor as creator takes on another dimension in work involving extensive use of improvisation, such as the work of John Cassavetes in the US and Mike Leigh in the UK.

Although views of the status of screen actors within the production process still vary widely, there is now more widespread agreement about its unique demands. The handling of the most searching CLOSE-UP and the need to hold character CONTINU-ITY when shooting out of sequence have helped give screen actors some parity with those in theatre, but there are still marked differences between the winners of best actor awards at major European FESTIVALS and the recipients of ACADEMY AWARDS. In recent years the CANNES FILM FESTIVAL has honoured lesser-known British actors such as Peter Mullan for *My Name is Joe* (dir. Ken Loach, 1998) and Kathy Burke for *Nil By Mouth* (dir. Gary Oldman, 1997), performances which remain largely unknown in HOLLYWOOD.

Actors Studio Founded in 1947 in New York by Elia Kazan and others, The Actors Studio became arguably the single most important influence on screen ACTING, principally associated with THE METHOD, a philosophy of teaching acting originating in the work of Konstantin Stanislavski and predominantly about the achievement of NATURALISM in performance. Lee Strasberg became the director of the studio in 1948 and remains the individual most commonly linked to its aims.

ACTT (Association of Cinematograph, Television and Allied Technicians) Founded 1931 (as ACT, the Association of Cine-Technicians, its name changing to ACTT in 1956), the British trade UNION representing film, and later TELEVISION, technicians in negotiations with PRODUCERS and others, with a long history, especially during the 1930s and the 1960s and 1970s, of left-wing political activity. Uniquely , the ACTT had its own production unit, ACT Films. In 1991, ACTT merged with BETA (the Broadcasting and Entertainment Trade Alliance, itself the product of a 1989 merger between ABS, the Association of Broadcasting Staff – originally the BRITISH BROADCASTING COMPANY's staff association – and NATTKE, the National Association of Theatrical, Television and Kine Employees, established in the 1890s as a union for theatre and MUSIC HALL employees). The result of the merger was the formation of BECTU (Broadcasting Entertainment Cinematograph and Theatre Union) which is now the major union representing craft workers in the film, television and theatre industries in the UK.

Actualité, actuality As well as its general use in English to mean reality, a very specific film term: in very EARLY CINEMA an actuality was a SHORT FILM of some everyday subject, part of a larger film programme – the LUMIÈRE PROGRAMME consisted of actualités. Although actuality has been seen as an early form of DOCU-MENTARY FILM, John Grierson, the influential documentary PRODUCER, DIRECTOR and commentator, writing in the 1930s (*The First Principles of Documentary*, Grierson, 1966) famously describes documentary as 'the creative interpretation of actuality', distinguishing between the raw material of actuality and the creative process by which it becomes documentary.
Further reading: Winston (1995)

Adult film See PORNOGRAPHY.

Adventure film Loosely, movies that involve CHARACTERS thrust out of their quotidian existence into a world of danger, excitement and exoticism, often with characters who are MYTHIC, like Tarzan, James Bond, or Indiana Jones. The adventure film is a loose amalgam of GENRES that includes SWASHBUCKLERS, jungle movies and many of the popular SERIALS of the STUDIO era. Although it oftens overlap with ACTION FILMS (the action-adventure film), in adventure the narrative focus may be as much spiritual as physical, as in *Lord Jim* (dir. Richard Brooks, 1965) or *Seven Years in Tibet* (dir. Jean-Jacques Annaud, 1997). Nevertheless, the NARRATIVES of such films usually involve male STARS in a fast-paced story featuring fights, chases and danger-ous stunts. Adventure films are often concerned with political IDEOLOGY, displaced into the past, as in, for example, *The Adventures of Robin Hood* (dir. Michael Curtiz, 1938) and *The Man in the Iron Mask* (dir. James Whale, 1939): heroes often find their loyalty torn between the good State and the bad king or ship's captain. Brian Taves (1993, p. 4) argues that 'the valiant fight for freedom and a just form of government, set in exotic locales and the historical past ... is the central theme of adventure', which he divides into five types: swashbuckler, pirate, sea, empire, and fortune hunter stories. In the 1980s, Steven Spielberg's Indiana Jones movies (*Raiders of the Lost Ark*, 1981; *Indiana Jones and the Temple of Doom*, 1984; *Indiana Jones and the Last Crusade*, 1989) – HOMAGES to and PASTICHES of classic adventure films – achieved wide popularity and inspired both a CYCLE of new tongue-in-cheek adventure movies such as *Romancing the Stone* (dir. Robert Zemeckis, 1984) and the develop-ment of the contemporary ACTION FILM. See also COSTUME DRAMA.
Further reading: Cawelti (1976), Gehring (1988), Landy (1991a), Richards (1977), Slotkin (1990)

Advertising The strength of the advertising campaign that distributors and exhibitors mount for any given film can be the primary factor behind its success or failure. Konigsberg (1997) points to the impact of TELEVISION advertising: like all products involving large financial investment, major film releases are almost automatically advertised on television, the cost of which necessitates widespread SATURATION RELEASE to maximise the advertising's impact, so that first-run houses and staged releases are becoming much rarer, inducing a financial caution with films withdrawn quickly if they fail to make a healthy BOX-OFFICE return in their first week. A film needs, in the words of Turner (1999), to 'specify its audience', and a major means is its advertising campaign. Advertising campaigns can go wrong: Turner cites the misrepresentation of *The Chant of Jimmy Blacksmith* (dir. Fred Schepisi, 1978), a relatively sensitive, liberal story focusing on Australia's problematic race-relations history, whose advertising campaign chose to focus on the brutal murder at the heart of the film's NARRATIVE – featuring an axe dripping with blood on all campaign print material – identifying the film with the HORROR GENRE and leading to its failing to find its audience.

Advertising today goes far beyond straightforward advertisements. Children's films in particular are likely to feature widespread MARKETING campaigns embracing a range of ways in which the film's name and CHARACTERS enter public consciousness, such as the relationship between MacDonald's fast-food outlets and the release of new films by the WALT DISNEY Corporation. MERCHANDISING represents a key element in the advertising strategy of big-budget films. Films thus form a symbiotic relationship with a range of other products which cross-promote each other. A specialized form of this is direct PRODUCT PLACEMENT in films. As well as the general shift towards more frequent, expensive television campaigns – though partly determined by the nature and budget of the film – there are signs that the Internet is being taken seriously as a medium: many films now offer websites, complete with TRAILERS and strong identifying IMAGES. However, campaigns are still heavily dependent on more conventional forms of print media, poster campaigns, commercial radio advertising and TRAILERS.

Aerial shot A SHOT taken from an aeroplane or helicopter. Normally such shots function as a sweeping ESTABLISHING SHOT, the extreme distance of such shots and the CAMERA MOVEMENT taking a lofty, possibly detached perspective, as in the opening shots of *American Beauty* (dir. Sam Mendes, 1999).

AFI (American Film Institute) Founded in 1967, funded primarily by the National Endowment for the Arts (plus funding from the film and TELEVISION industries) and based in Washington. D.C., with the objective of 'preserving the heritage and advancing the art of film in America' (compare the BRITISH FILM INSTITUTE). The AFI preserves films, offers training in film-making and supports, promotes and co-ordinates activities relating to the moving IMAGE, presenting an annual Life Achievement Award. The AFI's Center for Advanced Film and Television Studies in Los Angeles, originally intended to promote both critical work and film training, now concentrates on training students in direction and other production skills – beneficiaries have included directors David Lynch, Tim Hunter, Terrence Malick and Kathryn Bigelow.

African American film See BLACK FILM.

Agency, agent More properly, talent agency/agent. Like literary agents, talent agents represent the interests of ACTORS and DIRECTORS (and SCREENWRITERS,

PRODUCERS, CINEMATOGRAPHERS etc.). Agents seek work for clients and strike deals on financial terms and conditions in return for a percentage of their clients' earnings (typically 10 per cent). Major agencies in the movie business include CAA (Creative Artists Agency), ICM (International Creative Management) and the William Morris Agency. Although agents often played an important role during the STUDIO SYSTEM era, their importance has grown since the end of the CONTRACT SYSTEM. Agencies now perform many roles previously performed by the studios, nurturing careers and putting together PACKAGES, typically involving PROPERTIES, writers, producers, directors and STARS. Arguably, since the 1970s the agencies have become the driving force in Hollywood film-making, wielding more power than the studios: the powerful founder and head of CAA, Michael Ovitz, for example, masterminded Matsushita's purchase of MCA UNIVERSAL in 1990, was briefly head of WALT DISNEY, and during the 1990s advised major studios on links with telephone companies, whose importance lay in telephone lines for carrying programming.

Aleatory technique   The incorporation into the artistic process of the element of chance – in film ACTION and SOUND that were neither planned nor scripted but are allowed to remain in the final film. Such images, though fortuitous, may nonetheless be expressive. In many early films Jean-Luc Godard employed improvisational interview techniques with his actors, questioning the very distinction between ACTING and being, fiction and DOCUMENTARY, in the cinema, and some of Andy Warhol's films also involve chance occurrences. Aleatory techniques are commonly used in the CINÉMA VÉRITÉ and DIRECT CINEMA forms of documentary, to preserve the integrity of PROFILMIC events. See also OBSERVATIONAL CINEMA.

Alienation effect   Common English translation of playwright and theorist Bertolt Brecht's influential concept of *Verfremdungseffekt* or *V-effekt,* developed particularly in *A Short Organum for the Theatre* (1949, in Brecht, 1964), though 'distancing effect' better expresses Brecht's idea. See also BRECHTIAN, DISTANCIATION.

Allied Artists Pictures Corporation   American film production company, originally a subsidiary of MONOGRAM Pictures, founded in 1946 as Allied Artists Productions. After joining with Monogram in 1953, Allied Artists produced a series of SCIENCE FICTION movies, including *Invasion of the Body Snatchers* (dir. Don Siegel, 1956). During the 1970s the company concentrated more on TELEVISION production, ceasing production by 1980.

Alternative film   Alternative to what? The clearest answer is to MAINSTREAM FILM as defined by HOLLYWOOD and its imitators. Alternative films depart from classical Hollywood traditions in their approach to NARRATIVE and film language, with resulting difference in IDEOLOGY. If CLASSICAL NARRATIVE offers a form of REALISM, emphasizing clarity, linear PLOT structures and a high degree of CLOSURE, then alternative film seeks to disrupt such CONVENTIONS. In terms of narrative the key is ambiguity: if mainstream film satisfies us with explanations, alternative film often asks that we accept certain kinds of experience as partially unknowable, at the basic level of narrative asking far more of AUDIENCES than the mainstream. More obvious for spectators used only to mainstream film is alternative film's tendency to use cinematic CODES and languages in radically new ways, from EDITING devices such as the

JUMP-CUT by Jean-Luc Godard and others, to the appropriation and intensification of conventional forms in work by David Lynch like *Blue Velvet* (1986). A primary effect of new ways of employing cinematic languages has been to disrupt CONTINU-ITY – the hallmark of the mainstream Hollywood tradition – and draw attention to the processes of film-making, making much alternative practice REFLEXIVE. IDEO-LOGICALLY, alternative cinema not only explores marginalized political positions, but in Godard's phrase tries to make 'political films politically' (Hayward, 1996, p. 22), laying bare the realism of dominant cinema as not natural, but rather as highly constructed within the context of a particular dominant ideological position.

Mainstream DISTRIBUTION and EXHIBITION systems help to create misleading notions of alternative – films in languages other than English, for example, face great difficulties in gaining widespread distribution in North America and the UK. SUB-TITLES on a film sometimes seems enough to define it as alternative, whereas European films can be highly conventional in their narrative strategies and use of film language. See also AVANT-GARDE, COUNTER CINEMA.

Further reading: Bordwell & Thompson (1997)

Ambient light   The general, environmental light in a SCENE, emanating from a variety of sources and aspiring to provide a sense of natural light. The term can also be used for the low level of LIGHTING that remains in a cinema after the house lights have been turned off and the film is being projected. See also AMBIENT SOUND.

Ambient sound   The environmental or atmospheric noise that contributes a natural or authentic background to, say, a dialogue scene. Though its presence is usually not noticed, its deliberate absence can remind us of the constructed nature of IMAGE and sound, as when Jean-Luc Godard switches off the background sound in *Vivre sa vie* (1962). Ambient sound – or 'ambient air' – may be recorded during shooting, using a MICROPHONE separate from that recording the dialogue, or, more often, separately and later MIXED into the scene's SOUNDTRACK. See also AMBIENT LIGHT.

American International Pictures (AIP)   American film distribution/ production company specializing in B MOVIES, TEENPICS and EXPLOITATION FILMS, founded in 1954 by James H. Nicholson and Samuel Z. Arkoff, one of the independent companies that showed the way in the 1950s towards targeting market segments. AIP initially concentrated on HORROR FILMS and SCIENCE FICTION, made by DIRECTORS like Roger Corman, some designed to fill the bottom half of DOUBLE BILLS, then moving into production and eventually making movies with higher PRODUCTION VALUES, beginning in 1960 with Corman's *House of Usher*, a loose adaptation of Edgar Allan Poe's short story starring Vincent Price and shot in COLOUR and CinemaScope. Corman made several other Poe adaptations with Price for AIP, including *The Masque of the Red Death* (1964), with CINEMATOGRAPHY by British CULT director Nicolas Roeg. AIP also popularized a CYCLE of beach movies beginning in 1963 with *Beach Party* (dir. William Asher), but its fortunes declined after Corman's departure and it was eventually subsumed by ORION Pictures Corporation.

Further reading: Doherty (1988), McCarthy & Flynn (1975)

American Mutoscope and Biograph   See BIOGRAPH.

American shot See PLAN AMÉRICAIN.

Analogue A technology for recording and transmitting pictures and SOUND, deriving from the signal used for recording or transmission being 'analogous' to the actual light or sound waves given off by the subject. Analogue is currently being overtaken by DIGITAL technology, whose sound and IMAGES are of superior quality and, recorded digitally, are less liable to deteriorate over time.

Anamorphic lens An anamorphic lens on a CAMERA compresses, or squeezes, the width of a WIDESCREEN image to about half its size to fit the standard 35MM film FRAME. An anamorphic lens on a projector expands, or 'unsqueezes', to project a widescreen image with an ASPECT RATIO of 2.35:1 (instead of the standard 1.33:1). Originally developed by Frenchman Henri Chrétien during World War I for military purposes, rights to the system were bought by TWENTIETH CENTURY-FOX in 1952 and developed commercially as CINEMASCOPE, first used for *The Robe* (dir Henry Koster, 1953). The great advantage of the anamorphic system over earlier widescreen systems using more than one camera or special equipment was that it could be used with normal 35mm cameras and PROJECTORS, needing only a special LENS. Other STUDIOS developed their own anamorphic or 'scope' systems. See also PANAVISION. Further reading: Belton (1992), Gomery (1992)

Anarchic comedy See COMEDY.

Ancillary rights The primary destination for most commercial FEATURE films remains EXHIBITION in cinemas. Ancillary rights allow the exploitation of films in other markets, particularly other means of exhibition or DISTRIBUTION, mainly HOME VIDEO and SATELLITE, CABLE and network TELEVISION, and rights to related commercial activity such as music recording, television SPIN-OFFS, NOVELIZATION, computer games and MERCHANDISING such as toys and clothes. Since the BLOCKBUSTER era initiated by *Jaws* (dir. Steven Spielberg, 1975) and *Star Wars* (dir. George Lucas, 1977), ancillary rights have become increasingly important in the MARKETING and profit potential of major HOLLYWOOD films; profits from ancillaries now often exceed those from THEATRICAL exhibition.

Angle See CAMERA ANGLE.

Animal comedy See COMEDY.

Animation In its purest definition, animation is simply an exaggerated version of the practice of all film-making. Literally it gives life (or the illusion of life) to REPRESENTATIONS of objects, people and animals by recording them on film and then projecting them at such a speed as to give a sense of real movement. Differences between branches of animation lie in the choice of medium for the originals to be photographed: drawings, cut-outs, models, puppets or real objects.
　　Animation has changed fundamentally (and is still changing) through the application of various computer technologies. Computer generated IMAGES have created not only a separate branch of animation but also profoundly affected the way that other kinds of animation work. The traditional method of producing animated

CARTOONS was labour intensive and very expensive, involving the production of thousands of extremely precise individual drawings for even a SHORT FILM: 'For ten minutes of animation, 14,400 individual drawings or set-ups are theoretically necessary' (Konigsberg, 1997, p. 14). Computer-based methods of reproducing and 'moving' drawings have radically altered the economics of animation and made feature-length cartoons not only viable, but highly profitable, especially given the enormous international youth market and range of MERCHANDISING TIE-INS. Animation composed entirely of computer-generated images has now graduated from being an important component within films to being the medium for feature length productions, the two most commercially successful examples of which have both been produced by WALT DISNEY – *Toy Story* (dir. John Lasseter, 1995) and *A Bug's Life* (dir. John Lasseter, 1998).

Whilst the PRODUCTION VALUES of Disney's recent work are predictably very high, arguably they are directed towards a rather unambitious view of the potential of animation. As Paul Wells puts it, Disney animation 'for all its personality and comic energy, conforms to a certain kind of reality, which in turn conforms to a dominant IDEOLOGICAL position' (Nelmes 1996, p. 194). By contrast, a wide-range of animation practices, for example the work of the Czech SURREALIST Jan Svankmajer, both challenge Disney's orthodoxy and give a sense of animation's unique possibilities.

Many see an important part of animation's future bound up with other kinds of feature production, as computer-generated images play greater parts in the production of live-action features. The dinosaurs in *Jurassic Park* (dir. Steven Spielberg, 1992) are probably the best-known example of this kind of work, but it is becoming ever more widespread as costs come down. See also COMPUTER ANIMATION.

Anthology film A FEATURE-length film comprised of excerpts from other, longer films or of complete SHORT FILMS or independent episodes. *That's Entertainment* (dir. Jack Haley, Jr., 1974), which contains famous scenes from approximately one hundred classic MGM MUSICALS, is an example of the former, while *Bodybags* (1993), featuring two horror tales directed by John Carpenter and one by Tobe Hooper, and *Paris vu Par* (1964), containing six episodes, each focusing on a different section of Paris and each made by a different FRENCH NEW WAVE DIRECTOR, are instances of the latter type.

Anthology Film Archives (AFA) Organization established by EXPERIMEN-TAL FILM-MAKER and critic Jonas Mekas in New York City in 1970, the Anthology Film Archives collects, promotes and hosts screenings of experimental and AVANT-GARDE cinema.

Anti-trust One of the characteristics of capitalist societies is that while encouraging business success, they also legislate against 'trust' practices, monopolistic collaboration between companies to defeat competition. The US Supreme Court has several times invoked anti-trust legislation against the movie industry, the best known being the United States vs. PARAMOUNT Pictures suit (instituted 1938, concluded in the PARAMOUNT DECISION, 1948), in which the BIG 5 MAJOR STUDIOS were accused of conspiring to restrain trade in the movie industry, but anti-trust suits were also brought against the MOTION PICTURE PATENTS COMPANY (MPPC), declared illegal in 1915, and against TECHNICOLOR, forced to release its basic patents in 1950. See GATT.

AOL Time Warner See WARNER BROS.

Aperture The LENS aperture (i.e. opening) regulates – via the diaphragm – the amount of light passing through the LENS to the light sensitive FILM STOCK, while in shooting and PROJECTION the CAMERA or projector aperture (or gate) determines the area of the FRAME to be exposed or projected.

Apparatus In film theory, the physical attributes – from the film strip itself to the PROJECTOR to the theatre space in which it is projected – that constitute the medium of cinema, as well as the relation between these mechanisms and the viewing experience. Further, it refers to the manner in which, as Jean-Louis Baudry (1970, in Rosen, 1986) argues, the viewer is constructed by the CODES and CONVENTIONS of CLASSICAL HOLLYWOOD CINEMA as a transcendent SUBJECT carried along effortlessly through the NARRATIVE by the CAMERA and EDITING, in which sense apparatus theory is concerned with how cinema provides a fantasy of plenitude and wholeness for the spectator and a structured way of looking at films. As Christian Metz (1975, p. 2) puts it, 'The cinematic institution is not just the cinema industry . . . it is also the mental machinery – another industry – which spectators "accustomed to the cinema" have internalised historically and which has adapted them to the consumption of films.'
Further reading: Cha (1981), De Lauretis & Heath (1980)

Arbeiterfilm See NEW GERMAN CINEMA.

Arc lamp, arc light High intensity lamp which produces light from the electronic flow between two electrical poles. The carbon arc light – with electrodes made from carbon – has been used widely in both STUDIO and LOCATION work, especially for its ability to simulate sunlight.

Archetype A basic CHARACTER type or ACTION that has appeared repeatedly in the history of NARRATIVE art, whether literature, drama or film. The descent MYTH, for example, in which a hero must journey to the underworld and wrestle with his dark forces, is an archetypal event that informs works ranging from the Greek myth of Orpheus to *The Searchers* (dir. John Ford, 1956), *Apocalypse Now* (dir. Francis Ford Coppola, 1979) and *Desperately Seeking Susan* (dir. Susan Seidelman, 1985).
Further reading: Frye (1957)

Archival film or footage DOCUMENTARY or NEWSREEL footage, which can be incorporated into new films or TELEVISION programmes. See also FOUND FOOTAGE, STOCK SHOT.

Archives Film archives collect and preserve films (and related material such as STILLS, posters and scripts) for future use and reference. It took many years for many people to think of films as something worth collecting and preserving, and film also poses special problems for archiving: most commercial films were released on highly flammable NITRATE STOCK and the task of copying such material on to SAFETY FILM remains a large one; recently, a problem has emerged with the rapid fading of COLOUR films made in the EASTMANCOLOR process. Archives must also try to balance the demands of preservation and the demands of access. Though the future of archival activities may lie in digitization, it will be a long and costly process to convert existing material. MAJOR STUDIOS and major broadcasting companies have their own archives, especially now that the value of old films has become clear, and some companies sell archival film to television and film production companies. Many countries now have national archives to preserve the film heritage of their own and other nations and the international archives federation FIAF plays an important role. See also CINÉMATHÈQUE FRANÇAISE, NATIONAL FILM ARCHIVE.

Arriflex Brand name of motion picture CAMERAS made by the Arriflex Corporation of Germany. Lightweight and relatively compact, Arriflex cameras were popular with FRENCH NEW WAVE, CINÉMA VÉRITÉ and DIRECT CINEMA film-makers because of their versatility for shooting on LOCATION, and consequently were significant in the historical development of DOCUMENTARY film.

Art cinema A term related to ALTERNATIVE cinema, but with more specific CONNOTATIONS of cultural status, since calling a piece of work 'art' carries a particular set of meanings. The term originated in cinema's earliest battles to be taken seriously – with the French production company FILM D'ART, founded 1908, producing largely film recordings of prestigious theatre events. To an extent the term is relative: for UK and US audiences much European cinema is associated with 'art', and key movements of the post-World War II period form the cornerstones of what most people would term art cinema – FRENCH NEW WAVE, NEW GERMAN CINEMA and Italian NEOREALISM. However, there are strong traditions of art cinema in all the major English-speaking countries, though their films may be associated less with any NATIONAL CINEMA movement than with particular interest groups or individuals. Art cinema is sometimes automatically associated with AUTEURISM – 'art' as personal expression – but this would ignore, for example, the work emerging from the 1980s UK workshop movement under the nurturing influence of CHANNEL 4, much of which was done in companies formed and run as collectives. It is perhaps more useful to think of art cinema as striving for a distinctive voice either in terms of its overt political position or, more commonly, through its foregrounding of cinematic forms and CONVENTIONS.

For some the term art cinema is close to being archaic in a postmodern world where categorization of art forms has both become more difficult and fallen into critical disrepute. However, contemporary patterns of DISTRIBUTION and EXHIBITION tend to reinforce the boundaries that the term exemplifies: while cinema AUDIENCES continue to rise after the low point of the 1970s, they do so through large numbers of people watching an increasingly narrow range of commercial films. See also REPERTORY CINEMA. Further reading: Bordwell (1985), Neale (1981)

Art direction The definition of art direction in the making of a film depends to some extent on the scale of the production. On larger budget films the art director's role is to make sure that the PRODUCTION DESIGNER's ideas are fully realized in terms of SETS; on smaller scale work, the roles of art director and production designer are often merged. On most FEATURE FILMS the art director heads an art department with a range of craft skills from model-builders to interior designers, working closely with other design departments like COSTUME and make-up towards an overall vision of the film's 'look'.

Art house A cinema that specializes in showing art films or non-MAINSTREAM CINEMA.

ASA (standard or number) A numerical rating (e.g. 200 ASA, or 400 ASA) of the sensitivity of film EMULSION to light as determined by the American Standards Association (ASA), now the American National Standards Institute (hence ratings now sometimes given as ANSI rather than ASA). The ratings are popularly seen as a measure of FILM SPEED. Other internationally agreed measuring codes are DIN – Deutsche Industrie Norm – and ISO – International Standards Organization.

ASC The American Society of Cinematographers, the professional body of film and TELEVISION directors of photography. Membership – generally about 200 – is by invitation and A.S.C. is commonly used after the names of DIRECTORS OF PHOTOG-RAPHY in a film's CREDITS. The Society publishes a professional handbook and a monthly journal, *American Cinematographer*, often of great interest to non-professionals or specialists.

Aspect ratio The ratio of width to height of the film IMAGE – on film and in PROJECTION. The ratio of 1.33: 1 pioneered by Thomas Edison persisted internationally as a norm throughout the era of SILENT CINEMA. To maintain this ratio – generally accepted as classical and pleasing – when the addition of a SOUNDTRACK on the edge of the 35mm film strip made the image almost square, the ACADEMY OF MOTION PICTURE ARTS AND SCIENCES introduced in 1932 a MASKING of the top and bottom of the FRAME to re-establish the 1.33:1 ratio, which became known as the Academy ratio (or Academy aperture) – the international standard for shooting and exhibiting films. From the 1950s, WIDESCREEN innovations introduced different ratios.

Assembly, assembly edit The first stage in the EDITING of a film, in which unwanted material is eliminated and the usable or best TAKES are edited and arranged into approximately the intended final length and shape of the film. See also FINAL CUT, FINE CUT, ROUGH CUT.

Assistant director The role of the assistant director varies enormously from film to film. Most FEATURE FILMS have at least a second assistant director and probably a third, plus trainees. Many of the tasks performed by the assistant are logistical: scheduling shooting, arranging appropriate personnel to be in the right place at the right time and making sure the SET is kept well-organized, ready for the next TAKE. They may also 'direct' in the sense of organizing the roles of EXTRAS and crowds within a SCENE or rehearse performers.

Asynchronous sound Term most generally used for SOUND belonging to a particular SCENE which is heard while the IMAGES of the previous scene are still on screen, or which continue over a following scene. The term can also apply to DIEGETIC sound whose source cannot be seen on screen and to sound unintentionally out of SYNC with the IMAGE track. After the coming of sound film Sergei Eisenstein and others argued for asynchronous or nonsynchronous sound as an essential counterpoint to the image, to oppose the growing tyranny of synchronized sound TALKIES.

Audience The strong interest in audiences since the earliest days of film THEORY and CRITICISM stems in part from the cinema's status as a genuine mass medium with what some saw as a sinister power to influence, producing numerous alarmist studies based on 'hypodermic-needle' models of the ways audiences are influenced by what they see (see, Watson & Hill, 2000, p. 142). Simplistic notions of what film can do have never entirely disappeared from the popular consciousness, as evidenced by controversies surrounding films like Oliver Stone's *Natural Born Killers* (1995) or by the (partially successful) calls for increased CENSORSHIP of VIDEOS in the UK following the murder of James Bulger by two ten year-old boys who had allegedly watched films depicting similar acts.

As film studies grew in the 1960s, the audience was at first largely ignored by critics anxious to establish the medium's seriousness by treating film TEXTS as AUTEUR-produced, while the energies of social scientists interested in audiences had shifted to TELEVISION. The 1970s, though, saw not only a rapid growth in film as an academic discipline, but also its incorporation of influences from disciplines such as philosophy, sociology and PSYCHOANALYSIS and via these influences grew an interest in studying the audience. Although initially interest focused on what films did to audiences, there was a growing awareness that while films may seek to 'position' audiences, audiences had active, even if constrained, responses.

FEMINIST FILM THEORY had the greatest impact on the way film audiences were considered during the key 1970s, drawing heavily on ideas from psychoanalysis in general and Jacques Lacan in particular, with the focus not on audiences in the sense of a mass, but rather the individual SUBJECT or spectator. Since the 1980s there has been a less exclusively text-centred approach to audiences and spectators with the rise of, for example, ethnographically based studies of actual audiences (as opposed to purely theoretical ones). Such studies have been more widespread for TELEVISION (see, for example, Ang, 1985), but have also been influential in film.

Additionally, since the film industry depends on successfully targeting the maximum possible audience, it expends a great deal of energy on market research techniques designed to monitor the changing patterns of who cinema-goers are and what they want.

Further reading: Jenkins in Gledhill & Williams (2000), Mayne (1993)

Aura Term used by German cultural theorist Walter Benjamin in his influential 1936 essay, *The Work of Art in the Age of Mechanical Reproduction* (Benjamin, 1968) to describe the singularity and the direct experience of a work of art. In the era of mass media, popular art, including cinema, is pervasive and easily accessible and thus lacks aura. As TEXT, films are neither unique (since multiple PRINTS or VIDEOcassettes circulate simultaneously) nor intimate (since they are viewed in the social context of the theatre).

Auteur, auteurism, auteur theory An auteur (French for author) is, usually, a DIRECTOR whose work is characterized by distinctive thematic concerns and stylistic traits discernible across a number of films. True auteurs elevate style to a thematic level and stamp each work with their personality. Auteur CRITICISM looks at films as the personal expression of the director, interpreting individual movies in the context of the film-maker's entire *oeuvre*, assuming that the major creative decisions on a film are the responsibility of the director – although certain PRODUCERS, SCREENWRITERS, ACTORS and even CINEMATOGRAPHERS have also been discussed as auteurs. Although controversial initially, and attacked later for its excessive romanticism, the auteur concept has been and remains a crucial development in film THEORY and criticism, shifting attention away from sociological and literary analyses of films' narrative content to MISE-EN-SCÈNE and other aspects of style specific to film art.

Auteurism developed in the 1950s among critics writing for the French journal CAHIERS DU CINÉMA. François Truffaut's January, 1954 polemical article, *Une certaine tendance du cinéma français* (*A Certain Tendency of the French Cinema*) (in Nichols, 1976) attacked the 'tradition of quality' in French cinema and called for a *cinéma d'auteurs*, with creative responsibility shifting from screenwriters to directors. Truffaut's *politique des auteurs* became a rallying point for many *Cahiers* critics, who considered Alfred Hitchcock, Nicholas Ray, Samuel Fuller, Budd Boetticher, Anthony Mann, Howard Hawks and other American directors as artists on the same level as European film-makers such as Ingmar Bergman and Jean Renoir.

In Britain in the late 1940s Lindsay Anderson and others wrote about films as the artistic expression of the director in the magazine *Sequence*, which ceased publication in 1950. The first issue of MOVIE, May, 1962, revealed a similar preference to that of *Cahiers* for the American cinema and was in its own way as confrontational as Truffaut's article, offering 'the editorial board's taste in directors' (Cameron, 1972), a PANTHEON in chart form. For *Movie*, only Hawks and Hitchcock were in the 'great' category; Joseph Losey, a transplanted American, made the second rank of 'brilliant,' but most British directors were either merely 'competent' or 'ambitious' or lumped together in 'the rest.' *Movie*, however – publishing auteur criticism by V.F. Perkins, Ian Cameron, Robin Wood and others – was somewhat more sober than *Cahiers*, attempting to combine auteur analysis with a humanist tradition associated with the literary critic F.R. Leavis.

In the US, Andrew Sarris published *Notes on the Auteur Theory in 1962* in FILM CULTURE, translating Truffaut's *politique des auteurs* as 'the auteur theory' and attempting to lay a theoretical foundation by establishing three criteria any director must meet to be an auteur: technical competence, personal style and interior meaning. Despite not wishing to seem 'unduly mystical,' Sarris failed to explain interior meaning other than to suggest that it arises from a 'tension between the director's personality and his material' (Sarris in Braudy & Cohen, 1999, pp. 516–17). Sarris's 1968 book *The American Cinema* ranks and briefly discusses virtually every American director, as well as foreign directors who worked in Hollywood, within evaluative categories reminiscent of *Movie*.

The initial resistance to auteurism arose partly from the excesses of its practitioners. Chabrol, for example, argued that the smaller a film's theme, the more able the auteur to express his personality ('the smaller the theme is, the more one can give it a big treatment') (Chabrol, 1959, in Graham, 1968, p. 77). Similarly, Sarris's commitment to American directors led him to claim that a director such as George Cukor has a more developed style than an ART CINEMA film-maker like Ingmar Bergman because, unlike Bergman, Cukor had to work with someone else's scripts (Sarris, 1962, in Braudy & Cohen, 1999, p. 516). In his own article on the *politique des auteurs*, *Cahiers* editor André Bazin cautioned that auteurism risked becoming a cult of personality, since it seemed that any director designated as an auteur was incapable of making a bad movie. Bazin concluded by asking, in opposition to Chabrol, the rhetorical question, 'Auteur yes, but what of?' (Bazin, 1957 in Graham, 1968, p. 155). In its zeal to find personal expression in the cinema, classic auteurism often neglected to evaluate the specific nature of a given director's vision. It seemed sufficient simply to show and appreciate the 'vision' in the films of Raoul Walsh or Frank Tashlin. The reputations of certain directors – most notably, Fred Zinnemann and John Huston (ranked by Sarris as 'less than meets the eye') – suffered seriously because they seemed to disappear within their projects rather than impose a discernible stylistic consistency from film to film.

Romantic and apolitical, auteurism came under attack in the 1970s and 1980s as film theory became more concerned with IDEOLOGY. In Peter Wollen's famous formulation, critics now distinguished between Howard Hawks (biological author) and 'Howard Hawks' (a critical construct that unites a series of texts) (Wollen, 1998). As John Caughie notes, the author moves from 'standing behind the text as a source [to become] a term in the process of reading and spectating' (Caughie, 1981). Geoffrey Nowell-Smith argued that the critic should focus not on authorial vision, but 'uncover behind the superficial contrasts of subject and treatment a structural hard core of basic and often recondite motifs' (Nowell-Smith, 1973). Influenced by theories of PSYCHOANALYSIS, MARXISM and STRUCTURALISM, critics now saw the author's personality as itself shaped by ideology and merely one of numerous CODES informing a given TEXT. In France, in the wake of the events of May, 1968, the newly politicized editorial board of *Cahiers du Cinéma* took a position opposed to classic auteurism, with a collectively written analysis of *Young Mr. Lincoln* (dir. John Ford, 1939), showing how the film was affected by studio politics, the Depression, and cultural codes of representation, all of which are seen as influencing the film as much as the director's personal artistry (*Cahiers du Cinéma*, 1972). Roland Barthes and others claimed that the author was dead and carried no authority over the meaning of the text, and that textual meaning thus could be appropriated by readers and AUDIENCES. (Barthes, 1973).

The denial of the author as embodied person was as excessive as earlier auteurists' exaggerated claims of greatness. Today critics, whilst acknowledging the collaborative nature of the film-making process, still discuss directors and others as auteurs, although such discussions are more grounded in historical and industrial contexts. Auteurism, although changed, has survived because, as Bruce Kawin points out, 'The problem with the auteur theory is that it *may* allow the critic to ignore creative collaboration and leap straight to the director. The special merit of the auteur theory is that it is *capable* of acknowledging the collaborative structure of the cinematic enterprise *and* the evidence of patterns of coherence that have the integrity of authorship' (Kawin, 1987, p. 293).
Further reading: Hollows *et al.* (2000), Kael (1965)

Authorship See AUTEUR, AUTEURISM, AUTEUR THEORY.

Available light Most SCENES, INTERIOR or EXTERIOR, in most commercial FEATURE films are SHOT using artificial LIGHTING but a scene shot with 'available light' uses only light naturally available on the LOCATION or SET – sunlight for exterior shots and household or office lighting for interior shots. The less light available, the FASTER the FILM SPEED required and the more GRAIN visible in the finished IMAGE so, to achieve the clearer, 'glossy' look that most commercial features aspire to, artificial light is often used.

Avant-garde film Often today the term is seen as interchangeable with INDEPENDENT CINEMA or even ART CINEMA. It is more useful to think of it as applying more accurately to some key movements in twentieth century European and North American cinema, though there will always be debates about what is truly the 'advanced guard' (the term's literal translation) at any moment in the history of an art form. The single unifying feature of avant-garde practice in film has been the exploration of the possibilities inherent in the medium itself. Though most would now accept that all avant-garde practice constitutes a political act in a general sense, scholars and practitioners have differed widely over the true relationship between formal artistic experimentation and politics at given historical moments. Recent debates have included the idea that seeing the avant-garde as the true source of oppositional practice in art ignores the possibility of POPULAR CULTURE being read in such a way and that classically defined avant-garde practice can never be truly progressive as it remains within the domain of an artistic elite (Lapsley & Westlake, 1988).

Widely accepted landmarks of the cinematic avant-garde include: 1920s French IMPRESSIONISM and GERMAN EXPRESSIONISM, concerned with questions around the SPECTATOR, AUTHORSHIP and SUBJECTIVITY; 1920s Soviet cinema (despite the movement's avowed opposition to what they saw as the avant-garde's bourgeois and elitist conception of art); mid-century US experimental cinema as exemplified by Maya Deren, Stan Brakhage, Kenneth Anger and Andy Warhol and the STRUCTURAL filmmakers; and the work of Jean-Luc Godard, Jean-Marie Straub and others in the 1960s. See also ABSOLUTE FILM, ABSTRACT FILM, COUNTER CINEMA, MONTAGE.
Further reading: Curtis (1971), LeGrice (1977), Macdonald (1993), Peterson (1994), Rees (1999), Renan (1967)

Axis of action See 180° RULE.

B

B movie (B feature, B picture) Term used to designate the second film in a DOUBLE BILL, accompanying the A FEATURE (though any low budget film is sometimes referred to as a B movie). Initially, B movies were made both by MAJOR STUDIOS (often in special UNITS, such as Val Lewton's HORROR unit at RKO, which produced films like Jacques Tourneur's *Cat People*, 1942 and *I Walked With a Zombie*, 1943) and by PRODUCTION/DISTRIBUTION companies like MONOGRAM Pictures and REPUBLIC Pictures (the so-called POVERTY ROW studios) which specialized in these lower budgeted and quickly-made films (which often provided good training for DIRECTORS and ACTORS). Whereas A features generated revenue for their PRODUCER/DISTRIBUTOR as a percentage of the BOX-OFFICE take, and therefore had big profit potential, most second features were booked for a standard flat fee, so profits were smaller, though assured (provided budgets were low enough), and AUDIENCE attendance figures were less crucial. As befitted their status, B movies had shorter running times than A pictures (generally 60–75 minutes), tended to be GENRE pictures (especially CRIME and HORROR films, but also COMEDIES and others) and usually had lesser STARS (or no stars). The 1948 PARAMOUNT DECISION meant that the majors no longer programmed their own theatres and theatre owners were more free to choose what they showed, and this (plus other factors) eventually spelled the end of the double feature system and B movie production. In the 1950s both Monogram and Republic tried to take advantage of the freer distribution situation by making more expensive features (as well as making material for television, which became the new home for B movie type material).

The term B movie is also applied to low-budget 1950s films like those made by AMERICAN INTERNATIONAL PICTURES (AIP), though these were often intended as equal halves of double bills aimed at youth audiences and DRIVE-IN THEATRES. Paradoxically, B movie production during the STUDIO SYSTEM period – financially constrained but less risky, so less supervised – could offer greater creative freedom than A features, and tested the ingenuity and creativity of film-makers. Many B movies are now acknowledged classics in their genres and inspiration for contemporary film-makers. *Detour*, a 1945 FILM NOIR directed by Edgar G. Ulmer, running 69 minutes, SHOT in six days on a very low budget by PRC (Producers Releasing Company) and virtually unnoticed at the time of its release, is now a CULT classic. Paul Kerr discusses the role of the B movie in *film noir* in Kerr (1986).
Further reading: Gomery (1986), McCarthy & Flynn (1975)

Backdrop   As in theatre, a scene painted on to a cloth or scenery flats, or a photographic blow-up, placed at the back of a SET as background for a SCENE, used extensively in SILENT FILMS. Later films were more likely to use REAR PROJECTION, though a film like *Marnie* (dir. Alfred Hitchcock, 1964) uses both rear projection and backdrops in fairly obvious ways, provoking debate as to whether Hitchcock sought to undermine AUDIENCES' sense of convincing reality or merely underestimated their sophistication.

Background music   MUSIC on the SOUNDTRACK of a film that derives from no discernible source within the DIEGESIS, typically used to heighten the emotional effect of a given SCENE.

Back light   A light, usually a bright spotlight, positioned behind and usually above an ACTOR or object and in line with the CAMERA. Its function is to make the actor or object stand out from the background by providing a sharper edge or outline. Backlighting can provide a noticeably dramatic effect.

Back lot   The open air area of a studio's grounds, used primarily for shooting exteriors, whether natural – such as WESTERN landscapes – or urban/suburban street SCENES on standing SETS which could be adapted and re-used. Sometimes, back lots ran to areas of open country for exteriors. Back lots offered economic and controlled conditions for exterior shooting and were important during the STUDIO SYSTEM era, but the growth of LOCATION shooting and studios' desire to realise the asset value of prime real estate has meant a decline in their use.

Back projection   See REAR PROJECTION.

Back story   A term used mainly by SCREENWRITERS to describe the accruing of detail around the main PLOT lines of a film that will flesh out the lives of characters or communities. The key to a successful back story is subtlety and information – about a person's past, for example – given in hints and asides rather than lengthy and contrived dialogue.

Backstage musical   See MUSICAL.

BAFTA The British Academy of Film and TELEVISION Arts, founded in 1959 (originally the Society of Film and Television Arts). The term 'a BAFTA' is also used to describe one of the annual awards given by the Academy in recognition of achievement in one of its many categories. To some extent BAFTA also acts as a pressure and opinion-forming group within the British film industry.

Barney, Sound barney See BLIMP.

BBC See BRITISH BROADCASTING CORPORATION.

BBFC, BBFVC (British Board of Film Censors, British Board of Film Classification, British Board of Film and Video Classification) The British Board of Film Censors was established in 1913 as the film industry's response to inconsistent local authority practices to the licensing of cinema theatre premises and their effects on film EXHIBITION, following the 1909 Cinematograph Act and the need to establish common standards. Although this was industry self-regulation, without official governmental status, the board issued CERTIFICATES, and in practice BBFC certificates became esssential for films to be shown, although at various times – during the 1920s with film societies, and in the 1960s and 1970s with film clubs – ways for people to see non-certificated films were found. Historically, film CENSORSHIP by the Board has been very conservative in both political and sexual matters, although in 1975 films were removed from the common law offence of indecency and brought under the Obscene Publications Act (allowing a defence against obscenity on artistic grounds). An (in)famous decision to refuse a certificate for the French avant-garde film *The Seashell and the Clergyman* (dir. Germaine Dulac, 1928) ran: 'This film is so cryptic as to be meaningless. If there is a meaning, it is no doubt objectionable'. In 1982 'Censors' was changed to 'Classification' – though 'Censors' remained in the popular imagination – and in 1985 the Video Recording Act brought VIDEO within the Board's orbit. In 1994 guidelines for censorship and powers for the classification and re-classification of videos were established. Over time, systems for classification of certificates, or ratings, have changed, and are at present very much in line with those used in the US. Board policy has been influenced by debates in society, particularly around the depiction of violence. See also A/AA CERTIFICATE, G RATING, H CERTIFICATE, PG, RATINGS, U CERTIFICATE, X RATING.
Further reading: Mathews (1997), Robertson (1989)

BBS Small HOLLYWOOD production company (named after the first names of its three principals, Bert Schneider, Bob Rafelson and Steve Blauner), active in the late 1960s/early 1970s. Under the aegis of COLUMBIA Pictures, BBS produced films like *Head* (dir. Bob Rafelson, 1968), *Easy Rider* (dir. Dennis Hopper, 1969), *Five Easy Pieces* (dir. Rafelson, 1970), *The Last Picture Show* (dir. Peter Bogdanovich, 1971), *The King of Marvin Gardens* (dir. Rafelson, 1972) and Oscar-winning Vietnam War documentary *Hearts and Minds* (dir. Peter Davis, 1974). These productions – especially the commercially successful *Easy Rider* – characterized Hollywood's uncertainty about its AUDIENCES, what kinds of films it should make, and its readiness to risk innovation (at least on low-budget films) during this period.
Further reading: Grimes (1986), Riley in Roud (1980)

Beaver shot A shot in a soft-core PORNOGRAPHIC film or MAINSTREAM FILM that shows (usually) female genitalia.

BECTU (Broadcasting Entertainment Cinematograph & Theatre Union) See ACTT.

Below-the-line costs The costs incurred on a film production once shooting has actually begun, continuing into the costs of POST-PRODUCTION (as opposed to costs incurred before shooting begins: see ABOVE-THE-LINE COSTS). Below-the-line costs include salaries for members of the CREW, the renting of equipment, catering, etc., as well as the costs of EDITING, lab work, etc.

Benshi In Japanese cinema, the *benshi* was a live narrator who explained to the audience and commented on SILENT FILMS while they were shown. At the height of their popularity, *benshïs* were as popular an attraction as the movies themselves (Anderson and Richie 1960, p. 23). Richie (1971, p. 6) argues that the survival of the *benshi* well into the era of SOUND was a serious obstacle to the development of film art in Japanese NATIONAL CINEMA.

Best boy A member of the electrical team working on a large-scale production who generally acts as the assistant to the chief electrician or GAFFER.

Big 5 Term used to describe the five MAJOR STUDIOS in HOLLYWOOD – MGM, PARAMOUNT, RKO, TWENTIETH CENTURY-FOX and WARNER BROS. – which were fully VERTICALLY INTEGRATED – i.e. combined PRODUCTION, DISTRIBUTION and EXHIBITION – during the Hollywood STUDIO SYSTEM period 1920s–1940s. See also 'LITTLE 3'.

Big close-up (BCU) More selective view than a CLOSE-UP, showing only part of an object filling the FRAME. In terms of the human figure, a big close-up would isolate part of the face such as an eye or the mouth. Also called DETAIL SHOT and EXTREME CLOSE-UP (ECU).

Billing The relative position, agreed by contract, in which actors and other participants in a film's production appear in its CREDITS and publicity material, such as posters. The terms 'bill' and 'billing' were adapted directly from theatre and VAUDEVILLE/MUSIC HALL to cinema.

Binary opposition Term used in STRUCTURALIST criticism to describe two conflicting aspects of a culture as expressed in cultural MYTHS and TEXTS, originally developed by French structural anthropologist Claude Lévi-Strauss, who claimed that all cultural myths worked by establishing such mythic constructs. The theory is inviting for film analysis, particularly GENRE films, which are frequently regarded as the contemporary version of cultural myth. In his influential study of the WESTERN, Kitses (1969) maps out a series of binary oppositions – variations of the conflict between wilderness and civilization. See also GENRE, SEMIOTICS.

Biograph Originally named KMCD, then American Mutoscope and Biograph, this American film production company is remembered today primarily because of the films made for it by influential film pioneer D.W. Griffith. A member of the MOTION PICTURES PATENTS COMPANY (MPCC) and located in New York City, Biograph was founded in 1895 by four men including W.K.L. Dickson who worked with Edison on the invention of the KINETOSCOPE. By the turn of the century Biograph was the major film-making rival to Edison in the US. In addition to Griffith, Mary Pickford and Mack Sennett also began their careers with Biograph. Griffith worked at Biograph from 1908–1913, making more than four hundred ONE- and TWO-REELERS at the standard rate of one or two per week. Biograph also employed G.W. 'Billy' Bitzer, who became Griffith's personal CINEMATOGRAPHER, and a group of ACTORS, including Lillian Gish and Bobby Harron, who became part of Griffith's stock company and among the first movie STARS. Griffith himself began working for Biograph as an actor in a number of one-reelers including *Rescued from an Eagle's Nest* (dir. Edwin S. Porter, 1908), but was soon invited to direct. Despite the popularity of Griffith's work, the DIRECTOR often found himself at odds with company management in his wish to make longer and more complex films, a tension that came to a head when Griffith left Biograph after the six-reel *Judith of Bethulia* (1913). Within two years of the departure of Griffith in 1913 and those associated with him, the company ceased production.

Biopic A slang term, widely used in the American film industry in particular, formed from biography and picture, first used in the 1930s to describe a succession of films produced by WARNER BROS. based on a real person's life (though approaches have varied widely). The mainstream biopic tradition is best exemplified by *Lawrence of Arabia* (dir. David Lean 1962), whilst *The Music Lovers* (dir. Ken Russell, 1971) perhaps demonstrates the outer limits of the term in that it is based upon the life of Tchaikovsky, but depends heavily on speculation and fantasy.

Bird's-eye shot See OVERHEAD SHOT.

Black-and-white film Film with an EMULSION that renders COLOURS as a range of greys. Orthochromatic FILM STOCK, used almost throughout the period of SILENT FILM, was sensitive to only blue and green and tended to produce the sharp black and white contrasts typical of silent film, although with a FAST FILM speed, and consequent DEPTH OF FIELD, silent film also often produced DEEP FOCUS. By the late 1920s, orthochromatic stock had been largely replaced by PANCHROMATIC stock, sensitive to the full range of colours and producing a wider range of greys, but also with a slower FILM SPEED and tending to produce SHALLOW FOCUS – at least until LENSES, emulsions and LIGHTING improved, making deep focus once again more possible by the 1940s. Overall, black-and-white film proved a versatile and expressive resource from the beginnings of cinema, even before the more obviously bravura use made of it by Orson Welles (with films like *Citizen Kane*, 1941, with CINEMATOGRA-PHER Gregg Toland, and *The Magnificent Ambersons*, 1942) and by the makers of FILM NOIR (with directors of photography like John Alton and Nicholas Musuraca). COLOUR FILM took a long time to perfect and become accepted as a general purpose stock, and most films continued to be made in black and white until the 1960s, when the US TELEVISION networks switched to colour transmission, significantly increas-ing the demand for colour films. Since then, almost all professionally made films are made in colour as standard practice, though important films have been made in black-and-white, as a matter of aesthetic choice or to evoke the past, e.g. *The Last Picture Show* (dir. Peter Bogdanovich, 1971), *Lenny* (dir. Bob Fosse, 1974), Woody Allen films like *Manhattan* (1979) and *Zelig* (1983), *Raging Bull* (dir, Martin Scorsese, 1980), *Schindler's List* (dir. Steven Spielberg, 1993), and *The Addiction* (dir. Abel Ferrara, 1994).

Black film   Loose term for films made by black film-makers in the context of US cinema. Although the term has come into wide usage only since the 1980s, 'African-American' film would probably be the preferred term today. Although black film may seem of fairly recent origin, as early as 1916 the NAACP (National Association for the Advancement of Colored People) campaigned against the racist REPRESEN-TATION of blacks in *The Birth of a Nation* (dir. D.W. Griffith, 1916) and black film-makers made a riposte in *Birth of a Race* (1919). During the 1920s and 1930s a lively black movie business produced low-budget RACE FILMS for black audiences. After the coming of SOUND, the range of roles for black ACTORS in HOLLYWOOD films widened slightly and some all-black films were made, such as *Hallelujah* (dir. King Vidor, 1929) and *Cabin in the Sky* (dir. Vincente Minnelli, 1943). However, the NAACP 1942 annual convention, held in Hollywood, demanded more and different roles for black actors as well as for black film-makers who were almost completely absent from the mainstream. Although black CHARACTERS – played, pre-eminently by Sidney Poitier – were prominent in many 1940s and 1950s PROBLEM FILMS made by the STUDIOS, it was not until the late 1960s that black film-makers in any number began making industry films.

By this time, the US AUDIENCE had declined dramatically from its mid 1940s peak, and black audiences played a more important role in the success or failure of films. In 1970 *Cotton Comes to Harlem*, directed by black DIRECTOR (and actor) Ossie Davis, did well at the BOX OFFICE and *VARIETY* estimated that seventy per cent of its rentals came from black audiences. This – along with the success of the inde-pendently made *Sweet Sweetback's Baadasssss Song* (dir, Melvin Van Peebles, 1970) – started off the BLAXPLOITATION phase of the 1970s, including several films by other black directors such as Gordon Parks (*Shaft*, 1971, *Shaft's Big Score*, 1972) and Gordon Parks Jr (*Superfly*, 1972). Although black film-makers continued working in the film and TELEVISION industries throughout the 1970s and 1980s, it was not until the late 1980s that Hollywood again took significant notice of black film-makers, principally as a result of the success of Spike Lee's first feature, *She's Gotta Have It* (1986) – made independently for around $175,000 and grossing around $8 million. The financial success of Lee's subsequent films (*School Daze*, 1988, and *Do The Right Thing*, 1989, distributed by COLUMBIA and UNIVERSAL, respectively) and of *House Party* (dir. Reginald Hudlin, 1989) created a fashion in Hollywood for black film-makers, best exemplified by Columbia taking on novice, 23 year-old John Singleton to direct *Boyz N the Hood* (1991). During the early 1990s, many new black directors made their first films, some socially oriented, such as *Juice* (dir. Ernest Dickerson, 1992), some frankly black versions of commercial GENRE films, such as *New Jack City* (dir. Mario Van Peebles, 1991). Within INDE-PENDENT black film, two very different film-makers with backgrounds in the black activist 'Los Angeles school', Charles Burnett and Julie Dash, both precede and parallel the more Hollywood black film wave. *Killer of Sheep* (dir. Burnett, 1977) and *My Brother's Wedding* (dir. Burnett, 1983) are NEO-REALIST inspired accounts of working class black life, while *Daughters of the Dust* (dir. Dash, 1991) aspires to poetic and symbolic history. Though the fashion for black films and film-makers has receded, and black film has less identity than in the early 1990s, it is clear that black film-makers will remain a more important force within Hollywood than in the past, and continue to make important contributions to independent film-making. There has been little in British cinema to compare with these developments, but distinctive black work has emerged from independent groups such as the Black Audio Film Collective and SANKOFA. See also RACE.

Further reading: Cripps (1978), Diawara (1993), Guerrero (1993), Hillier (1993), Guerrero in Lewis (1998), Lott in Neale & Smith (1998), Pines (1975), Reid (1993), Smith (1997)

Blacklist From the 1940s to at least the 1960s many qualified film industry employees, including ACTORS and DIRECTORS, were prevented from working in HOLLYWOOD because their names appeared on an unofficial blacklist operated by the MAJOR STUDIOS, compiled largely as the result of the work of the HOUSE UN-AMERI-CAN ACTIVITIES COMMITTEE (HUAC). The committee's main declared aim was to root out alleged communist subversion in all areas of American public life and Hollywood became a high-profile target because of its ability to produce covert PROPAGANDA. The best known blacklisted employees were those forming the HOLLYWOOD TEN. As a result of the blacklist some writers worked under different names for many years, including the young Martin Ritt, who drew on this experience in *The Front* (dir. Ritt, 1976), starring Woody Allen as a blacklisted SCREENWRITER.

Further reading: Belton (1994), Ceplair & Englund (1980)

Black Maria The first film studio – for shooting films for KINETOSCOPE parlours – built by Thomas Edison in Orange, New Jersey, in 1893, to a design by William K. Laurie Dickson. The roof could be removed, and the studio revolved, to catch sunlight at different times of the day. Covered in tar paper inside and out, the Black Maria was said to resemble the kind of van used by the police, known as the Black Maria.

Further reading: Robinson (1996)

Blaxploitation Term coined by the American trade paper *VARIETY* for a CYCLE of FEATURE films made from the late 1960s to the mid 1970s targeted specifically at black AUDIENCES. Encouraged by the success of *Cotton Comes to Harlem* (dir. Ossie Davis) in 1970, the first wave of popular American BLACK CINEMA to feature black ACTORS in major roles tended to be ACTION FILMS with sensationalist PLOTS featuring stories of CRIME and VIOLENCE in the inner city. As the civil rights movement gained momentum and edged into the more militant black rights movement, many black viewers, reacting to what Bogle refers to as the 'integrationist' IMAGE of Sidney Poitier and Harry Belafonte, welcomed a new wave of action movies featuring more macho black STARS such as ex-football great Jim Brown. *Sweet Sweetback's Baadasssss Song* (1971), an angry, militant INDEPENDENT FILM about racism and STEREOTYPING directed by black DIRECTOR Melvin van Peebles, helped open the door for new representations of blacks in popular cinema. Richard Roundtree became famous as *Shaft* (dir. Gordon Parks, 1971) and Ron O'Neal as *Superfly* (dir. Gordon Parks Jr., 1972), both films inspiring a couple of SEQUELS. *Coffy* (dir. Jack Hill,

1973) and *Cleopatra Jones* (dir. Jack Starrett, 1973), starring Pam Grier and Tamara Dobson respectively, applied the same formula to female CHARACTERS, creating 'supermacho females' (Guerrero, 1993, p. 4).

Although some blaxploitation films were made by black film-makers, many had white PRODUCERS and directors and were made to cash in on the trend. Consequently, many of the black characters in these films are also stereotypes, although different from the 'toms, coons, mulattos, mammies and bucks' (Bogle, 1973) of the past. The constraints of blaxploitation characterization are parodied in Robert Townsend's *Hollywood Shuffle* (1987), in which blacks go to ACTING school only invariably to be cast as pimps and drug dealers. The question of the extent to which blaxploitation was politically progressive has been a matter of debate, but some of these movies, such as *Blacula* (dir. William Crain, 1972), have been of continuing interest to film scholars.
Further reading: Reid (1993)

Blimp A soundproof CAMERA housing that muffles the noise of the camera's motor so that it is not picked up by a MICROPHONE on the SET. In the early SOUND period blimps were used because the cameras were bulky and microphones omnidirectional; but this resulted in making the camera immobile compared to the freedom of movement it had attained in such late SILENT FILMS as *The Last Laugh* (dir. F.W. Murnau, 1924). The practice of blimping cameras in early sound film is parodied in *Singin' in the Rain* (dir. Gene Kelly and Stanley Donen, 1952) when Kelly and Jean Hagen attempt to shoot a dialogue SCENE for their first sound film with comic results. Many newer cameras are self-blimped or operate relatively noiselessly. Also called barney, sound barney. See also CAMERA MOVEMENT.

Blind bidding A film rental forced upon an EXHIBITOR by a DISTRIBUTOR (normally one with muscle, such as a MAJOR STUDIO) even though the exhibitor has not seen the film. See also BLOCK BOOKING.

Block booking Film industry business practice in which exhibitors, to get access to films they wanted, were made to agree to rent and show other material which they may not have seen or wanted (see BLIND BIDDING). This arrangement advantaged the MAJOR STUDIOS whose successful films enabled them to find EXHIBITION for less attractive material. This was one of the long established (since at least 1916) practices that the majors were forced to abandon after the 1948 PARAMOUNT DECISION, but the system continued to operate outside the US.

Blockbuster Although the term has a long history in HOLLYWOOD and elsewhere for any film which becomes a resounding BOX-OFFICE success, it was particularly during the 1950s and 1960s, when Hollywood was struggling to win back or retain declining audiences, that blockbusters – big, expensive films, normally combining WIDESCREEN, COLOUR, long running times (sometimes with intermissions) and EPIC subjects – were made. Films like *The Ten Commandments* (dir. Cecil B. DeMille, 1956), *Ben-Hur* (dir. William Wyler, 1959), *El Cid* (dir. Anthony Mann, 1961), often released on a ROADSHOW basis, were regarded as films with the potential to do block-busting business. From the 1970s, the term shifted back to mean any film which achieves – and is designed to achieve – outstanding box office success. *Jaws* (dir.

Steven Spielberg, 1975), for example, was a blockbuster under this later definition but not under the earlier one, while, for example, *Terminator 2: Judgment Day* and *Titanic* (both dir. James Cameron, 1991 and 1998) are perhaps blockbusters in both senses – very expensive productions, EPIC subjects and very successful at the box office. Rather than the earlier selective, gradual roadshowing release schedule, blockbusters since the 1970s owe much of their success to SATURATION RELEASE.

Further reading: Balio (1976a), Schatz in Collins (1993), Cook (1996), Wyatt in Lewis (1998), Biskind in Miller (1990)

Blocking A term taken from legitimate theatre – the way the positioning of ACTORS and the way they will move on stage, or SET – is planned, though the term can be extended to the process of explaining this blocking to the actors, and to the process of arranging the CAMERA placement, LENSES, etc. for a SCENE to be SHOT.

Blow up The process by which a larger DUPLICATE PRINT is made from a smaller GAUGE. 16MM can be blown up to 35MM for THEATRICAL RELEASE and 35mm is often blown up to 70MM for special EXHIBITION purposes. The term can also be used for enlarging some small portion of an IMAGE – which informs the PLOT of *Blow-Up* (dir. Michelangelo Antonioni, 1966) – and is a printing procedure in some AVANT-GARDE film-making, such as *Tom, Tom, the Piper's Son* (dir. Ken Jacobs, 1968).

Blue movie Sometimes synonymous with PORNOGRAPHIC FILM, the term is also used to distinguish soft-core or less explicit movies. See also STAG FILM.

Bolex A lightweight, HAND-HELD 16MM CAMERA manufactured in Switzerland. Sometimes used for TELEVISION news coverage, the Bolex has also been popular with OBSERVATIONAL film-makers.

Bollywood Colloquial term combining 'Bombay' with 'HOLLYWOOD', taking Bombay as the centre of Indian popular cinema, produced at one time in a number of MAJOR STUDIOS and heavily reliant on STARS and GENRES, like Hollywood. Indian cinema's continuing output of 600–700 FEATURE FILMS a year makes it the largest film industry in the world and Bombay could still be claimed as the main centre for film-making in Hindi as well as other Indian languages. However, film production in other parts of India, particularly Madras, Hyderabad and Calcutta, for different Indian languages, has become almost as important. Although during the 1930s and 1940s Bombay production was based on studios such as New Theatres, Prabhat Studios and Bombay Talkies, this is no longer the case. See also MASALA FILM.

Further reading: Cook & Bernink (1999), Vasuderan in Gledhill & Williams (2000), Kasbekar in Nelmes (1999), Rajadhyaksha in Nowell-Smith (1996), Thompson & Bordwell (1994)

Boom A long 'arm' or other kind of extension device that is used for getting MICROPHONES, CAMERAS or lights into position during shooting, varying from the simple pole used by a SOUND operator to hold a microphone out of SHOT over the performer's head to a complex mechanical mounting that enables a camera to be positioned at a variety of heights, ANGLES and distances.

Boom shot A SHOT made using a BOOM or CRANE. Also known as CRANE SHOT.

Box-office Literally, the term originally referred to the small booth at the front of cinemas where tickets were sold, but today likely to mean the takings earned by a film during its THEATRICAL release. The term is also often used in relation to potential earning power, a particular STAR being considered 'good box-office'. See also GROSS.

Brat pack Refers principally to a group of young ACTORS who appeared in a loosely linked series of films during the early 1980s dealing with teenage angst and the problems of entry into adulthood, but also identified with the films themselves – 'brat pack movies'. The actors most identified with this group included Demi Moore, Emilio Estevez, Molly Ringwald, Ally Sheedy, Matt Dillon and Rob Lowe, whilst the most prominent films include *The Outsiders* (dir. Francis Ford Coppola, 1983), *St Elmo's Fire* (dir. Joel Schumacher, 1986) and a succession of FEATURES by the DIRECTOR most firmly associated with this group, John Hughes, including *The Breakfast Club* (1985), *Pretty in Pink* (1986) and *Ferris Bueller's Day Off* (1986).

Breakdown Describes the way a SCENE has been, or will be, edited, 'cut up', broken down, or arranged, into SHOTS. See also *DÉCOUPAGE*.

Brechtian Deriving from, or influenced by, the ideas and practice of German dramatist and theorist (and occasional SCREENWRITER) Bertolt Brecht. His thinking about politicized, reflexive forms of theatre has been almost as influential on film-making as it has been on theatre, particularly during the 1960s and 1970s. Film-makers such as Jean-Luc Godard, Jean-Marie Straub and Danièle Straub-Huillet were heavily influenced as is shown in such films as *Tout va bien* (dir. Jean-Luc Godard & Jean-Pierre Gorin, 1972) which begins with a discourse about the aesthetic and economic conditions of narrative film-making and contains many other 'Brechtian' elements. See also ALIENATION, COUNTER CINEMA, DISTANCIATION, EPIC, REFLEXIVITY. Further reading: Brecht (1964), Elsaesser in Kleber & Visser (1990), Polan in Nichols (1985), Stam (2000)

Breen Code See also CENSORSHIP, MOTION PICTURE ASSOCIATION OF AMERICA.

Bricolage Putting objects or SIGNS into new contexts to give them fresh meanings – one of the chief characteristics of POSTMODERN culture, which relies heavily on the 're-cycling' of meanings from the past. Bricolage is perhaps most visible in contemporary ADVERTISING, which frequently draws upon 'high art' sounds and IMAGES and associates them with anything from washing powder to cars. In film studies the term describes the frequent use of such practice within films as well as the borrowings from classic cinema that appear in different ways across contemporary cultural practices. David Lynch, for example, draws heavily on re-cycled meanings from Hitchcock to *The Wizard of Oz* (dir. Victor Fleming, 1939), which famously underpins the entire plot of his *Wild at Heart* (1990).

Bridge As the name suggests, 'bridges' or 'bridging' devices connect SCENES. A bridging SHOT links two SEQUENCES which are separated by TIME and/or SPACE, such as the reverse calendar shots which take us back in time after the prologue in *Written* *on the Wind* (dir. Douglas Sirk, 1956). A 'sound bridge' links two scenes either by continuing MUSIC over the TRANSITION ('bridge music'), or by beginning the dialogue of the next scene over images of the previous scene – also referred to as a 'sound advance', and very common in contemporary cinema.

Brighton school Name for the British film-makers active in Brighton 1900–1908, associated by film historians with significant developments in film form in EARLY CINEMA related to EDITING and the use of CLOSE-UPS, especially in the work of G.A. Smith and James Williamson. Williamson appears to have used a form of PARALLEL EDITING in films like *Attack on a Chinese Mission Station* (1900) and *Fire!* (1901). Early American DIRECTOR Edwin S. Porter saw films of the Brighton school and his famous *The Great Train Robbery* (1903) shows their influence, but producer Cecil Hepworth's *Rescued by Rover* (dir. Lewis Fitzhamon, 1905), the most sophisticated British film up to that time in its use of CONTINUITY EDITING, was in turn probably influenced by Porter's work.
Further reading: Thompson & Bordwell (1994)

British Broadcasting Corporation (BBC)   The state SUBSIDIZED and regulated British TELEVISION and radio company which is obliged in its charter to perform a public service function, defined by its famous early Director-General, John Reith, as providing a 'balanced diet' of education, information and entertainment. The BBC's once enormous output of all kinds of drama has frequently been a training ground for prominent British film DIRECTORS, including Ken Loach and Stephen Frears, whilst the BBC has also produced, or co-produced, a number of FEATURE FILMS during the last decade.

British Film Institute (BFI)   Founded in 1933 to promote the art of film in the UK, including its role in education. Funded through a combination of membership subscriptions and direct government support, it operates the NATIONAL FILM AND TELEVISION ARCHIVE, the NATIONAL FILM THEATRE (NFT) and the Museum of the Moving Image on London's South Bank, and publishes the journal *SIGHT AND SOUND*. It also runs an education department and library, providing services to teachers and film scholars, distributes films through its DISTRIBUTION library and is responsible for a network of regional film theatres. The BFI has an important voice within debates about the role and status of film in the UK, and the AMERICAN FILM INSTITUTE (AFI) was based partly on the BFI.

British New Wave   Name given to the output of a relatively tight-knit group of young British DIRECTORS – Lindsay Anderson, Karel Reisz and Tony Richardson, and to a lesser extent Jack Clayton and John Schlesinger – and independent production companies, particularly Woodfall Films, originally set up by Richardson and theatre writer John Osborne, from the late 1950s to the mid-1960s. 'New Wave' derived from the roughly contemporaneous FRENCH NEW WAVE. Woodfall's output included Richardson's *Look Back in Anger* (1959), *The Entertainer* (1960), *A Taste of Honey* (1961) and *The Loneliness of The Long Distance Runner* (1962) and Reisz's *Saturday Night and Sunday Morning* (1960). Anderson, Reisz and Richardson had been co-founders of FREE CINEMA in the mid 1950s – principally dedicated to the production of 'personal' DOCUMENTARIES – and the New Wave is seen as a crucial phase in the documentary and REALIST strain of British cinema. Early accounts of the movement tended to view it as a radical break with what preceded it and as progressive in its treatment of mainly working-CLASS characters centred on the industrial north of England. More recent critics (Hill, 1986) have questioned this analysis, focusing particularly on the films' treatment of GENDER and sexuality. Most of the New Wave directors had backgrounds in the British establishment and Oxbridge, and although there was an attempt to treat honestly previously marginalized subjects, it was from an outsider's perspective, leading to romantic and individualized portrayals of (almost exclusively) male working-class heroes rather than a radical analysis of class relations.

Buddy film A male-oriented ACTION GENRE, especially popular in the 1970s, depicting the adventures of two or more men and emphasizing male bonding and camaraderie. Often overlapping with the ROAD MOVIE, buddy films frequently depict a pair of men on a journey, either randomly episodic or motivated by a specific quest. Tellingly, the buddy film achieved its greatest popularity in the 1960s and 1970s, coinciding with the rise of the modern women's movement, suggesting that it expressed something of a cultural backlash against feminism. George Roy Hill's *Butch Cassidy and the Sundance Kid* (1969) and *The Sting* (1973), both pairing male STARS Robert Redford and Paul Newman, were among the most successful movies of the period, the latter taking seven OSCARS. The masculine bias of the buddy film was addressed directly in *Thelma and Louise* (dir. Ridley Scott, 1991), featuring the adventures of two outlaw women fleeing the police through the American Southwest and an ending that deliberately invokes that of *Butch Cassidy*. More recently, beginning in 1987, the four *Lethal Weapon* movies (dir. Richard Donner) starring Mel Gibson and Danny Glover, have been particularly successful inter-racial buddy movies.
Further reading: Fuchs in Cohan & Hark (1993), Hark in Cohan & Hark (1997), Wood (1986)

Buff A film enthusiast with much detailed knowledge of facts about cinema, implying a certain pedantry or tendency to list-making. 'Buff' is not specific to cinema, and apparently owes its (US) origins to enthusiasts for watching fires, after the buff-coloured uniforms worn by New York's volunteer firemen. See also CINEASTE.

Burlesque See PARODY.

C

CAA Creative Artists Agency, one of the two most powerful talent AGENCIES in the USA entertainment industry.

Cable television The use of underground cables as a means of delivering TELE-VISION signals for domestic consumption. Before the widespread use of DIGITAL trans-missions cable was also the only delivery system providing the possibility of interactivity for home shopping and banking, etc. The importance of cable for the

film industry has been clearest in the US where a number of channels – preeminently HBO (HOME BOX OFFICE) and the Movie Channel – provide premium film services to subscribers. Originally, cable providers only had to compete with VIDEO rental services for the supply of movies after the end of their THEATRICAL release, but with the coming of SATELLITE delivery and now digital systems, there are many different ways for the domestic consumer to see recently released films on demand (see PAY-PER-VIEW). HBO in particular has been heavily involved in 'pre-buying' – investing in films in exchange for exclusive early rights to screen them on television – while others have purchased STUDIO back catalogues for their exclusive use. The phrase 'straight to cable' (or 'STRAIGHT TO VIDEO') is used derogatorily to describe films that were originally intended for theatrical release, but which were not considered strong enough on completion.
Further reading: Wasko (1994)

Cahiers du Cinéma French FILM JOURNAL, founded in 1951 by Lo Duca, Jacques Doniol-Valcroze and André Bazin, but in many ways the successor to *La Revue du Cinéma* (edited Jean-George Auriol, 1929–31 and 1946–49). Bazin and others had developed much of their thinking before *Cahiers*, but it became influential mainly for its criticism in the 1950s and early 1960s when Bazin, Doniol-Valcroze and young critics like François Truffaut, Claude Chabrol, Eric Rohmer, Jacques Rivette and Jean-Luc Godard were re-evaluating HOLLYWOOD cinema via the *POLITIQUE DES AUTEURS*, which championed the DIRECTOR as *AUTEUR* or 'author' of films as much in Hollywood as in Europe (though the critics' admiration for American cinema above other cinemas has been overplayed). The views of the *Cahiers* critics were given particular credence by Truffaut, Chabrol, Rohmer, Rivette and Godard, from the late 1950s, becoming the core of the critically acclaimed FRENCH NEW WAVE movement. *Cahiers* enjoyed a second period of influence in the late 1960s and early 1970s when its work was heavily influenced by MARXIST thinking about IDEOLOGY and emerging work on PSYCHOANALYSIS, much of which found its way into English via the pages of the British journal *SCREEN*.
Further reading: Browne (1990), Hillier (1985), Hillier (1986)

Cameo Term used to describe a brief appearance or very small role in a film by a STAR or other celebrity. Films such as *The Player* (dir. Robert Altman, 1992) feature a host of HOLLYWOOD figures playing themselves in cameo roles, and Alfred Hitchcock was celebrated for his brief cameo appearances in his films.

A 'cameo SHOT' evokes the effect of the relief carving associated with, for example, the cameo brooch, by photographing someone – usually head and shoulders – or something, against a neutral or dark background, with 'cameo lighting' to help him or her 'stand out'.

Camera The film camera enables IMAGES to be recorded onto CELLULOID, which when projected at the correct speed onto a screen will give the illusion of movement. The basic principles of recording onto film have changed very little since their invention at the end of the nineteenth century, which in turn drew heavily on the principles of still photography which had been developed in France in the 1820s. The two earliest cameras used successfully for recording motion were Thomas Edison's KINETOGRAPH and the lumière CINÉMATOGRAPHE, both of which employed a camera body that excluded light and which stored the film which was then passed through an APERTURE equipped with a LENS exposing it briefly to record the image that was in front of it.

To record images that can then be projected with a convincing illusion of motion requires that the film is exposed at a constant speed (today, 24 FRAMES per second, but earlier 16) and without movement within the aperture. This is achieved by extremely precise mechanisms that hold the film steady using SPROCKET wheels to stop it long enough behind the aperture for it to be exposed and move it at a constant, though intermittent, speed. Early films sometimes get their 'jerky' quality from the imperfections of the mechanism holding the film steady as it is being exposed. Many purely mechanical problems began to be ironed out when the early wooden cameras changed to metal ones in the 1920s, enabling moving parts to be made and secured with greater precision. The twentieth century saw ever greater refinements and miniaturization of the earliest designs. Virtually all cameras now use electric motors as a power source though some very small cameras still use a spring-wound device housed in sound-proof chambers to enable the simultaneous recording of SOUND. Camera bodies today are lighter and able to be HAND-HELD or used remotely on some form of BOOM or other controlled mechanical object and there are now a number of different film GAUGES suitable for different kinds of work and budgets.

Most professional cameras today consist mainly of a camera body with lenses, VIEWFINDER and magazines (containing film) as separate, detachable parts. As these bodies in particular have become lighter, the range of situations where film is able to be SHOT has increased enormously which has therefore profoundly affected the aesthetic history of film. The FRENCH NEW WAVE directors and CINÉMA VÉRITÉ and DIRECT CINEMA DOCUMENTARY film-makers of the 1960s employed the developing technology to their advantage by using hand-held shooting techniques more frequently and for a greater range of purposes.

The advent of first ANALOGUE and now DIGITAL VIDEO technology has meant that the film camera is unable to compete in terms of sheer portability or ease of operation. Domestic digital cameras are already capable of recording images that are able to be broadcast as news items at least. However, the film camera remains sacred for most fiction FEATURE FILM production: in the UK it is now standard for all except the most routine TELEVISION drama productions and worldwide it is probably some time yet before any electronic means of recording images will rival the quality of celluloid film projected onto a cinema screen. See also ARRIFLEX, BOLEX, ECLAIR, MITCHELL.

Camera angle Part of the basic grammar of film-making, most camera angles derive their descriptions from the degree to which they vary from a mythical 'standard' SHOT, best described as a CAMERA positioned at the shoulder height of the average human straight on to the subject. Below this would be LOW ANGLE, above it high angle and from this derive extreme low and high angles. Clearly, the use of mechanical equipment, such as BOOMS or helicopters, increases the possibilities here.

One common, though often reductive, way of reading camera angles is to see them as expressions of power relations between characters, with a POINT-OF-VIEW SHOT from the position of one CHARACTER looking down at another indicating the dominance of one over the other. In practice there are a number of languages at work in any SCENE and a performer's body language or facial expression might well be working in an ironic relationship to a camera angle's apparent reading.

An example of the use of camera angles to suggest power relationships and the emotions engendered by them comes early in *Witness* (dir. Peter Weir, 1985). A young Amish Boy, visits the big city with his mother – the first time that he has been outside of his religious community that rejects most of the trappings of modern civilization. Weir films the boy in an extended SEQUENCE as he wanders around Philadelphia's 30th Street railway station while he and his mother wait for a connection. Many of the shots are at low angles, from the boy's point of view; we see adult legs moving quickly in CLOSE-UP, reflecting a sense of confusion and vulnerability. Alfred Hitchcock used camera angles to suggest a kind of omnipotence: in a well-known scene from *The Birds* (1963) his camera pulls back from a disastrous fire at a filling station to take up a god-like perspective hovering over the small town of Bodega Bay. As the fire has taken place through a combination of human stupidity and a fresh vengeful attack by a flock of seagulls, Hitchcock seems to be suggesting that elemental forces have been unleashed and that a vengeful god sits and watches.

Unorthodox angles have been used by conventional film-makers to suggest altered mental states, such as the stereotypical drunk's perspective wandering down a street, whilst SURREALIST and other kinds of EXPERIMENTAL practice use angles as part of a vocabulary designed to disorientate the spectator. *Blue Velvet* (dir. David Lynch, 1986) opens with a man suffering a heart attack whilst mowing his impossibly green lawn, surrounded by its white-picket fence. The suburban idyll is disturbed and Lynch graphically reminds us what lies behind its fragile facade by offering an ultra-low angle shot that takes us right down into the grass that was about to be mowed, showing the teeming insect life that inhabits it. See also DUTCH ANGLE.

Camera movement Any motion of the CAMERA during a SHOT, both physical movement of the camera, as in PANNING, TILTING, or HAND-HELD CAMERA, or movement of the camera fixed on a moving vehicle such as a DOLLY or CRANE. ZOOM SHOTS or RACK FOCUS are sometimes considered an aspect of camera movement since there is a change of viewing perspective within the same shot, although technically the camera is stationary.

Camera movement serves several expressive purposes. Most basically, it allows for variation of perspective for the viewer, breaking up the ACTION of a SCENE for dramatic purposes (see CLASSICAL HOLLYWOOD CINEMA). Camera movement also works in relation to the BLOCKING of CHARACTERS: for the embrace between the two lovers at the end of *A Man and a Woman* (dir. Claude Lelouch, 1966) the camera sweeps in circles around them, amplifying the lyricism of the moment and giving the audience a sense of the CHARACTERS' vertiginous elation. Camera movement also enhances the use of the SUBJECTIVE CAMERA, allowing us to move along with characters with whom we are meant to identify. In *Der Letzte Mann* (*The Last Laugh*, dir. F.W. Murnau, 1924), the mobile camera consistently expresses the protagonist's POINT OF VIEW, eliminating the need for INSERT TITLES to explain what he is thinking or feeling.

Camera movement also may provide editorial comment on the part of the DIRECTOR. In the opening shot of Douglas Sirk's *All that Heaven Allows* (1955), the camera cranes down from the church steeple to the level of the characters in the street, establishing at the outset that the prohibitions on female desire that the story explores are not divine but socially determined. Similarly, in *Frenzy* (1972), just as the viewer realises that a woman is about to be killed as she goes into the apartment of the man we now know is a serial killer and the door closes on them, Alfred Hitchcock slowly tracks the camera down the stairway, into and across the street, observing people going about their business, forcing us to dwell on our helpless position as spectators and the cruel indifference of fate.

On a more practical level, in DOCUMENTARY the hand-held moving camera allows film-makers to follow PROFILMIC events as they happen, as it does in *Primary* (dir. Drew Associates, 1960) when it moves behind John F. Kennedy at a political rally through a thick crowd, up a narrow flight of steps, and onto the stage where he begins to speak. Camera movement also may eliminate the need for many CUTS, as the camera can pan, tilt, track or dolly to a new SPACE or subject, revealing new information to the viewer. The LONG TAKES that open *Touch of Evil* (dir. Orson Welles, 1958) and *The Player* (dir. Robert Altman, 1992) are celebrated examples. The moving camera is crucial to André Bazin's conception of REALISM as a combination of several stylistic elements or techniques that preserve space and TIME in PROFILMIC events. In the early years of SOUND, the camera became temporarily less mobile, as cameras had to be placed in BLIMPS so that MICROPHONES would not pick up the sound of their motors. See also AERIAL SHOT, BOOM SHOT, IDENTIFICATION, SUBJECTIVE CAMERA.

Camera Obscura Film journal founded in 1976 by former members of the journal *Women and Film*. *Camera Obscura* was a product of a second phase of FEMINIST critical interest in cinema, edited by a collective and working towards a feminist analysis of MAINSTREAM FILM (and, later, TELEVISION) drawing on the theoretical discourses of IDEOLOGY, SEMIOTICS and PSYCHOANALYSIS. *Camera Obscura* has also explored feminist work (or work of interest to feminists) in the AVANT-GARDE and COUNTER CINEMA. The journal's title comes from the device by which light passing through a small hole at the end of a darkened room is focused to throw an (inverted) IMAGE at the opposite end.

Camera operator On larger scale productions the CAMERA operator – often known by the looser title of camera man – is a key member of the camera CREW operating under the guidance of the CINEMATOGRAPHER or director of photography. The operator is responsible for the physical control and movement of the camera whilst shooting, including looking through the VIEWFINDER to see that the IMAGE is correct in terms of ANGLE, FOCUS and FRAME. On smaller scale productions the camera operator and the cinematographer may well be the same person. Again, the larger the production the more assistants the operator him/herself will have, including assistants to perform tasks like loading the film or adjusting the FOCUS, which may be done by a first assistant cameraman. See also FOCUS PULLER, CLAPPER LOADER.

Caméra stylo, le Literally, 'camera pen', the phrase was used by Alexandre Astruc in his historically important essay *The Birth of the Avant-Garde: Le Caméro Stylo*, originally published in 1948, in which he envisioned a maturation of FILM as an art to the point that 'the cinema will gradually break free from the tyranny of what is visual, from the IMAGE for its own sake, from the immediate and concrete demands of the narrative, to become a means of writing just as flexible and subtle as written language.' (Astruc in Graham, 1968, p. 18). Astruc's essay has been seen as influencing the ideas of the FRENCH NEW WAVE and the development of the AUTEUR THEORY.

Camp As Richard Dyer puts it (1992, p. 133), 'Arguments have lasted all night about what camp really is', but Dyer also offers a useful definition of the term's relevance to cinema: 'a certain taste in art and entertainment, a certain sensibility.' It could therefore be said that camp is not inherent in a TEXT or a person, but is rather to be found in the way the viewer or reader reacts, in reading the surface or style of something in a way that might be quite separate from its generally accepted content. Where artists set out to produce art that is camp, there is a a pre-occupation with style.

Whilst a camp sensibility can be turned on to almost anything there are certain artists, GENRES and actual films that invite such responses more clearly than others, from the 'trash' cinema of John Waters – from the relatively 'acceptable' *Hairspray* (1988) to the outrageous *Pink Flamingos* (1974) – to Marlene Dietrich, Doris Day, Bette Davis and the films of Russ Meyer such as *Faster, Pussycat! Kill! Kill!* (1966). Within this range, both Davis and Dietrich made films that involved content that people cared about as well as revelling in the leading actors' style of performance, whereas it is unlikely that many people ever took a Russ Meyer PLOT very seriously. Jack Babuscio explains why camp's ability to undermine rigid definitions of GENDER has often associated it with the concerns of gay men: 'Camp, by focusing on the outward appearances of role, implies that roles and in particular sex roles are superficial – a matter of style. Finding STARS camp is not to mock them; it is more a way of poking fun at the whole cosmology of restrictive sex roles and sexual identifications which our society uses to oppress its women and repress its men' (Dyer, 1977, p. 44).

Cannes Film Festival First held in 1946, Cannes is probably the most prestigious of surviving film FESTIVALS. It awards an ever-evolving array of prizes in various categories for films released in the previous twelve months. The most important of these is the Palme d'Or for best film, though the Jury Prize and those for direction and performance also carry considerable weight. The major prizes at Cannes are second only to the American ACADEMY AWARDS in terms of worldwide importance, though for some the prestige of success at Cannes is worth more. Cannes represents a different set of values within world cinema, in some ways representing the European AUTEUR-based ART CINEMA tradition, reflected in those who have won the Palme d'Or in recent times: Mike Leigh (UK), Bille August (Sweden), Emil Kusturica (Yugoslavia) and Lars Von Trier (Denmark). However, prize-giving is only the official face of Cannes: for many it is a hard-nosed trade fair with people from all levels of the industry scrambling to clinch deals and sell projects.

Canted shot See DUTCH ANGLE.

Caper film A SUBGENRE of the CRIME FILM featuring a narrative emphasis on the planning and commission of a major crime, usually a theft. Typically, as in *Ocean's Eleven* (dir. Lewis Milestone, 1960) and *Topkapi* (dir. Jules Dassin, 1964), the criminals' target has top security and is seemingly impregnable. The heist, and the preparations for it, are often shown in elaborate detail, and the CHARACTERS are usually a disparate group of criminals, brought together for their individual expertise and a single purpose. According to Kaminsky (1974), the caper film evolved out of the GANGSTER FILM and movies about charming jewel thieves, but did not become a recognizable FORMULA until the 1950s with such movies as *The Asphalt Jungle* (dir. John Huston, 1950), *The Lavender Hill Mob* (dir. Charles Crichton, 1951) and *The Killing* (dir. Stanley Kubrick, 1956). He argues that these movies, repeatedly setting off a small unlikely group against institutionalized authority, are rebellious tales about a combination of individualism and Hawksian professionalism challenging state power.

Caption Words either superimposed over IMAGES on the screen or appearing against a plain background. The most common use of captions in the SOUND era is probably to indicate TIME and place, particularly when a dramatic time shift has taken place, such as 'seven years later'. Used injudiciously, captions can seem a rather lazy way of conveying information that could be made to emerge more subtly from the images or dialogue, but dialogue can be wittily counterpointed to images: in one scene from *Annie Hall* (dir. Woody Allen, 1977) Woody Allen's and Diane Keaton's CHARACTERS chat aimlessly while captions reveal their real thoughts. Known as INTERTITLES, captions were integral to SILENT CINEMA.

Carnivalesque A complex term derived from the work of Russian critic and theorist Mikhail Bakhtin: 'Carnival embraces an anti-classical aesthetic that rejects formal harmony and unity in favour of the asymmetrical, the heterogeneous, the oxymoronic, the miscegenated. Carnival's "grotesque realism" turns conventional aesthetics on its head in order to locate a new kind of popular, convulsive, rebellious beauty, one that dares to reveal the grotesquerie of the powerful and the latent beauty of the "vulgar" ' (Stam, 2000, p. 18). Stam (1989) uses the idea to discuss films by Luis Buñuel, Jean Vigo and Lina Wertmuller – seen not as simply as ALTERNATIVE but as reaching back to the older tradition of carnival – and to comic films by Mel Brooks and Monty Python.
Further reading: Bakhtin (1968).

Cartoon Popular name given to any ANIMATION film, though the name 'cartoon' is especially associated in the popular imagination with the short programme fillers made by the MAJOR STUDIOS of HOLLYWOOD during the STUDIO SYSTEM era, particularly those starring anthropomorphized animals such as Donald Duck, Mickey Mouse, Bugs Bunny, Daffy Duck, Tom and Jerry, etc. Up until the 1950s some specialized cinemas in London, for example, showed nothing but such cartoons.

Cast All the performers appearing in a film; as a verb, choosing those performers, as in CASTING. The cast list generally appears in the list of CREDITS at the end of a film with performers' names alongside the CHARACTERS they play.

Casting The process of choosing performers to fill the roles in a film, always an area of conflict and controversy in the film industry – folklore about the 'casting couch' has passed into common currency. Certainly young female (and sometimes male) performers have at times been asked for sexual favours on the 'casting couch' in return for parts in films. Standard auditions or SCREEN TESTS are still important parts of the process, though for major roles today auditioning may be as much under the control of the STAR as the DIRECTOR or PRODUCER, perhaps in a private meeting with elements of more conventional auditioning playing a part. Outside MAINSTREAM commercial cinema variations to standard casting procedures can make casting a more integral and systematic part of the creative process: British film-maker Ken Loach has often operated a strict policy of not using established star ACTORS and sometimes of not using actors at all. At the other extreme, much casting of commercial cinema is entirely influenced by BOX OFFICE considerations and the current popularity of any given star.

Casting director On most major productions, the person responsible for casting all except the leading roles, which would normally be cast by the DIRECTOR in conjunction with the PRODUCER (see CASTING). A casting director will also negotiate contracts with AGENTS and sometimes the performers.

Cel A thin sheet of cellulose acetate or similar clear plastic on which IMAGES are painted in one process of ANIMATION. The technique most commonly used in CARTOONS, involves a series of cels, each with slight differences, superimposed on a painted background and photographed one at a time to achieve the effect of motion.

Celluloid Term used to describe the flexible base which is coated with light-sensitive EMULSION to form the strip of film which passes through the CAMERA and, as a print, the projector. Until 1951 the celluloid base was made from highly flammable cellulose NITRATE, then replaced by cellulose acetate, or SAFETY film. Celluloid has also been commonly used as a term for cinema as medium, or more commonly popular cinema, as in Vito Russo's book on homosexuality in cinema, *The Celluloid Closet* (1987).

Censorship In literal terms, deciding whether or not a film, or part of a film, may be shown in public or on TELEVISION. Censorship takes many forms and the history of cinema is full of controversial moments which tell us much about the social and political history of the times in which particular censorship decisions were made. The most visible and clear-cut kinds of film censorship today are the industry-centred systems of CERTIFICATION in the UK and US which allot every RELEASE a CERTIFICATE indicating its official suitability for showing to children and young adults. Scenes of explicit VIOLENCE or SEXUALITY are the most common reasons for excluding younger audiences, though the use of 'bad' language is also common.

Currently there is no direct political censorship of films among western democracies though political considerations can contribute greatly to other forms of censorship. There have been numerous examples of governments and regimes banning films deemed to be threats to the state, from Nazi Germany and the former Soviet Union and some of its Warsaw Pact allies, to South Africa under apartheid. Many governments do ban films under a range of laws though there are prominent examples, such as the US and Germany, which make it unconstitutional to apply any form of direct censorship, though the US leaves a large loophole around the question of 'obscenity'.

Apart from the certification system the UK has various laws that can be used to prevent certain kinds of films being shown: laws on obscenity are frequently applied by Customs and Excise to prevent particular kinds of PORNOGRAPHY entering the country, libel laws can be used to prevent statements being made about individuals which they can prove to be both untrue and damaging to their reputation and the law on blasphemy is designed to prevent public statements of insult or hatred about the (Christian) church. All of these have caused controversies because of the wide scope for interpretation that they offer. Local authorities sometimes attempt to apply censorship of their own, even when a film has been certificated, by applying local by-laws on the licensing of buildings for entertainment to exclude material that it is felt would somehow disturb the general public. Recent attempts at local censorship have involved such high-profile films as *The Last Temptation of Christ* (dir. Martin Scorsese, 1988), *Natural Born Killers* (dir. Oliver Stone, 1994) and *Crash* (dir. David Cronenburg, 1996).

Arguably more significant for FEATURE FILMS are the different forms of self-censorship when a film is being conceived and eventually made. Though difficult to quantify, such self-censorship can happen at every level of the development of a project from original idea right through to POST-PRODUCTION and MARKETING. Some of this results from certification systems; in the US, for example, it is considered cata-strophic for most films to receive the so-called NC-17 certificate rather than the milder 'R', so that calculations are constantly made on perception of what is needed to avoid the NC-17.

The advent of cheap, easily available copies of feature films on VIDEO to rent or buy has posed new questions of censorship for the feature film industry: it is clearly impossible to control the age of viewers of films watched in a domestic context and the UK government has responded by introducing greater censorship powers for video recordings than those available for films on THEATRICAL release. It is therefore possible to find video versions of films different from those shown in cinemas (while television broadcasters also censor, for example, nudity and language). See also BBFVC, HAYS CODE, MOTION PICTURE ASSOCIATION OF AMERICA (MPAA).
Further reading: Black (1994), Leff & Simmons (1990), Lyons (1999).

Central Casting The Central Casting Corporation was set up by the MAJOR HOLLYWOOD STUDIOS in 1925 to provide EXTRAS for movies, establishing a reputa-tion for CASTING performers by type – 'tough guy', 'executive type', 'dumb blonde', etc. Such casting by type led to the phrase 'straight out of Central Casting', implying that someone fitted to perfection a certain type or STEREOTYPE (in movies or life). Though run independently since 1976, alongside many other casting agencies, 'Central Casting' retains a metaphorical force.

Certificate A rating given to a film in order to inform the public about the nature of its content. In the UK and the US, RATINGS are established by bodies set up within the film industry – in the UK, the BRITISH BOARD OF FILM CENSORS (BBFC) and in the US, the MOTION PICTURE ASSOCIATION OF AMERICA (MPAA). RATINGS are gener-ally based upon the age at which it is considered suitable for the film to be seen, either alone or accompanied by an adult. In the UK, the '18' RATING is given to films consid-ered to have the most explicit material, usually sex or VIOLENCE, meaning that nobody under the age of eighteen can legally be admitted to a programme which contains a film so rated. See also CENSORSHIP, RATINGS, RATING SYSTEM.

Certification See CENSORSHIP, CERTIFICATE, RATINGS, RATING SYSTEM.

Channel 4 UK TELEVISION station, launched in 1982 with a brief to innovate and to address AUDIENCES not previously catered to by the existing three British television stations. In Wales the fourth channel was dedicated to Welsh language broadcasting and was called Sianel Pedwar Cymru (S4C).

Channel 4 has had considerable impact on the British film industry, and is perhaps the single most important reason why any UK film industry has survived during the 1980s and 1990s. Channel 4's *Film on Four* arm was set up to invest in British INDEPENDENT films and to seek investment partners for films it commissioned, retaining exclusive rights to their television transmission and their sale for foreign transmission. The aim of *Film on Four* productions was to secure a limited THEATRICAL DISTRIBUTION followed reasonably quickly by a showing on Channel 4. The length of the holdback from television transmission depended largely on the distribution deal achieved and subsequent BOX-OFFICE performance.

Channel 4 patronage has been crucial to both the development of young British DIRECTORS and to more established figures wanting to make films with a distinct contemporary British identity, who found it difficult to find reliable long-term sources of investment. The latter group includes Stephen Frears, Mike Leigh and Ken Loach, whose work since the 1980s has depended at least partly on Channel 4's involvement. Newer directors who benefited from Channel 4 include Neil Jordan, Michael Radford, Peter Greenaway and Terence Davies. In keeping with Channel 4's remit, the films often dealt with 'outsiders' – often in terms of RACE, CLASS or GENDER – offering opportunities for the positive REPRESENTATIONS of minorities within the broader frame of British media.

As well as *Film on Four*, Channel 4 also housed a department of Independent Film and VIDEO with its own commissioning editor, who sought out low-budget innovative production from small-scale production companies and fostered the growth of this sector in general in the UK. Central to these activities was the Workshop Movement, a loosely defined group of small, mostly politically oppositional, film-making collectives and organizations. The Workshop Movement grew out of late 1960s politics, with groups making issue-based films, often rooted in the location of the particular workshop and committed to broadening access to the means of film production. Channel 4 provided a high-profile source of work for this sector, reaching agreements with the then powerful television unions for an agreed number of commissions for television by the workshops with CREWS working for less than agreed union minimum wages and with lower staffing levels. However, a change in Channel 4's funding at the start of the 1990s brought much of this to an end. Channel 4 has now launched Film Four, a subscription television channel available on CABLE, satellite and DIGITAL devoted entirely to the screening of independent cinema.

Character At one level, a straightforward term meaning a person from the fictional world of the film represented by a performer on the screen. During the late nineteenth and twentieth centuries traditional Western notions of character and characterization have centred on performance styles which hold that an ACTOR'S greatest achievement is to become the character, to leave as little space as possible between the performance and the person being represented. In cinema particularly, this is disrupted by the notion of the STAR performance, in which the actor's persona, carried over from hir or her other films and public appearances, predominates, producing a hierarchy amongst film actors in which stars become famous, rich and glamorous, but CHARACTER ACTORS get kudos and respect for their ability to impersonate others.

Dyer (1977) suggests that the development of the notion of character in film has roughly paralleled that in the novel and the theatre – a trajectory away from types and towards the idea of 'individualization'. MAINSTREAM CINEMA in the twentieth century has moved from being almost entirely PLOT-oriented to focusing more on character (though the emergence of technology-based BLOCKBUSTERS is a challenge here).

It is now common to see the idea of 'character' as the basis of fiction as an IDEO-LOGICALLY loaded one, the product of a capitalist bourgeois conception of the world. A drama based on the highly individuated actions of individuals implies a world that revolves around individuals rather than the much larger forces of CLASS, RACE or GENDER: in *Battleship Potemkin* (dir. Sergei Eisenstein, 1925), in place of an individual hero who performs heroic deeds to save a situation or person, we have the heroic ship's crew and people of Odessa victimized. However, some theorists and film-makers have operated on the basis that characters can perform the same functions as 'types' and reveal the underlying forces of a particular social and historical moment whilst retaining the features of a fully individuated human being (see EPIC).

Dyer (1977, pp. 110–111) argues that star IMAGES 'behave' in many of the ways traditionally associated with character including ideas such as development, the promotion of identification and 'particularity', but the parallel is not exact and development of a star's image is much more problematic than that of a character within a conventional narrative. Marilyn Monroe was an example of a star whose image 'behaved' most satisfyingly (from an AUDIENCE'S point of view) like a character in that she changed and developed, though with a degree of consistency, always allowing us a glimpse of the earliest stages of her visible persona. See also THE METHOD.

Character actor An ACTOR who generally plays minor roles, full of (usually) unglamorous physical detail and repeated over a range of films, often contrasted with a STAR, whose CASTING is generally in leading roles with scope for star IMAGE to show through. See also ACTING, CHARACTER.

Chase film A GENRE of early SILENT CINEMA, chase films featured stories built around a pursuit as the main ACTION. Chases were popular because they provided the kinetic excitement of movement along with motivation for fast EDITING featuring CROSS-CUTTING. Many of the films of French film-makers Fernand Zecca and Max Linder were chase films, as were some of the Mack Sennett COMEDIES for KEYSTONE. Geduld and Gottesman (1973, p. 74) extend the term to cover such later SOUND films as *Odd Man Out* (dir. Carol Reed, 1946) and *Night of the Hunter* (dir. Charles Laughton, 1955).

Chaser In the early years of the twentieth century – when it seemed as if cinema might have already peaked in popularity and might prove a passing craze – motion pictures 'moved to the bottom of the bill in VAUDEVILLE theatre and assumed the role of "chasers" – a vaudeville term denoting the concluding act on a programme, during which large portions of the audience left the theatre. It sometimes had a more pejorative sense, as when managers purposely put a bad act on the bill to "chase" patrons out of the theatre so that new customers could be seated' (Musser 1990, p. 298). 'Chaser' was also used as an alternative to CHASE FILMS.

Cheat, cheat shot The rules or CONVENTIONS of CONTINUITY EDITING and the flexibility of shooting in a studio allow for some 'cheating' about the placing of CHARACTERS in SPACE. To 'cheat' is to slightly change the position of a character from one SHOT to the next to exclude unwanted background or make possible a better ANGLE, or to enable an ACTOR to apparently turn to look at someone or something when in fact repositioning him/herself for a more attractive shot. A 'cheat shot' is any shot that seeks to persuade the spectator, via EDITING, that something has happened when it has not.

Chiaroscuro The term comes from a combination of two Italian words that translate as 'light' and 'dark'. It has come to refer to a LIGHTING design using heavy contrasts, creating a *MISE EN SCÈNE* dominated by heavy shadow. Originally the technique was most strongly associated with GERMAN EXPRESSIONIST cinema, but it is now more often mentioned as a defining characteristic of the look of FILM NOIR, where its deep shadows are seen as both a source of hidden danger and a more expressionistic signifier of the general psychological tone of the GENRE.

Children's Film Foundation Originally part of the RANK ORGANIZATION and called the Children's Entertainment Films Division, it became an organization funded directly by the British Film Production Fund in 1957, generally making low-budget FEATURE length films or shorts shown mainly in the SUBSIDIZED sector.

Chopsocky GENRE term coined by the American trade paper VARIETY to describe Kung Fu or MARTIAL ARTS movies.

Choreographer The person who plans, rehearses and stages movements in a dance (CHOREOGRAPHY), whether for the stage or film – Jerome Robbins and Bob Fosse, for example, worked in both forms. Dancers can devise their own choreography, as did Fred Astaire and Gene Kelly, or work with different choreographers. Kelly, Fosse and others may be considered AUTEURS who use dance, and its relationship to the CAMERA, as personal expression.

Choreography The art of creating and directing a dance, of planning and directing the movement of a dancer or group of dancers either on stage or in the cinema. In film, choreography may involve not only the dancer(s) but also the CAMERA, which can move in relation to the dance, as it does in many of Busby Berkeley's MUSICALS, CRANING and TRACKING around the troupe of chorines. Through the use of SPECIAL EFFECTS choreography may extend beyond the physical limitations of the real world, as when Gene Kelly dances with an animated Jerry the mouse in *Anchors Aweigh* (dir. George Sidney, 1945) or Fred Astaire dances on the ceiling in *Royal Wedding* (dir. Stanley Donen, 1951). See also CHOREOGRAPHER.

Cineast(e), cinéaste Properly speaking, an enthusiast (hence the suffix '-ast' or, in French, '-aste') or devotee of cinema, or cinephile (see also BUFF), and someone with considerable knowledge about film history, the choice of a foreign term possibly implying some pretension in such a person. Confusingly, cinéaste is now more commonly used to describe film-makers (though this is more in line with its original use – it was, apparently, coined by 1920s French experimental film-maker Louis Delluc – to describe anyone involved in the making of a film).

Cineaste Quarterly film journal, with a left-wing political orientation, published in New York City. Since its inception in 1967, *Cineaste* has given equal attention to MAINSTREAM FILM, DOCUMENTARY, ART CINEMA, and THIRD CINEMA in a writing style that seeks to bridge the gap between popular film CRITICISM and academic analysis.

Cinecittà The largest Italian STUDIO complex (with 15 SOUND stages), opened in 1937 by Mussolini, and more or less state-controlled in the late 1930s and during World War II, which led to its identification with Fascism and falling out of favour in the immediate post-war period. In the 1950s Cinecittà re-established itself as the centre for Italian film production, for example, for PEPLUM FILMS, and Federico Fellini made most of his films there – it was the main setting for his fantasy/autobiographical 1963 film *8½*. Popularly known as 'HOLLYWOOD on the Tiber' during the 1950s and 1960s, when many RUNAWAY Hollywood productions (e.g. *Quo Vadis?*, dir. Mervyn LeRoy, 1951, *Ben-Hur*, dir. William Wyler, 1959) exploited the lower costs and other advantages of working in Europe. Cinecittà remains today but has been less used since the 1970s by both Italian and foreign producers. See also NEO-REALISM.

Cinema Journal Academic film journal published by the University of Texas Press for the Society for Cinema Studies, the largest academic association of film studies in North America. First published in 1959 as the *Journal of the Society of Cinematologists*, the journal changed to its present name in 1966 (although the organization did not change its name to the Society for Cinema Studies (SCS) until three years later). Published quarterly, the journal features articles on all aspects of cinema and also features *Professional Notes* and *Archival News* columns with information about conferences and research activities.

Cinema Nôvo Brazilian film movement beginning in the late 1950s, combining elements of HOLLYWOOD cinema and European ART FILM in an attempt to make a politically-oriented cinema that would speak to and for the poor and disenfranchised, both within Brazil and in the Third World generally. Especially influenced by the political views and aesthetic techniques of Italian NEO-REALISM, the movement included film-makers like Glauber Rocha, Ruy Guerra and Nelson Pereira dos Santos. Rocha's *Antonio das mortes* (1969), one of the *Cinema Nôvo* films to achieve international DISTRIBUTION, uses elements of the WESTERN GENRE to present a stylized tale of the oppression of peasants by wealthy landowners. By the early 1970s political pressure had severely limited the group's activities – its major figures either exiled by an oppressive military government or constrained by working in a state-controlled film industry. See also THIRD CINEMA.

Further reading: Chanan (1983), Johnson & Stam (1982), Chanan in Nowell-Smith (1996)

Cinema of attractions Term popularized by film historian Tom Gunning (1986) to describe the visual appeal of much early or primitive SILENT cinema. A reference to Sergei Eisenstein's notion of 'a MONTAGE of attractions', the phrase describes the tendency of early cinema to create a vivid impression on the viewer through IMAGES of SPECTACLE, similar to the aesthetic of carnivals, amusement parks and other such events, rather than literature, upon which NARRATIVE cinema most heavily depends. Gunning argues that many early films offer an alternative form of address to the narrative mode that superseded it, offering the viewer 'exhibitionist confrontation rather than diegetic absorption.'

Cinéma vérité A style of OBSERVATIONAL CINEMA that uses available LIGHTING, FAST FILM STOCK and a minimum of unobtrusive equipment, especially the HAND-HELD CAMERA and portable SOUND recording equipment, to record PROFILMIC EVENTS as they unfold using ALEATORY TECHNIQUES. French film historian Georges Sadoul may have been the first to use the term, although it became more widely known when anthropologist/film-maker Jean Rouch and sociologist Edgar Morin used it as the subtitle for their influential film *Chronique d'un été* (*Chronicle of a Summer*, 1961).

Although the term is sometimes used interchangeably with DIRECT CINEMA, there is a significant difference between the two approaches. As Barnouw (1993) points out, 'the direct cinema documentarist took his camera to a situation of tension and waited hopefully for a crisis; the Rouch version of *cinéma vérité* tried to precipitate one. The direct cinema artist aspired to invisibility; the Rouch *cinéma vérité* artist was often an avowed participant. The direct cinema artist played the role of uninvolved bystander; the *cinéma vérité* artist espoused that of provocateur.' Rouch believed that the camera functions as a 'psychological stimulant' that, while perhaps affecting the behaviour of people in front of the camera, actually reveals a deeper truth about their personality. A literal translation of Dziga Vertov's newsreel *Kino Pravda* – literally, 'film truth' – *cinéma vérité*, like Vertov's *Man with a Movie Camera* (1929), boasted of its own presence in and influence upon profilmic events.

The tradition of *vérité* has been used by such subsequent film-makers as Michael Rubbo (*Waiting for Fidel*, 1974), Marcel Ophuls (*The Sorrow and the Pity*, 1970) and, more recently, to ironic effect, by Michael Moore (*Roger and Me*, 1989). Pseudo-*vérité* movies such as *The War Game* (Peter Watkins, 1966) and *The Blair Witch Project* (dir. Eduardo Sanchez and Daniel Myrick, 1999) employ the CONVENTIONS of *verité* to achieve a greater sense of realism and immediacy.

Further reading: Eaton (1979), Marcorelles (1973), Winston (1995)

CinemaScope See WIDESCREEN.

Cinémathèque Française One of very few well-known film ARCHIVES, due largely to its curious history. Founded in 1936 by Henri Langlois – drawing on Langlois's own collection of films – with later film-maker Georges Franju and later theorist Jean Mitry. During World War II Langlois and Lotte Eisner, who became later a major film historian, hid films from the occupying Germans and after the war rewarded by government grants. The Cinémathèque was always as interested in showing its films as in preserving them and its screenings influenced the tastes of French critics, especially those associated with *CAHIERS DU CINÉMA*, who later formed the core of the FRENCH NEW WAVE. Langlois's methods alienated him from

the international film archive body, FIAF, and the French government attempted to oust Langlois – events which became mixed up in the May 1968 Paris uprising which almost brought down the French government. The government later withdrew funding, establishing its own official state film archive in 1969, though the Cinémathèque itself continues (and also runs the Paris Musée du Cinéma).
Further reading: Roud (1983)

Cinematic Term describing something taken to have qualities associated with, characteristic of, or specific to cinema. Used when a film is considered to exhibit particular qualities of cinema, such as striking EDITING, though the way the term is used can tend to be rather precious. The term can also be used to refer to 'cinematic' qualities in other art forms such as theatre, painting or the novel: inter-war novelists such as John Dos Passos have been described as 'cinematic' in their methods of description and structure.

Cinématographe The name given by brothers Louis and Auguste Lumière to their machine which both photographed and projected moving pictures. The Cinématographe marked a significant advance on Thomas Edison's KINETOSCOPE by introducing the intermittent motion of film through the CAMERA (inspired by the mechanism of the sewing machine). The term 'cinema' – both the medium of film and the place where films are shown – derives from Cinématographe, coined from the Greek for 'movement' and 'writing'. See also LOOP, LUMIÈRE PROGRAMME.
Further reading: Neale (1985), Robinson (1996), Thompson & Bordwell (1994), Winston (1996)

Cinematographer The person with overall responsibility for the LIGHTING and photography of a film, including setting up and moving the CAMERA, positioning lights, composing the IMAGE and selecting LENSES – also sometimes described as director of photography or lighting cameraman – on larger productions with a whole department working under him. The cinematographer is second only in importance to the DIRECTOR in terms of responsibility for the look of the film and the two are likely to have worked closely together before shooting as well as on the SET or location itself. Many directors happily give credit to the role of the cinematographer in a film's success, as Orson Welles did after *Citizen Kane* (1941), acknowledging the huge contribution of Gregg Toland to the film's cinematic innovations such as the extensive use of DEEP-FOCUS photography. A number of important cinematographers have gone on to direct their own FEATURES including Haskell Wexler (*Medium Cool*, 1969) Nicolas Roeg (*Performance*, 1970, co-directed with Donald Cammell), and Chris Menges (*A World Apart*, 1988), though rarely with the same degree of success.

Cinematography The work of the CINEMATOGRAPHER, including both technical procedures such as the operation of the CAMERA, LIGHTS, film STOCK and LENSES as well as aesthetic concerns such as composition, COLOUR and CAMERA MOVEMENT. The creative possibilities of cinematography have been greatly enhanced by technical advances, particularly the invention of lightweight and silent cameras, smaller, more powerful lights, film stocks offering ever-increasing possibilities in the size and brilliance of the IMAGE and the plethora of devices for SPECIAL EFFECTS photography. Cinematography is one of the key elements of cinema, best seen in its contribution to the dominant look or visual tone of a film. Turner (1999, pp. 54–55) talks of LIGHTING having two functions within a film, one being 'expressive', the other to do with REALISM, and the same could be said of all the work of the cinematographer.

The expressive function of cinematography, though never entirely absent from a film, can sometimes dominate the look of a film. The principal cinematographer on Terrence Malick's *Days of Heaven* (1978) – the story of a group of people's relationship with a particular landscape, the Texas Panhandle – was Nestor Almendros, with additional photography by Haskell Wexler. Both men are among the most accomplished cinematographers of the modern period, and their work gives the landscape a sense of size, emptiness and great beauty while the dialogue in the film is spare, with humans dwarfed by place in an American tradition that includes John Ford's use of Monument Valley.

Cinematography's function in a realist aesthetic is, like other elements of film language, to be as invisible as possible, creating the illusion of naturally occurring events. Realist cinematography would generally include the use of predominantly HIGH KEY LIGHTING, without the EXPRESSIONISTIC shadows that dominated FILM NOIR, and quiet, unobtrusive camera movement SHOT from human heights and angles, though realism is as full of CONVENTIONS as any other style, and as difficult to achieve. Further reading: Bordwell & Thompson (1997)

Cinerama WIDESCREEN process invented in 1935 – used for training anti-aircraft gunners during World War II – but first introduced commercially in 1952 with the special presentation, *This Is Cinerama*. Cinerama used three 35MM cameras and three 35mm projectors, on a wide, curved screen with an ASPECT RATIO of 2.5:1, with stereophonic SOUND to give a SURROUND SOUND effect, so that both IMAGE and sound enveloped the spectator. The three separate projected images merged on the screen into one, although the system never perfectly solved the problem of joins where the images overlapped. *This Is Cinerama* and the Cinerama system were a success but the cost of equipping theatres meant that it could only ever be used in a few prime locations, and the early films were no more than travelogues designed to exploit the system, such as showing a roller coaster ride. It was some years before narrative films were made in Cinerama, the most successful being *How The West Was Won* (dir. Henry Hathaway, John Ford, George Marshall, 1962). The complications and expense of the system – together with competition from widescreen systems like CinemaScope – forced Cinerama to adopt a single film ANAMORPHIC process, using UltraPanavision, with a 65MM NEGATIVE and 70MM prints, though the brand name Cinerama was retained. As with other experiments with widescreen systems such as CinemaScope, TODD-AO and other 1950s innovations, Cinerama was a novelty response to declining cinema AUDIENCES.
Further reading: Belton (1992)

City symphony film A particular GENRE of DOCUMENTARY FILM that provides an impressionistic view of a specific urban place. City symphony films usually lack a narrative, tending to be ABSTRACT FILMS structured loosely as 'a-day-in-the-life-of' a city or place, relying on MONTAGE to provide a sense of rhythm and movement. The first such film was *Mannahatta* (1921), a poetic short about New York City made by photographer Paul Strand and painter Charles Sheeler. *Berlin: Symphony of a Great City* (dir. Walter Ruttmann, 1927) and *Man with a Movie Camera* (dir. Dziga Vertov, 1929) are among the most well-known city symphony films. More recent films such

as *Koyaanisqatsi* (dir. Godfrey Reggio, 1983) and *Baraka* (dir. Ron Fricke, 1992) use the same approach on a global scale.

Clapper board A slate with spaces for recording information including the name of the film and DIRECTOR, the date and the numbers of both the SCENE and TAKE. Two hinged 'clapsticks' on top of the slate are banged together by a CLAPPER LOADER when a take begins. This seemingly theatrical gesture – widely known outside the film industry – has very practical purposes, allowing an EDITOR to identify each take accurately, but also to synchronise SOUND and image in POST-PRODUCTION through the simultaneous appearance of both the board and the sound of the banging clapsticks. Nowadays various electronic devices perform roughly the same function, but the clapper board is still widely used.

Clapper loader A member of the CAMERA CREW whose most public responsibility is to mark the beginning of each TAKE by 'clapping' the sticks on the CLAPPER BOARD whilst holding it in front of the CAMERA. Sometimes referred to as a second assistant CAMERA OPERATOR, the person may also be responsible for other relatively mundane jobs associated with the camera such as loading the magazines with film.

Class An important term for the study of film in two principal ways. First, the concept of class is central to MARXIST film CRITICISM. Secondly, class as the overt subject matter of actual film TEXTS is important to certain key moments of film production in some countries including Britain. According to Marxist thinking, class is never absent from the concerns of any film and one of the key functions of analysis is to reveal the way that class relations are represented or concealed. In Marxist terms, class is a term used to identify groups of people with common economic interests within a capitalist system because they occupy the same place within the system that creates and consumes wealth. Crudely, the working class produces wealth through its labour and the ruling class consumes it, though there are many variations within this – hence terms like middle class, petit bourgeois and lower middle class. Although these class relations are based on places within an economic system, they also describe power relations. In a capitalist system power is generally denied to the working class. At one level a straightforward class analysis can be applied to the film industry itself where class relations are very clear: the craft level of film production – including SET construction, electrical operations, make-up and so on – remains hidden and invisible, whereas the final product, the film, is sold as something glamorous and almost 'natural', without reference to the intensive labour that in practice is required.

Perhaps the most telling point to be made about class and the cinema is the way that most classical or MAINSTREAM FILM obscures true class relations, primarily because of the tendency of CLASSICAL NARRATIVE to be constructed around cause and effect patterns based upon individual actions and motivations. Hill (1986) illustrates this by focusing on a period of British cinema that was, ostensibly, centrally concerned with class. One of the claims of the BRITISH NEW WAVE – films like *Room at the Top* (dir. Jack Clayton, 1959), *Saturday Night and Sunday Morning* (dir. Karel Reisz, 1960) and *The Loneliness of the Long Distance Runner* (dir. Tony Richardson, 1962) – was that it sought to represent working-class life truthfully in ways not previously seen in the cinema. However, while the films might be set in places that were at the time under-represented in cinema, they still resorted to individual, rather than class-based, explanations for what happens to their protagonists. This is not to argue that these are bad films, simply that their ability to represent class-based narratives is strictly limited by their adherence to a form of drama that is, finally, about individuals.

Significantly, Hill has to go back to Sergei Eisenstein and films like *Strike* (1924) and *Battleship Potemkin* (1925) to find examples which escape the failure of cinema to deal adequately with class relations. Most mainstream cinema has struggled to deal with class because it operates within a REALIST aesthetic that mitigates against it. At various historical moments since Eisenstein the AVANT-GARDE has sought to deal with class relations through radical cinematic means and Jean-Luc Godard's work in the late 1960s and early 1970s is a strong example (see for instance *Tout Va Bien*, 1972). Further reading: Miller & Stam (1999)

Classical Hollywood cinema, Classical narrative, Classic narrative cinema
A style of film-making prevalent in HOLLYWOOD between 1930 and 1960, many features of which survive as the dominant form of MAINSTREAM FILM today. The fact that the style is particularly associated with Hollywood should not obscure the fact that it also dominated (and continues to dominate to some extent) all commercial film production, certainly in the West. A key feature of classical Hollywood cinema is that it prioritizes narrative over any concern with form and its appearance is one of reality – a highly constructed reality which hides the manner of its making by carefully worked-out film-making strategies. One of the most important of these is the system of CONTINUITY EDITING, or INVISIBLE EDITING, the principal objective of which is to hide the fact that the film has been EDITED at all, aiming for an effect of seamlessness in which spectators are 'stitched' into the reality with which they are presented – hence the critical notion of SUTURE.

In terms of narrative, classical Hollywood cinema has a number of elements that make up a clear recurring pattern. Most STORIES are based upon the disruption of order by an event or series of events, setting in motion a chain of cause and effect until harmony is restored by the resolution of difficulties. Narratives are CHARACTER-led, with events seen as the result of individual motivations, goals and drives and any wider explanations in politics and history are subsumed within this. Hayward (1996, p. 46) cites the example of the mainstream liberal VIETNAM MOVIES made in the USA during the 1970s and 1980s. Whilst these films often took quite bold anti-war positions, none offered any kind of explanation or critique of the war's causes, instead dramatizing it as the experience of individuals and the consequent disruption of their lives, as in *Platoon* (dir. Oliver Stone, 1986). Classical Hollywood cinema is also characterized by a high degree of CLOSURE – endings that tend to resolve all the conflicts that have been the subject of the narrative. Hollywood films are popularly seen as always having a 'happy ending': while this is something of a distortion, they do tend to have endings which leave little room for moral or narrative ambiguity. This is also relevant to film style, where the use of MISE-EN-SCÈNE, CAMERA and editing serve to give viewers a firm sense of where they are, rather than leaving them with any sense of spatial or temporal ambiguity.

The IDEOLOGICAL function of classical Hollywood cinema has been the focus of much theoretical work since the 1970s. Through the combination of its narrative trajectories and its stylistic construction of a natural, realistic world, Hollywood could be said to have been a major contributor to common-sense notions about questions of GENDER, RACE, SEXUALITY and the economics of capitalism. Put simply, the endless repetition of the Hollywood pattern of romantic heterosexual love ending in marriage and stability tends to naturalize this as the normal way to live and, by extension, marginalizing other forms of human relationships. This should not be taken to mean that the patterns of such a cinema are entirely resistant to change or to re-interpretation. Several theorists have speculated about the 'cracks and fissures' that can appear in the apparently seamless vision of the classical Hollywood narrative, allowing for a variety of readings, particularly when viewing takes place in a fresh historical context, such as the subversive power of a female STAR's performance within a narrative that seeks to objectify and control the character that plays (see Dyer 1979, 1986).

The stylistic system in operation within this kind of cinema is, however, subject to a limited degree of change and the gradual importation of ideas from EXPERIMENTAL and AVANT-GARDE film. The POSTMODERN context of a much freer exchange between cultural forms and TEXTS of all types has led to a contemporary mainstream cinema that remains predominantly REALIST, but which also borrows more freely from less conventional forms.

Further reading: Bordwell (1985), Bordwell, Staiger & Thompson (1985), Hollows *et al.* (2000)

Click track   A SOUNDTRACK on which a series of clicks have been recorded to get the exact tempo for the post-recording of MUSIC to accompany a film. The musical conductor usually listens to the click track with earphones.

Cliffhanger   A term used to describe either a whole film that depends heavily on suspense for its effects or a SCENE from a film that leaves the fate of a CHARACTER hanging in the balance. It is the basis of the SERIAL form, which today survives only on TELEVISION. The origins of the word are fairly literal and come from one of the most common forms of suspense whereby somebody is actually hanging from a cliff while the AUDIENCE waits anxiously to see if s/he will be rescued. *North by Northwest* (dir. Alfred Hitchcock, 1959) climaxes with Eve Marie Saint dangling off a cliff holding onto Cary Grant's arm, but Hitchcock then playfully CUTS to Grant hauling Marie Saint not up a cliff, but on to the top bunk of a sleeper car as they start their honeymoon – generally thought to be an affectionate HOMAGE to the cliffhanger.

Clip   A short segment of a film used for a variety of purposes such as ADVERTISING. A film TRAILER will typically consist of a number of clips edited together to give an audience a strong impression of a film's qualities. Clips are also an important part of a new film's promotion on TELEVISION talk shows.

Closed set   A SET, whether in a STUDIO or on LOCATION, where a film is being SHOT, which is closed to visitors, including studio executives, the only people allowed being those necessary to shooting the SCENE. A set might be closed when an intimate scene is being shot, or when film-makers wish to maintain secrecy about the precise contents of a film or scene (or about problems with the film).

Close-up   An IMAGE in which an object or part of the human body, usually the face or hands, fills most of the FRAME. Close-ups are often used to isolate details from the surrounding environment for emphasis and to direct the viewer's attention to a particular detail or an ACTOR's expression in order to enhance IDENTIFICATION with a CHARACTER.

Closure In narrative construction, the extent to which a STORY's ending reveals the consequences of the major ACTION, either depicted or provided in exposition – as, for example, at the end of *American Graffiti* (dir. George Lucas, 1973) – or offers resolution to its various dramatic conflicts. A film with closure leaves the viewer with no unanswered questions about the fate of the major CHARACTERS or the consequences of their actions. Closure, usually in the form of an upbeat or happy ending, is considered a CONVENTION of HOLLYWOOD or MAINSTREAM cinema, although such closure may be ironic, as Wood (1965) argues of *Psycho* (dir. Alfred Hitchcock, 1960), where the psychiatrist's concluding explanation of Norman Bates's mental illness reduces him to a mere 'case' but cannot possibly contain the dark impulses the film has encouraged in the audience. Lack of closure, suggesting that the lives of the characters carry on after the film ends, is associated with REALIST films, such as those of Jean Renoir (the final LONG SHOT of the two French soldiers in *La Grande Illusion*, 1937, escaping into Switzerland, presumably to return ultimately to their units to fight again, is perhaps the most famous example) and the Italian NEO-REALIST films of Vittorio De Sica (*Bicycle Thieves*, 1947; *Umberto D*, 1952). In the wake of European ART CINEMA, definitive closure has become less common in Hollywood film today than in the past.
Further reading: Bordwell & Thompson (1997)

Code A term central to SEMIOTIC and STRUCTURALIST approaches to film study – a way in which individual signs are organized in order to generate meaning. Although it belongs to early studies of language as a system of signs, the term has long been applied to almost all ways of structuring meaning. The range of codes that apply to film is enormous and includes both those that are unique and specific to the medium and those that form part of everyday communication but which are also part of the language of film. The former includes codes associated with CAMERA MOVEMENT and EDITING whilst the latter includes written and spoken language, codes of non-verbal behaviour, performance, COSTUME and interior DECOR. There is also a sense in which film generates sets of codes within GENRE.

The generally accepted version of the way that codes come to embody meanings is that they work on two levels: that of DENOTATION and CONNOTATION. Denotation is the literal meaning derived from a sign, whereas connotation refers to the suggestions made by an individual sign or code. Hayward (1996, p. 310) refers to Roland Barthes' and John Hartley's identification of a third level of meaning, where a set of connotations becomes IDEOLOGY. The complex, interlocking signs and codes in a scene from, say, *The Searchers* (dir. John Ford, 1956) could be read in terms of excessive male VIOLENCE and racism or alternatively in terms of a kind of heroic nobility and a mythic quest for identity. Either way they ultimately reflect the ideological position(s) taken by the interpreters which are likely to result from their own origins in terms of CLASS, RACE and GENDER. Inevitably, this is an over-simplification and experience of the WESTERN genre would also be vital to the way an individual would read *The Searchers*, for there are internal generic codes operating as well as wider cultural ones.

The ideological dimension to the reading of film codes shifts over time and the development of FEMINIST thought is a clear example of how this can impact on the way an AUDIENCE views a film TEXT, ranging from dress codes and attitudes to quasi-PORNOGRAPHY to more complex work on the role of the CAMERA in producing a male-orientated cinema based upon the male GAZE dominating conventional CINE-MATOGRAPHY.

Although semiotics has at times aspired to a kind of scientific status, the question of where codes begin and end needs to be seen flexibly. To take costume in film as an example, a garment might be seen as a sign and a whole outfit as a code, but it could be more useful to see each individual CHARACTER'S clothing as part of the overall code of the film's costume design, particularly in a genre film. Thus Humphrey Bogart's suits and hats as Sam Spade or Philip Marlowe could be seen as part of a broader FILM NOIR dress code which in turn depends on codes associated with clothing at certain historical moments and subject to constant reinterpretation. See also ICONOGRAPHY, SIGNIFIER.

Further reading: Aumont (1992), Rowe in Nelmes (1999)

Collage film A form of EXPERIMENTAL or AVANT-GARDE FILM in which individual IMAGES taken from other visual media (newspapers, magazines, other films, TELE-VISION or VIDEO) provide all of the film's visual content or a significant part of it. Arthur Lipsett's *Free Fall* (1961) and *Very Nice, Very Nice* (1964) are comprised entirely of FOUND FOOTAGE on both the SOUND and image tracks, while *Letter to Jane* (dir. Jean-Luc Godard and Jean-Piesse Gorin, 1972) uses the repeated image of Joseph Kraft's famous photograph of actress/activist Jane Fonda and other media images to examine the IDEOLOGY and CODES of journalism and MAINSTREAM CINEMA.

Colorization A trademark name (another being Color Systems Technology) – but now also a generic term – for computer-based programmes that add COLOUR to BLACK-AND-WHITE FILM for broadcast and VIDEO transmission – a sort of electronic version of TINTING in SILENT CINEMA. The prime motive for colorization was the appetite of NETWORK TELEVISION for COLOUR FILM, but what threatened to become a major trend, with colorized versions of popular classics like *It's a Wonderful Life* (dir. Frank Capra, 1946), has somewhat subsided, partly due to the industrial and critical outcry at the effects on film-makers' original intentions.

Further reading: Klawans in Miller (1990)

Colour, colour film Although colour film may seem a relatively recent inno-vation – from the late 1930s or even as late as the 1950s – a colour option for motion pictures was available and exploited from very early on in cinema history, just as with SOUND. Maxim Gorky's observations on the LUMIÈRE PROGRAMME (Leyda, 1960) remind us that spectators did notice that the world represented was in BLACK-AND-WHITE, not colour. Although colour photography posed large technical problems for film-makers, the early desire for colour was clear in the popularity of colour TINTING throughout the period of 'SILENT' FILM.

The principles of colour photography have been understood since the mid-nine-teenth century and a movie colour system, Kinemacolour, was patented in 1906, leading to some early colour films. Early processes however, involved considerable technical problems in photography and/or projection. Kinemacolour, for example, was a two-colour additive process using a rotating red-blue filter to add colour to black-and-white film. Kodachrome, adopted for movies in 1916, was a subtractive process, with unwanted colours taken away from white light through layers of subtractive colours on a single filmstrip, rather than in projection. Similarly, TECHNI-COLOR's two-colour process, developed in the mid-1920s, used a beam splitter and two negatives, one red, one green, joined together. Overall, the problems with colour and the apparently small advantages, plus the problems and costs of adapting to SOUND, were such that the MAJOR STUDIOS showed little interest in the use of colour for FEATURE FILM purposes, despite examples such as the Douglas Fairbanks movie *The Black Pirate* (dir. Albert Parker, 1926). Technicolor, however, produced SHORT FILMS and collaborated with MGM and WARNER BROS. on short subjects and colour SEQUENCES within black-and-white films (e.g. *Ben Hur*, dir. Fred Niblo, and *The Phantom of the Opera*, dir. Rupert Julian, both 1925). Technicolor then introduced a three-colour process and made exclusive agreements with INDEPENDENT companies like WALT DISNEY, which acquired exclusive rights to colour CARTOONS (such as the *Silly Symphonies* and *Snow White and the Seven Dwarfs*, 1937) and Pioneer Films, which released the first three-colour feature, *Becky Sharp* (dir. Rouben Mamoulian, 1935) before joining forces with independent producer David O. Selznick, whose SELZNICK International Pictures went on to make successful PRESTIGE PICTURES in Technicolor, most notably *Gone with the Wind* (dir. Victor Fleming, 1939).

Although World War II delayed the full exploitation of colour (by 1947 still only 12 per cent of US features were being made in colour), these successes effectively established the viability of colour. However, not until the early 1950s, primarily under the pressure of competition from TELEVISION, was more than half of HOLLY-WOOD's output in colour, and that percentage fell to only 25 per cent by the end of the 1950s, rising again (to 94 per cent by 1970) once the leasing of major studio movies to television became standard practice and the television networks switched to colour broadcasting in the mid 1960s. Technicolor jealously guarded control of its processes, providing its own cameramen, colour consultants and equipment for Technicolor productions, but in 1950 was forced by anti-trust decree to release its basic patents. Other colour systems emerged, notably Eastman Kodak's single NEGA-TIVE EASTMAN COLOR STOCK, introduced in 1952. Eastman Color used the same 3-colour subtractive process as Technicolor but combined three layers of colour dye in the same EMULSION and coupled them in the developing and printing process. This meant that a low-cost negative could be used in a normal CAMERA thereby reducing costs – an important factor in that in 1935, shooting in colour added 30 per cent to production costs (though falling to 10 per cent by 1949, when it was also reckoned that colour could add up to 25 per cent to BOX-OFFICE receipts). So successful was Eastman Color that the brand names developed by both MAJOR STUDIOS (Warnercolor, Metrocolor, Pathecolor) and laboratories (Movielab, Deluxe and even Technicolor) all used the system. After 1955 'Technicolor' refers only to the laboratory process which produced three separately dyed negatives, and since the mid 1970s even Technicolor has converted to an Eastman-based system. In the 1960s it was discovered that the Eastman Color images were more prone to fading than Technicolor's older process, posing major new preservation problems for film ARCHIVES.

The way that colour has been used by film-makers has changed over time according to the degree and nature of its use, its technical possibilities and factors such as cost. Colour film will never be able to register colour accurately, though it can be argued that improvements in colour stocks over the last 100 years have significantly altered their look and have been designed generally to produce more subtle and natural colours, or greater REALISM. Within the technical possibilities offered, film-makers can seek an acceptable approximation to natural colours or, alternatively, emphasize its artifice. Historically, colour was initally considered suitable for ADVEN-TURE FILMS and MUSICALS, rather than for straight dramas or COMEDIES and this tended to mean that colour was used in relatively stylized, gaudy or artificial ways. Certainly, many 1940s/1950s musicals such as *An American in Paris* (dir. Vincente Minnelli, 1951) or *Singin' in the Rain* (dir. Gene Kelly and Stanley Donen, 1952) and melodramas like *Leave Her to Heaven* (dir. John M. Stahl, 1945) or *Some Came Running* (dir. Minnelli, 1958) often emphasised the artifice of colour. Artifice is particularly striking in the family melodramas directed by Douglas Sirk, such as *All That Heaven Allows* (1955) and *Written on the Wind* (1956), and in the 1940s work of Michael Powell and Emeric Pressburger in Britain (*A Matter of Life and Death*, 1946; *Black Narcissus*, 1947; *The Red Shoes*, 1948). Such expressive use of colour contrasts with the often more 'naturalistic' colour in other films of the period, such as the WESTERNS directed by Anthony Mann (*Bend of the River*, 1952, *The Man from Laramie*, 1955), though colour is clearly stylized in westerns such as *Duel in the Sun* (dir. King Vidor, 1946) and *Shane* (dir. George Stevens, 1953). Despite exceptions like *Bram Stoker's Dracula* (dir. Francis Ford Coppola, 1992), since the 1970s the main trend in US films and elsewhere is for colour to appear more naturalistic. It may be that colour has come to signify generally the real, as black-and-white was able to (and still can, to some extent).

Generally speaking (other than for prestige productions), the widespread use of colour came later to Europe and other film-making countries like Japan. 1950s and 1960s European ART CINEMA was often strongly associated with black-and-white film and contrasted with popular cinema's use of colour. However, in the early 1960s film-makers like Jean-Luc Godard, Alain Resnais, Ingmar Bergman and Michelangelo Antonioni made their first colour films, often exploring the possibilities of stylized or expressive use of colour, as in films like *Cries and Whispers* (dir. Bergman, 1972), *The Red Desert*, dir. Antonioni, 1964) or *Two or Three Things I Know About Her* (dir. Godard, 1966).

Further reading: Bordwell & Thompson (1997), Branigan and Buscombe in Nichols (1985), Cook & Bernink (1999), Gomery (1992), Branigan in Kerr (1986), Maltby (1995), Neale (1985), Winston (1996)

Columbia American film company, originally known as CBC Sales Corporation when founded in 1920 by brothers Harry and Jack Cohn and Joseph Brandt. Renamed Columbia Pictures in 1924, the company, under the direction of Harry Cohn, worked by borrowing most of its STARS, DIRECTORS and SCREENWRITERS from other STUDIOS. Among its biggest successes in the 1930s were several films by Frank Capra, including *It Happened One Night* (1934), which swept the top five OSCARS at that year's ACADEMY AWARDS ceremonies. In the 1950s Columbia moved into TELE-VISION production with its subsidiary company, Screen Gems, and began backing some INDEPENDENT productions (*On the Waterfront*, dir. Elia Kazan, 1954) and foreign films (*Lawrence of Arabia*, dir. David Lean, 1962). Columbia had a number of subsequent major BLOCKBUSTER successes, including *Close Encounters of the Third*

Kind (dir. Steven Spielberg, 1977). The company, which also founded CBS, HBO and Tristar Pictures, was purchased by Coca-Cola in 1982 and then by Sony Corporation in 1991.

Further reading: Finler (1988), Gomery (1986)

Comedy Most generally, any film that treats its subject matter in a humorous way. Although sometimes referred to as a GENRE, comedy is really a tone that cuts across genres, so that there are comic WESTERNS (*Blazing Saddles*, dir. Mel Brooks, 1974), comic GANGSTER FILMS (*The Ladykillers*, dir. Alexander Mackendrick, 1955), even comic DISASTER FILMS (*Airplane*, dir. Jim Abrahams, 1980) and comic HORROR FILMS (*Young Frankenstein*, dir. Brooks, 1974). Nevertheless, there are several distinct comic genres, including SLAPSTICK COMEDY, SCREWBALL COMEDY, ROMANTIC COMEDY, and PARODY.

The comic impulse was apparent in film from the beginning. In the first LUMIÈRE PROGRAMME was the SHORT FILM *L'Arroseur arrosé* (*Watering the Gardener*, 1895), which features the SIGHT GAG of a gardener getting sprayed in the face when he looks at the nozzle of his hose. Max Linder was the first film comedian to combine a CHARACTER with comic gags, making over 350 comic SHORT FILMS, first in his native France from 1905–15 and then in the US from 1917–22. His films were an important influence on Charlie Chaplin, perhaps the most artistically ambitious of the comedians during the Golden Age of SILENT FILM comedy that also includes Buster Keaton, Harry Langdon and Harold Lloyd, and Mack Sennett's KEYSTONE comedies. Keaton explored the complex mechanics of elaborate sight gags, as in his pursuit by a landslide of falling rocks and a mob of aspiring brides in *Seven Chances* (1925), while Chaplin explored character development and the sentiment of MELODRAMA, as well as social criticism, particularly in his later FEATURES such as *Modern Times* (1936) and *The Great Dictator* (1940).

Many comedians came to Hollywood from VAUDEVILLE and the music hall during the early period as well as after the arrival of SOUND, bringing to cinema the tradition of the comic team, the most well-known of which were Laurel and Hardy and later, in the 1940s and 1950s, Abbott and Costello. With the arrival of sound, the emphasis of comedy shifted from the primarily physical to the verbal, relying on wit, puns and *double entendres*. W.C. Fields became a STAR with his caustic, mumbling asides, as did Mae West with her sexual innuendo. The Marx Brothers made a series of anarchic comedies, with fast-paced verbal assaults that, combined with destructive pranks, made language a weapon with which to assault the pretensions and values of their upper-CLASS victims, whether in academe (*Horse Feathers*, dir. Norman Z. McLeod, 1932) or the opera (*A Night at the Opera*, dir. Sam Wood, 1935).

In the 1930s, ROMANTIC COMEDY and SCREWBALL COMEDY also depended upon language to articulate a sophisticated sparring between the sexes in such movies as *It Happened One Night* (dir. Frank Capra, 1934), *Bringing Up Baby* (dir. Howard Hawks, 1938) and *His Girl Friday* (dir. Hawks, 1940). In the 1940s, WRITER-DIRECTOR Preston Sturges made a series of sharply satirical comedies, including *The Great McGinty* (1940), *Miracle of Morgan's Creek* (1944) and *Hail the Conquering Hero* (1944) that anticipated the films of Billy Wilder and the development of black comedy twenty years later. In the 1960s black comedy, both in fiction and film, befitted the cynical and anxious period of the Vietnam War. Preceded by Chaplin's *Monsieur Verdoux* (1947), a comedy about a serial wife murderer, and Alfred Hitchcock's *The Trouble with Harry*

(1955), a farce about a corpse that refuses to stay buried in a picturesque New England town, a series of iconoclastic comedies broke taboos of taste by mocking serious subjects. Among them, Stanley Kubrick's *Dr. Strangelove: Or, How I Learned to Stop Worrying and Love the Bomb* (1963) lampooned the government and the military, as well as the Cold War and nuclear holocaust, while *The Loved One* (dir. Tony Richardson, 1964) derided the commercialization of death and funeral rites in contemporary America. More recently, Quentin Tarantino has carried black humour's uneasy combination of comedy and VIOLENCE into the GANGSTER FILM, combining IMAGES of graphic violence with stylized banal dialogue in *Pulp Fiction* (1994).

In England, EALING studios was known for its comedies, beginning with *Kind Hearts and Coronets* (dir. Robert Hamer, 1949) and in such other notable films as *The Man in the White Suit* (dir. Alexander Mackendrick, 1951) and *The Lavender Hill Mob* (dir. Charles Chricton, 1951). Roy and John Boulting, twin brothers who produced and directed their own films, made a series of popular anarchic comedies including *Lucky Jim* (1957) and *I'm All Right, Jack* (1959). In the 1960s and into the early 1970s came the series of *Carry On* films, including ribald spoofs of EPICS (*Carry On Cleo*, 1965) and SPY FILMS (*Carry on Spying*, 1965), all directed by Gerald Thomas. Elsewhere in Europe, Luis Buñuel's *The Discreet Charm of the Bourgeoisie* (1972) and *The Phantom of Liberty* (1974), made in France, were satires aimed at the bourgeoisie, and Italian film-maker Lina Wertmuller made a big impact in the international ART CINEMA with a series of innovative comedies starring Giancarlo Giannini that combined romantic comedy with gender politics (*Swept Away . . . by an unusual destiny in the blue sea of August*, 1975) and political philosophy (*Seven Beauties*, 1976).

With frankly sexual comedies of manners like *Carnal Knowledge* (dir. Mike Nichols, 1971), romantic comedy became virtually impossible (Henderson 1978). In the late 1970s however, Woody Allen emerged as the most important comic AUTEUR in contemporary cinema, writing, directing and starring in a series of films that combined romantic comedy with modern insecurities, among them *Annie Hall* (1977), which won several ACADEMY AWARDS, including Best Picture, Best Director and Best SCREENPLAY. Romantic comedy has regained popularity in recent years, as it finds ways to be more up-to-date in its attitude toward SEXUALITY and GENDER, as in *Chasing Amy* (dir. Kevin Smith, 1977), *As Good as it Gets* (dir. James L. Brooks, 1997), and *There's Something About Mary* (dir. Peter & Bobby Farrelly, 1998).

There have been innumerable theoretical attempts to define comedy, the comic and humour, beginning with Aristotle, but thankfully none of them are definitive. For example, Henri Bergson's notion of comedy as the blending of the human and mechanical explains much of slapstick comedy (Bergson, 1956), but not romantic comedy or parody. However, there is no doubt that comedy and the laughter it elicits can be liberating, if not subversive, as in Mikhail Bakhtin's notion of the CARNIVALESQUE (Bakhtin, 1968).

Further reading: Cook & Bernink (1999), Durgnat (1972), Gehring (1996), Horton (1991), Horton (1994), Horton (2000), Jenkins (1993), Karnick & Jenkins (1994), Landy (1992), Mast (1979), Murphy (1992), Neale & Krutnik (1990), Palmer (1987), Paul (1994), Schatz (1981), Shumway (1991), Seidman (1994), Sennett (1985), Siegel & Siegel (1994), Sikov (1995), Weales (1985), Winokur (1996)

Commentary A VOICE-OVER, speaking from outside the ACTION of the film to offer some kind of explanation of the events on the screen. The voice-over can carry a degree of implicit authority through the sense of objectivity that comes from standing outside events, however illusory that might be. There are therefore potentially powerful IDEOLOGICAL implications to adding a commentary to, say, DOCUMENTARY footage. In the case of fiction films commentary is often used as a device to clarify and explain, sometimes as the result of an inability to trust either an AUDIENCE'S intelligence or the power of ambiguity as a dramatic device. An example of the latter is the last-minute superimposition of a voice-over to the final version of *Blade Runner* (dir. Ridley Scott, 1982), something which the DIRECTOR resisted and had removed on the release of the DIRECTOR'S CUT in 1993. See also NARRATOR, NARRATION.

Compilation film A film made largely or entirely from FOOTAGE from other films or visual media. Unlike COLLAGE FILMS, compilation films tend to be DOCUMENTARIES rather than EXPERIMENTAL or AVANT-GARDE films, and to be structured rhetorically, to explain or persuade, rather than lyrically.

Composition in depth See DEEP FOCUS.

Computer animation See ANIMATION.

Conglomerate A large company with interests in a wide range of commercial activities. Since the 1960s, conglomerates have had a determining effect on the film industry in the US and worldwide: the MAJOR STUDIOS are multinational or transnational companies. In the 1960s, when most major studios were hit by financial crises engendered by overambitious production expenditure and falling audience figures, several studios were taken over by conglomerates attracted by the studios' assets (real estate, film libraries) and (temporary) undervaluation. In 1966 Gulf +Western Industries, with hundreds of companies from paper and sugar mills to sports teams and metal products, as well as publishing and VIDEO games, bought PARAMOUNT Pictures; in 1967, Transamerica, Inc., with interests in life insurance and car rentals, bought UNITED ARTISTS (sold in 1981 to MGM, to form MGM/UA); in 1969, Kinney National Services, with interests in car rentals, funeral parlours, parking lots and much else, bought WARNER BROS. which, as a sign of coming times, renamed itself Warner Communications in 1971. Signalling the restored financial health of the movie and related industries (see SYNERGY), in 1989 Gulf+Western shed a number of its other interests to concentrate on film, TELEVISION and publishing, changing its name to Paramount Communications Inc., bought by VIACOM, in 1993.
Further reading: Balio (1990), Gomery in Nowell-Smith (1996), Izod (1988), Lewis in Lewis (1998), Maltby, Gomery and Balio in Neale & Smith (1998), Miller in Miller (1990)

Connotation A key concept in the SEMIOTIC approach to film analysis. The connotations produced by a set of signs or CODES such as written or spoken language, COSTUME, SETS and LIGHTING are those aspects of meaning that are suggested rather than literal. Connotations are produced from the way that we read films and are therefore affected by a range of factors such as the CLASS, RACE or GENDER of the spectator and by the socio-historical context in which they are read. It follows, then, that the connotative level of meanings is IDEOLOGICAL.

Within a film internal factors will affect the way that we read the connotations produced by the codes in operation as well as the larger forces mentioned above. In a famous scene from *Double Indemnity* (dir. Billy Wilder, 1944) Barbara Stanwyck's character makes a grand entrance, walking slowly down a curving staircase, having already exchanged suggestive remarks with Fred McMurray's insurance salesman, and the CAMERA fixes her in its GAZE including focusing on an ankle bracelet. Though such bracelets have long lost their specific association with prostitution, the generic CONVENTIONS of FILM NOIR, the connotations of the earlier 'hard-boiled' conversation, the non-verbal behaviour of the two CHARACTERS, and even the way in which the SCENE is lit, lead us inescapably to read this innocent piece of jewellery as one of many signs of Stanwyck's promiscuity. We may then, however, read that promiscuity in a number of ways, including delight in a woman so up-front about her own SEXUALITY and desire and, for now anyway, in control of the situation. See also DENOTATION, SIGNIFIER.

Constructivism An AVANT-GARDE art movement in the Soviet Union shortly after the Revolution. Influenced by FUTURISM and its embrace of technology, constructivists viewed the artist as an engineer whose responsibility it was to make 'useful objects' – the artist's task in building the new socialist society. Vsevolod Meyerhold, a theatre DIRECTOR with whom Sergei Eisenstein worked early in his career, applied constructivism to the stage, although the most important constructivist film is Dziga Vertov's *The Man with the Movie Camera* (1929), which shows the CINEMATOGRAPHER and EDITOR as part of the work force necessary to produce the film that we are seeing, and also emphasises the importance of machinery in daily Soviet life, the relation of human movement to machinery, and the motion picture CAMERA itself as a machine.
Further reading: Petric (1987)

Continuity editing Film editing that maintains a sense of uninterrupted and continuous narrative ACTION within each SCENE, maintaining the illusion of reality for the spectator. Because it seeks to maximize CONTINUITY, to be seamless and not call attention to itself – as in the case of, say, the JUMP CUT or THEMATIC MONTAGE – continuity editing is often referred to as INVISIBLE EDITING. At the same time, though, continuity editing also seeks to direct the viewer's response by structuring dramatic emphasis and controlling IDENTIFICATION with CHARACTERS. Specific techniques of continuity editing include MATCH CUTS involving screen direction, EYELINE MATCH, and SHOT/REACTION SHOT. This system of narrative film construction is the foundation of CLASSIC NARRATIVE FILM. See also CLASSICAL HOLLYWOOD CINEMA, SUTURE.
Further reading: Bordwell & Thompson (1997)

Continuity A quality possessed by a film that is designed to make it look as seamless and natural as possible with no attention drawn to the processes behind its making. On SET a continuity clerk will have responsibility for ensuring that all the fine details in each TAKE, such as the exact position of PROPS and objects, the position of ACTORS and the state of hair and make-up, are recorded and matched when the SCENE is SHOT again. The practice of shooting most FEATURE FILMS out of narrative SEQUENCE to minimize costs makes the job of ensuring continuity vital to the creation of a seamless narrative REALISM. AVANT-GARDE and ART CINEMA practices have sometimes focused on the deliberate shattering of the illusion of reality established by continuity. See also CLASSICAL HOLLYWOOD CINEMA, CONTINUITY EDITING, JUMP CUT.

Further reading: Aumont (1992), Bordwell & Thompson (1997)

Contract player An ACTOR under contract to a production company, paid a regular wage rather than for a specific performance. The term is most often used for actors on long-term contracts during the STUDIO SYSTEM era; contract players, including STARS, normally had little say in what films they appeared in, and were assigned by their STUDIOS to whatever they considered suitable.

Contract system During the STUDIO SYSTEM period, the STUDIOS, as well as maintaining studio facilities on a permanent basis, also maintained on long-term contract most of the personnel it needed to sustain continuous production – PRODUCERS, EDITORS, CINEMATOGRAPHERS, all kind of technicians, as well as STARS and other performers. See also CONTRACT PLAYER.

Convention In any art form, a frequently used technique or content that is accepted as standard or typical in that tradition or GENRE. MAINSTREAM cinema features numerous conventions for the REPRESENTATION of CHARACTER, CLASS, RACE, GENDER or narrative construction, some associated with specific genres, others informing CLASSICAL HOLLYWOOD CINEMA generally. In the WESTERN, for example, the cowboy who dresses in black and wears two guns is invariably a villainous gunfighter. Conventions also include stylistic qualities associated with particular genres: MELODRAMA is characterized by an EXCESS in the *MISE EN SCÈNE*, whereas FILM NOIR commonly employs LOW-KEY LIGHTING and FLASHBACKS. Sometimes stylistic conventions are referred to as CODES to distinguish them from conventions of narrative. Conventions function as an implied agreement between makers and consumers to accept certain artificialities. So, for example, in the MUSICAL the PLOT halts as characters suddenly break into song and dance accompanied by the sudden manifestation of NON-DIEGETIC MUSIC. Conventions can be used in movies for subversive purposes precisely because we expect them. George Romero's undermining of numerous conventions of the classic HORROR FILM in *Night of the Living Dead* (1968) is one of the main reasons the film had such a powerful effect upon contemporary AUDIENCES (Grant, 1995). Changes in conventional representations are a result of several factors, including social and cultural change, audience familiarity, and the evolving vision of AUTEURS working within particular genres.

Co-production Collaboration between two or more production companies, often today based in different countries and arising out of financial necessity, sometimes leading to inappropriate aesthetic decisions, such as the CASTING of someone of a particular nationality in order to secure co-production money from that country. See also EUROPUDDING.

Costume As Church Gibson (Hill & Church Gibson, 1998, pp. 36–42) points out, film costume is simultaneously a neglected area of academic study and a major source of PLEASURE for film spectators. This she associates with costume's perceived relationship to fashion and hence, until comparatively recently, with a kind of frivolity.

However, film costume is more properly seen as an integral part of the creation and study of a film's MISE EN SCÈNE. This in turn extends to the role of costume in relation to GENRE or in the creation of individual CHARACTERS. There are, however, films in which the display of costume (and other aspects of *mise en scène*) almost becomes an end in itself, hence the terms COSTUME DRAMA or HERITAGE FILM.

Film costume has been area of particular interest to feminist film critics through its role in the construction of gender and its centrality to the study of STARS.

Costume designer The person specifically responsible for designing the COSTUMES on a production. On most FEATURE FILMS s/he will be a member of a team headed by the ART DIRECTOR and will work closely with both the DIRECTOR and CINEMATOGRAPHER, particularly on questions of LIGHTING and other aspects of COLOUR design.

Costume drama A film in which authentic period COSTUME is an important part of overall PRODUCTION VALUES. The term is often used pejoratively today to mean that the film is somehow superficial in appealing to its audience through the SPECTACLE of its lavish costumes. In practice, costume dramas vary greatly and while some may be the cinematic equivalent of a tour around a royal palace, others are innovative and interesting. *Barry Lyndon* (dir. Stanley Kubrick, 1975), for example, is both conventionally beautiful to look at and striking in the detachment with which it treats its production values. See also HERITAGE FILM.

Counter cinema A term for films that somehow challenge or subvert the CODES, CONVENTIONS and/or IDEOLOGY of MAINSTREAM CINEMA. Such films may be EXPERIMENTAL or NARRATIVE, and are often distributed and exhibited outside the normal commercial venues. Counter cinema films often engage in DISTANCIATION and DECONSTRUCTION, in that they tend to be concerned, as Jean-Luc Godard would say, less with the illusion of reality than with the reality of the illusion. While earlier AVANT-GARDE and experimental films may be examples of counter-cinema, the term was coined by British film-maker and theorist Peter Wollen (1982) to describe Godard's early 1970s work with the DZIGA VERTOV GROUP (*Vent d'est/Wind from the East*, 1972) and its resistance to the methods and values of CLASSICAL HOLLYWOOD CINEMA. FEMINIST THEORY took a particular interest in the idea of counter cinema later in the 1970s, with critics such as Laura Mulvey (1975) and Claire Johnston (1974) arguing that mainstream film is a patriarchally constructed way of seeing and that a feminist counter cinema has the potential to dismantle a masculine GAZE. See also REFLEXIVITY.

Cover shot See ESTABLISHING SHOT.

Coverage Also known simply as 'cover' – the collection of different SHOTS of a SCENE from a variety of ANGLES and distances, the purpose of which is to provide enough shots to choose from to cover the ACTION of the scene smoothly during EDITING. A cover shot – usually a long MASTER SHOT – offers a way out if CONTINUITY cannot be achieved during the editing of the scene. In a different meaning, coverage is also the name for a reader's report/evaluation of a script for PRODUCERS.

Crab dolly See DOLLY.

Crane shot A shot made using a CRANE or BOOM. Also known as BOOM SHOT. See also BOOM, CRANE.

Crane A mechanical arm-like trolley used to move a CAMERA through space above the ground or to position it at a place in the air. A SHOT taken from a crane allows the camera to vary distance, angle and height during the shot. Also known as BOOM.

Crawl, crawling title A type of film TITLE, CREDITS or written TEXT, as at the beginning of *Star Wars* (dir. George Lucas, 1977) ('Long ago in a galaxy far away . . .') that looks as if it were moving slowly across the screen either vertically or horizontally. Also called creeper title.

Creative geography EDITING process whereby SHOTS taken in different LOCATIONS at different times can be combined to suggest a unity of SPACE and TIME. One of the experiments carried out by Lev Kuleshov's workshop at the Moscow State Film School in the early 1920s involved editing together five separate SHOTS, taken in different places at different times, into a narrative sequence: 1. man walking right to · left; 2. woman walking left to right; 3. man and woman meet, shake hands, man points off-screen; 4. shot of a white building; 5. shot of man and woman ascending steps outside a building. These unrelated shots – the shots of the man and the woman were shot in different places, the white building was the US White House (stolen from an American film), and the steps belonged to a church in another part of the city – were apparently read by AUDIENCES as constituting a SEQUENCE unified in time and space. See also KULESHOV EFFECT.
Further reading: Cook (1996), Pudovkin (1970)

Credits At one level simply a list of people on both sides of the CAMERA who were involved in making a film, appearing at the start or end of the film, or both. A common pattern has the major credits (for performance, direction and production) at the start and a complete list at the end. Over time credit sequences have become more elaborate and are now often an important and interesting part of the film itself. In some cases the SEQUENCES themselves have aspired to being art in their own right: Saul Bass, who worked extensively with Otto Preminger and Alfred Hitchcock in the 1950s and 1960s, is generally credited with being a pioneer of such work (for example, *Psycho*, dir. Hitchcock, 1960). The actual credits themselves can become fraught with sensitivities because of the implied BILLING it gives one performer over another and the resultant tensions are often the stuff of contractual disputes.

Creeper title See CRAWL.

Crew A loose term meaning the whole team of technicians and craft workers involved in the production of a film, subdivided into smaller groups such as the CAMERA crew or SOUND crew.

Crime film Any film involving the planning, commission or solving of a crime in its narrative. Too amorphous to be considered a GENRE, the crime film includes CAPER FILMS, DETECTIVE FILMS, GANGSTER FILMS, POLICE FILMS, SPY FILMS and

THRILLERS. All crime film genres allow viewers the vicarious excitement of IDENTIFI-CATION with CHARACTERS who test the limits of the law.

Further reading: Cawelti (1976), Clarens (1980), Murphy (1986), Murphy (1992), Shadoian (1977), Schatz (1981)

Criticism The most common use of the term refers to non-academic writing on contemporary films, usually in newspapers and magazines, taking the form of anything from a short tabloid assessment of a new film accompanied by a star rating to a longer piece accompanied by other material, such as a retrospective look at the work of the DIRECTOR or leading ACTOR. A piece written in immediate response to a film's release is more properly referred to as a review, though these are commonly included in the general category of criticism. Until relatively recently film critics were seen as crucial to a film's BOX-OFFICE success and critics do wield some power and influence. However, current trends suggest that large-scale investment in ADVERTIS-ING and MARKETING are much more important and have the power to appeal to AUDI-ENCES over the heads of critics, as with George Lucas' revival of the *Star Wars* series, which was not reviewed particularly favourably but nevertheless broke box-office records.

Film critics now operate through all the media, not only print, and some TELEVI-SION reviewers, including Roger Ebert in the USA and Barry Norman in the UK, have been seen as influential. Some newspaper and magazine critics have endured long enough to become key figures in the history of the industry: Pauline Kael, for many years reviewer for *The New Yorker*, is one such figure, and others, including Dilys Powell of *The Sunday Times*, have inspired much reverence.

Cropping Any process by which the original size and shape of a film IMAGE is changed, whether by MASKing on the film itself or by means of the projector APER-TURE. Mostly the term has referred to the cropping of film IMAGES for TELEVISION transmission, since WIDESCREEN film images needed to be cut down to fit the ASPECT RATIO of the television screen (though increasingly masking and widescreen televi-sion have changed the practice).

Further reading: Neale in Neale & Smith (1998)

Cross ownership The ownership by one corporation of different media outlets, such as News Corporation's ownership of both press (*The Sun, The Times*) and TELEVISION (BSkyB) interests in the UK. Cross ownership – considered danger-ous for putting opinion-forming into too few hands – is in many ways the basis of the SYNERGY generated by the media CONGLOMERATES that dominate film produc-tion and DISTRIBUTION.

Crosscutting In EDITING, the alternation of SHOTS from at least two different SCENES, usually implying that the multiple events are occurring in different SPACES but simultaneously. Sometimes called PARALLEL EDITING, crosscutting often implies PARALLEL ACTION, although Hayward (1996, p. 78) suggests that parallel editing refers to the intercutting of actions occurring at different times. D.W. Griffith was known for crosscutting in many of his ONE-REELERS, gradually increasing the tempo of the editing in his last-minute rescues to create suspense. As well as temporal simultane-ity, crosscutting can also imply thematic comparison or contrast, as in the end of *The*

Godfather (1972) where Francis Ford Coppola – borrowing from the end of Sergei Eisenstein's *Strike* (1924) – crosscuts between the assassination of several rival gangsters and the ritual slaughter of a bull, suggesting that such murders are part of a sacrificial rite of VIOLENCE in the gangster underworld.
Further reading: Bordwell & Thompson (1997)

Crossing the line See 180° RULE.

Crossover When a film aimed at a specific AUDIENCE is a success and then becomes a success with a more general audience, it is said to be a 'crossover', just as country music, though aimed at a particular audience, can cross over and become a success in the general charts. For example, BLAXPLOITATION pictures, initially aimed at black audiences, crossed over and gained success with mainstream white audiences.

Crowd scene A SCENE in a film involving a large number of people including EXTRAS. As Turner (1988, p. 60) points out, crowd scenes can become 'a performance of cinema, a celebration of its ability to trap so much of the world in its FRAME'. Turner cites the funeral sequence near the start of Richard Attenborough's *Gandhi* (1982) as a prime example – its centrepiece a helicopter SHOT showing the million people that lined the route of Gandhi's cortege.

Crown Film Unit In August 1940, the GPO FILM UNIT, a leading player in the 1930s British DOCUMENTARY production, was renamed the Crown Film Unit and put under the aegis of the Ministry of Information, making it an arm of government war PROPAGANDA. At the start of World War II, there was much uncertainty about the role of film in the British war effort, although the GPO Film Unit made some early SHORT FILMS (such as *The First Days*, dir. Humphrey Jennings, Harry Watt and Pat Jackson, 1939). Notable work by the Crown Film Unit included many short films, including those by Humphrey Jennings (such as *Words for Battle*, 1941, *Listen to Britain*, 1942, and *A Diary for Timothy*, 1945) as well as what we would now call feature length drama documentaries, like *Target for Tonight* (dir. Harry Watt, 1941), *Fires Were Started* (dir. Jennings, 1943) and *Western Approaches* (dir. Pat Jackson, 1944). After the war the Crown Film Unit continued to make documentary films, but much of the energy, social consciousness and belief by government which marked the 1930s and the war was missing, and the Unit was closed down in 1951.

Cult film A film with an especially devoted following, but unlike BLOCKBUSTERS, which appeal to a broad AUDIENCE, cult films tend to construct a subcultural community of admirers, as with *Easy Rider* (dir. Dennis Hopper, 1969) or *Rocky Horror Picture Show* (dir. Jim Sharman, 1975). The term loosely refers to a variety of films, both new and old, which tend to be of two types: rediscovered classics such as Joseph H. Lewis' *Gun Crazy* (aka *Deadly is the Female*, 1949) and the films of Josef von Sternberg, and newer MIDNIGHT MOVIES such as *Rocky Horror* and *Night of the Living Dead* (dir. George Romero, 1968), credited as the first film to be so exhibited. Telotte (1991) has observed that there is a close enough relation between the cult film as TEXT and as experience to allow us to conceive of both aspects together as what he calls the cult 'supertext', a feature that distinguishes the cult film from the more traditional film GENRES.

One of the central appeals of cult movies, despite their stylistic and thematic heterogeneity, is that they tend to involve some form of transgression. It may be the REPRESENTATION of the taboo, as in *Freaks* (dir. Tod Browning, 1932), the distasteful graphics of violated bodies in the SPLATTER FILM, or a reversal of aesthetic norms, as in the sleazy *Pink Flamingos* (dir. John Waters, 1973). The films of Edward D. Wood, Jr., widely acknowledged as the worst DIRECTOR of all time, are cult because they transgress basic technical competency. Wood's 1956 effort (?) *Plan 9 From Outer Space* is a cult favourite because it is so *obviously* awful in the context of the well-made CLASSICAL NARRATIVE FILM.
Further reading: Eco (1986), French & French (1999), Hoberman & Rosenbaum (1983), Mendik & Harper (2000), Peary (1981, 1983 & 1989)

Cut (1) The most common method of connecting IMAGES – the physical act of SPLICING the end of one SHOT to the beginning of the next. A cut appears as an instantaneous transference from one shot to another. (2) In a completed film, the particular type of EDITING, which is a direct change from one image to another. (3) A particular version of a film that is different from the released version, as in the DIRECTOR'S CUT of *Close Encounters of the Third Kind* (dir. Steven Spielberg, 1977), known as *The Special Edition*, or *Blade Runner* (dir. Ridley Scott, 1983), which dropped the VOICE-OVER and added a different ending. (4) As a verb, to eliminate FOOTAGE or SCENES in the final film. (5) The director's signal for stopping the CAMERA during a TAKE.

Cutaway A SHOT that briefly interrupts the main narrative or temporal flow of events to show something else, sometimes used to reveal what CHARACTERS are thinking or to show what they see, as in a REACTION SHOT, or to provide a TRANSITION between SEQUENCES. Cutaways also may provide a comment on the ACTION, as in *The Thin Red Line* (1998), in which director Terrence Malick several times CUTS between images of battle and CLOSE-UPS of natural objects such as seashells to contrast the chaos of war with the harmony of nature. Cutaways are also used to avoid showing something that may be considered objectionable, such as sex or VIOLENCE. In *Bring Me the Head of Alfredo Garcia* (1974), Sam Peckinpah cuts from an interior SCENE of the Mexican patriarch's dishonoured daughter as she is about to have her hands broken to an exterior LONG SHOT of the ranch house in which this vengeful act is occurring, although the SOUND of bones crunching is carried over on the SOUNDTRACK. Cutaways are commonly used in OBSERVATIONAL CINEMA to hide JUMP CUTS that eliminate parts of PROFILMIC EVENTS. See also INSERT.

Cycle A brief but relatively intense period of production within a particular GENRE in which the individual films share a particular approach. Examples include the 1930s WARNER BROS. BIOPICS, beginning with *Disraeli* (dir. Alfred E. Green, 1929), and the vigilante CRIME FILMS in the 1970s, including *Walking Tall* (dir. Phil Karlson, 1973) and *Death Wish* (dir. Michael Winner, 1974). Altman (1999) suggests that cycles are distinguishable from SUBGENRES in that, while the latter are shared among different STUDIOS, the former tend to be proprietary, and that cycles provide adjectival inflections upon existing genres that may themselves evolve into full-fledged genres, as in the case of MUSICAL romance.

Czech New Wave Brief period of distinctive work in the mid 1960s by a group of young DIRECTORS including Jiri Menzel, Ivan Passer, Milos Forman and Vera Chytilova. These film-makers were able to make their most important films at a time of relative political tolerance of the arts known as the Prague Spring, which ended abruptly when Soviet tanks rolled into the city in 1968. Although their films were diverse in style, the Czech film-makers shared a knowledge of, and were influenced by, such preceding movements as Italian NEO-REALISM, the FRENCH NEW WAVE and DIRECT CINEMA. Because the country's cinema was controlled by the State, Czech New Wave directors found a way to offer political comment subtly, through seemingly light-hearted comedies that featured sharply observed characters engaged in the common activities of everyday life. Films such as *Intimate Lighting* (dir. Passer, 1965) and *The Fireman's Ball* (dir. Forman, 1967) emphasized an ironic gap between the capriciousness of their CHARACTERS and the prosaic platitudes of official state policy. Other Czech films, such as Chytilova's *Daisies* (1966), moved more in the direction of fantasy and formal experimentation. Some Czech New Wave films, such as Menzel's *Closely Watched Trains* (1966), achieved substantial international success in the ART CINEMA market. Both Passer and Forman moved to the USA and entered the film industry, the latter more successfully with such films as *One Flew Over the Cuckoo's Nest* (1975) and *Man on the Moon* (1999).
Further reading: Hames (1985)

D

Dadaism An art movement centring in France from World War I to the 1920s that reacted to conventional art in its emphasis on the spontaneous, irrational and the subconscious. The movement influenced literature and painting, as well as the cinema, with a few AVANT-GARDE FILMS such as *Le Retour à la raison* (*Return to Reason*, dir. Man Ray, 1923) and *Entr'acte* (dir. René Clair, 1924) that challenged conventional narrative structure and CONTINUITY EDITING. See also AVANT-GARDE FILM, SURREALISM.
Further reading: Kuenzli (1987), Rees in Nowell-Smith (1996), Rees (1999)

Dailies Prints of each day's successful TAKES, usually with synchronized SOUND, printed and delivered by the laboratory, usually the day after shooting, and viewed particularly by the DIRECTOR and the CINEMATOGRAPHER, in order to keep track of LIGHTING levels and, often, performance. Often referred to as RUSHES.

Day for night (or day-for-night, or D/N) Process by which SCENES supposed to be taking place at night are SHOT in daytime but, by using some combination of under-exposure, FILTERS and under-printing, are made to look as if they are taking place at night. Routinely used for films, especially HOLLYWOOD films, either because it avoided the LIGHTING problems of shooting at night or because it was cheaper to shoot in daytime, or both. 'Day for night' provides the English language title of François Truffaut's 1973 film about film-making *La Nuit américaine*, 'American night' being the French term for 'day for night'.

Deconstruction Critical THEORY term, associated with the French philosopher Jacques Derrida and with POST-STRUCTURALISM in general, applied to anything that can be construed as a TEXT and, as the name implies, about dismantling the structures that lie beneath the surface of, in this case, a film in order to understand how it works. It is therefore diametrically opposed to a cinema that seeks to retain its 'magic' through the power of illusion to conceal the process of 'construction'. A process of deconstruction focused on GENRE and narrative might reveal how GENRE films draw on features common to all films from the same genre and how they relate to wider social structures. This, in turn, might reveal the relationship of a particular film to a dominant IDEOLOGY, though deconstruction is not a tool allowing the critic access to a more profound truth about a given text, but rather the logic of a philosophical position that dismantles the notion of a finite, knowable world – including the very idea of the self.

Film-makers produce film texts that are in themselves partly acts of deconstruction. COUNTER CINEMA is based upon deconstruction in that its function is always partly to raise questions about the assumptions of DOMINANT CINEMA by laying bare the means of its construction. Hayward (1996, p. 63) mentions the claim by Noël Burch that deconstruction in the cinema was being practised long before the term was coined, notably by the GERMAN EXPRESSIONISTS in films like *The Cabinet of Dr Caligari* (dir. Robert Wiene, 1919). Wells (in Nelmes, 1996, p. 200) analyses deconstruction in the Chuck Jones CARTOON, *Duck Amuck* (1953), which in the course of its ACTION 'reveals all the aspects of its own construction'. See also SEMIOTICS, STRUCTURALISM.

Decor   The total effect of the ART DIRECTION and all its contributing skills in a particular SCENE, or even a whole film – the look created by the combined contributions of PROPS, furniture, COSTUMES and the overall COLOUR scheme adopted for a particular scene. Decor can have a straightforward narrative function such as the establishment of place and CHARACTER or be part of an EXPRESSIONIST or symbolic design.

Découpage   French term to describe the way in which a film, or a SCENE, has been edited (literally, 'cut up'), or broken down into SHOTS. Although it could describe any such breaking down into shots, *découpage*, or *découpage classique*, often describes specifically the classic style of CONTINUITY EDITING exemplified by HOLLYWOOD cinema, as opposed to the MONTAGE approach to editing. Like other French terms such as *MISE EN SCÈNE* and *PLAN SÉQUENCE*, *découpage* exists in the language of film CRITICISM in English because of the influence of French film criticism during the 1960s and 1970s.

Deep focus   A way of shooting that keeps a number of planes of ACTION in any one SHOT in sharp FOCUS, allowing a number of significant actions to take place simultaneously in different planes, as opposed to SHALLOW FOCUS where only the plane of action nearest the CAMERA is sharply in focus (though others may be visible though slightly blurred). By allowing a greater range of possibilities and choices for the spectator, deep focus has been seen as one of the techniques of REALISM in cinema, particularly when used in conjunction with the LONG TAKE. André Bazin (1967), for example, argued that a cinema based upon techniques that constantly drew attention to themselves and directed the spectator where to look, such as MONTAGE, defied the essentially realist possibilities of cinema, whereas deep focus left spectators with the power to direct their GAZE to a number of different parts of the shot or *MISE EN SCÈNE*. Deep focus was used in early SILENT CINEMA, but changes in film STOCK made it more difficult until the pioneering work of CINEMATOGRAPHER Gregg Toland in the 1930s, particularly on *Citizen Kane* (dir. Orson Welles, 1941), which remains the textbook illustration of the use of deep focus. See also CINEMATOGRAPHY, FOCUS.

Further reading: Ogle in Nichols (1985)

Degradation Term for the progressive deterioration of the quality of the photographic IMAGE through the various stages of printing: a PRINT made from a duplicate NEGATIVE, or from another print, lacks the definition and contrast shading of a print made from the original negative. Degradation is generally seen as a negative quality but, as a sign of the specific nature of the film material and process, it has been used REFLEXIVELY in AVANT-GARDE film-making.

Denotation A term widely used in SEMIOTICS as one of the principal ways that any sign or unit of meaning – a word or IMAGE – actually works. Denotation can be seen as the simplest or literal level of meaning or signification, as opposed to CONNOTATION – the level of associations and suggestions. If a film started with a blank screen and the caption 'Texas' and a date in the 1860s, it would denote that the fictional world of the film was set in that specific TIME and place, but the connotations of the name 'Texas' are manifold, as are those of that particular date, for spectators familiar with the conventions of the WESTERN GENRE.

Dénouement Literal translation from the French for 'untying', the dénouement of a narrative is the moment where all mysteries are solved and explanations given, implying a high degree of CLOSURE with the main PLOT and all sub-plots fully concluded. A high degree of REALISM is usually associated with a low-key dénouement with much left unresolved in the lives of the main CHARACTERS. One of the most repeated dénouements in cinema, and a CONVENTION of the MUSICAL and ROMANTIC COMEDY GENRES, involves one or more marriages after a series of difficulties placed in front of the leading characters.

Depth of field The area remaining in acceptably sharp FOCUS both in front of and behind the main area of focus in the FRAME, which is affected by the LENS APERTURE, the FOCAL LENGTH of the lens, the distance between the CAMERA and the main focus area, the amount of LIGHTING and the FILM SPEED.

Greater depth of field – and DEEP FOCUS – can be achieved by WIDE ANGLE lenses (with shorter focal lengths), narrower apertures, greater distance between camera and primary area of focus and faster film speed (as was standard in early SILENT CINEMA). Changes of CHARACTER positioning in shallow depth of field require FOLLOW FOCUS or RACK FOCUS to remain in focus.

Further reading: Aumont (1992), Comolli in Nichols (1985)

Detail shot Also called EXTREME CLOSE-UP. See BIG CLOSE-UP.

Detective film Film GENRE featuring a detective hero, whether an official law-enforcement agent or a private eye, seeking to solve crimes and identify and apprehend criminals. Bordwell (1985) sees detective stories as a structured play of the delay and disclosure of knowledge. Such narratives offer viewers heroic protagonists and the opportunity to match wits with both the CHARACTERS and the film-makers in sorting out the clues to solve the mystery. The genre's primary literary antecedent was the Gothic novel, with its mysterious, seemingly supernatural occurrences often explained in the rational light of day and DÉNOUEMENT. Some of the short stories of American writer Edgar Allan Poe, which he called 'tales of ratiocination,' featured the first detective figure, Auguste Dupin, a character type that would be given wider popularity by Conan Doyle's Sherlock Holmes, first in fiction and then in numerous films, the most well known of which is the SERIES of movies starring Basil Rathbone as Holmes and Nigel Bruce as Dr. Watson beginning with *The Hound of the Baskervilles* (dir. Sidney Lanfield) in 1939. With the coming of SOUND, the private detective movie became a staple in both British and American film production, the two countries turning out countless series, many of them B MOVIES from minor STUDIOS. Most of these detectives were morally upright characters who represented an unproblematic view of justice and the law, though already in 1929 Alfred Hitchcock explored in *Blackmail* the ethical ambiguities within the detective hero.

A SUBGENRE of the detective film, the private eye film, involves a loner hero moving through a corrupt world to solve crime. Unlike the detective, the private eye is more individualistic, like the WESTERN hero, working outside the institutionalized police system and in fact often in conflict with official detectives. In 1930s HOLLYWOOD films the private detective character, influenced by the British genteel school of detective fiction, tended to be debonair and sophisticated – personified by ACTOR William Powell in a series of films as Philo Vance (the best of which is *The Kennel Murder Case*, dir. Michael Curtiz, 1933), and, paired with Myrna Loy, as Nick Charles in *The Thin Man* (dir. W.S. Van Dyke, 1934) and its SEQUELS. In the 1940s, with the adaptation to the screen of the fiction of the American 'hard-boiled' writers such as Raymond Chandler, Dashiell Hammett and, later, Mickey Spillane, the private detective became more cynical and tough, solving crime as much with his fists as with deductive logic. Hammett's Sam Spade and Chandler's Philip Marlowe were both played by Humphrey Bogart, in *The Maltese Falcon* (dir. John Huston, 1941) and *The Big Sleep* (dir. Howard Hawks, 1946) respectively.

By the 1960s even official detectives had grown cynical, as much with the corruption and cumbersome procedures of the legal system as with the increase in crime. Popeye Doyle (Gene Hackman) in *The French Connection* (dir. William Friedkin, 1971) and Harry Callahan (Clint Eastwood) in *Dirty Harry* (dir. Don Siegel, 1972) find themselves at odds with their superiors. In the first of three Dirty Harry sequels, *Magnum Force* (dir. Ted Post, 1973), Callahan discovers that the police force itself is responsible for the multiple murders he is investigating. More recently the detective film has adapted to social change: *V.I. Warshawski* (dir. Jeff Kanew, 1991), based on Sarah Paretsky's novels, presents a tough female dick, while *Bad Lieutenant* (dir. Abel Ferrara, 1992) presents the detective as a full-blown psychotic. See also CRIME FILM, MYSTERY FILM.
Further reading: Tuska (1978), Tuska (1988)

DGA The Directors Guild of America. See GUILD.

Dialectical montage Also called INTELLECTUAL MONTAGE, Soviet film-maker Sergei Eisenstein's term for his approach to THEMATIC MONTAGE, based on Karl Marx's theory of history and CLASS struggle (itself adapted from Hegel's philosophy) as a dialectical system involving a pair of opposite forces (thesis, antithesis) that generate a synthesis which in turn becomes the first term in a new dialectical conflict. In *A Dialectic Approach to Film Form* (1949, p. 49), Eisenstein argues that MONTAGE 'arises from the collision of independent SHOTS – shots even opposite to one another.' In *October* (1927), Eisenstein intercuts shots of Kerensky, leader of the Provisional Government, and a preening peacock, suggesting Kerensky's vanity. The idea of vanity is contained in neither of the individual shots, but rather in their juxtaposition through EDITING. As Eisenstein argues in *The Film Sense* (1947), 'in every such juxtaposition the result is qualitatively distinguishable from each component viewed separately.' Although dialectical montage tends to interrupt the seamless flow of the narrative DIEGESIS, such editing can also be found in narrative cinema. In the famous opening of *Modern Times* (1936), for example, Charles Chaplin follows a shot of workers crowding into a factory for the morning shift with a shot of sheep being crowded into a pen.
Further reading: Bordwell (1993)

Diegesis, diegetic The 'fictional world' of a fictional TEXT (film, novel, play, comic book, etc.), from the Greek for narrative, a useful critical tool for making distinctions between what may be considered diegetic – belonging to the fictional world of the text – and what may be considered non-diegetic – extraneous to the fictional world of the text. In terms of film MUSIC, for example, where the distinctions are usually clear, music from an identifiable source within the fictional world of the film, from a radio or juke box, is diegetic, while SOUNDTRACK music is non-diegetic. In terms of the film IMAGE, the norm, certainly for most illusionist fiction films, is for IMAGES to be diegetic – clearly part of the fictional world of the film. However, in some anti-illusionist film-making, non-diegetic images can serve symbolic or metaphorical purposes: during the massacre of the workers at the end of *Strike* (1924), Sergei Eisenstein cuts in a shot of a bull being slaughtered, which has no fictional relationship to the main action, but works as a metaphor for the workers' fate. Directors like Jean-Luc Godard introduce non-diegetic elements – book covers, scenes from unrelated films or real-life interviews – into their fictions as distancing or anti-illusionist devices. Film credits, though a well-established CONVENTION, are also clearly non-diegetic. See also DISTANCIATION.
Further reading: Aumont (1992), Bordwell & Thompson (1997)

Digital, digitalization, digitization Digital refers to the electronic coding of information for processing by computer: data is broken down into a binary system of 0s and 1s (offs and ons), rather than being represented in ANALOGUE form. IMAGE and/or SOUND which has been recorded digitally is reproduced anew each time it is seen and/or heard, so that quality does not deteriorate in relation to the original. Digital sound recording has long established itself as standard and DVD technology for sound and image looks set to replace VIDEO. Digital methods are increasingly used for computer generated ANIMATION and for SPECIAL EFFECTS, where photographed images can be digitized and then infinitely manipulated to remove unwanted elements of the image – like the removal of wires and other stunt paraphernalia in

Terminator 2: Judgment Day (dir. James Cameron, 1991) or to add new ones, such as backgrounds. Thus, following the death of ACTOR Oliver Reed during the shooting of *Gladiator* (dir. Ridley Scott, 2000), it was possible to create digitally scenes which Reed had not performed. Digital technology has made possible the restoration of old films (such as *Snow White*, dir. Walt Disney, 1937) by removing scratches and other imperfections and as a storage medium, digitization offers future solutions for ARCHIVES in the storage of film. Ditigal technology will also allow the transmission of HDTV (High Definition TELEVISION) and the beaming of digital motion pictures directly to cinemas.

Digital video See DV.

Direct cinema Type of OBSERVATIONAL DOCUMENTARY practice developed in the United States during the 1960s in which PROFILMIC EVENTS are recorded as they happen, without rehearsal or reconstruction, using portable 16MM and sync-SOUND equipment such as the NAGRA and directional MICROPHONES. Many of these film-makers, including Richard Leacock (*Happy Mother's Day*, 1963), D.A. Pennebaker (*Dont Look Back*, 1966) and the Maysles Brothers (*Salesman*, 1969), first worked together within the DREW ASSOCIATES making documentaries for the ABC TELEVISION network.

The term is credited to director/cinematographer Albert Maysles to distinguish it from the French CINÉMA VÉRITÉ. For unlike vérité, direct cinema sought to be as unobtrusive as possible – like a FLY ON THE WALL, as American documentary film-maker Richard Leacock put it. Accordingly, direct cinema films employ LONG TAKES and minimal EDITING, and prefer a chronological structure that preserves profilmic events as much as possible. In this approach, subjects are allowed to speak for themselves and the CAMERA observes, hoping to capture a PRIVILEGED MOMENT that penetrates the persona to the truth of the person behind it. Direct cinema films also eschew a VOICE-OF-GOD NARRATION, a technique associated with the rhetorical manipulation of the earlier Griersonian style of documentary.

Further reading: Allen & Gomery (1985), Issari & Paul (1979), Mamber (1974), Winston (1995)

Directional mic See MICROPHONE.

Director of photography See CINEMATOGRAPHER.

Director The person with ultimate responsibility for everything that takes place on a film SET, from technical aspects such as choosing the right LENS or LIGHTING set-up to the movement of the ACTORS. In practice, the director works in conjunction with a range of other creative artists, in particular the CINEMATOGRAPHER or director of photography as well as the film's PRODUCERS. The precise nature of the relationship between the director and the rest of the creative team working on a film has varied enormously in terms of the historical development of the industry and the individual styles of particular directors.

The practical working methods of directors can vary from the extreme of Alfred Hitchcock, who claimed that all the creative work went on before shooting started, in the STORYBOARDING of SHOTS, to those such as John Cassavetes, who relied a great deal on the creative power of improvising actors in the creation of a SCENE. Some directors supervise every edit during POST-PRODUCTION, others will adopt (or be forced to adopt) a more hands-off approach once the film is shot. Critical debates surrounding the 'idea' of a director are discussed below, but it is inescapable that film directing is essentially a collaborative process on everything except the lowest budget SHORT, and even the most determinedly AUTEURIST director is dependent on a range of other talents and skills to realise a vision.

From the earliest days of film there existed a tension between the role of the director and the degree of control exercised by the STUDIO making the film. The earliest days of SILENT CINEMA saw directors as central figures exercising a powerful controlling influence over all aspects of a film's production. The rise of the studios in HOLLYWOOD, though, meant more restraint on the creative power of the director as economics played an ever-increasing role in the direction of a film. The period following the introduction of SOUND is probably when the director's power and status diminished most rapidly (in Hollywood at least): the cost of making films rose rapidly, leading to a much greater caution on the part of investors in a picture; the coming of sound meant that directors were more likely to be working closely to somebody else's blueprint in the form of a SCREENPLAY; and the sheer number of films being produced meant the emergence of a kind of factory system with the director often little more than a hired hand producing films to a more or less set formula. Some directors were able to maintain their influence whilst others experienced an almost total loss of control.

The modern theoretical debate about the role and nature of the director was effectively begun in the 1950s in France with the emergence of a new school of thought about Hollywood – the POLITIQUE DES AUTEURS, the loose title for debates conducted around CAHIERS DU CINÉMA – which sought to establish the role and identity of the director as AUTEUR (author), largely through recurring patterns in the MISE EN SCÈNE across a series of films. Previously, the idea of director as auteur was largely restricted to film-makers who also originated the idea behind the film. The Cahiers critics argued that directors working within the Hollywood system could also be auteurs, but through the distinctive patterns in which they used film language.

The politiques des auteurs had some indirect effect on the perception of the director within the MAINSTREAM industry, particularly as it spread via US critics like Andrew Sarris. More significant for the director in an industry context was the gradual decline of the power of the STUDIO SYSTEM. TELEVISION's impact on film audiences meant a drastic reduction in the number of films made and spiralling production costs meant that films could no longer be made as if on a production line. A sense of each film being an independent entity developed, and this required a controlling directorial figure on each production.

Alongside this the 1950s and 1960s saw the European ART CINEMA reach a wider audience through the work of film-makers like Jean-Luc Godard and François Truffaut in France, Federico Fellini in Italy and Ingmar Bergman in Sweden, a tendency taken up in the USA in the 1970s by the emerging MOVIE BRATS, including Peter Bogdanovich, Francis Ford Coppola, Brian de Palma, George Lucas, John Milius, Martin Scorsese and Steven Spielberg.

Interestingly, since the 1970s the idea of the director has been marked by two almost opposite tendencies. On the one hand, film studies, embracing a range of influences from cultural studies and philosophy in particular, came largely to reject the idea of the director as a single creative force seeing directors rather as part of a larger system, as defined by, for example, MARXISM, STRUCTURALISM and POST-STRUCTURALISM. Furthermore, the twin notions of the death of the author and spectators as active creators of the TEXT questioned the very notion of the individual artist working in any context, especially in a collaborative medium like film. On the other hand, in terms of the industry's own perspective, directors have often been marketed as a kind of STAR whose name can be used as the active selling point of a film. See also *METTEUR-EN-SCÈNE*.

Director's cut The EDITED version of a FEATURE FILM that is wholly approved by the DIRECTOR. Many directors make it a contractual obligation that the released version of a film is their cut, though in practice they may come under pressure from the PRODUCERS to make compromises for commercial reasons. Probably the most common reasons for disputes in this area are over the length of the film or the nature of the ending. It has recently become fashionable to release a new director's cut of a film some while after the original THEATRICAL release. Major films to have received this treatment include *Blade Runner* (dir. Ridley Scott, 1982) and *Dances with Wolves* (dir. Kevin Costner, 1990). A cynical view of directors' cuts is that they are yet another way of squeezing the commercial potential of a film, though fans of *Blade Runner* in particular have made strong claims for the superiority of the later version.

Disaster film A film that features in its narrative a great catastrophe, whether natural or the result of human error. Movies in the disaster GENRE often feature PLOTS with a cross-section of CHARACTER types that reflect various social values. The main appeal of disaster films is the REPRESENTATION of the disaster itself, hence they often employ elaborate, state-of-the-art SPECIAL EFFECTS and typically reserve the SPECTACLE of the disaster for the climax. As the characters are confronted with disaster, some survive while others die, their fates an index to the films' social attitude.

Yacowar (1977 in Grant, 1995) identifies eight types of disaster movies, including natural attacks, monster attacks and the ship of fools, all of which reflect contemporary issues. During the Depression of the 1930s, such movies as *San Francisco* (dir. W.S. Van Dyke, 1936) and *The Hurricane* (dir. John Ford, 1937) appealed to AUDIENCES that were all on shaky ground and in the same boat. In the 1940s the disaster film was displaced by the real disaster of world war, in the 1950s by the SCIENCE FICTION film's depiction of nuclear holocaust, and in the 1990s by the ACTION FILM. The genre flourished in the 1970s however, beginning with *The Poseidon Adventure* (dir. Ronald Neame, 1972). The Watergate scandal, defeat in Vietnam and other divisive issues in American culture were expressed in the movies' depictions of mass disaster. In *The Towering Inferno* (dir. John Guillermin, 1974) a new office building catches fire because of inferior wiring, suggesting the corruption of capitalism, while *Earthquake* (dir. Mark Robson, 1974), featuring the technological gimmick of SENSURROUND, metaphorically shows the very foundation of society crumbling. *The Poseidon Adventure* literally turns society upside down when the ship is overturned by a tidal wave and the band of survivors must make their way from the top to the bottom of the ship in order to escape. Ecological disaster films such as *No Blade of Grass* (dir. Cornel Wilde, 1970) and *Frogs* (dir. George McCowan, 1972) emerged with growing awareness of environmental pollution. The recent CYCLE of disaster films – *Dante's Peak* (dir. Roger Donaldson, 1997), *Volcano* (dir. Mick Jackson, 1997),

Deep Impact (dir. Mimi Leder, 1998) and *Armageddon* (dir. Michael Bay, 1998) – suggest a millennial anxiety that also appears in some apocalyptic science fiction movies.

Further reading: Ryan & Kellner (1988)

Discontinuity CONTINUITY EDITING organizes the flow of EDITING to make SPACE and TIME appear in an apparently logical and natural way so that the spectator barely notices the editing techniques, while the organization of narrative in a classical film also stresses continuity and logic. *Dis*continuity, therefore, works against the effects of continuity: the JUMP CUT, for example, reminds the spectator about the artifice of the CONVENTIONS by the mismatching of filmic elements which are generally matched. Although jump cuts can be deliberate or accidental, discontinuity is generally something consciously worked for. Discontinuity tends to provoke DISTANCIATION rather than involvement and is a common feature of COUNTER CINEMA; a film like *Tout va bien* (dir. Jean-Luc Godard and Jean-Pierre Gorin, 1972) works for noticeable discontinuity at the level of both the editing and the flow of STORY and PLOT.

Further reading: Bordwell & Thompson (1997).

Discours See ENUNCIATION.

Discourse The means by which meaning is produced and exchanged in a particular context. Cinematic discourses are made up of both IMAGES and SOUNDS, themselves the products of other kinds of CODES (fashion, non-verbal behaviour, etc.). Within the frame of cinematic discourse there are competing discourses that broadly reflect power relations. For example, one might speak of the discourse of dominant HOLLYWOOD-based cinema versus new discourses offered by THIRD CINEMA or American INDEPENDENT CINEMA. One way of explaining the wider cultural importance of discourse is that it is the way we keep making sense of the world to ourselves through the repeated narratives that are constantly circulating. Where this becomes problematic is that, in a media-dominated world, the discourses of the broadcasting organizations become those of common-sense, excluding certain kinds of alternatives. Once ideas are seen as common-sense, their IDEOLOGICAL nature becomes concealed. Alternative discourses are then extremely important in the constant process of questioning ideas that stem only from the established centres of power. From this it will be obvious that the range of discourses in circulation at any one time is vast, but that a much smaller number are actually dominant. See also STRUCTURALISM, SEMIOTICS.

Disney See WALT DISNEY COMPANY.

Dissolve A TRANSITIONAL device in which one SHOT appears to FADE out as the next shot fades in over the first, eventually replacing it altogether. The first shot becomes increasingly indistinct as the second becomes increasingly more distinct, and there is a moment when the two IMAGES are evenly blended or superimposed, usually at the midpoint. Dissolves are commonly used to suggest change of setting or a longer lapse of TIME than typically implied by the straight CUT, hence it is often used to begin and end FLASHBACKS. Also called LAP DISSOLVE.

Distanciation The process of distancing the audience from the SPECTACLE in front of it, as opposed to the drawing in of the spectator which characterizes CLASSI-CAL HOLLYWOOD and other MAINSTREAM cinema. The idea of distancing or distanciation was developed particularly during the 1920s by Soviet artists in film, theatre and photography, through the concept of 'making strange' (*ostranenie*), and by Bertolt Brecht in Germany, with ideas about EPIC THEATRE and, later, the *verfremdungseffekt*, or ALIENATION EFFECT: the aim was to produce active, politicized spectators aware of the processes of art and the IDEOLOGICAL work they performed, rather than the passive, unpoliticized, unaware spectators taken as typical of classical cinema (or theatre). An obvious way to break the spell of a CLASSICAL NARRATIVE might be for a character to turn from the DIEGETIC world on the screen and speak directly to the AUDIENCE, thus breaking the usually watertight illusionistic world of the narrative. Distancing effects can also be achieved by, for example, deliberate breaks with the CONVENTIONS of CONTINUITY EDITING, such as the use of overlapping ACTIONS or JUMP CUTS, or the introduction of non-DIEGETIC material. At the level of overall narrative, distancing can be achieved by 'dedramatization', by loosening the ties of cause and effect, and so on, producing a heightened awareness of the 'constructedness' of narrative, a characteristic of COUNTER CINEMA, especially in the work of Jean-Luc Godard. Further reading: Elsaesser in Kleber & Visser (1990), Stam (2000)

Distribution The sector of the film industry responsible for getting films actually shown in cinemas (EXHIBITION), involving everything from the most basic logistics such as getting the right number of PRINTS to the right place at the right time to complex issues such as the timing of a film's RELEASE and, most controversially of all, which films get shown where. The control of film distribution has always generated controversy and debate. A major distribution deal is central to a film's success and the comparatively small number of companies involved gives them enormous power over the kinds of films that AUDIENCES get to see. Predictably, worldwide distribution is predominantly US-based, dominated by a small number of companies – PARA-MOUNT, WARNER, WALT DISNEY, TWENTIETH CENTURY-FOX, COLUMBIA (though now owned by Japanese company Sony), UNIVERSAL, new versions of the old HOLLYWOOD STUDIOS, now characteristically parts of international CONGLOMERATES with interests across the entertainment industries and beyond. A major PRODUCER-distributor controls the international marketplace by a simple mechanism: exhibitors need HOLLYWOOD BLOCKBUSTERS which guarantee BOX-OFFICE success, and must therefore agree to the terms offered by the major distributors, including box-office splits (see GROSS) and BLOCKBOOKING. Outside the US it is also common for major distributors to work together to secure deals in foreign territories, giving them even more power over the kind of material that gets shown.

Control extends to when and with what kind of publicity and MARKETING films are released. Distribution patterns linked to different marketing strategies include exclusive runs at prestigious locations (increasingly confined to ART HOUSE releases) as well as SATURATION RELEASE in given territories. The cost of TELEVISION ADVER-TISING, now deemed essential to a film's success, is such that most releases are on a big enough scale to take advantage of a short blitz of commercials during the film's first week. Though not impossible, it is now extremely difficult for a film to do well without a major distributor's marketing power, and the economic judgment of the distributor therefore becomes central to a film's success or failure. Exceptions to the

HEGEMONY of the major distributors include companies principally concerned with INDEPENDENT or art house releases, such as, in the UK, Artificial Eye (mainly concerned with non-English language films) and Film Four, set up to distribute films in which CHANNEL 4 has a major financial stake.

Distribution today extends beyond theatrical release and newer distribution windows include VIDEO retail and rental, SATELLITE, CABLE and terrestrial ANALOGUE television; currently DIGITAL technology is opening up new possibilities for movies-on-demand in the home as well as DVD, but patterns of ownership and control over distribution are similar if not identical to those relating to theatrical release.

Divorcement See PARAMOUNT DECISION.

Docudrama A film – often a TELEVISION film or drama – that dramatizes actual events or an actual person's life with fictional devices. Sometimes referred to as 'faction,' docudramas may deal with either topical events, important moments in history, or the lives of famous or obscure people (see BIOPIC). Whichever the case, the subject is deemed to be of sufficient interest to warrant recreating. A hybrid of DOCUMENTARY and drama, docudramas purport to be factual but staged. AUDIENCES accept as a CONVENTION of the GENRE that dramatic elements will be infused into the factual material, but at the same time expect that known facts will not be violated in the process – which is what distinguishes it from fiction, after all. However, sometimes docudramas, in situations where all the facts are not known, ask us to consider their particular enacted version as the way things *might* have happened, as in *JFK* (dir. Oliver Stone, 1991), which presents a conspiracy explanation for Kennedy's assassination. Elements of docudrama go back to early NEWSREELS and to the carefully composed IMAGES that recreate American Civil War paintings and photographs in *Birth of a Nation* (dir. D.W. Griffith, 1915). However, the space between fact and fiction is vague, and debate is ongoing about which films are in fact docudrama as well as how to define it. MAIN-STREAM releases such as *Schindler's List* (dir. Steven Spielberg, 1993) and *In the Name of the Father* (dir. Jim Sheridan, 1993) may also be considered docudramas.
Further reading: Rosenthal (1999)

Documentary Broadly speaking, any film practice that has as its subject persons, events or situations that exist outside the film in the real world; also referred to as NON-FICTION FILM. Documentary films exploit the CAMERA's affinity for recording the surface of things. REALIST film theorist Siegfried Kracauer (1965) refers to the 'affinity' of film as a photographic medium to capture 'life in the raw'.

Documentary has been central to film history from the beginning. The *ACTUAL-ITÉs*, short slices of life by the Lumière Brothers, were, in 1895, not only the first films exhibited to the public, but also the first documentaries. The LUMIÈRE PROGRAMMES proved so popular that within two years they had approximately one hundred operators at work around the world, both filming and exhibiting (Barnouw, 1993). Many of the new enterprising film companies that sprang up at the beginning of the twentieth century featured non-fiction titles, particularly TRAVELOGUES; but when film-makers such as Edwin S. Porter and D. W. Griffith perfected the EDITING techniques that have come to characterize the CLASSICAL HOLLYWOOD CINEMA, documentary was quickly eclipsed in popularity by narrative film. Assuming a subsidiary position within the institution of cinema, documentary survived as NEWSREELS, one of a series of SHORTS shown before the DOUBLE BILL. Yet newsreels retained a distinct appeal. Pathé News, for example, begun in the US in 1910, proved so popular that within two years several other STUDIOS, including UNIVERSAL, PARAMOUNT and FOX, entered the field. Orson Welles' *Citizen Kane* (1941) assumed that newsreel CONVENTIONS were familiar enough to movie audiences to begin with a mock newsreel which is at once a clever device of exposition and a PARODY of such newsreels generally and of Louis de Rochemont's *The March of Time* specifically.

The first FEATURE-length documentary was *Nanook of the North* (1922), about Inuit life in the Canadian north. Directed by Robert Flaherty, a former explorer and prospector with little prior training in CINEMATOGRAPHY, *Nanook* demonstrated that fictional techniques could be successfully employed in the documentary as well. Flaherty borrowed techniques from narrative film practice to powerful effect. Moving beyond the picturesque detachment of the conventional travelogue, *Nanook* had a commercially successful run on Broadway (as the second feature with a Harold Lloyd COMEDY, *Grandma's Boy*, dir. Fred Newmeyer, 1922). Documentary remained on the margins of HOLLYWOOD cinema, however, which has only rarely produced a feature-length work, such as *Woodstock* (dir. Michael Wadleigh, 1970), that has managed to find DISTRIBUTION in commercial theatres.

John Grierson, who spearheaded the British documentary movement in the 1920s, coined the term 'documentary' in a review of Flaherty's subsequent *Moana* (1926). The film, he wrote, 'being a visual account of events in the daily life of a Polynesian youth and his family, has documentary value' (Grierson, 1976, p. 11). Grierson believed that documentary film had great value as social PROPAGANDA and mass education. Unlike Flaherty, whom he chastised for his romanticism, Grierson wanted 'to make drama from the ordinary' in films that were 'social not aesthetic'. He headed the EMPIRE MARKETING BOARD FILM UNIT and the GPO FILM UNIT, defining its characteristic exhortatory style – often, as in *Coalface* (dir. Alberto Cavalcanti, 1935), with a VOICE-OF-GOD NARRATION and a pro-industrial, capitalist IDEOLOGY. Still, documentaries such as *Night Mail* (dir. Basil Wright and Harry Watt, 1936), with its use of MONTAGE along with the rhythmic verse by W.H. Auden and MUSIC by Benjamin Britten, showed that social relevance and aesthetic concerns need not be antithetical.

Documentary films are different from fiction precisely because they possess an indexical bond, a referent, to the historical real. They are unique in engaging what documentary theorist Bill Nichols calls our 'epistephilia', a pleasure in knowing about the real world (Nichols, 1991). No matter how marvellous the SPECIAL EFFECTS in a fiction film, a death scene will never produce the same kind of horror as that generated by, say, the Zapruder footage of Kennedy being assassinated or the explosion of the space shuttle Challenger as caught by TELEVISION news cameras. Every documentary makes some claim about the real world and, to some degree, seeks to bring about change in the AUDIENCE, whether to influence attitudes, increase understanding, or persuade to action.

So in the 1930s, as the world geared up for war, documentary emerged as a dominant form of cultural expression and political propaganda. Even the United States government, which had kept at arm's length from the country's film industry so as not to interfere with private enterprise, experimented briefly with a US Film Service branch, for which Pare Lorentz made *The Plow that Broke the Plains* (1936) and *The River* (1937) in support of New Deal policies. By the end of the decade, film-making in Germany and other countries had come under government control. Hitler commissioned Leni Riefenstahl to make *Triumph of the Will* (1936), a celebration of Nazi ideology for which the monumental Nuremberg Party rallies were deliberately staged. In the US, Frank Capra, a major Hollywood DIRECTOR, oversaw for the military the production of *Why We Fight* (1942-44), a SERIES of seven documentaries designed to provide background information about the global conflict and help shake Americans from their strong isolationist position. Many Hollywood professionals were involved in the various aspects of the films' production. Shown as a required part of military training, *Why We Fight* effectively simplified the political complexities by cleverly invoking patriotic MYTH and national fervour. In England, toward the end of the war the CROWN FILM UNIT's documentaries helped boost morale on the home front, particularly with the strikingly poetic approach of Humphrey Jennings in such films as *Fires Were Started* (1943) and *A Diary for Timothy* (1945).

By the 1950s the various newsreel series had ceased production, as their function was increasingly taken over by television, where daily news reports were able to show world events more quickly. But inspired by the powerful immediacy of the location photography and actuality FOOTAGE of wartime films, a renewed embrace of REALISM began to emerge in Italian NEO-REALISM and British 'kitchen sink' realism in the BRITISH NEW WAVE. Also, INDEPENDENT film-makers such as Morris Engel (*The Little Fugitive*, 1953) and John Cassavetes (*Shadows*, 1961) began making feature films with lightweight portable equipment as a way of rivalling the studios.

With the development of this new portable 16mm equipment in the 1960s, the documentary film underwent a significant revolution. Lightweight REFLEX CAMERAS meant that the camera no longer had to be the centre of PROFILMIC EVENTS, but could follow them as they happened. For the first time film-makers could enter a situation directly and be a part of the very situation being documented. The camera gained a new mobility, and as further improvements were perfected, the tape recorder and the camera, which before had been connected by a cumbersome cable, were able to operate entirely independently. The CREW required to make a documentary was reduced to only two people, one to operate the camera, another for SOUND. Not only did IMAGES gain a new freshness and immediacy, but so did the SOUNDTRACK, featuring as never before the unscripted speaking voices of documentary subjects.

A new OBSERVATIONAL style developed, one that allowed film-makers to abandon the omniscient voice-over narration and rhetorical structure associated with the Griersonian tradition. As a result, documentary experienced a revitalization internationally. Although there are differences between the various national movements, they shared the premise that truth could now be discovered rather than imposed. In Great Britain Lindsay Anderson (*Every Day Except Christmas*, 1957) and Karel Reisz (*We are the Lambeth Boys*, 1959) made films of everyday life and British POPULAR CULTURE as part of the FREE CINEMA movement. In Canada in the early 1960s, both English and French Canadian film-makers working for the NATIONAL FILM BOARD OF CANADA, founded by Grierson in 1939, concentrated on making films about ordinary people and events. In France, anthropologist/film-maker Jean Rouch turned his camera closer to home, filming a cross-section of Parisians in *Chronicle d'été* (*Chronicle of a Summer*, 1961), beginning the movement known as CINÉMA VÉRITÉ.

An entire generation of documentarians embraced the new style and valorized the technology. In the US, DIRECT CINEMA film-makers such as Richard Leacock, D.A. Pennebaker, and the Maysles Brothers sought to reveal the truth of events by preserving their temporal integrity as much as possible. Most advocated an unproblematic view of cinematic realism whereby the camera could apprehend the world directly, penetrating surface reality to reveal deeper truths. The presence of the camera was not seen as affecting the profilmic event to any significant degree, and if it did, film-makers could search for those PRIVILEGED MOMENTS that would reveal the real person hiding behind the social personae of their subjects.

Many film-makers have sought to use documentary politically for cultural legitimization, to help create a sense of shared purpose. In the 1950s, Québecois film-makers discovered that training the camera on themselves facilitated the Quiet Revolution, the province's discovery of itself as a proud and distinct culture within Canada. Subcultures and various interest groups have used the documentary successfully to help develop a sense of identity and solidarity. In the 1970s FEMINIST documentary film-makers developed a distinctively intimate, TALKING HEAD style that promoted the shared rediscovery of mutual experience with the viewer, as in *With Babies and Banners* (dir. Lorraine Gray, 1977) and *The Life and Times of Rosie the Riveter* (dir. Connie Field, 1980) (Lesage, 1984). More recently, documentaries about gayness and AIDS have appeared with the emergence of the gay movement in the 1980s. Much documentary practice continues to be politically engaged and some films, such as *Harlan County, USA* (dir. Barbara Kopple, 1976) and *Roger and Me* (dir. Michael Moore, 1989), have been able to find limited commercial distribution.

While for many viewers documentary still means objectivity, today it is much more commonly accepted that documentaries are inevitably biased. Documentary makers and viewers are more sensitive to the politics of REPRESENTATION, of how other people are represented and how they might represent themselves. Thus most film-makers have abandoned the certainties implied by the Griersonian style, using a variety of techniques to address their relative position in the process of documentation. This condition is probably less a POSTMODERN crisis in signification than the result of the proliferation of camcorders and a greater increase in basic visual literacy. Many recent documentaries, such as *The Thin Blue Line* (dir. Errol Morris, 1987), seek to uncover ambiguities of truth rather than a unified, singular Truth (Williams, 1993).

Because of their stylistic heterogeneity, ranging from the poetic expressionism of the CITY SYMPHONY film to ETHNOGRAPHIC minimalism, documentary cannot be considered a GENRE in any sense equivalent to those of commercial fiction cinema. As Nichols has concluded, 'Documentary as a concept or practice occupies no fixed territory. It mobilises no finite inventory of techniques, addresses no set number of issues, and adopts no completely known taxonomy of forms, styles, or modes' (Nichols, 1991, p. 12). Unsurprisingly, all attempts to provide inclusive definitions of documentary have been fraught with difficulty. The simplest and most useful has remained John Grierson's 'the creative treatment of actuality,' since it allows for a combination of actuality and the inevitable shaping hand of the film-maker. Documentary style is potentially unlimited, and since Flaherty virtually every technique familiar in fiction film has been used in documentary film practice as well. But whatever their genre or style, all documentary films implicitly argue for the Keatsian equation of truth and beauty.

Further reading: Barsam (1973, 1976), Corner (1996), Ellis (1989), Grant &

Sloniowski (1998), Jacobs (1979), Lovell & Hillier (1972), Macdonald & Cousins (1996), Renov (1993), Swann (1989), Winston (1995)

Dolby sound In the 1970s the Dolby company developed a high-quality SOUND recording system, originally for audio magnetic tape, to reduce the amount of tape 'hiss' or interference audible during playback. Dolby has also long been associated with the production of 35mm film SOUNDTRACKS and is used as a relatively low-key MARKETING device by both film DISTRIBUTORS and EXHIBITORS, as in 'with full Dolby sound'. In common DISCOURSE 'Dolby' is used as a generic term for a number of technical devices now associated with the company and Dolby has firmly entered the DIGITAL arena through its production of advanced sound systems that now contribute to the very high quality of reproduction of sound in practically all cinemas.

Dolly A platform on wheels most often used to move the CAMERA and CAMERA OPERATOR around while filming to allow for smooth motion of the camera. In a TRACKING SHOT, the dolly, mounted on rails, allows for smooth changes in the distance of the CAMERA to the subject within the same SHOT. Also used as a verb to describe the ACTION of moving the camera on such a platform while filming.

Dolly grip A GRIP specializing in moving the CAMERA on a DOLLY.

Dolly shot A SHOT made using a DOLLY. See also TRACKING SHOT.

Dominant cinema See MAINSTREAM CINEMA.

Dominant, dominant contrast The particular element of the visual composition of an IMAGE, or the way a SHOT is FRAMED, that draws the viewer's eye.

Double bill The showing of two FEATURE FILMS, one after the other, a practice historically associated with the HOLLYWOOD STUDIO era, but a rarity in today's patterns of DISTRIBUTION and EXHIBITION. Its origins can be traced to the US in the Great Depression when two films for the price of one was designed to lure hard-up people back to the cinema. The phenomenon is also associated with the so-called B-MOVIE; whereas to show two major films at once would have been prohibitive for the exhibitor, the cheaper B-MOVIE made the double bill possible. It still survives in certain contexts such as REPERTORY CINEMAS that might show two films together, revealing interesting links or contrasts between them. The term is also referred to as 'double feature'.

Double exposure See SUPERIMPOSITION.

Double A person filmed in place of a leading ACTOR or STAR – a procedure often adopted for difficult stunts, but also used for long distance SHOTS where the presence of the actual performer is not necessary. More frequent nudity on screen since the 1960s has also made more common the use of 'body doubles', in which supposed shots of the body of the leading actors (particularly women) will in fact be of doubles, as with Angie Dickinson in *Dressed to Kill* (dir. Brian de Palma, 1980).

Downtime, down time The period during which PRODUCTION, especially shooting, is halted by equipment failure or some other unavoidable factor. The existence of a special term probably stems from the great costs involved in film production, where, more than in most arts, time is money.

Dream film The ability of EDITING to play with SPACE and TIME and the ability of the film medium to speed up, slow down and freeze time, have long been closely associated with the structure of dreaming, as evidenced by the dream framing structure of early films like *The Life of an American Fireman* (dir. Edwin S. Porter, 1903). The relationship between film, dream and the unconscious was perceived during the 1920s by the French IMPRESSIONISTS and was especially savoured by the DADAISTS and SURREALISTS; 'Film seems an involuntary imitation of dreams. The cinema might have been invented to express the life of the unconscious' (Luis Buñuel, as evidenced by *Un Chien andalou*, 1928) (Hammond, 1978). René Clair, co-director of the Dada-ist *Entr'acte* (1924), commented that 'the spectator's mind is not unlike that of a dreamer. The darkness of the hall, the enervating effect of the MUSIC, the silent shadow gliding across the luminous screen – everything conspires to plunge us into a dreamlike state in which the suggestive power of the forms playing before us can become as imperious as the power of the IMAGES appearing in our veritable sleep' (Petric, 1981). Later US AVANT-GARDE film-maker Maya Deren's films (*Meshes of the Afternoon*, 1943; *At Land*, 1944; *Ritual in Transfigured Time*, 1949) and Kenneth Anger's *Fireworks* (1947) are strongly dream-like in structure. Although Surrealists found dream-like elements in HOLLYWOOD films like *Peter Ibbetson* (dir. Henry Hathaway, 1935), dream sequences within Hollywood films tended to be clearly separated off from reality (as in the dream sequence designed by Salvador Dali for Hitchcock's *Spellbound*, 1945).
Further reading: Eberwein (1984)

Drew Associates Group of young DOCUMENTARY film-makers organized by PRODUCER Robert Drew and based in New York City, known for their pioneering work in DIRECT CINEMA. The group, including major figures of American OBSERVATIONAL CINEMA like D. A. Pennebaker, Albert Maysles, and Richard Leacock, began making films for Time, Inc. in 1958. They sought to be invisible observers of PROFILMIC events – ideally, like a FLY ON THE WALL in Leacock's famous phrase. One of their best known films, *Primary* (1960), about the Wisconsin presidential campaigns of senators John F. Kennedy and Hubert Humphrey, so impressed ABC executives that the network contracted with Time, Inc., to broadcast their films on national TELEVISION. The group made nineteen pioneering and influential films for the network, beginning with *Primary* and ending with *Crisis: Behind a Presidential Commitment* in 1963, tending to favour famous and exciting figures as their subjects, such as race car drivers (*Eddie*, 1961).

Drive-by A drive-by SHOT is a shot of a generally static person, object or place taken from a moving CAMERA, typically a camera located in a vehicle, as it passes or drives by.

Drive-in, drive-in theatre An outdoor cinema theatre (as opposed to indoor hard top theatres) where patrons watch a large screen from their parked

cars, listening to small speakers placed in each car (or, these days, tuning in the car radio for sound). Drive-ins were very popular in the US from 1945–1960s, especially in the warmer regions: there were some 4,000 drive-ins by 1958, most holding 500–700 cars, though larger ones held as many as 2,000. The popularity and growth of drive-ins, which during this period were generally oriented to family audiences, related to increased car ownership and suburbanization in the post-war period. In 2000 only some 800 US drive-ins are left, aimed at youth audiences and generally devoted to EXPLOITATION films. Reasons for the decline of the drive-in are many: competition from TELEVISION and, more recently, CABLE and HOME VIDEO; smaller size cars; the development of suburban MALL CINEMAS and MULTIPLEXES; and the rising price of real estate. The drive-in is mythologized by film itself, often as a convenient location for a romantic encounter, using the greater privacy afforded by watching a film from a car, as evocation of the past or, as in the case of *Targets* (dir. Peter Bogdanovich, 1968), a place full of possibilities for the HORROR genre.
Further reading: Gomery (1992)

Dub, dubbing The process of adding SOUND to a film after the original shooting has finished, or mixing a range of sounds recorded from different sources to form a film's final SOUNDTRACK. The most visible kind of dubbing is when dialogue in one language is substituted on the soundtrack for the one spoken by the ACTORS on the screen – used as an alternative to SUBTITLES, though for many the effect completely destroys the film as it is impossible to make the sound appear 'in SYNC' with the IMAGE. Most dubbing takes place for more credible reasons such as adding additional atmosphere (crowd noise, crickets in the desert, a storm, etc.) or spoken dialogue when the original recording turns out not to have been of high enough quality. See also FOLEY ART/ARTIST.

Dupe, duplicate negative Duplicate of an original NEGATIVE made from a master positive. Dupes are made to safeguard the original and for making RELEASE PRINTS.

Dutch angle Also known as a canted shot, a CAMERA ANGLE that noticeably deviates from the normal vertical or horizontal axis, so that vertical and horizontal lines within the IMAGE appear at a tilted angle in relation to the film FRAME, most frequently used to evoke a sense of disequilibrium in the spectator, often linked with the subjective lack of mental balance in a CHARACTER.

DV/Digital video VIDEO recording format aimed primarily at the amateur or domestic market, and fast replacing ANALOGUE formats such as Hi8 and S-VHS. Digital video offers a higher quality of IMAGE that suffers negligible DEGRADATION from copying, and programs are available for EDITING on personal computers. Higher quality DV formats, such as Panasonic's DVCPro, Sony's DVCam and JVC's Digital-S, are used professionally.

DVD DIGITAL versatile disc (originally known as 'digital VIDEO disc') – the same size as a CD or CD-Rom – from which digital information is read by a laser. DVD is capable of holding a huge amount of information and replaying at very high quality. At present, DVDs can only be used for playback, but they are replacing LASER DISCS for

quality transmission, especially for HOME CINEMA systems, and are likely to replace the relatively low quality video once capable of recording.

Dynamic frame   A technique suggested by Sergei Eisenstein in 1930 (Eisenstein, 1988), positing that the ideal film IMAGE should be square, rather than the rectangular ACADEMY ASPECT RATIO norm, and that the size and shape of the image should be able to be changed – 'dynamic' – as film-makers saw fit. Eisenstein's idea found little support, despite some isolated experiments (just as his radical thinking about SOUND found few sympathetic ears).

Dziga Vertov Group   Radical film collective formed shortly after the political unrest in France during May, 1968. The group, whose best-known member was the FRENCH NEW WAVE DIRECTOR Jean-Luc Godard, named itself after Soviet DOCUMEN-TARY film-maker and theorist Dziga Vertov (*Man with the Movie Camera*, 1929), whose philosophy of the KINO EYE was harnessed to political activism and PROPA-GANDA in the decade after the Russian revolution. The collective aimed to make films politically rather than to make political films – that is, to make films that were polit-ical in form as well as content. The films were also made in a politically radical manner – filmed in 16MM on low budgets and shown non-theatrically to student and activist groups. The Dziga Vertov Group completed five films, including *British Sounds (See You at Mao)* (1969) and *Vent d'est/Wind from the East* (1970), before disbanding the following year.

E

Eady Levy   A levy by the British government on all cinema admissions and placed in a fund to support British film-making, named after the Treasury official, Wilfred Eady, responsible for its introduction. Started by the Labour government in 1950, firstly on a voluntary basis in return for a reduction in entertainment tax, then made statutory in 1957, the fund was distributed to PRODUCERS according to BOX-OFFICE returns through the National Film Finance Corporation. The Levy was abolished in 1985 by the Conservative government and the NFFC replaced by a private-sector body with some small initial state subsidy. Its abolition was seen by many as an important indicator of government attitudes to the survival of a British film indus-try at a time when it was already struggling to maintain a significant output.

Ealing   One of the most famous British STUDIOS, taking its name from the area of West London in which it operated for most of its existence between 1931 and 1955. Ealing's output before and during World War II was relatively prolific and high profile, including musical-based vehicles for Gracie Fields and George Formby. However, the studio is best known for the series of early 1950s COMEDIES which are still firmly iden-tified as among the key films of British cinema, including *The Lavender Hill Mob* (dir. Charles Crichton, 1951), *The Man in the White Suit* (dir. Alexander Mackendrick, 1951) and *The Maggie* (dir. Mackendrick, 1954). Other significant DIRECTORS associ-ated with Ealing included Basil Dearden and Robert Hamer. T.E.B. Clarke was the scriptwriter associated with most of the comedies. Stylistically Ealing belongs to the British REALIST tradition with its roots in DOCUMENTARY. Key social-problem films

such as *The Blue Lamp* (dir. Basil Dearden, 1950) employ a number of the structural features of documentary, including an authoritative VOICE-OVER and more extensive location shooting than was common at the time, while the comedies tend to use a realist base to launch the comic fantasy that is at their centre.
Further reading: Barr (1977), Barr (1986)

Early cinema See SILENT CINEMA.

Eastman Color The single NEGATIVE COLOUR FILM STOCK introduced by Eastman Kodak in 1952 which, for 35MM FEATURE FILM production, by the mid-1950s had supplanted the three colour separation negative system developed and perfected by TECHNICOLOR – mainly because it could be used in a normal CAMERA and was cheaper. Eastman Color remains the main COLOUR stock in use today. Though fading occurred with early Eastman Color stock, improvements have lessened the problem.
Further reading: Neale (1985)

Éclair Motion picture CAMERA made by the French company, Eclair International Diffusion. The company makes both 16MM and 35MM cameras that are very lightweight and reliable, and so have been used extensively in OBSERVATIONAL CINEMA.

Editing The process by which SHOT film FOOTAGE is assembled to create sets of meanings not wholly contained in the separate shots themselves. The majority of edits appear on the screen as a series of CUTS with one SCENE ending and another beginning with no visible break, though transitional devices such as DISSOLVES, FADES and WIPES, all of which are visible on the screen in different ways, are also common.
   The physical processes of editing have recently undergone a series of changes as the result of developments in VIDEO editing systems, particularly with DIGITAL technology. Earlier, editing consisted of cutting up and SPLICING back together pieces of celluloid, using increasingly refined versions of flat-bed editing tables like the STEENBECK. Though this remains the dominant method of high quality film editing, it is now common for RUSHES to be transferred to video tape (now usually digital) and for a rough ASSEMBLY of the film to be made using tape. Digital technology offers the further advantage of allowing random access to SHOTS and virtual edits on a computer to try out different ways of assembling a particular SEQUENCE or indeed the whole film. Because of the time and cost savings, video-based editing now plays a part in the POST-PRODUCTION of virtually all FEATURE FILMS, and for many low-budget features it will be the sole method until the very last stage of the process.
   In a standard commercial feature film the main aim of the editing process is to create CONTINUITY, to let the film tell a STORY as straightforwardly as possible, though this makes a complex process sound simple and CONTINUITY EDITING – or INVISIBLE EDITING – requires much careful planning so that the film is shot in a way that makes this kind of editing possible (see 180° RULE, 30° RULE). Among established techniques used to disguise the transition from one shot to the next are the use of bridging devices such as SOUND that overlaps the CUT and cutting at a point in the ACTION when there is movement towards the edge of the FRAME. This does not mean that all

the editing in a conventional piece of storytelling will be motivated by continuity: moments when the editing is much more visible – such as a series of rapid edits to MUSIC in certain kinds of action SEQUENCES – are common.

MONTAGE is less about presenting a film sequence as the illusion of reality, than about reconstructing segments of the recorded world in order to comment on it, or represent it in a new way. It is in some ways the opposite of continuity editing, though commercial cinema also employs montage as an editing technique – one example being the shower scene in Alfred Hitchcock's *Psycho* (1960).

The debate about editing and film art has concerned critics and theorists at various moments in the history of film. Sergei Eisenstein argued in the 1920s that it was during the editing process that real creativity took place, that footage was simply raw material, like paint, for the artist to assemble to create aesthetic effects: for Eisenstein montage was about the collision of IMAGES creating powerful effects. André Bazin (Bazin, 1967, 1971), in the 1940s and 1950s, considered this approach too manipulative, arguing that film's purpose was the recording of physical reality as faithfully as possible, allowing spectators to freely direct their vision via composition in depth using DEEP FOCUS and LONG TAKES, edited together as seamlessly as possible. Here the editing process becomes subservient to the creation of the *MISE EN SCÈNE* within the shot.

Today the DIRECTOR'S CUT draws attention to the fact that even well known DIRECTORS will not automatically have total control over the editing process. Ideally, editing is a close collaboration between a director and skilled EDITOR who respect each other's skills and creativity. See also BRIDGE, CROSSCUTTING, DAILIES, DUB, NEO-REALISM, PARALLEL EDITING, SHOT-REVERSE-SHOT.

Further reading: Aumont (1992), Bordwell & Thompson (1997), Miller & Stam (1999)

Editor The person ultimately responsible for assembling the FOOTAGE SHOT during the various stages of a film's production, from simply putting together a SCENE, or set of scenes, from the DAILIES or RUSHES, to the final version of the whole film. The power and status of editors can vary greatly from film to film, but their role automatically involves close liaison with the film's DIRECTOR and, probably, PRODUCER. It is now more widely recognized that an editor's most important skills are less technical than those associated with patterns and rhythms, though it is still rare for an individual editor to achieve a high public profile, with one or two key exceptions such as Thelma Schoonmaker, Martin Scorsese's long-term collaborator since *Raging Bull* (1980), and editors who went on to become directors such as David Lean, Hal Ashby and Robert Wise. See also EDITING.

Educational film A type of DOCUMENTARY produced with the primary purpose of teaching a subject or skill. Educational films are often made explicitly for viewing in the classroom. See also INSTRUCTIONAL FILM.

Ellipsis A passage of TIME that is missing from the film's ACTION on screen, but which is implied through various cinematic means. This can range from the most obvious such as a CAPTION indicating that it is 'Twelve Years Later' to more subtle indicators of ageing or other kinds of narrative exposition. FADES or DISSOLVES on the screen are common ways of indicating ellipsis, whilst the JUMP CUT is an uncomfortable way of drawing the spectator's attention to time having passed without providing any kind of smooth transition through a CUTAWAY to another viewpoint. See also EDITING.

Empire Marketing Board (Film Unit) The Empire Marketing Board existed to market the British Empire. Between 1928 and 1933, under its Public Relations head, Sir Stephen Tallents, John Grierson laid the foundations for the important output of British DOCUMENTARY films in the 1930s, bringing together key film-makers like Basil Wright, Arthur Elton, Harry Watt, Paul Rotha and Edgar Anstey. The unit produced important early documentaries such as *Drifters* (dir. John Grierson, 1929), *Industrial Britain* (dir. Robert Flaherty, 1932), and *Aero-Engine* (dir. Elton, 1933) – almost 100 short films in all. When the EMB was wound up in 1933, Tallents moved to the General Post Office and took Grierson's film unit with him, to found the GENERAL POST OFFICE FILM UNIT.
Further reading: Grierson (1966), Lovell & Hillier (1972), Winston (1995)

Emulsion The light-sensitive material fixed to the strip of cellulose ACETATE (until 1951, cellulose NITRATE), consisting of light-sensitive silver salts suspended in gelatine. The photographic IMAGE is formed when the EMULSION is exposed to light and then becomes visible when developed. Emulsion is easily scratched and some AVANT-GARDE film-makers (such as Len Lye, Norman MacLaren and Stan Brakhage) have experimented with scratching the emulsion, thus letting light through, or removing the emulsion and painting directly on to the acetate strip.

Enunciation In SEMIOTICS, a term that refers to the analysis of any film or other TEXT as DISCOURSE. Based on the work of Emile Benveniste, any given film is seen as a speech act (*énoncé*) which is distinct from both the speaker and SUBJECT constructed by the text. Enunciation is either *HISTOIRE* or *DISCOURS*, roughly a distinction between fictional and factual texts, respectively. The latter present themselves as history, masking their enunciation; hence the textual work of enunciation is fundamentally IDEOLOGICAL and consequently a focus of DECONSTRUCTION. The concept has important implications for RECEPTION THEORY and how we think of the dynamics of SPECTATORSHIP, particularly in the context of MAINSTREAM CINEMA, which cloaks its status as enunciation through such techniques as CONTINUITY and SUTURE.

Epic (epic theatre, epic novel) In his essay *The Modern Theatre is the Epic Theatre* (Brecht, 1964), Bertolt Brecht – developing a theory and practice of MARXIST aesthetics – argued for the replacement of conventional dramatic (or Aristotelian) theatre, with its striving for illusion and the AUDIENCE'S emotional involvement, by 'epic theatre'. Via MONTAGE instead of linear development, reason instead of feeling, 'epic theatre' would appeal to the intellect, limit empathy and invite critical appraisal of the narrative, so that the full political and IDEOLOGICAL implications of the drama would be available through some form of DISTANCIATION. Brecht's distinction between conventional drama and 'epic theatre' has clear similarities in film to the distinction between illusionist CLASSICAL NARRATIVE CINEMA and montage and various forms of REFLEXIVITY. This should not be surprising: Brecht was developing his ideas while the Soviet film-makers were experimenting with montage, and Brecht's writings on theatre became available in the West only in the late 1950s and early 1960s, when FRENCH NEW WAVE and other kinds of NEW CINEMA began to emerge.

Brecht's thinking about theatre has been widely influential on film-making, particularly in COUNTER CINEMA, with its combination of political subject matter and a reflexive approach to film form. Confusingly, another influential Marxist theoretician, Georg Lukács, was also developing ideas about the epic qualities of certain kinds of novel (exemplified by Honoré de Balzac and Thomas Mann) and their potential for critical REALISM, as compared to much nineteenth century drama. Though Brecht, arguing for modernism, explicitly opposed Lukács, Lukács argued persuasively (in ways later echoed by literary critic Raymond Williams) for the epic novel's ability to render the movement of historical forces through an 'intensive totality' of life and 'typical' protagonists. A Lukácsian approach has been interestingly applied to some films, such as Luchino Visconti's *Rocco and his Brothers* (1960) (Nowell-Smith, 1973; Rohdie, 1992).

Further reading: Lukács in Burns & Burns (1973), Lukács (1970), Sobchack (1995), Stam (2000)

Epic film   A film GENRE characterized by sweeping visual IMAGES with large casts ('a cast of thousands'), frequently involving a NARRATIVE that unfolds over many years or generations and involving events of major historical significance. Epics are usually set in ancient or Biblical times, but not necessarily. The epic actually overlaps with such other genres as the WESTERN, MUSICAL and WAR FILM, and is defined more by its scale of treatment than by inherent CONVENTIONS and ICONOGRAPHY. Like MELODRAMA, their emphasis is less on CHARACTER development than on visual SPECTACLE, often with large-scale battle SCENES and ACTION set-pieces like the chariot race in *Ben-Hur* (dir. William Wyler, 1959). As befits their scope, epics tend to be filmed in WIDESCREEN format and feature lavish PRODUCTION VALUES. *The Robe* (Henry Koster, 1953) was the first film made in CinemaScope, while *How the West Was Won* (1962), a CINERAMA production, was directed by no less than three big-name Hollywood directors (John Ford, Henry Hathaway and George Marshall). *The Ten Commandments* (dir. Cecil B. DeMille, 1956) was over four hours long with an intermission. Often, as was the case with *Cleopatra* (dir. Joseph L. Mankiewicz, 1963), epic films tout their expense and EXCESS. Sobchack (1995) observes that their bloated length and shamefully expensive production values are part of their experience and pleasure.

Like the sweeping heroic tales of the classic literary epics, the genre quickly developed in the SILENT CINEMA. The multi-reel Italian PEPLUM FILM *Cabiria* (dir. Giovanni Pastrone, 1914), featuring the destruction of a palace by an exploding volcano, was followed by D.W. Griffith's two ground-breaking films, *Birth of a Nation* (1915) and *Intolerance* (1916), for which the mammoth Babylonian set for a while dominated the Los Angeles landscape. While epics did appear steadily, they became a prominent genre in the 1950s. Not only did a new CYCLE of epics come from Italy, such as *Hercules Unchained* (dir. Pietro Francisci, 1960) with American ACTOR Steve Reeves, but HOLLYWOOD looked to the epic as it began using WIDESCREEN and COLOUR to combat the competition of TELEVISION by luring back AUDIENCES with the kind of scale impossible on the small screen. Also, the remote historical setting of epics allowed them to explore with relative ease both contemporary GENDER politics and Cold War IDEOLOGY. The latter is the focus, for example, of *Spartacus* (dir. Stanley

Kubrick, 1960), with its SCREENPLAY by Dalton Trumbo, one of the HOLLYWOOD TEN. Ancient Rome and Egypt are often depicted as having military regimes that oppress innocent Christians. In his prologue to *The Ten Commandments*, Cecil B. DeMille, one of the few AUTEURS to work with any consistency in the genre, speaks directly to the CAMERA, making explicit the metaphorical connection between the film's STORY and contemporary politics.

The cycle of epics in the 1950s and 1960s inevitably came to an end because of rising costs, falling profits and the changing nature of audience demographics. Still, the epic has remained largely an American genre, since HOLLYWOOD alone of all NATIONAL CINEMAS has the financial means to produce them. Yet epics have declined somewhat in recent years as Hollywood has embraced the economics of the BLOCK-BUSTER, which seeks in effect to make any movie with a large enough budget an 'epic event.'
Further reading: Babington & Evans (1993), Elley (1984), Hirsch (1978)

Episodic narrative The ideal CLASSICAL NARRATIVE flows smoothly and logically, helped on its way by CONTINUITY EDITING, effects follow causes and enigmas move to a resolution with a high degree of narrative economy in which very little is irrelevant. However, stories do not need to be told in this familiar way, even if this is the way that most AUDIENCES are most used to. Film-makers refusing this approach argue that reality is not structured like a (classical) narrative, and claim greater REALISM for a more episodic approach in which there might be gaps, or scenes may not seem to advance the plot. André Bazin (1971) argued that such an approach was a major innovation of Italian NEO-REALISM, and it is characteristic of much 1950s and 1960s ART CINEMA and much of Godard and other NEW CINEMA of the 1960s and 1970s. These more episodic styles found their way into US cinema in the 1960s and 1970s (for example, *Easy Rider*, dir. Dennis Hopper, 1969; *Five Easy Pieces*, dir. Bob Rafelson, 1970) and remain characteristic of much INDEPENDENT CINEMA, such as Jim Jarmusch's films (*Stranger Than Paradise*, 1984; *Mystery Train*, 1989). See also BBS.
Further reading: Bordwell (1985)

Equity The abbreviated name of the only significant ACTORS' union in the UK and one of the main ones in the USA.

Erotic film See PORNOGRAPHY.

Erotic thriller While the THRILLER is a film that generates suspense, mystery and excitement, the erotic thriller does so by focusing specifically upon problems in heterosexual relationships. The GENRE developed quickly as a result of the impressive BOX-OFFICE success of *Fatal Attraction* (dir. Adrian Lyne) in 1987 and then *Basic Instinct* (dir. Paul Verhoeven) in 1992. Earlier thrillers featuring heterosexual couples depicted a romantic relationship that grew as the suspenseful PLOT unfolded, as in Alfred Hitchcock's *The 39 Steps* (1935) or *North by Northwest* (1959). The erotic thriller tends to turn romance into sex, with more explicitly erotic SCENES of love-making, and then turn the tensions and ambiguities of the relationship itself into the suspense. *Fatal Attraction* generated considerable controversy about its adulterous affair that goes sour when an initially competent professional woman, becomes a crazed, jealous monster who stalks a man's family. Movies such as *Jagged Edge* (dir.

Richard Marquand, 1985), *Body of Evidence* (dir. Uli Edel, 1993), *Indecent Proposal* (dir. Lyne, 1993) and *Disclosure* (dir. Barry Levinson, 1994) depict fear, distrust and dangerous and deadly games as the result of sexual relationships, and express the confusion over changing sexual attitudes, the institutionalization of harassment guidelines in the workplace, and the anxieties over AIDS. Because of their SOFT-CORE SEQUENCES, many erotic thrillers are made STRAIGHT-TO-VIDEO.
Further reading: Eberwein (1998), Williams (1993)

Essanay American film company founded in 1907 by George K. Spoor and G.M. Anderson, initially known for its WESTERNS, especially the almost four hundred Bronco Billy SHORTS starring Anderson. The company managed to lure Charles Chaplin away from KEYSTONE with a contract for a weekly salary of over $1,000. Chaplin made fourteen shorts for Essanay, including one of his most well-known, *The Tramp* (1915). It was also at Essanay that Chaplin formed his productive association with CINEMATOGRAPHER Rollie Totheroh. In 1916, however, Chaplin moved to MUTUAL, and Essanay, its fortunes now declining, was bought out the following year by VITAGRAPH.

Essay film A form of DOCUMENTARY and/or AVANT-GARDE film which emphasizes argument over storytelling, often with strong autobiographical or personal elements. A prime exponent of the form is French film-maker Chris Marker with films like *Sans Soleil* (*Sunless*, 1983) and *The Last Bolshevik* (1993). Other documentary film-makers have also dabbled in the form, such as Ross McElwee (*Sherman's March*, 1985; *Time Indefinite*, 1992), in which, as with Marker, the strongly autobiographical/personal merges with the meditative, and Errol Morris (*The Thin Blue Line*, 1988; *Fast, Cheap and Out of Control*, 1997), where the autobiographical is largely absent. Arguably, many earlier documentary films – such as *Coal Face* (dir. Alberto Cavalcanti, 1935) – could be included, and Phillip Lopate (Warren, 1996) includes *Nuit et brouillard* (*Night and Fog*, dir. Alain Resnais, 1955) in his discussion of the essay film. Related to the form are films like *Deux ou trois choses que je sais d'elle* (*Two or Three Things That I Know About Her*, dir. Jean-Luc Godard, 1966) or *Kuhle Wampe* (dir. Slatan Dudow, 1931), which are more arguments than fictions. Within more obviously avant-garde work, Michael Renov (James, 1992) argues for Jonas Mekas (*Diaries, Notes and Sketches*, also known as *Walden*, 1969) as an essayist, and the equally personal work of Su Friedrich (*The Ties That Bind*, 1984; *Sink or Swim*, 1990) also qualifies for the 'essay' rubric.

Establishing shot A SHOT, usually at the beginning of a SCENE, that situates where and sometimes when the ACTION that is to follow takes place before it is broken up through EDITING. Establishing shots also make clear the spatial relations among CHARACTERS and the SPACE they inhabit. Such shots are common in EPIC FILMS, which feature sweeping narratives and many CROWD SCENES. Establishing shots are usually LONG SHOTS or EXTREME LONG SHOTS, although not necessarily so. Also known as COVER SHOT.

Ethnographic film Anthropological DOCUMENTARY that seeks to present and describe other cultures with a minimum of interpretation and IDEOLOGICAL distortion. Robert Flaherty's *Nanook of the North* (1922), the first documentary FEATURE, is usually considered one of the foundational ethnographic films despite the romanticization of the Inuit people by its DIRECTOR. The use of cinema for purposes of explicit cultural investigation was pioneered by anthropologists Margaret Mead and Gregory Bateson in New Guinea and Jean Rouch in Africa. Film-makers such as David and Judith MacDougall (*Nawi*, 1971) have used a MINIMALIST approach to allow for a more uncorrupted anthropological observation. At their worst, ethnographic films are condescending, as in the African films of Martin and Osa Johnson. Indigenous peoples are presented in their documentaries as exotic OTHERS displayed for the more civilised spectator. Luis Buñuel PARODIED the Eurocentric perspective commonly displayed in such films in his *Las Hurdes* (*Land Without Bread*, 1932). Recently, more politically-minded film-makers such as Trinh T. Minh-Ha (*Naked Spaces: Living is Round*, 1985; *Surname Viet Given Name Nam*, 1989) have used a variety of techniques such as CAMERA MOVEMENT and ASYNCHRONOUS SOUND to undermine the spectator's sense of cultural superiority and to allow documentary subjects to speak for themselves.

Further reading: Eaton (1979), Heider (1976)

Europudding A derogatory term to describe a film produced at least partly through funds provided by the European Union to encourage CO-PRODUCTION initiatives between member states. Alternatively, it may refer to a film with complex funding arrangements involving co-production money from sources based in a number of European states. It is claimed that the need to satisfy so many PRODUCERS, as well as different AUDIENCES, from different cultural contexts often ends up denying the film any clear identity at all.

Excess Borrowing from Roland Barthes's discussion of 'the third meaning' in IMAGES as meaning that cannot be 'conflated with the dramatic meaning of the episode' (Barthes, 1977, p. 53) and from Stephen Heath's notion that there is always a tension in any film between the unifying drive of its narrative CODES and the abundance of information photographic images inevitably offer (Heath, 1981), NEO-FORMALIST film theorist Kristin Thompson defines excess as 'those aspects of the work which are not contained by its unifying forces' (in Rosen, 1986, p. 130) – that is, aspects which are not justified by the film's compositional motivation. The term has been applied to *MISE EN SCÈNE*, particularly in the case of the GENRES of MELODRAMA and the EPIC FILM. In Elsaesser's influential 1973 analysis of melodrama (in Grant, 1995), the florid elements of style – CAMERA MOVEMENT, COLOUR and so on – are considered excessive of narrative function and a kind of textual symptom of IDEOLOGICAL repression experienced by the CHARACTERS. Similarly, the pronounced EXPRESSIONISM of FILM NOIR is often thought of as excessive because of its pronounced stylization, but Bordwell argues that noir films 'blend causal unity with a new realistic and generic motivation,' without subverting the structural logic of the CLASSICAL HOLLYWOOD FILM (Bordwell, Staiger & Thompson, 1985, p. 77). More loosely, the term is used as an adjective to describe any element of a film, such as a highly stylized, vivid performance by an ACTOR, or use of the CAMERA or MUSIC, that is 'over the top', that stands out beyond the rest of the film, or is beyond the bounds of good taste. Some people regard everything about HOLLYWOOD as objectionably excessive.

Executive producer See PRODUCER.

Exhibition The actual showing of a film to an AUDIENCE in a cinema or other commercial context. The importance of this sector of the industry has been the control it has exercised over the kinds of films that have reached the public at various times during the industry's history. Such control is at its most complete when a high level of VERTICAL INTEGRATION is prevalent. This means that the PRODUCERS of films not only distribute them, but also own the places of exhibition. In the United States various kinds of ANTI-TRUST judgments have attempted to restrict such practices, most importantly the PARAMOUNT DECISION, 1948, which ruled that the major HOLLYWOOD STUDIOS had to sell off their film theatres. This decision had major consequences for the industry in that it meant that INDEPENDENT companies would have enhanced access to film exhibition and that studios could no longer monopolize what the public saw. However, the ending of this particular kind of control has not meant an end to exhibition being controlled by a narrow range of companies. In the USA there is evidence that the studios (in reality, large cross-media CONGLOMERATES) are again securing substantial footholds in the ownership of exhibition, though today the accepted centre of power is in DISTRIBUTION.

Arguably the key to the narrowness of distribution and exhibition patterns is the scale and cost of MARKETING. Even if small independent exhibitors want to show less conventional films they have to do so without the benefit of the multi-million pound campaigns, including blanket TELEVISION ADVERTISING, that accompany any major RELEASE. There are obvious exceptions to this in ART CINEMAS that cater to a specific market around larger and more affluent centres of population and which deal with the small number of distributors that specialize in this area.

The context in which films are exhibited has been one of the most widespread and rapid changes in the industry in the past two decades. The rise of the MULTIPLEX – containing not only a large number of separate cinema screens under one roof, but very often cafés, bars and shops as well – has been the most visible change, and has meant real improvements not only in comfort, but also in the standard of film PROJECTION and SOUND reproduction.

Expanded cinema Term coined by Gene Youngblood (Youngblood, 1970), arguing that 'the definition of cinema must be expanded to include VIDEOtronics, computer science, and atomic light' and exploring 'computer films, TELEVISION experiments, laser movies and multiple-PROJECTION environments'. Youngblood's main subjects were computer-based ABSTRACT EXPERIMENTAL film-makers like Alex Jacobson, John and James Whitney and Jordan Belson, but he also refers to related work by film-makers such as Stan Brakhage and Andy Warhol and Stanley Kubrick's *2001: A Space Odyssey* (1968). The term 'expanded cinema' has also been used to refer to experiments in mixed media performance combining live ACTORS, live MUSIC and projected film IMAGES. Further reading: LeGrice (1977)

Experimental film A film that is not part of the MAINSTREAM and that seeks to expand film language or technique in some way. Virtually synonymous with AVANT-GARDE FILM, experimental films range from the intensely personal, as in the psychodramas of Maya Deren or the early films of Stan Brakhage, to the detached STRUCTURAL FILMS of Paul Sharits and Michael Snow. SURREALIST, DADAIST, and FUTURIST films are all experimental. These films are usually shown in such venues as museums, art galleries and universities rather than in commercial theatres. See also ABSTRACT FILM, UNDERGROUND FILM.

Further reading: Battcock (1967), Curtis (1971), Peterson (1994), Rees (1999), Renan (1967), Sitney (1979), Tyler (1970)

Exploitation film A film with sensationalist value that exploits a contemporary issue or subject or capitalizes on more prurient aspects of hit MAINSTREAM movies. BLAXPLOITATION is an example of a particular issue, the REPRESENTATION of blacks and RACE in American cinema, which was exploited to the extent that it became a virtual GENRE. Other recognizable exploitation genres include women-in-prison films and rock n' roll movies. SLASHER MOVIES developed largely as an exploitation of commercial movies like *Halloween* (dir. John Carpenter, 1978). Until recently, exploitation films had a market niche as B MOVIES in urban downtown areas and at DRIVE-IN CINEMAS, and certain PRODUCERS and STUDIOS, such as AMERICAN INTERNATIONAL PICTURES, specialized in making them. Originally the term had a negative CONNOTATION, with an implication that such films were cheaply made with poor PRODUCTION VALUES, and that they were crass or crude in tone. But as Cook (1976) argues, the institutionalized marginal nature of exploitation films in fact allowed for more relaxed relation to the IDEOLOGICAL constraints facing mainstream film-makers, as the feminist work of such DIRECTORS as Stephanie Rothman (*Student Nurses*, 1970; *The Velvet Vampire*, 1971) suggests. As well, the opportunity to work in exploitation films for Roger Corman's NEW WORLD PICTURES, another company that specialized in them, provided invaluable experience for many DIRECTORS, including John Sayles, Jonathan Demme and Peter Bogdanovich. See also SEXPLOITATION, TEENPICS.

Further reading: McCarthy & Flynn (1975), Meyers (1983), Schaefer (1999)

Expressionism Generally, an approach to film-making in which film-makers seeks to give their inner experiences, thoughts or feelings, or those of a CHARACTER, objective expression through stylization (SETS or performances), symbolism and/or manipulation of IMAGES at the expense of cinematographic REALISM. More specifically, a particular movement in the arts in Europe from approximately the beginning of the twentieth century through the 1920s, which in film became a dominant style in Germany (see GERMAN EXPRESSIONISM). Expressionist films will exploit any stylistic technique or aspect of the medium – COLOUR, SOUND, ANGLES, LENS, and so on – for its symbolic potential. Expressionist cinema is often contrasted to realism as the two primary tendencies of film style: whereas the short *ACTUALITÉS* of the Lumière Brothers, which mark the beginning of film history, are considered the beginning of DOCUMENTARY and realism, the hundreds of 'artificially arranged scenes' of Georges Méliès that followed shortly after, with their numerous CAMERA tricks, SPECIAL EFFECTS and fantastic narratives, are the first expressionist films.

Exterior A SHOT or SCENE in what is supposed to be taken as an outdoor LOCATION, which might be in fact outdoors – on location or in an outdoor studio SET, but which could also be shot inside a STUDIO but intended to appear as being outdoors. In a SHOOTING SCRIPT, such shots would be marked 'Ext'. See also INTERIOR.

Extra A person used as part of crowd or background SCENES in a film, generally uncredited and speaking no lines. Very often extras have no dramatic experience at all and are taken on locally at the LOCATION where the scene is being SHOT.

Extreme Close-up (ECU) Also called DETAIL SHOT. See BIG CLOSE-UP.

Extreme long shot (ELS) A panoramic exterior view from a distance even greater than that of the LONG SHOT or ESTABLISHING SHOT. Unlike these SHOTS, the great distance of the extreme long shot often dwarfs human figures rather than situates them for the viewer. As a result, extreme long shots tend to be used to emphasize human vulnerability and to view human endeavour within a larger perspective, as in the famous ending of Jean Renoir's *La Grande Illusion* (1937), showing two soldiers trudging through the snow, nature oblivious to the political boundaries established by men.

Eyeline match A CUT that uses a performer's eyeline to provide the match with the next SHOT. The simplest example would be CUTTING from one shot with a CHARACTER looking at something outside the FRAME to a second shot with an object or person at the same level as the eyeline of the character in the first shot, implying that the second shot reveals what the character in the first shot is looking at. See also CONTINUITY EDITING.

F

Faction See DOCUDRAMA.

Factual film See DOCUMENTARY.

Fade, fade-in, fade-out The gradual disclosure or obscuring of an IMAGE as the screen becomes progressively illuminated (fade-in) or darkened (fade-out). Fade-ins are usually preceded by a moment of darkness with no discernible image, fade-outs followed by darkness. Fades are often used to indicate the passage of TIME or change of location within a narrative, and as TRANSITION between SCENES or SEQUENCES. They may also work as POINT-OF-VIEW SHOTS or as instances of a SUBJECTIVE CAMERA where it suggests lapsing into or awakening from unconsciousness on the part of a CHARACTER. Although images most often fade to or from black, they may be used with any COLOUR, such as the fades to red in Ingmar Bergman's *Cries and Whispers* (1972). Fades are also used in relation to SOUND, as volume is audibly raised (fade-in) or lowered (fade-out).

Famous Players American film production and DISTRIBUTION company founded in 1912 by Adolph Zukor. In 1914 Zukor hired Mary Pickford, one of the biggest STARS of the day, luring her away from BIOGRAPH with an astronomical salary of $2,000 per week. In 1916 the company merged with the Jesse Lasky Feature Play Company to become the Famous Players-Lasky Corporation, with Zukor as president. Many other important stars of the silent era made films for Famous Players-Lasky, which in 1927 incorporated into PARAMOUNT, one of HOLLYWOOD's MAJOR STUDIOS.

FAMU The Film Faculty of the Academy of Dramatic Arts, Prague, founded in 1947, the film school at which many members of the 1960s CZECH NEW WAVE trained.

Fantasy film   A film that posits some violation of the real world in its narrative, whether imaginary creatures (the mermaid in *Splash*, dir. Ron Howard, 1984); the alteration of natural laws (*The Witches of Eastwick*, dir. George Miller, 1987); alternate worlds (*Conan the Barbarian*, dir. John Milius, 1982) or the existence of superheroes (*Superman*, dir. Richard Donner, 1978). Fantasy films feature stories with impossibilities rather than, as in SCIENCE FICTION, possibilities. Fantasy is often different as well from HORROR, in that while both GENRES feature supernatural beings – ghosts and angels – in fantasy these creatures are often benevolent or non-threatening whereas in horror they are, by definition, frightening. Fairy tales from *Alice in Wonderland* (dir. Norman Z. McLeod, 1933) to *The NeverEnding Story* (dir. Wolfgang Petersen, 1984), sword-and-sorcery movies such as *Dragonslayer* (dir. Matthew Robbins, 1981) and *Krull* (dir. Peter Yates, 1983) and mythological stories such as *Jason and the Argonauts* (dir. Don Chaffey, 1963) are all fantasy films.

Death and the afterlife is a common theme in the fantasy genre, and is the subject of such films as *Death Takes a Holiday* (dir. Mitchell Leisen, 1934), *Here Comes Mr. Jordan* (dir. Alexander Hall, 1941), *A Matter of Life and Death/Stairway to Heaven* (dir. Michael Powell, 1946), and *Meet Joe Black* (dir. Martin Brest and Alan Smithee, 1998). Ghosts and spirits appear in many fantasy films, from the DADAIST SHORT film *Ghosts Before Breakfast* (dir. Hans Richter, 1928) to HOLLYWOOD BLOCKBUSTERS such as *Ghostbusters* (dir. Ivan Reitman, 1984) and *Ghost* (dir. Jerry Zucker, 1990) to the German ART FILM *Wings of Desire* (dir. Wim Wenders, 1986). Such STORIES are popular because they offer comfortable fantasies about life after death, divine justice and order in the universe. As in the TRICK FILMS and *voyages extraordinaires* of Georges Méliès, fantasy films often employ elaborate SPECIAL EFFECTS to depict their otherworldly aspects.

Further reading: Donald (1989), Fowkes (1998), Slusser & Rabkin (1985), Todorov (1975)

Farce   A form of COMEDY that relies on highly improbable PLOTS and situations as well as exaggerated characterization usually involving some element of physical performance such as SLAPSTICK. Farce has a very long history in the theatre and became one of the dominant forms of SILENT CINEMA where its visual qualities made up for the lack of SOUND. This is not to imply that farce is a simple form and the work of the Marx brothers during the 1930s is amongst the clearest evidence that some of the cleverest and most enduring comedy is dominated by farce. In more recent times the British *Carry On* SERIES of films, starting in the late 1950s, are amongst the best known of modern farces, though the influence of the form can be seen in a much wider range of film comedy, such as some early films by Woody Allen or those written as vehicles for the comic talents of Eddie Murphy. Today it is perhaps rare to find pure farce in FEATURE FILMS though elements of it are present in most forms of film comedy.

Fast film   FILM SPEED describes the degree of light sensitivity of film EMULSION. Fast film STOCK is more sensitive to light, with higher exposure numbers (e.g. 400 ASA), while slow film, less sensitive to light, has lower exposure numbers (e.g. 100 ASA). Fast film is therefore particularly useful in low, often natural, light conditions and tends to look more grainy than slower speed film. See also GRAIN.

Fast motion ACTION filmed at fewer FRAMES per second than the norm (24 frames per second for SOUND film, 18 frames for SILENT FILM), so that when PROJECTED at normal SPEED it seems accelerated. Fast motion is often used for comic effect, particularly in silent cinema, and to enhance ACTION SEQUENCES. The technique also may be used expressively, as in the SCENE in *A Clockwork Orange* (dir. Stanley Kubrick, 1971) in which, accompanied by the *William Tell Overture* on the SOUNDTRACK, the fast motion emphasizes the impersonal haste with which the protagonist Alex has sex. Shooting at fewer frames than normal is still often referred to as 'undercranking' – a reference to the silent cinema era, when CAMERAS were cranked by hand.

Feature, feature film In the SILENT FILM period, 'feature' originally signified the 'featured' attraction in a programme of several films; by the 1910s this meant a longer film, generally over 75 minutes – the feature film – as distinct from a number of accompanying SHORT SUBJECTS. During the 1930s and 1940s, DOUBLE BILLS, or double features, were standard, with the A FEATURE generally longer in running time than the B FEATURE. Today, the term 'feature film' describes any full-length fictional feature film shown in a commercial cinema; they are usually shown in a commercial cinema (though DOCUMENTARY features, such as *Roger and Me*, dir. Michael Moore, 1989, are also shown) and on their own, without the support of a second feature or any short subjects. Officially, a film needs to run over 34 minutes to qualify as a feature – films running under 34 minutes are classed as short films; most features today run between 90 and 130 minutes, although many run longer. Most early production was of ONE REELERS or TWO REELERS and the longer, feature format was pioneered by European producers in Italy (e.g. *The Last Days of Pompeii*, dir. Luigi Maggi, 1908; *Cabiria*, dir. Giovanni Pastrone, 1914) and France (see FILM D'ART). Resistance to the production of longer films was one of the causes of the downfall of the MOTION PICTURE PATENTS COMPANY; the INDEPENDENTS who fled to HOLLYWOOD soon began to make the longer, feature films.
Further reading: Cook (1996), Pearson in Nowell-Smith (1996)

FEKS 'The Factory of the Eccentric ACTOR' (founded St Petersburg, formerly Leningrad, 1921, disbanded 1929) – an important source of ideas and works in 1920s Soviet theatre and cinema. Though begun as an attempt to radicalize Soviet theatre, film and theatre were very closely linked at this time and founders Grigori Kozinstev and Ilya Trauberg later became best known as film-makers. The work of FEKS was a major influence on film-makers such as Sergei Eisenstein and Lev Kuleshov and theatre practitioners like Vladimir Mayakovsky and Vsevolod Meyerhold. FEKS borrowed from the break with the past represented by FUTURISM, and its eccentrism owed much to circus and VAUDEVILLE traditions – emotions might be represented by acrobatic movements – and to the SLAPSTICK COMEDY of American silent comics like Charlie Chaplin and Mack Sennett's KEYSTONE Kops; its experimental approach to cinema also owed something to the shortages of material and equipment and the improvisation such shortages required. Probably the best known FEKS-influenced films are *The Extraordinary Adventures of Mr West in the Land of the Bolsheviks* (dir. Lev Kuleshov, 1924) and *Strike* (dir. Eisenstein, 1924), in which Eisenstein's eccentric work in theatre is more evident than in his later works. Eccentrism should also be

seen in the context of *ostranenie* – making strange, associated with DISTANCIATION – and to comparable movements in other parts of Europe, such as DADAISM.
Further reading: Thompson & Bordwell (1994)

Feminist film Films that specifically seek to address the role of GENDER in film from a woman's perspective. The rise of feminist practice dates mainly from the 1970s and to some extent parallels the development of a significant body of feminist film THEORY, though part of the work of feminist film scholars has also been to uncover feminist film-making from the past – the attention paid to the HOLLYWOOD work of Dorothy Arzner (see Mayne, 1995) and the AVANT-GARDE work of Maya Deren being clear examples. The brief account that follows is therefore mainly concerned with the growth of a consciously feminist film practice and it should not be taken to imply that no feminist work existed until the 1970s.

Unsurprisingly, a great deal of the work was (and still is to a large extent) confined to the EXPERIMENTAL and avant-garde. One of the key practitioners from the 1970s, Laura Mulvey, was also the author of texts vital to the development of feminist theoretical debates. In films such as *Penthesilea* (1974) and *Riddles of the Sphinx* (1977) (both co-directed with Peter Wollen) Mulvey attempted to DECONSTRUCT traditional film language to demonstrate the nature of its dependence on the idea of a theoretically male look or GAZE. This involved incorporating ideas about anti-illusionism and the exposure of the means of construction from the European avant-garde into new ways of looking at the SUBJECT that avoided a sense of addressing the male spectator. The work of Mulvey and others avoided simple substitutions of positive IMAGES of women for the supposed negative ones of MAINSTREAM film (see Haskell, 1973) and instead sought to develop an entirely new way of making film by breaking the traditional rules of the male-orientated MAINSTREAM CINEMA.

Parallel to this, women were also foremost amongst those seeking to challenge the ways that film production worked institutionally. A number of films were made by women working collectively and co-operatively and, whilst men were also attempting the same thing, there was a sense in which this disruption of traditional hierarchical patterns of working was of particular relevance to attempts to find a new cinematic language. Key texts from this 1970s strand include the Berwick Street Collective's *Nightcleaners* (1975) and the Film and History Project's *The Song of the Shirt* (1979). A further group of feminist film-makers were at this time working on more extended ways to find a new specifically feminist voice, both in DOCUMENTARY and fiction. Chantal Akerman's *Jeanne Dielman, 23 Quai du Commerce. 1080 Bruxelles* (Belgium, 1975), Michelle Citron's *Daughter Rite* (US, 1978) and Sally Potter's *Thriller* (UK, 1975) are key examples of the emergence of a feminist voice anxious to break free not only from mainstream cinema, but also from simply adopting the methods of the male European avant-garde.

To some extent the period following an initial burst of EXPERIMENTAL activity was characterized by debates about the need for a more accessible feminist cinema that would speak to those without any strong background in film or art practice. Two examples of films that attracted a measure of mainstream attention without breaking out of the ART CINEMA distribution circuit were *Question of Silence* (dir. Marleen Gorris, 1982) and *Born in Flames* (dir. Lizzie Borden, 1983), both of which used elements of traditional GENRE practice only to subvert them from within a feminist perspective. At the other end of the commercial spectrum, the 1980s was also a time of further growth for the Workshop Movement, given new impetus by the funding provided by CHANNEL 4. A number of women were either prominent in mixed workshops or in those set up as women-only collectives. Nelmes (1999) provides an interesting case study of the work of one of the latter, Red Flannel, based in South Wales.

Feminist film practice is a broad area with highly diverse aims. For some practitioners the aim is not to enter the mainstream at all because of the obvious and extensive compromises that it involves, while for others, the whole point is to address as wide an AUDIENCE as possible. The number of women in genuine positions of power within the film industry, whilst remaining shamefully small, has increased over the last twenty years. Whether this means that genuine traces of feminist practices have entered the mainstream is a matter of debate. See also GAY AND LESBIAN FILM, QUEER THEORY, WOMEN'S FILM.

Further reading: Hollows *et al.* (2000), Kuhn (1994)

Feminist film theory A key area of development in film studies since the 1970s which has foregrounded GENDER as central to a wide range of approaches to the study of film. It is essential to think of feminist film theory not as a unified body of work, but rather as a collection of approaches under a broad umbrella. The earliest identifiable work associated with feminist THEORY was done mainly in the USA in the 1970s: Molly Haskell's *From Reverence to Rape* (1973) is typical of an approach centrally concerned with the analysis of IMAGES of women in the cinema and exposing an accumulation of female STEREOTYPES with little basis in external reality. This work might be considered 'pre-theory' in that its perspectives were largely empirical and assumed a true feminine that male-dominated cinema conceals or misrepresents.

Two of the key representative TEXTS of feminist work from the 1970s onwards were essays by Claire Johnston (1973) and Laura Mulvey (1975). Johnston argued strongly against simply reading bad REPRESENTATIONS of women against an assumed reality, urging instead the STRUCTURAL reading of films as made up of interconnected signs and CODES that are powerfully inflected by the historical moment of their production. Such factors as GENRE and AUTEUR THEORY also informed Johnston's work, which urged women to produce not only CRITICISM that exposed the underlying IDEOLOGICAL function of much film language, but to start to produce a cinema which would stand as an alternative to MAINSTREAM practice.

Mulvey's work was most significant for its incorporation of PSYCHOANALYTIC theory into feminist thought and for the consequent change of emphasis from the film TEXT to the film spectator's interaction with it. For Mulvey, most work on the relationship between the subconscious and the cinematic experience has implicitly assumed that the spectator was male, because of its roots in Freudian ideas of male 'completeness' and feminine 'lack'. Mulvey raised for the first time the problem of the female spectator experiencing a mainstream cinema that is constructed around a male GAZE with female CHARACTERS positioned as its object. VISUAL PLEASURE – one of Mulvey's key concepts – comes from SCOPOPHILIA (looking) and cinematic pleasure is founded on a male look. As Mulvey later made clear, it was not that film was constructed to please men, but rather that it was constructed around a theoretical MASCULINE position that had to be negotiated by any real spectator who wanted to identify with the ACTIONS of the central characters. For many, the logic of Mulvey's earlier position – though she has herself contributed to its later revisions – was that the female spectator had to adopt a masochistic position in order to take pleasure from the structures of mainstream cinema. In short, if woman is reduced to fetishized object by the film and only male heroes are allowed agency, then women are denied anything but masochistic pleasure.

Subsequent debates have taken issue with this key formulation in a number of ways. One is that the performance of the female 'object' in the form of the STAR can in itself subvert the idea that she can only remain a passive object. Here the films of Marlene Dietrich directed by Josef von Sternberg have been among the most heavily scrutinized: at one level, Dietrich's characters are wholly fetishized and objectified, but their sheer power and dominance over the film makes them hard to contain in the way that psychoanalytic theory would maintain that they must be, and the threat of woman is anything but neutralized and destroyed (see, for example, *The Devil is a Woman*, 1935). Perhaps even more importantly came the notion that not all female spectators were alike. Feminist theory has addressed the idea that it was important to study not only the abstract notion of spectatorship, but also actual AUDIENCES. The positions of both GAY AND LESBIAN male spectators are simply the most explicit challenges to the idea of an audience divided on simple gender lines. The position of the black female spectator has also come to be clearly recognized as very different in relation to HOLLYWOOD's exclusive use of white women stars. Contemporary work on audiences has moved further towards ethnographic approaches originally associated more with the study of TELEVISION and other mass media. Patricia White cites a study of black women viewers of *The Color Purple* (dir. Steven Spielberg, 1985) by Jacqueline Bobo and comments that 'She finds their familiarity with Alice Walker's novel, the opportunity to see a high-budget film with a black female protagonist, and the community in which they viewed and discussed the film contributed to a more nuanced and positive reception of the film than that of many liberal reviewers, both black and white' (White in Hill & Church Gibson 1998, p. 124).

This is a simplified account of the efforts of feminist theorists to continue the debate started by Mulvey and others and to seek more complex and pluralistic ways to understand the idea of the gendered spectator. Detailed examples of such work can be found in Mayne (1993) and Modleski (1988). See also FEMINIST FILM, QUEER THEORY, WOMEN'S FILM, VOYEURISM.

Further reading: Erens (1990), Hayward (1996), Humm (1997), Kuhn (1989), Stam (2000), Stam & Miller (2000), Thornham (1997)

FEMIS The Institut de Formation et d'Enseignement pour les Métiers de l'Image et du Son (Institute for the Training and Teaching of the Audio-visual Professions), the French national film school, combining practical training with theoretical studies, which replaced IDHEC (Institut des Hautes Etudes Cinématographiques/ Institute for Higher Cinematographic Studies) in 1986. IDHEC was founded in 1943 and provided training for many notable DIRECTORS and others, including Alain Resnais, Louis Malle and Jacques Demy and CINEMATOGRAPHER Henri Decae). During the 1950s and 1960s it was regarded by many as being rather formal and unadventurous in approach and very few FRENCH NEW WAVE directors trained there (while others, like Resnais, failed to complete their courses).

Femme fatale From the French for 'fatal woman', a female CHARACTER who uses her SEXUALITY to lure and entrap men, leading to their downfall and, usually, death. The *femme fatale* is particularly associated with 1940s and 1950s FILM NOIR, and NEO-NOIR films, though she exists in other genres as well. The *femme fatale* is the modern version of the vamp – deriving from vampire – as this character was known during the SILENT FILM period (and, curiously, 'vamp' remains the term for *femme fatale* in French). The archetypal silent cinema vamp star was Theda Bara, in films like *A Fool There Was* (dir. Frank Powell, 1915). Naturally, there is no male equivalent.

Festivals Events (usually annual) which invite films into competition and offer prizes. Around this basic function are gathered activities which range from the celebration of film through themed RETROSPECTIVES and the like, to much more blatant trade fairs at which production and DISTRIBUTION deals are struck. Around the bigger festivals such as CANNES there is also a considerable amount of glamorous social activity of much interest to the international mass media. Apart from Cannes there are major festivals in Venice, Berlin, Toronto, London, Edinburgh and SUNDANCE, whilst the number of smaller festivals proliferates each year.

FIAF The Fédération Internationale des Archives de Film, or International Federation of Film Archives – the union of national film ARCHIVES founded in 1938 between the four then major archives: the CINÉMATHÈQUE FRANÇAISE, the British NATIONAL FILM ARCHIVE, the Berlin Reichsfilmarchiv and the New York Museum of Modern Art film archive. FIAF re-established itself and rapidly expanded after World War II, actively co-ordinating the work of national archives and establishing archive standards.

Fifth Generation Chinese Cinema The Chinese define their film history by generations, and the Fifth Generation refers to a new wave of films made in the 1980s in reaction to the Cultural Revolution (1966–1976). Signalling the recovery of the film industry in China, many of these films were distributed internationally and were successful in the ART CINEMA market. Among the most well known of the Fifth Generation DIRECTORS are Chen Kaige (*King of the Children*, 1987; *Farewell My Concubine*, 1993) and Zhang Yimou, whose collaborations with actress Gong Li in such films as *Red Sorghum* (1987), *Ju Dou* (1990) and *Raise the Red Lantern* (1991) made her an internationally recognized actress. The Beijing Film Academy, closed in 1968, reopened in 1978 and graduated its first class in 1982. In 1984 *Yellow Earth*, directed by Chen with CINEMATOGRAPHY by Zhang, provided the commercial breakthrough for new Chinese films.

Fifth Generation films are characterized by an exploration of political issues combined with an EXPRESSIONIST richness new to Chinese cinema. Influenced by European art cinema, these films were criticized by the Chinese authorities as inappropriate for the Chinese masses that make up their primary audience. Although many Fifth Generation films were commercial and critical successes abroad, the group's impetus was impeded by political pressure to produce more conventional, popular movies. In 1989, the Chinese Government cracked down on internal dissent at the pro-democracy demonstrations in Tiananmen Square. For their subsequent films, directors such as Chen and Zhang turned to international CO-PRODUCTIONS in order to secure funding.

Further reading: Browne *et al.* (1994), Yau in Nowell-Smith (1996)

Fill light A smaller, softer light, generally positioned near the CAMERA but on the opposite side from the KEY LIGHT, to which it is complementary. The function of the fill light is to fill in any areas left underlit by the key light, or to soften any shadows it casts. Also known as filler light, fill-in light, filler, fill. See also LIGHTING.

Film and Photo League A national network of leftist, politically active DOCU-MENTARY film-makers in the US in the early 1930s. They co-operated to shoot FOOTAGE for NEWSREELS of labour activities for union organizing and other leftist gatherings. Some of the members of the New York Film and Photo League formed the Nykino collective in 1935, which two years later evolved into FRONTIER FILMS.

Film Comment Bi-monthly magazine, published by the Film Society of Lincoln Center in New York City, which seeks to cover the range of film-making practices, from INDEPENDENT to MAINSTREAM, from both HOLLYWOOD and around the world, in a punchy house style that, while avoiding the dry jargon of academic DISCOURSE, often collapses into the excessively subjective.

Film Culture American film journal founded in New York City in 1955 by film-maker Jonas Mekas. Published irregularly, *Film Culture* focused primarily on American EXPERIMENTAL and AVANT-GARDE film, although in its early years it published some important work by Andrew Sarris (including his foundational essay *Notes on the Auteur Theory in 1962*) and Peter Bogdanovich on AUTEUR THEORY and HOLLYWOOD cinema.

Film d'Art The name of both a French film company, founded in 1908 and oper-ative until 1911/1912, and the kind of films it produced (subsequently imitated by other companies) – a conscious effort to make PRESTIGE PICTURES which would elevate cinema to high art by the use of stage ACTORS and historical subjects, filmed more or less as if on a THEATRICAL stage. The best known *film d'art* is probably *L'Assassinat du Duc de Guise* (*The Assassination of the Duc de Guise*, 1908), with a musical score by composer Saint-Saëns, and later, longer productions (FEATURE length films before the longer form was taken up in the US) included *Germinal*, *Les Misérables* and *La Reine Elizabeth* (dir. Louis Mercanton, 1912), featuring Sarah Bernhardt. See also SILENT CINEMA.
Further reading: Hayward (1993), Williams (1992)

Film noir French for 'black film,' the term refers to a GENRE or style of film depict-ing a dark, corrupt and VIOLENT world characterized by an EXPRESSIONIST mood and *MISE EN SCÈNE*. Named after the *roman noir* or *série noire*, a SERIES of pulp novels published in France dealing with crime and the underworld, French critics in the 1940s used the phrase to refer to a new wave of cynical and stylized American movies that appeared across several GENRES, including CAPER FILMS, DETECTIVE FILMS, GANG-STER FILMS and THRILLERS. The question of whether noir itself is actually a genre, or a style, period or movement, has been a subject of ongoing debate among critics. Naremore (1998) argues that the term in fact is a cultural attitude that transcends cinema.

Schrader (1972 in Grant, 1995) and others have enumerated well the narrative and visual CONVENTIONS of noir, which were drawn from several influences: the influx to HOLLYWOOD of many DIRECTORS, ACTORS, and CINEMATOGRAPHERS fleeing Nazi Germany who had been involved in the GERMAN EXPRESSIONIST movement; ITALIAN NEO-REALISM; the American, 'hard-boiled' fiction of such 1930s writers as Dashiell Hammett, Raymond Chandler and James M. Cain; and post-war disillusionment, a delayed reaction to the IDEOLOGICAL optimism of POPULAR CULTURE during the Depression and the war years. Noir narratives are about crime, corruption and passion, both their allures and dangers. CHARACTERS in film noir are often motivated by greed, lust and selfishness, or else they serve as the innocent dupes of others who are. The noir world is an irredeemably fallen one, with characters caught in a web of circumstances beyond their control, as exemplified by the protagonist of *Detour* (dir. Edgar G. Ulmer, 1945), an unfortunate drifter who inadvertently commits murder.

The films are frequently SET in impersonal urban spaces that reflect the alienation and decadence of the characters, as suggested by the titles of such noirs as *The Asphalt Jungle* (dir. John Huston, 1949) and *While the City Sleeps* (dir. Fritz Lang, 1956). In some noirs, such as *The Naked City* (dir. Jules Dassin, 1948), the city is a palpable presence, taking on a menacing quality that threatens to overwhelm the characters trapped within it. PLOT construction in film noir is often complex, featuring numerous FLASH-BACKS, as in'*The Big Sleep* (dir. Howard Hawks, 1946), which features over a half-dozen intricately plotted murders. The flashbacks, which emphasise that the ACTION has already been determined, further underscore the genre's sense of fatalism and doom. In *D.O.A.* (dir. Rudolph Maté, 1950), the main character searches for the man who has already murdered him with a lethal dose of poison. Noir protagonists are almost exclusively male, and many critics have suggested that the genre reflects the disturbances to traditional notions of GENDER and sexual politics caused by the war. Anxiety over the new-found independence of women in the work force found its expression in the backlash STEREOTYPE of the *FEMME FATALE*. Krutnik (1991), for example, argues that film noir expresses a crisis in masculinity that reveals male anxiety about loss of power in a changing society.

SCENES often take place at night or are darkly lit, employing CHIAROSCURO and LOW-KEY LIGHTING. The *MISE-EN-SCÈNE* is expressionistic, with canted or DUTCH ANGLES, stark contrasts of dark and light in the IMAGES, imbalanced compositions that suggest powerlessness and geometric compositions that imply entrapment and fate. Many film noirs were B MOVIES, which ironically added to, rather than detracted from, their expressiveness, as their frequent lack of high PRODUCTION VALUES tended to amplify the seamy nature of their fictional worlds. Bordwell argues that film noir, despite its stylistic distinctiveness, does not in fact seriously challenge the structural rules of CLASSIC HOLLYWOOD CINEMA (Bordwell, Staiger & Thompson 1985). Yet these films do stand apart from Hollywood family fare and escapist FANTASY because of the cynical and seamy view of American life they emphasize.

Initially film noir was said to have had a specific time span, conventionally bounded by *The Maltese Falcon* (dir. John Huston) in 1941 and *Touch of Evil* (dir. Orson Welles) in 1958. However, in 1974 the commercial and critical success of Roman Polanski's *Chinatown* brought about a renewed interest in noir that has continued unabated, in such NEO-NOIRS as *Blood Simple* (dir. Joel Coen, 1984) and *Pulp Fiction* (dir. Quentin Tarantino, 1994).

Further reading: Cameron (1993), Copjec (1993), Hirsch (1981), Kaplan (1998), Martin (1997), Maxfield (1996), Palmer (1994) (Palmer, 1996), Place & Peterson (1974), Silver & Ursini (1996), Telotte (1989)

Film Quarterly Durable film journal published by the University of California Press, *Film Quarterly* first appeared in 1945 as *Hollywood Quarterly*. The journal features a comprehensive book review section in its summer and fall issues each year.

Film school An institution specializing in the teaching of all aspects of film production but also offering courses in FILM THEORY and history. In the United States there are film schools associated with a large number of universities including New York, Southern California and California at Los Angeles. In the UK the leading film school, the National Film and TELEVISION School at Beaconsfield, is independent of any larger institution whilst a number of others are now part of either university departments or leading colleges of art.

Film speed A term for the degree of light sensitivity of film EMULSION. FAST FILM, more sensitive to light, has higher exposure numbers (e.g. 400 ASA), while slow film, less sensitive to light, has lower exposure numbers (e.g. 100 ASA). Film speed can also mean film running speed, that is the speed at which a strip of film moves through the CAMERA or projector, usually measured in FRAME exposures per second, or fps. SILENT FILM, cranked by hand rather than mechanically, was SHOT at any speed between 12 fps and 20 fps, and normally projected at 16 fps, which produced relatively normal movement without flicker (though silent projectors now run at 18 fps). SOUND film, in order to accommodate a reasonably audible SOUNDTRACK, runs at 24 fps (and TELEVISION at 25 fps). See also GRAIN.

Film stock Unexposed film, i.e. film that has not yet been used to shoot IMAGES, also referred to as raw film. Film stocks are differentiated according to FILM SPEED, GAUGE, and whether NEGATIVE or positive and BLACK-AND-WHITE or COLOUR.

Filmic See CINEMATIC.

Filmography A chronological list of films with which an individual has been associated. Though the word derives from bibliography it is more problematic because of the issue of AUTHORSHIP that has always surrounded films: a film can appear in the filmography of its DIRECTOR, its STARS, its CINEMATOGRAPHER, etc. The word's existence is emblematic of the emergence of film studies as an academic discipline.

Filter In photography, filters, made from glass or gelatine, normally in the form of an attachment to the LENS (but pieces of glass or gelatine can simply be held in front of the lens) change the nature of the light passing through the CAMERA lens. Filters are of many different kinds: for example, COLOUR filters change contrast and colour in COLOUR FILM and are used in DAY-FOR-NIGHT shooting, while diffusion filters create SOFT FOCUS.

Final cut Sometimes used interchangeably with FINE CUT, but usually used to describe the final version of the EDITED film, either the IMAGE track or the SOUND-TRACK separately, or image and sound combined. A DIRECTOR with contractual rights to the final cut has – at least in theory – complete control over the final form of the film.

Fine cut An edited version of the film at its most advanced stage before given final approval and completion.

First National Film company founded in 1917 by Thomas L. Tally and John D. Williams initially for EXHIBITION. First National was for a short period a company of some importance, owning over three thousand theatres, and also began producing films. Charles Chaplin made eight films for the company, including *The Kid* (1921) and *The Pilgrim* (1923), and Mary Pickford, Mack Sennett, Thomas Ince and King Vidor, all major figures in SILENT CINEMA, at one point made films there. The company was bought out by WARNER BROS. in 1929.

First-person camera See SUBJECTIVE CAMERA.

Fisheye lens An extreme form of WIDE ANGLE LENS that takes in virtually a 180° view, distorting the IMAGE by making the centre more prominent and rounding the edges – hence used primarily to create the impression, in a POINT OF VIEW SHOT, of seeing the world through a mind altered by drugs or by extreme emotion such as fear.

Fixed camera A static camera that remains in one position while shooting a SHOT or SCENE. Conventional wisdom claims that AUDIENCES are so used to relatively short shots edited together into scenes, or to a mobile camera which PANS, DOLLIES or TRACKS, that only relatively short fixed camera shots are acceptable. However, much of the work of Japanese director Yasujiro Ozu (e.g. *Tokyo Story*, 1953; *An Autumn Afternoon*, 1962) consists of relatively extended static camera shots, and directors like Orson Welles and William Wyler often used lengthy static shots with composition in depth and DEEP FOCUS (such as the 'strawberry shortcake' sequence in Welles's *The Magnificent Ambersons*, 1942, in which the camera remains static for a SEQUENCE SHOT of some four minutes).

Flash pan See ZIP PAN.

Flashback The representation of some ACTION or SCENE which occurs in the PLOT previous to the present TIME of a film's narrative. Also, a SEQUENCE within a film, used to relate the cause of events, provide necessary exposition or to show remembered scenes or actions. A flashback can be either an instance of a SUBJECTIVE CAMERA, as when a CHARACTER remembers something from the past, or an example of omniscient NARRATION. Flashbacks are CONVENTIONally coded by being bracketed by an aural effect such as a noticeable echo on the SOUNDTRACK or an optical effect such as a FADE or DISSOLVE. In addition, flashbacks are often introduced with a VOICE-OVER narration by the character to whom the flashback belongs.

Turim (1989) discusses the narrative logic of the flashback, its 'naturalizing process' within CLASSIC HOLLYWOOD CINEMA and its REPRESENTATION of memory and history. While flashbacks are usually embedded within the present-tense part of a film's narrative, occasionally they constitute the primary structuring device of the entire STORY, pushing the present into the background, as in the non-chronological tableaux structure of *Two For the Road* (dir. Stanley Donen, 1967) or the overlapping, at points contradictory, accounts in *Citizen Kane* (dir. Orson Welles, 1941). Sometimes, too, flashbacks are revealed as told by an unreliable narrator, as in Alfred

Hitchcock's *I Confess* (1953). Flashbacks are used often in FILM NOIR to add to the GENRE's sense of a predetermined, enclosed world. See also FLASHFORWARD.
Further reading: Bordwell & Thompson (1997)

Flashforward The REPRESENTATION of some ACTION or SCENE which occurs at some point in the future of the present TIME of a film's narrative. Much less common than the FLASHBACK, the flashforward tends to call attention to the process of narrative construction since it is often not understandable until the end of the film when narrative time catches up to it. The protagonists of both *La Jetée* (Chris Marker, 1962) and *Don't Look Now* (dir. Nicolas Roeg, 1973) witness their own deaths in flashforward, although neither they nor the viewer understands the meaning of these IMAGES until the moment arrives in the climax. Jean-Luc Godard uses flashforwards twice in *Weekend* (1968) to show the fate of his bourgeois couple as the inevitable outcome of CLASS struggle.

Flick pan See ZIP PAN.

Flicker film A form of STRUCTURAL FILM that emphasizes the effect produced by the fluctuation in the intensity of the light falling upon the SCREEN during film PROJECTION as the individual FRAMES pass through the shutter at a slightly slower rate than persistence of vision requires to create the illusion of MOVEMENT. The most famous flicker film is Tony Conrad's appropriately titled *The Flicker* (1966).

Flicks Slang term, no longer in widespread use, for cinema or, in the singular, a film, generally reserved for popular cinema – people still talk of seeing a 'flick'. The term originates in early cinema, in which the slower PROJECTION speed (16–18 frames per second as opposed to the usual 24 frames per second today) gave a more discernible 'flicker' effect.

Fluxus 1960s neo-DADA film-making group, a precursor of STRUCTURAL FILM and a variation of PURE FILM, aiming at 'radical filmic reductions . . . in which this or that single element in the register of the CODES of filmic SIGNIFICATION has been isolated', such as white light, LEADER, FLICKER (James 1989, p. 242). Led by George Maciunas, experiments with single FRAME films, static single SHOT films and CAMERA-less films were made by film-makers such as Yoko Ono (such as her 'bottoms' film No.4), Paul Sharits and Nam June Paik.
Further reading: Curtis (1971), LeGrice (1977)

Fly-on-the-Wall Phrase credited to American DOCUMENTARY film-maker Richard Leacock to describe the unobtrusive ideal of DIRECT CINEMA, which was to record PROFILMIC EVENTS as faithfully as possible. See also DIRECT CINEMA, OBSERVATIONAL CINEMA.

Focal length LENSES are designated by their focal length, measured in millimetres. The focal length of a lens is the distance from the optical centre of the lens to the point when a distant object comes into FOCUS. A long focal length produces a narrower angle of view, allowing a smaller area to be focused (as with a telephoto lens), while a shorter focal length produces a wider angle of view (as with a WIDE ANGLE lens).

Lenses can be of a fixed focal length, or have variable focal length, as with a ZOOM LENS.

Focus puller The assistant, usually the first assistant CAMERA operator, responsible for adjusting the focusing of the camera LENS during a shot. See RACK FOCUS.

Focus The point behind the LENS at which rays of light reflected from a subject converge to form an IMAGE. The sharpness of that image is variable: DEEP FOCUS keeps both background and foreground in sharp focus, whereas SHALLOW FOCUS has a foreground subject in sharp focus but the background less defined, and SOFT FOCUS gives a slightly blurred or hazy effect overall. CAMERAS and projectors have focus control mechanisms, normally an adjustable barrel, which can change the FOCAL LENGTH of the lens. See also RACK FOCUS.

Foley art, Foley artist The term given to the production of SOUND SPECIAL EFFECTS in POST-PRODUCTION, by specialist technicians able to mimic the sound of, for example, walking on different kinds of surfaces, in synchronization with ACTIONS on the screen. Considerable ingenuity is used in producing sounds which, experienced in conjunction with the moving IMAGE on screen, are barely noticed and simply accepted as real. The name derives from Jack Foley, credited as the pioneer of modern techniques for producing such sound effects.

Follow focus Term used to describe the progressive adjustment of FOCUS during the shooting of a SCENE in order to keep a figure or object in focus as he/she/it moves around. See also DEPTH OF FIELD.

Footage The amount of film SHOT over a particular period. The term relates to the traditional way of measuring this in feet. A foot of 35MM film contains 16 FRAMES and film is shot at 24 frames per second. Film CAMERAS are all equipped with counters to measure the number of feet and frames that have been shot.

Formalism An EXPRESSIONIST approach to any art form, including film-making, in which aesthetic considerations take precedence over content. In formalist works, emphasis is typically placed on symbolism and composition as opposed to REALISM. Formalist works are often lyrical and self-conscious, deliberately calling attention to their own IMAGES. Cinema formalists tend to work in EXPERIMENTAL FILM (ABSTRACT FILM, PURE CINEMA); by contrast, with rare exceptions such as British film-maker Peter Greenaway – while many MAINSTREAM DIRECTORS may be preoccupied with formal considerations in individual SHOTS, SCENES or SEQUENCES, few maintain such an approach given the requirements of narrative.

Because formalism, whether in THEORY or practice, tends to be more concerned with the *how* of artistic expression rather than with *what* is expressed, in the 1930s the Soviet regime under Stalin embraced the principles of SOCIALIST REALISM, which viewed an excessive preoccupation with formal matters as a decadent use of art. Directors such as Sergei Eisenstein, who was especially concerned with the formal implications of EDITING and MONTAGE, found themselves pressured by the government to make less experimental films. Soviet cinema in the 1920s is often referred to as formalist, though arguably form did not take precedence over content in their films.

Formula film A predictable film that follows CONVENTIONS and patterns established in previous films. Such films might be less inspired GENRE movies, or any
MAINSTREAM movie that baldly copies popular elements (CHARACTERS, PLOT, *MISE EN
SCÈNE*) from earlier movies. The term has negative CONNOTATIONS, implying that a
film so described lacks originality.

Found footage Any film footage in a film or TELEVISION programme, whether a
COMPILATION FILM or a film on some specific event, that has been SHOT originally for
some other purpose. For example, much NEWSREEL material shot in Britain in World
War II was re-used in DOCUMENTARY and PROPAGANDA films made during the period
as in Humphrey Jennings' *Listen to Britain* (1942), *Fires Were Started* (1943) and *A
Diary for Timothy* (1945). Somewhat differently, experimental film-makers like Su
Friedrich (*Sink or Swim*, 1990), Michelle Citron (*Daughter Rite*, 1979) and Derek
Jarman (*The Last of England*, 1987) have incorporated (their own) family HOME
MOVIE footage into their films. An unusual use of found footage in a MAINSTREAM
FILM occurs in *Forrest Gump* (dir. Robert Zemeckis, 1994) where the central CHARAC-
TER played by Tom Hanks is inserted into a number of key historical scenes using a
combination of real historical footage and DIGITAL SPECIAL EFFECTS. See also
ARCHIVAL FILM, STOCK SHOT/FOOTAGE.

Four-walling Industry term used in the USA for a particular kind of DISTRIBUTION-
EXHIBITION deal. Normally, the distributor rents the film to an exhibitor, and the GROSS
(gross receipts) from the BOX-OFFICE are divided according to a predetermined
formula, once the exhibitor has subtracted the HOUSE NUT from the gross. In four-
walling, the distributor pays the exhibitor a flat rental fee for the theatre – the four walls
– takes responsibility for all the arrangements and expenses involved in ADVERTISING
and running the shows, and takes all the box-office receipts (less the guaranteed flat
rental fee and expenses). While this places a greater onus on the distributor, the distributor, in return, retains the vast majority of any profits. This practice, in existence since
the silent period, became popular in the 1960s for distributors of family entertainment
FEATURES like Sunn Classics, and became more widespread after the *Billy Jack* (dir. Tom
Laughlin, 1971) affair, in which Laughlin's complaints about WARNER BROS.' initial
RELEASE of the film led to very successful RE-RELEASE based on four-walling. In the
sense that short four-wall engagements depended on heavy ADVERTISING, they
provided a partial forerunner of the later strategy of SATURATION RELEASE.
Further reading: Wyatt in Lewis (1998)

Fox Film Corporation Film company founded in 1913 by William Fox, a
theatre owner in New York City, as part of his fight against the MOTION PICTURES
PATENTS COMPANY. Under Fox's leadership the company was involved in production,
DISTRIBUTION and EXHIBITION. The company was also aggressive in the development
of SOUND for films, introducing the Movietone Sound System that produced a popular NEWSREEL. Fox overspent on refitting theatres for sound and was forced out of the
company in 1931. In 1935 the company merged with Twentieth Century Pictures to
form TWENTIETH CENTURY-FOX.
Further reading: Finler (1988)

Frame The basic unit of film: a single, rectangular, still IMAGE, with a certain
ASPECT RATIO, separated from frames on either side by frame lines, recorded on a

strip of CELLULOID, which, when projected at a certain SPEED (16-18 frames per second for SILENT FILMS, 24 frames per second for SOUND film) gives the illusion, via persistence of vision, of pictures moving at an acceptably normal rate. The term frame presumably comes from the picture frame for painting, and 'to frame' means to position the camera to compose a desired image. More metaphorically, frame can be applied to a narrative or story, as in 'framing narrative'.

Free Cinema A short-lived movement in British cinema during the late 1950s which sought a new approach to DOCUMENTARY film-making, but which had a more lasting effect on the FEATURE FILMS of the BRITISH NEW WAVE in general. As Caughie (1996, p. 70) says, the movement actually consisted of six programmes of films shown at the National Film Theatre in London between 1956 and 1959, inspired in part by an earlier series of polemics about the nature of this kind of work mainly in the journal *Sequence*. The programmes centred on a group that went on to constitute the core of the BRITISH NEW WAVE – Lindsay Anderson, Tony Richardson, Karel Reisz and CINEMATOGRAPHER Walter Lassally – though the films shown included work by Roman Polanski and a number of emerging FRENCH NEW WAVE DIRECTORS such as François Truffaut and Claude Chabrol. One of the programme leaflets for the London seasons offered an explanation of the movement's title: 'These films are free, in the sense that they are entirely personal' (Caughie 1996, p. 70): this was a cinema that encouraged a more personal, often poetic, response to contemporary life rather than the kind of film-making that was restrained by commercial pressure or the CONVENTIONS of earlier documentary practice. The irony is that so many of the feature films that grew from Free Cinema's practice became associated with REALISM, which is in one sense contrary to the notion of any mediation between the world and its recording on film – a contradiction explored by John Hill (1986).
Further reading: Anderson in Barsam (1976), Lovell & Hillier (1972)

Freed Unit Named for songwriter and PRODUCER Arthur Freed, who at MGM was responsible for making many of the MUSICALS regarded as among the best in the GENRE, including *Meet Me in St. Louis* (dir. Vincente Minnelli, 1944), *An American in Paris* (dir. Minnelli, 1951) *Singin' in the Rain* (dir. Gene Kelly & Stanley Donen, 1952) and *The Band Wagon* (dir. Minnelli, 1953). Freed had worked at MGM since writing songs with Nacio Herb Brown for its first musical, *The Broadway Melody* (dir. Harry Beaumont) in 1929, and for many to follow. Assistant producer of *The Wizard of Oz* (dir. Victor Fleming, 1939), he was then the sole producer of *Babes in Arms* (1939), combining Judy Garland and Mickey Rooney and reviving the career of DIRECTOR Busby Berkeley. Freed also brought Broadway director Minnelli to the STUDIO, as well as ACTOR/dancer Fred Astaire and CHOREOGRAPHERS Michael Kidd and Bob Fosse. Many of Freed's best musicals were written by Betty Comden and Adolph Green. Freed's last film before leaving the STUDIO in 1970 was *Light in the Piazza* (dir. Guy Green, 1962).
Further reading: Fordin (1975)

Freeze frame A FRAME of film that is repeated numerous times, making it appear as if the movement in the SHOT has stopped although the film is still in the process of PROJECTION. Freeze frames are often used at the end of a film to suggest a lack of CLOSURE, as in *The 400 Blows* (dir. François Truffaut, 1959), where the freeze on a CLOSE-UP of Antoine Doinel (Jean-Pierre Léaud) as he stands by the sea suggests his indecision and uncertain future. George Roy Hill uses a freeze frame at the end of *Butch Cassidy and the Sundance Kid* (1969), as the two eponymous heroes burst out a door into a hail of bullets, so that the characters seem to transcend death and become figures of MYTH instead. Ridley Scott invokes the ending of Hill's film at the end of *Thelma and Louise* (1991) when the two women, surrounded by the pursuing police, purposefully drive their car over the edge of the Grand Canyon as the IMAGE of them in mid-flight freezes.

French New Wave   During 1958 and 1959, several new French film-makers hit the headlines as well as being successful at the BOX-OFFICE, in both France and abroad. Between 1960 and 1962 over one hundred more French film-makers made their first FEATURES. These are the essential facts for understanding the French New Wave, since there is little else to clearly define the phenomenon. The phrase *nouvelle vague* or 'new wave' had been used in 1957 as a journalistic description of changes in French society related to the role of youth, but became widely associated with cinema following the combined successes of François Truffaut's *Les Quatre cent coups* (*The 400 Blows*) and Alain Resnais's *Hiroshima mon amour* at the 1959 Cannes Film Festival. In reality, the French New Wave consisted of film-makers with very different backgrounds and aspirations, with very little in terms of articulated ideas holding them together as a coherent group, and it is even difficult to date both the beginning and the end of the period. Arguably, the New Wave could be dated from *La Pointe courte* (dir. Agnès Varda, edited by Alain Resnais, 1956), or from *Et Dieu créé la femme* (*And God Created Woman*, dir. Roger Vadim, 1956). But Varda's first, relatively experimental, feature made no commercial impact and Vadim's film, though very successful, as well as establishing Brigitte Bardot as a STAR, had little in common – other than a modern subject – with later New Wave films. Certainly, Louis Malle (who had trained at IDHEC) had made *L'Ascenseur pour l'échafaud* in 1957 and *Les Amants* (*The Lovers*) in 1958, with both a star – Jeanne Moreau – and a CINEMATOGRAPHER – Henri Decae – strongly associated with the New Wave (Decae also photographed Claude Chabrol's first feature, *Le Beau Serge*, in 1958).

Even so, it was the Cannes success of *Les Quatre cent coups* and *Hiroshima mon amour*, plus the appearance of Jean-Luc Godard's first feature, *A bout de souffle* shortly after, that made 1959 the year in which critics and AUDIENCES became finally aware of the changes in French cinema. These three films are in many ways very unlike each other, and their differences point to some of the main groups within the umbrella term French New Wave. The *Cahiers* group – Truffaut, Godard, Chabrol, Eric Rohmer (first feature: *Le Signe du Lion*,1959) and Jacques Rivette (first feature: *Paris nous appartient*, 1960) – had been critics, along with André Bazin and Jacques Doniol-Valcroze, on the journal CAHIERS DU CINÉMA and most of them had already made SHORT films. *Cahiers* promoted the idea of the DIRECTOR as AUTEUR or AUTHOR and films as embodying the personality of the director, largely through the MISE EN SCÈNE. They had mounted an often savage critique of the tradition of quality in French cinema – what they labelled the *cinéma de papa* ('daddy's cinema'), associated with film-makers like Claude Autant-Lara, André Cayatte, René Clément, Henri-Georges Clouzot – and especially its expensive, ponderous, often period literary adaptations, seen as technically proficient but soulless and out of touch with young audiences. There were more individual French film-makers they admired and wished to emulate – directors such as Robert Bresson, Jean Renoir, Jean-Pierre Melville, Jean Cocteau, Georges Franju, Jacques Becker, Jacques Tati. They also looked to 1950s Italian cinema – particularly the work of Roberto Rossellini – as a model of the kind of cinema they could make themselves. These critics and film-makers were also marked by their exposure to the wide range of cinema offered by Henri Langlois's CINÉMATHÈQUE FRANÇAISE.

There is much debate as to whether the French New Wave should be considered a 'movement'. To some extent, there was a shared set of ideas and tastes, expressed in their critical writing, and a fortuitous set of economic circumstances (in the form of government subsidies for film-making), and so on, but although they were a group in some ways, their films were in many ways different: *Les Quatre cent coups* owes much to Italian NEO-REALISM, though it stresses the personal rather than the social, while *A bout de souffle* is more REFLEXIVE in its breaking of the CONVENTIONS of CONTINUITY EDITING and its reference to the American CRIME FILM. The so-called 'Left Bank' group – primarily, Resnais, Varda and Chris Marker – had significantly more experience of film-making: all had made important DOCUMENTARIES, often with strongly social or political subject matter, such as Resnais's *Nuit et brouillard* (*Night and Fog*, 1955) and Marker's *Letter from Siberia* (1958), and this remained a stronger element in their New Wave period work. Their work related more clearly than that of the ex-*Cahiers* directors to a tradition of experiment and MONTAGE in cinema. Other influential New Wave film-makers, such as Jean Rouch and Jacques Demy, did not fit easily into either group. After the early 1960s, differences within the *Cahiers* group also became more manifest: Truffaut and Chabrol became relatively MAINSTREAM, for example, while Godard and Rivette, in different ways, became more resolutely experimental. If anything binds French New Wave film-making of the period 1958-1962 together, it is a sense of renewal of subject matter – usually contemporary and often more personal or more idiosyncratic – and of stylistic experiment, at the level both of SHOOTING and EDITING – with techniques like FAST and SLOW MOTION, FREEZE FRAMES, IRIS effects as had been used in SILENT CINEMA – and of narrative construction. Early New Wave films were generally SHOT cheaply, which encouraged LONG TAKES and SEQUENCE SHOTS, LOCATION shooting in AVAILABLE LIGHT – also made possible by advances in CAMERA and SOUND recording technology and FILM STOCKS – and convention-breaking solutions to editing problems, like the JUMP CUT, and so on.

Overall, New Wave films show a greater degree of self-consciousness about the conventions of cinema and part of the continuing importance of the New Wave lies in the greater filmic self-consciousness in cinema everywhere that it ushered in. The French New Wave played an important part – along with more strictly social and political changes, and the crisis of HOLLYWOOD cinema – in stimulating other 'new waves', such as the CZECH NEW WAVE and new directors in Japan like Nagisa Oshima, while a Hollywood film like *Bonnie and Clyde* (dir. Arthur Penn, 1967) shows very clear stylistic influences.

Further reading: Cook (1996), Douchet (1999), Hayward (1993), Hillier (1985), Hillier (1986), Monaco (1976), Thompson & Bordwell (1994), Vincendeau and Graham in Nowell-Smith (1996), Williams (1992)

Frontier Films In the 1930s many important DOCUMENTARY film-makers in the United States were associated with the New York FILM AND PHOTO LEAGUE, and in

1937 several of them, including Ralph Steiner and Paul Strand, formed Frontier Films, a socially committed production company that made a series of important films about political and social issues, such as *People of the Cumberland* (dir. Sidney Meyers and Jay Leyda, 1938), about unionization efforts in that region of the country. The group's last film was *Native Land* (dir. Strand and Leo Hurwitz, 1942), with MUSIC by Marc Blitzstein and narrated by black American ACTOR Paul Robeson, which contained acted SEQUENCES about the working CLASS's struggle against capitalist oppression.

F-stop, f-stop number, f-number As with a still CAMERA, the number on the LENS that indicates how far the lens aperture is open and therefore the amount of light reaching the unexposed film.

Full shot See LONG SHOT.

Futurism Art movement contemporaneous with World War I that celebrated speed and dynamism as a response to modern life in the industrial age. The movement was founded by Italian poet Filippo Tommasso Marinetti in a literary manifesto published in 1909 that called for a rejection of the past and the establishment of a new society based on the values of mechanization. The Futurist movement had particular influence in pre-revolutionary Russia and the new Soviet Union, which embraced similar values of the artist as worker and also placed considerable emphasis upon the importance of industrialization and machinery. Futurism was particularly amenable to the medium of cinema – a mechanical APPARATUS – and its influence in the Soviet Union is apparent in CONSTRUCTIVISM, particularly in Dziga Vertov's praise for the perceptual ability of the KINO EYE.

FX The normal abbreviation for effects. See SFX.

G

G rating One of the AUDIENCE-classification ratings introduced by the MPAA in the 1960s as a replacement for the MOTION PICTURE CODE (or BREEN CODE, originally the HAYS CODE). A G-rated film was deemed suitable for a general audience, with no age restrictions. As the demographics of audiences have changed, G-rated films, formerly the majority of films released, have been overtaken by R-RATED films, which are deemed suitable for those aged 18 and over. See also CENSORSHIP, CERTIFICATE.

Gaffer The chief electrician on a film CREW. The gaffer supervises and is responsible for all major electrical installations on the set including LIGHTING and power. Responsible to the DIRECTOR OF PHOTOGRAPHY, the gaffer has a number of electricians working under him or her.

Gainsborough British STUDIO founded in 1924 by Michael Balcon, closed in the late 1950s. Early Gainsborough is best remembered for the early career of Alfred Hitchcock; its later work has become part of the reappraisal of the less respectable side of British cinema. Much of the most prominent work from Gainsborough during the late 1930s and 1940s ran counter to the restraint and REALIST tendency in British cinema. Gainsborough MELODRAMAS, including *The Man in Grey* (1943), *Fanny by Gaslight* (1944) and *The Wicked Lady* (1945) are associated with a group of British ACTORS – the 'Gainsborough Foursome' of James Mason, Stewart Granger, Margaret Lockwood and Phyllis Calvert. Gainsborough melodramas were scorned by contemporary critics whilst proving very successful at the BOX-OFFICE. Their tone is deliberately at odds with the moral seriousness of much British wartime output and they are commonly thought of as cashing in on AUDIENCES' desire for escape from the war and the austerity that followed. Gainsborough melodramas' interest for feminist theorists lie in the space they allow for fantasy and their overt address to female spectators. As John Caughie puts it, 'The wicked ladies are punished in the end, but not before they have left their mark and cut a dash through decency and emotional restraint' (1996, p. 71).

Further reading: Aspinall & Murphy (1983), Cook (1998)

Gangster film A GENRE of CRIME FILM focusing on one or a group of criminals, often featuring a narrative pattern that traces their rise and inevitable fall. Initially an American genre, the gangster film reflects that country's ingrained fascination with rugged individualism, energy and VIOLENCE. But the genre also crystallized as a result of three converging historical factors: Prohibition, the Great Depression, and the arrival of SOUND FILM. The Volstead Act of 1920 made the manufacture, sale and transportation of alcohol illegal. Virtually overnight the 'bootlegging' of liquor became an illegal but popular industry, and the exploits of real gangsters made them into folk heroes who kept the spirit of American free enterprise alive during a period of economic collapse. Gangsters were capitalists engaged in corporate takeovers, Horatio Alger-like heroes who rose to the top of the company.

Gangster films were first made during the SILENT era, with films such as *Underworld* (dir. Josef von Sternberg, 1927) and *The Racket* (dir. Lewis Milestone, 1928), and the genre's lineage is typically traced back at least as far as D.W. Griffith's ONE-REELER *The Musketeers of Pig Alley* (1912). The genre really needed the arrival of SOUND to provide much of its distinctive appeal – the rat-a-tat of machine gun fire, the squeal of careening car tyres, and the quick urban patter of the CHARACTERS all were part of the gangster film's aggressive urgency. The first significant CYCLE of gangster films appeared in the early 1930s, beginning with *Little Caesar* (dir. Mervyn LeRoy, 1930), *Public Enemy* (dir. William Wellman, 1931) and *Scarface* (dir. Howard Hawks, 1932).

The changing nature of organized crime in America, as well as legitimate business, was reflected in later gangster movies. *Inside the Mafia* (dir. Edward L. Cahn, 1959) and *Murder, Inc.* (dir. Burt Balaban, 1960) show the shift in REPRESENTATION of the gangster from entrepreneur to business executive. Francis Ford Coppola's *Godfather* trilogy (1972, 1974, 1990) uses gangsterism as an explicit metaphor of American capitalism and imperialism. By contrast, outlaw couple movies such as *You Only Live Once* (dir. Fritz Lang, 1937), *Gun Crazy* (dir. Joseph H. Lewis, 1950) and *Bonnie and Clyde* (dir. Arthur Penn, 1967) depict gangsters as doomed romantics fighting the Establishment.

The gangster films of the 1930s allowed viewers the thrill of identifying with dashing gangster figures on the screen and vicariously enjoying violence committed by charismatic ACTORS such as Edward G. Robinson, James Cagney and Humphrey

Bogart. At the same time gangster films typically provide narrative CLOSURE, wherein the gangster ultimately pays for his crimes by suffering a violent death, as when Cagney is dumped unceremoniously at his mother's doorstep at the end of *Public Enemy* or is shot down in a hail of bullets on the church steps in the climax of *The Roaring Twenties* (dir. Raoul Walsh, 1939). As Warshow observed, 'we gain the double satisfaction of participating vicariously in the gangster's sadism and then seeing it turned against the gangster himself' (1970, pp. 131–32).

Early gangster films tended to explain gangsters as products of their environment, taking a social Darwinist approach to the urban jungle where the fittest survive. In the first scenes of *Public Enemy* we see little Tommy Powers filling buckets of beer and learning the ways of the street. But *Public Enemy*, like *Manhattan Melodrama* (dir. W.S. Van Dyke II, 1934) and numerous other gangster films, presents a parallel character of a brother or boyhood friend who has chosen the straight, law-abiding life, as if to suggest that while gangsters may be social victims, they are also tragic figures (Warshow, 1970) doomed because they are driven to succeed. Post-war gangster films, as in some of the adult WESTERNS of the period, sought more interior, psychological reasons for the gangster's violent behaviour. In *White Heat* (dir. Walsh, 1949) Cagney plays a gangster with an overbearing mother and an Oedipal complex.

Several other countries have produced a significant tradition of gangster films. In France, Jean-Pierre Melville made such austere gangster films as *Bob le flambeur* (1955) and *Le Samourai* (1967). In Japan gangster films have been especially popular since the end of World War II, many focusing on the Japanese yakuza. After the war England produced a number of excellent gangster and spiv films (*The Blue Lamp*, dir. Basil Dearden, 1950; *Night and the City*, dir. Jules Dassin, 1950), as well as several EALING COMEDIES about gangsters (*The Lavender Hill Mob*, dir. Charles Crichton, 1951) and *The Ladykillers* (dir. Alexander Mackendrick, 1955). See also HOOD FILM. Further reading: Clarens (1980), Cook & Bernink (1999), Karpf (1973), McArthur (1972), McCarty (1993), Rosow (1978), Schatz (1981), Shadoian (1979), Yaquinto (1998)

GATT The General Agreement on Tariffs and Trade, the international body for regulating world trade, founded in 1948, and replaced in 1995 by the World Trade Organisation (WTO). Historically, the GATT and the WTO, though dedicated to the liberalization of world trade, tended to enforce agreements favouring the rich industrialized nations of the West, and this has been true of the way in which US film PRODUCERS and DISTRIBUTORS, via the MPEA (a branch of the MPPA), have argued against subsidy and 'protectionism' in other film industries. In Europe, France and Italy – with significant but struggling film industries of their own – have argued most strongly against US dominance, against a background in which US audio-visual exports to Europe amounted to $3.7 billion in 1992, against US imports of only $288 million from Europe, and in which, by the 1970s, over 85 per cent of revenues from FEATURE film EXHIBITION in the UK were for US films.

Gauge The width of the strip of film, measured in millimetres. The best known and most used gauges have been 8MM, SUPER 8MM, 16MM, 35MM, 65MM and 70MM. In early days, a great variety of gauges were tried out: 9.5mm, for example, had a very strong amateur following before 8mm established itself as the main amateur gauge.

Gauze shot A method for achieving a SOFT FOCUS shot by placing gauze or similar material over the LENS of the CAMERA during shooting.

Gay and lesbian film Films that define themselves primarily in relation to their contribution to ideas about gay or lesbian identities. Alternatively, films that have become closely identified with gay or lesbian sensibilities by virtue of the way they have come to be read. To a large extent the history of gay and lesbian cinema has predictably paralleled changes in MAINSTREAM attitudes to homosexuality. However, many would argue that HOLLYWOOD's traditional conservatism has resulted in the film industry's handling of gay and lesbian REPRESENTATION lagging some way behind changing social attitudes.

The depiction of homosexuality was explicitly banned by the HAYS CODE from 1934 until the 1960s, though there are numerous examples of implicitly gay and lesbian CHARACTERS in mainstream films throughout the period. Very often these consisted of crude suggestions of effeminacy as SIGNIFIERS of a male character's wider corruption. A prominent example can be seen in *The Maltese Falcon* (dir. John Huston, 1941) where Joel Cairo (Peter Lorre) continuously displays STEREOTYPICALLY effeminate traits such as using a perfume smelling of gardenias and becoming hysterical at the sight of blood on his clothes. In the novel upon which the film is based the character is openly homosexual, but the HAYS CODE meant that the film had to resort to innuendo and suggestion. More sympathetic and complex suggestions of gay or lesbian relationships from inside HOLLYWOOD during this period are rare.

To find examples of positive representations of gay and lesbian characters before at least 1970 it is necessary to look at either the North American or European AVANT-GARDE. Among the best known early works are two German productions, *Anders Als Die Andern* (*Different From the Others*, dir. Richard Oswald, 1919) and *Mädchen in Uniform* (*Girls in Uniform*, dir. Leontine Sagan, 1931). In North America the work of Kenneth Anger, including *Fireworks* (1947), and Andy Warhol's films of the 1960s, are some of the most prominent examples.

A further category of representation of gay and lesbian characters is the so-called 'PROBLEM FILM' in which they are depicted with a kind of liberal sympathy, but with lives that lack any source of sustainable pleasure. *Victim* (dir. Basil Dearden, 1961) is in one sense a bold film in its implicit criticism of the contemporary UK laws on homosexuality that allowed a gang of blackmailers to prey on homosexual men, but it is also clearly a portrayal of gay men through male heterosexual eyes, seeing homosexuality as a kind of affliction to be 'tolerated'.

From the 1970s onwards mainstream film has openly used gay and lesbian characters and STORY lines with increasing frequency, but rarely have the films been made under the control of gay or lesbian men and women and they have proved largely unsuccessful in the eyes of the wider gay and lesbian community. Traditional landmarks include *The Boys in the Band* (dir. William Friedkin, 1970) which contains what seem now a largely hilarious collection of male gay stereotypes, and *Philadelphia* (dir. Jonathan Demme, 1993), which has been Hollywood's highest-profile attempt to deal with the impact of the AIDS crisis on the male homosexual community. To an extent, the debates around *Philadelphia* are very similar to those around *Victim* thirty years before, though it attempts to present a more positive view of a white middle-CLASS gay lifestyle. Arguably, both films are products of a sensibility that observes a social problem from a distance, however liberal their ultimate message.

The international ART CINEMA circuit has been the most obviously progressive arena for gay and lesbian representations during the last two or three decades. From Rainer Werner Fassbinder in Germany through Derek Jarman and Terence Davies in the UK and Pedro Almodovar in Spain, one of the strengths of European art cinema has been the strong showing of gay film-makers. Whilst there has also been an expansion in lesbian film-making, it has tended to remain less well-funded and lower-profile, reflecting the relative lack of opportunity still afforded to mainstream women filmmakers. Lesbian film-makers have often had to operate outside the feature-length sector with all the DISTRIBUTION problems that inevitably result from this.

More recent developments in thinking about gay and lesbian cinema have resulted in the re-appropriation of the term 'queer' to describe the more diverse and arguably more radical practices of film-makers anxious that representation should not be driven by the idea of a heterosexual AUDIENCE and parallel ideas of political correctness (see QUEER CINEMA). Gay audiences have created their own spaces within mainstream cinema through radical re-readings. Richard Dyer and others have chronicled the ways in which TEXTS as divergent as the films of Judy Garland and mainstream FILM NOIR have offered alternative points of identification for gay and lesbian audiences (Dyer, 1986, 1990, 1993).

Further reading: Dyer (1977), Gever, Greyson & Parmar (1993), Hollows *et al.* (2000), Jones in Nelmes (1999), Miller & Stamm (1999), Russo (1987), Wilton (1995)

Gaze   At one level a term simply referring to the acts of looking that take place as part of the experience of cinema: the patterns of looking between ACTORS on the screen and the spectators themselves looking at the film. However, since at least the 1970s, the term gaze has been a key one for film theorists, particularly those concerned with the application of PSYCHOANALYTIC thought to the study of cinema. Put simply, the kind of looking that we do as part of a cinema AUDIENCE and its relationship to our conscious and unconscious desires has become one of the most important branches of film studies. The adoption of the rather more intense phrase 'gaze' is perhaps reflective of the significance now attached to the quality and nature of what was once seen as simply 'looking' at a film.

Early scrutiny of the cinematic gaze, the look of the camera, was part of the attempt to explore the impact of cinema on the unconscious. This led to the widespread idea that the experience of cinema actually parallels the working of the unconscious mind through its enactment of our desire to look or gaze, sometimes in a VOYEURISTIC way. Furthermore, some have argued that cinema can give the illusion of a kind of control of the IMAGE, with the projector analogous to the imagination of the spectator playing out an unconscious fantasy world on the screen. Early work by theorists such as Christian Metz (1975) employed psychoanalytic THEORY in such a way as to position the spectator's gaze as an exclusively male phenomenon, or at least that the spectator as SUBJECT of a film was masculine, raising the question of how women spectators derived PLEASURE from films that seemed to assume only an active male audience, and this remains a key area of enquiry for FEMINIST FILM theorists even today.

The term gaze is a key one in asking such questions as to whom film is made for and by, and the power relations (particularly in the area of GENDER) that exist within the film industry. It forces us to consider, for example, the very basic question 'Who is assumed to be watching this film?' See also SCOPOPHILIA.

Gender The concept of gender – as opposed to sex – has been central to debates in film studies since the 1970s, just as it has been central to debates about all art forms and all social and political values. Whilst an individual's sex may be seen as a narrow biological concept, the meaning of a person's gender is IDEOLOGICAL and therefore open to scrutiny and re-definition. Traditionally, societies have attempted to equate sex and gender and in so doing have narrowly prescribed what it is possible for men and women to become during their lives. These definitions have often revolved around BINARY OPPOSITIONS relating to active and passive roles in society. The development of FEMINIST thought has been central in questioning these oppositions and from this process has emerged today's complex debates surrounding femininity and MASCULINITY.

The issue of gender in cinema has been explored by critics in a variety of ways, from the simpler questioning of the way women are represented on a screen (for example, Haskell 1973) to the more complex arguments about film's gendered SUBJECTIVITY offered by PSYCHOANALYTIC approaches (Mulvey 1975). Film historians have also played a key role in revising what had tended to be an almost exclusively male history of the development of film. Just as feminist literary historians have uncovered and published a new lineage of female novelists and poets, so FEMINIST FILM historians have rescued key women contributors to film history. Work on Dorothy Arzner, one of the few women DIRECTORS working in HOLLYWOOD during the 1930s, is a strong example here (Mayne, 1995). Conventional ideas on gender have also been shown to have played a significant role in the development of film language in areas such as LIGHTING and CINEMATOGRAPHY, with, for example, different techniques being used to light male and female STARS and women being much more casually objectified by the CAMERA through the isolation of parts of their bodies in individual SHOTS. Contemporary thinking on gender and film is also likely to seek to understand its construction in film in relation to other key contested social determinants, particularly RACE and CLASS.

Further reading: Stam (2000), Stam & Miller (2000).

Genre A category, kind or type of art or cultural artefact with certain elements in common. In film, common generic elements include subject matter, theme, narrative and stylistic CONVENTIONS, motifs, CHARACTER types, PLOTS, and ICONOGRAPHY. MAINSTREAM genre movies are commercial FEATURE FILMS which, through repetition and variation, tell familiar stories with familiar characters in familiar situations, so that, as Robert Warshow puts it, a genre 'creates its own field of reference' (Warshow, 1970, p. 130). In film studies the term serves simultaneously as: 1) an industrial approach, in which production, especially during the STUDIO SYSTEM era, is standardized, and MARKETING is geared toward generic labelling and packaging; 2) a consumer index, providing AUDIENCES with a sense of the kind of PLEASURES to be expected from a given film; a way of organizing product shelving in VIDEO rental shops; and 3) a critical concept, a tool for theorizing relations between films and groups of films, for understanding the complex relationship between popular cinema and POPULAR CULTURE, and for mapping out a taxonomy of popular film.

From the period of EARLY CINEMA, movies were loosely typed by PRODUCERS, audiences, and reviewers alike, although the generic landscape was different than it is now (Altman, 1999). According to Neale (1990), producers concentrate their marketing of a given film into a generic image that appears in posters, LOBBY CARDS, PRESS KITS, and other forms of promotion and marketing.

Genre films activate expectations in spectators based on the experience of previous similar movies. Some genre movies are FORMULA FILMS, merely deploying the appropriate generic elements with little creativity, while others are made by AUTEURS who use these elements in innovative and expressive ways. Buscombe (1970 in Grant, 1995) discusses how DIRECTOR Sam Peckinpah uses the iconography and conventions of the Western to criticize the values of civilization and mourn the passing of the West in the opening SCENE of *Ride the High Country/Guns in the Afternoon* (dir. Sam Peckinpah, 1962).

Genre THEORY has been plagued by problems of definition. The major genres are defined inconsistently, by rather different criteria: for example, the HORROR FILM and COMEDY by their intended affect, SCIENCE FICTION by the nature of its narrative premise, WESTERNS by their setting. FILM NOIR is particularly problematic, and is variously described by critics as a genre, period, movement and a style. Further, some theorists have argued that in the POSTMODERN era genre mixing has become common, although Staiger argues that generic hybridity has always been a feature of genre movies (Staiger, 1997). Many critics have accepted a model of generic evolution involving several phases – roughly, formative, classic, intellectual, parody – but this view has been questioned by Gallagher and others (Gallagher in Grant, 1995). Altman shows that specific generic designations are always in the process of change, evolving out of already established genres and alternating between genres and CYCLES (Altman, 1999). Alan Williams objects to the common usage of the term genre itself, suggesting that, comparable to literary criticism, genres in film should be conceived broadly, as narrative, AVANT-GARDE and DOCUMENTARY, while what we commonly refer to as genres are more accurately SUBGENRES (Williams, 1984).

Early critical writing approached film genres as cultural MYTHS. Warshow's essays on the GANGSTER FILM and the Western (Warshow, 1970) and André Bazin's two pieces on the Western (Bazin, 1971), all written in the late 1940s and early 1950s, similarly interpreted the cowboy and gangster as tragic incarnations of American cultural values. The fluctuating popularity in the production and reception of film genres is commonly understood as a reflection or anticipation of changing cultural values and the impact of particular historical events. The sudden and intense production of science fiction films in the 1950s, for example, is viewed by many critics as an expression of the decade's anxieties over atomic power, Communism, the Cold War and Fordist conformity, while the cycle of DISASTER films in the 1970 reflected Americans' fears for the future of the country during the period of the Vietnam War, the Watergate scandal and a series of political assassinations.

In the early 1970s, as the MOVIE BRATS were revising and reinvigorating the classic genres, auteurist criticism focused on how individual directors used generic traditions to express their personal vision; but as academic film CRITICISM developed, genre films were examined from other critical perspectives. Kitses (1969) and Wright (1975) took a STRUCTURALIST approach to the Western, identifying common features across a range of films by different directors. In his influential analysis of the HORROR FILM, Robin Wood combined both MARXIST and PSYCHOANALYTIC approaches to identify a universal structure for the genre, which can be examined for its IDEOLOGY

(Wood, 1979, also in Grant, 1984 and Nichols, 1985). Genres have also been subjected to FEMINIST criticism as well as examined for their conventional codings of GENDER. With the exceptions of musicals and MELODRAMAS – at one time referred to in the industry as WOMEN'S FILMS – movies in the various ACTION-oriented genres addressed an assumed viewer who was, like most of the film-makers themselves, male, white and heterosexual. In Westerns, SPY FILMS, THRILLERS, science fiction and horror movies, DETECTIVE and WAR FILMS, women and visible minorities assumed subsidiary and STEREOTYPED roles. Until recently, in all the male or action genres it was white men who had to get the job done, whether driving the cattle, solving the crime, capturing the spies, or defeating the aliens.

Although genre films are usually associated with American cinema, many NATIONAL CINEMAS are organized generically or have prominent genres, although they may be different from those of HOLLYWOOD. Japanese cinema, for example, developed according to two broad but rigid categories of film, the *jidai-geki* or period film, and the *gendai-geki*, or film about contemporary life, with a number of genres within each category (Richie 1971), while Indian cinema's MASALA FILM is a hybrid that has no true equivalent in HOLLYWOOD. Some national cinemas have established international market niches for themselves by focusing on distinctive variations of established American genres, as in the case of the SPAGHETTI WESTERN in Italy or HAMMER HORROR in Great Britain.

Further reading: Browne (1998), Cook & Bernink (1999), Gehring (1988), Gledhill in Gledhill & Williams (2000), Hollows *et al.* (2000), Neale (1980), Neale (2000), Schatz (1981), Tudor (1974)

German Expressionism A specific period or movement of German cinema from 1919–1932 which eschewed REALISM in an attempt to project onto the exterior world abstract REPRESENTATIONS of intense inner emotion, whether of CHARACTERS or the artists themselves. Characteristic techniques of German expressionist cinema include an emphasis on extreme CAMERA ANGLES, CHIAROSCURO LIGHTING, distorting LENSES and/or SETS and stylized ACTING and make-up. The films were SHOT mostly in the STUDIO, many at UFA, the largest studio in the country, with an artificial look that deliberately sought to exclude the natural world (Eisner, 1969, pp. 11–12). Also manifest in such other arts as literature and painting, EXPRESSIONISM in German film is generally agreed to have begun in 1919 with *The Cabinet of Dr. Caligari* (dir. Robert Wiene), a HORROR FILM about an evil mesmerist who forces a somnambulist to commit murder. Designed by expressionist artists Hermann Warm, Walter Reiman and Walter Röhrig, the film contains almost no right angles in its distorted buildings and streets, shadows are painted directly on the walls and floors rather than created by lighting and the make-up and acting are deliberately stylized.

Production of expressionist films in Germany peaked in the mid 1920s, and the movement dissipated in the early 1930s with the coming of SOUND and the emigration of many German film-makers to HOLLYWOOD as the Nazis rose to power. Many DIRECTORS (e.g., Fritz Lang), CINEMATOGRAPHERS (e.g., Karl Freund), ACTORS (e.g., Peter Lorre, Conrad Veidt) and other film workers fled to the USA and worked their way into the Hollywood STUDIO SYSTEM, where they contributed significantly to the development and look of the horror film, particularly those produced at UNIVERSAL, and later to FILM NOIR. Later films such as *The Blue Angel* (dir. von Sternberg, 1930) and *M* (dir. Lang, 1931) have expressionist elements, but the new emphasis on synchronized dialogue ultimately brought an end to the movement much as it did to the Soviet cinema's experiments in THEMATIC MONTAGE.

German expressionist films have often been seen as intimately related to the historical context of their production. The narratives of German expressionist films, as Kracauer (1974) observes, tended to focus either on STORIES of the fantastic and the supernatural, such as Fritz Lang's *Niebelungen* saga (1924) and *Nosferatu, a Symphony of Terror* (dir. F.W. Murnau, 1922), the first adaptation of Bram Stoker's 1898 novel *Dracula*, or on impulse films, stories of CHARACTERS who are seized by strong emotions that shatter the bourgeois order of their lives, as in *Der Letzte Mann* (*The Last Laugh*, dir. Murnau, 1924) or the previously mentioned *The Blue Angel*. For Kracauer, German expressionism's avoidance of the real world was both a harbinger and a cause of the rise of Fascism in Germany. He interpreted the elimination of nature as symptomatic of the German people's turning away from political responsibility in their embrace of Hitler's National Socialism. This impulse revealed the German's people's fear of their own inner selves, and their cinema's embrace of powerful tyrants and arch villains such as Caligari and Dr. Mabuse in Lang's *Dr. Mabuse, The Gambler* (1922) anticipated the success of Hitler. See also KAMMERSPIELFILM, STREET FILM.

Further reading: Barlow (1987), Coates (1991), Eisner (1969), Elsaaesser (2000), Elsaesser in Nowell-Smith (1996)

Ghost film See FANTASY FILM.

Giallo Italian term for graphic THRILLERS and HORROR FILMS of the 1950s and 1960s. Predating SLASHER FILMS, the *giallo* ('yellow') takes its name from the colour of the covers of pulp detective novels published in Italy in the 1940s and 1950s. The GENRE includes both POLICE FILMS (*giallo-poliziesco*) and horror films (*giallo-fantastico*), featuring an overtly EXPRESSIONIST stylization. The most well-known giallos outside of Italy are by DIRECTORS such as Mario Bava (*Black Sunday*, 1960; *Blood and Black Lace*, 1964) and Dario Argento (*The Bird with the Crystal Plumage*, 1969; *Suspiria*, 1977; *Tenebrae*, 1982).

Glass shot A SPECIAL EFFECTS shot in which the CAMERA shoots through the clear area of a sheet of glass with a partial painted or photographic IMAGE. This economical way of shooting in the STUDIO, adding a sense of depth and/or suggesting a setting, was much used in the 1920s and 1930s, e.g. for the miniature shots in *King Kong* (dir. Merian C. Cooper and Ernest B. Schoedsack, 1933). The term is also used for MATTING together scenery painted on to glass and LIVE ACTION, a technique still in common use.

Goldwyn American film company, founded by Samuel Goldwyn and bought shortly after his departure by theatre owner Marcus Loew in 1924, then merged with Metro Pictures Corporation and the Louis B. Mayer Company to become MGM (Metro-Goldwyn-Mayer), the largest STUDIO in HOLLYWOOD. The Goldwyn company provided MGM with a small roster of STARS, DIRECTORS, a small EXHIBITION chain and, most importantly, an expansive studio facility in Culver City, California, originally built by PRODUCER/director Thomas Ince in 1915. Goldwyn himself went on to become an important INDEPENDENT producer.

Gore film See SPLATTER FILM.

Government and cinema Since cinema first came to be seen as a mass medium with a great potential influence, governments have taken varying degrees of interest in controlling its impact on AUDIENCES, from direct involvement in production to the more indirect impact epitomized by the effects of the legal systems of contemporary Western democracies or the indirect investment governments make in indigenous film industries through forms of production SUBSIDY. Perhaps the most celebrated example of direct government-sponsored cinema is that produced in the Soviet Union of the 1920s, combining openly PROPAGANDIST intentions with radical aesthetic experimentation, particularly with MONTAGE (see KINO EYE). The films of Leni Riefenstahl and others in Nazi Germany are also clear examples of direct state interest at work, in this case Josef Goebbels's Propaganda Ministry. In Britain the wartime CROWN FILM UNIT produced innovative contributions to the war effort, the lyricism of Humphrey Jennings standing out as a contradiction of the idea that films made for a specific propaganda purpose are necessarily crude or dull.

The direct control or CENSORSHIP of films has always been scrupulously avoided in Britain and the US, where governments have preferred various systems of industry self-regulation, typified by the long-standing HAYS CODE, central to the regulation of cinema during the HOLLYWOOD STUDIO SYSTEM era, and the BRITISH BOARD OF FILM CENSORS (BBFC), awarding CERTIFICATES in a process divorced from government control. However, the degree to which a government can create pressure towards a particular censorship climate is a matter for debate; many argue that the 1980s British Conservative government attempted to create a moral climate less tolerant of sexually explicit material, particularly positive REPRESENTATION of GAY AND LESBIAN identities. It is certainly a peculiarity of the British system of government that local authorities have a *de facto* power of censorship through their licensing of places of public entertainment, resulting in high-profile cases of films being effectively banned in some towns but shown freely just across the border. *The Last Temptation of Christ* (dir. Martin Scorsese, 1988), *Natural Born Killers* (dir. Oliver Stone, 1994) and *Crash* (dir. David Cronenberg, 1996) are among examples in recent times.

Government investment in, or subsidy of, NATIONAL CINEMA has been of great importance, particularly in Europe. In France, it has at various times been part of a wider policy of investment in French culture as a bulwark against American cultural HEGEMONY; more recently the Irish government has followed a policy of tax breaks for both Irish film-makers and those making films in Ireland.

GPO Film Unit Between 1928 and 1933 John Grierson laid the foundations of the influential British DOCUMENTARY film-making movement of the 1930s at the EMPIRE MARKETING BOARD. When the Board was closed down in 1933, its public relations chief, Sir Stephen Tallents, moved to the General Post Office and took with him the Board's Film UNIT led by Grierson, to establish the GPO Film Unit, which went on to become the main body associated with British documentary in the 1930s. Although many subjects had some link to the work of the Post Office such as *Night Mail* (dir. Harry Watt and Basil Wright, 1936), its brief was wide. Stylistically, like the films made by the EMB Film Unit, the GPO films were heavily influenced by the MONTAGE experiments of the Soviet film-makers, who shared a commitment to drawing on reality, to ordinary working people's lives and to PROPAGANDA in favour

of the needs and purposes of the State. By the early 1930s, the approach to montage included not just the montage of IMAGES but also image and SOUND, especially after Alberto Cavalcanti joined the unit in 1934: *Coal Face* (dir. Cavalcanti, 1935) is a good example both of the influence of montage ideas and of a film about a subject more generally central to British life. By the mid 1930s there was some tension in British documentary between formal experimentation and a more straightforward approach to social subjects, and later 1930s GPO films tended to be less EXPERIMENTAL than early and mid 1930s films, though there was experimentation with what we would now call drama documentary – scripted dramas with real people playing themselves in real locations – such as *The Saving of Bill Blewett* (dir. Watt, 1936) and *North Sea* (dir. Watt, 1938). British documentary film-making during this period shared its overall attitude with the BBC, founded 1927, especially its commitment to public service and education. This helps to explain the contributions to GPO documentaries by leading British arts figures like composer Benjamin Britten and poet W.H. Auden who both contributed to *Coal Face* and *Night Mail*. Cavalcanti took over leadership of the GPO Film Unit from Grierson in 1937, and in 1940 the GPO Film Unit was renamed the CROWN FILM UNIT, under the aegis of the Ministry of Information.
Further reading: Barnouw (1993), Grierson (1966), Lovell & Hillier (1972), Macdonald & Cousins (1996), Winston (1995)

Grain The microscopic particles of silver salts in film EMULSION which respond to light and register IMAGES. The grains – unevenly distributed in the gelatine base – create different densities and the effect of graininess in the developed and PROJECTED image. Though graininess can result from overdevelopment or PRINT duplication, it is also particularly marked in narrower GAUGES such as 8MM and 16MM, the more so when FAST FILM STOCK is being used in low light conditions. Since 8mm and 16mm and low light are often associated with HOME MOVIES and DOCUMENTARY or NEWS-REEL FILM, a grainy effect can be consciously worked for to evoke a sense of authenticity or TIME past (for example, *Les Carabiniers*, dir. Jean-Luc Godard, 1963; *Cathy Come Home*, dir. Ken Loach, 1966).

Grip An on-SET worker who may be responsible for several different jobs, such as setting up equipment or scenery or laying DOLLY tracks, so called because a grip must have a firm grip. The leading grip is referred to as the key grip. See also DOLLY GRIP.

Gross, gross receipts, gross profits The total amount of money taken by a film at the BOX-OFFICE, though it may be calculated as the actual total amount or the total amount returning to the DISTRIBUTOR minus the agreed percentage taken by the EXHIBITOR to cover expenses (see HOUSE NUT). Since the advent of TELEVISION leasing, CABLE and VIDEO, gross can also be used in relation to the combined revenue from all sources. The gross thus represents, crudely, the profits accruing to a distributor on a film. As in accounting in other fields, net profits refers to the revenue remaining (if any), after NEGATIVE COSTS, distribution expenses (such as making RELEASE PRINTS and ADVERTISING) and any POINTS participation expenses have been deducted.

Guild The guilds are professional organizations representing various crafts and skills involved in the film and TELEVISION industry, such as the Directors Guild of America (DGA), representing DIRECTORS, the Screen Actors Guild (SAG), representing performers and stunt artists, the Writers Guild of America (WGA), representing SCREENWRITERS, the Motion Picture Editors Guild, representing editors, and so on. The guilds, many with both West and East coast offices, function as UNIONS, negotiating salaries and fees, working conditions and CREDITS, protecting members' interests and taking legal action on their behalf when necessary and, sometimes, organizing strikes, such as the (largely unsuccessful) SAG strike in 1980. As this volume goes to press SAG members are engaged in a high-profile strike over members' rights to payments for repeat showings of TV shows and commercials.

H

H certificate British censors' certificate for HORROR FILMS, introduced in 1937 and dropped in 1951, when it was replaced by the X CERTIFICATE, which applied to more than horror films. H certificate films – indicative of one of many moral panics – were not to be shown to children under 16. See also BBFVC (BRITISH BOARD OF FILM AND VIDEO CLASSIFICATION), CENSORSHIP.

Hammer horror A key British contribution to the GENRE of the HORROR FILM, taking its name from the production company set up in 1948 as part of Exclusive Films and named after Will Hammer, then head of Exclusive. From the start Hammer was an unashamedly POPULIST company, producing a series of B-PICTURES, but in 1955, with the success of *The Quatermass Xperiment* (dir. Val Guest), the company turned more intensively to the horror genre. Its best known contribution to cinema history is perhaps its re-discovery of both the Frankenstein and Dracula MYTHS which the STUDIO turned into two of its biggest successes, *The Curse of Frankenstein* (dir. Terence Fisher, 1957) and *Dracula* (dir. Fisher, 1958), and for the enduring partnership of the British ACTORS Peter Cushing and Christopher Lee. However, Hammer's output was both enormous and long-lived and Jackson (1998) reports that the company is still technically in existence.

Hammer horror is best characterized by the idea of EXCESS, in opposition to the MAINSTREAM British REALIST aesthetic. An early defence of the films by Jean-Paul Török compared them favourably with more the critically fashionable FREE CINEMA: 'There is much talk now of Free Cinema. However, by its power of suggestion, its frenzy, its invitation to voyage towards the land of dark marvels and erotic fantasy, isn't the English horror film the real Free Cinema' (in Barr, 1986, p. 115). In one of the key books on Hammer, David Pirie (1973) goes so far as to say that horror in general 'remains the only cinematic myth which Britain can claim as its own and which relates to it in the same way as the WESTERN relates to America' (quoted in Caughie & Rockett, 1996, p. 79). Hammer horror is important in two ways: first, it made its own distinctive and substantial contribution to the horror genre and, secondly, it has come to be seen as a corrective to a now outdated version of British cinema history as being entirely about restraint and a strong realist aesthetic.
Further reading : Hutchings (1993)

Hand-held camera The use of the CAMERA by the CAMERA OPERATOR without the support of a TRIPOD, DOLLY or CRANE for stability during shooting. The hand-held camera provides greater mobility than the predetermined unilateral direction offered by dollying, craning or TRACKING. However, the IMAGES produced in this manner, if not stabilized by a STEADICAM, are inevitably shaky. Because the hand-held camera is commonly used in CINÉMA VÉRITÉ and DIRECT CINEMA film-making in order to follow PRO-FILMIC EVENTS as they unfold, the hand-held approach is generally associated with DOCUMENTARY authenticity. Hence fiction films often use the hand-held camera to simulate documentary's sense of immediacy and actuality, as in the supposed VIDEO imagery that permeates *Natural Born Killers* (dir. Oliver Stone, 1994) or *The Blair Witch Project* (dir. Eduardo Sanchez and Daniel Myrick, 1999).

Hard ticket See ROADSHOW.

Hard-core film See PORNOGRAPHY.

Hays Code Widely used name for the code of practice adopted in 1930 by the Motion Picture Producers and Distributors of America (formed in 1922 and renamed the MOTION PICTURE ASSOCIATION OF AMERICA [MPAA] in 1945) to control the content of films, particularly in matters of sexual morality. The Code took its name from Will H. Hay, president of the organization from 1922 to 1945. Hay was a former Republican Postmaster-General and the Code can be seen as a conservative response to HOLLYWOOD's association with sex scandals like the Fatty Arbuckle case (in which a young actress died during a party).

The Code was originally drawn up by two Roman Catholics, Daniel Lord and Martin Quigley, and the influence of the strong Catholic lobby (particularly the Legion Of Decency) was crucial until the eventual replacement of the Code by an advisory RATINGS system similar to the one in use today. After an initial period of voluntary compliance, the MPPDA began in 1934 to enforce the code through fines on any movie theatre affiliated to it showing a film without the organization's prior consent. The system began to break down with the Supreme Court's 1948 PARAMOUNT DECISION, which ended the link between EXHIBITORS and PRODUCERS and meant that movie theatres could no longer be forced to abide by the code. The Hays Code remained in place until 1968, with numerous revisions in order to attempt to keep pace with changing standards of public taste and decency. See also CENSORSHIP, GOVERNMENT AND CINEMA.

HBO Home Box Office, the US pay CABLE TELEVISION service begun by Time Inc. in 1972, is now part of the media CONGLOMERATE AOL Time WARNER. HBO has been, and remains, a major player in the cable provision of FEATURE FILMS and sports. Initially very successful, as one of the cable pioneers, in the late 1970s and early 1980s – cabled households in the US increased from 6.5 million in 1972 to 29 million in 1982 – but faced hostility from HOLLYWOOD'S MAJOR STUDIOS and competition from their own cable channels (VIACOM's Showtime, Warner's Movie Channel and Nickelodeon) which resulted in various ANTI-TRUST suits. A shortage of new features led to HBO initiating its own production schedule and, for example, joining COLUMBIA PICTURES and the CBS Television network in setting up the new major studio triStar in 1983 (though by the end of the 1980s TriStar had become simply a Columbia subsidiary). Marking a new configuration in the film industry, TriStar (whose first feature was *The Natural*, dir. Barry Levinson, 1984) was to offer features for THEATRICAL DISTRIBUTION via Columbia, for cable via HBO, for HOME VIDEO release by Columbia and/or CBS and network television transmission via CBS. By the

end of the 1980s, Time Inc. and Viacom controlled over 80 per cent of the cable market. HBO has continued to be an important producer of modestly budgeted features, attracting film-makers by an often greater degree of artistic licence and freedom from CENSORSHIP than offered by major studios.
Further reading: Wasko (1994)

HDTV High definition TELEVISION. Although television has now been in widespread use for over 50 years and has undergone much technological development, more than a century after its invention, motion picture CINEMATOGRAPHY on CELLULOID still produces better quality IMAGES than electronic means. HDTV, using roughly twice as many lines per frame as television does at present, and with a wider ASPECT RATIO, aspires to produce an electronic image to rival the film image in quality, combined with the non-deterioration afforded by DIGITAL technology.
Further reading: Winston (1996)

Head The beginning of a REEL or strip of film, the opposite end of the TAIL.

Heavy A male CHARACTER of a criminal type, a thug or 'muscle', particularly in the GANGSTER FILM. The heavy, normally played by thick-set performers, connoted VIOLENCE or the potential for it. Heavies are usually played by CHARACTER ACTORS, though some ACTORS who began as heavies – such as Lee Marvin – graduated to major roles. The term derives from nineteenth century stage MELODRAMA, where actors specializing in villains were called the 'heavy lead'.

Hegemony Idea developed by Antonio Gramsci, hegemony describes the way that dominant CLASSES or groups maintain power over subordinate ones. Hegemony is most crudely exercised by visible means such as a repressive police or military regime, but more commonly is achieved by a form of consent in which the basic values of the dominant group are naturalized through the everyday workings of IDEOLOGY. Thus the education system and the media operate within a series of controlled parameters which, though shifting over time, generally constitute the range of a society's hegemonic controls.

There are two key ways in which the term is relevant to the study of film. First, MAINSTREAM or dominant cinema in all countries can be said to be part of the APPARATUS that maintains the norms of a given society by repeating and naturalizing REPRESENTATIONS of certain ways of living at the expense of others. This in turn is part of the process of hegemony. In the West, mainstream film loosely upholds the basic tenets of capitalism such as the desirability of land ownership, the profit motive and the nuclear family as the cornerstone of people's lives. Secondly, the dominance of the world's film industry by the US has been seen as part of the US's wider hegemonic influence over less-powerful nations. In certain European countries, most notably France, there have been official efforts to combat this involving among other things the heavy state SUBSIDY of a strong indigenous film industry. More recently the growth of powerful transnational media organizations, whose owners – like Rupert Murdoch – sometimes literally change nationality, has given a new twist to the idea of hegemonic control which is still exercised by one CLASS over another, but on a global scale and outside the (debatable) democratic controls of Western governments. See also GATT.
Further reading: Lapsley & Westlake (1988)

Heimatfilm German for 'homeland film,' a GENRE of sentimental, romanticized movies about rural Germany. Many heimatfilms offer pastoral escapism, although during the period of the NEW GERMAN CINEMA some DIRECTORS used the genre in subversive or critical ways, as did Werner Herzog in *Herz aus Glas* (*Heart of Glass*, 1976). Edgar Reitz's 16-hour, 11-part SERIES for TELEVISION, *Heimat* (1980-84), was telecast widely in Europe and North America.

Heist film See CAPER FILM.

Heritage film Lez Cooke succinctly sums up the most prominent features of the British films of the 1980s that brought the term into use: 'the nostalgic celebration of a moment in British history when Britain still had an Empire and was still a world power, a preoccupation with the cultures and values of the upper echelons of society and the adoption of high PRODUCTION VALUES in the REPRESENTATION of the period detail and costumes' (Nelmes, 1999). The film that best exemplifies these characteristics for Cooke is the multi-ACADEMY AWARD winner *Chariots of Fire* (dir. Hugh Hudson, 1981). Though 1980s British films in general can be seen as dominated by films of this type, *Chariots of Fire* may be distinctive in its foregrounding of their IDEOLOGICAL dimension. The heritage film is closely associated with the work of the Ismail Merchant/James Ivory PRODUCER/DIRECTOR team, in which it is apparent that the heritage film is not confined to British themes: both *The Europeans* (1979) and *The Bostonians* (1984) have North American settings. The greatest critical and Academy Award success has come though from the team's 'British' work such as *Howard's End* (1992) and *The Remains of the Day* (1995), while their return to an American setting for *Jefferson in Paris* (1995) was generally seen to exemplify the emptiness of a form that at its worst can seem more like a tour around a country house rather than cinema. Further reading: Hill (1999)

High concept A NEW HOLLYWOOD term, originating in the 1970s but most current in the 1980s and 1990s. 'The term originated with the MADE-FOR-TELEVISION MOVIE in the 1970s, which needed stories that could be promoted and summarized by a thirty-second TELEVISION spot. A high concept movie has a straightforward, easily PITCHED and easily understood narrative. While PRODUCERS of high-concept movies emphasise their idea's uniqueness, their critical detractors stress the extent to which they rely on the replication and combination of previously successful narratives: *Robocop* is *Terminator* meets *Dirty Harry*. Production executives might reasonably justify high concept as a way of packaging previously tested and reliable ingredients, particularly for the global market' (Richard Maltby in Neale & Smith, 1998, pp. 37–38). The opening sequence of *The Player* (dir. Robert Altman, 1992) neatly satirises some of the absurdities involved in the pitching of high concept movies. Despite its origins, the high concept tag is now most usually applied to big-budget BLOCKBUSTERS involving big name STARS (such as Arnold Schwarzenegger, Sylvester Stallone, Keanu Reeves) and/or DIRECTORS (such as Steven Spielberg, James Cameron, Paul Verhoeven) whose films would be considered as almost certain hits. Further reading: Wyatt (1994).

High key lighting A LIGHTING design that emphasizes brightness with little use of shadow or strong contrasts. It is most often associated with MUSICALS or particular

kinds of COMEDIES where it works in conjunction with other aspects of ART DIREC-
TION (the use of strong COLOURS, for example) to create an overall sense of cheerful-
ness or optimism. The main source of light in such a design would come from the
KEY LIGHT placed near the CAMERA in front of the scene with FILL LIGHT being used to
eliminate shadow.

Hindi cinema See BOLLYWOOD, MASALA FILM.

Histoire See ENUNCIATION.

Hollywood The official centre of film production in the US, home of all the
country's MAJOR STUDIOS. Film companies began moving into this small suburb of
Los Angeles, California in 1911, especially following DIRECTOR D.W. Griffith's move
there after leaving BIOGRAPH in 1913 to work for MUTUAL, attracting INDEPENDENT
film companies seeking to escape the constraints of the eastern-based MOTION
PICTURES PATENT COMPANY.

Regularized EXHIBITION, which developed as a result of the popularity of NICK-
ELODEONS, increased demand for new films and made a year-round production
schedule necessary. Southern California had obvious appeal to the film companies
because of its warmer climate, relatively little rain, and varied topography that allowed
for a diversity of LOCATIONS. Labour was cheaper than in the east and the relatively
inexpensive real estate market allowed incoming production companies to buy large
tracts of land on which to build their STUDIOS for interior shooting. According to
Cook (1996), by 1915 the Hollywood film industry employed 15,000 people and
accounted for 60 per cent of the country's film production, rising to almost 90 per
cent a decade later.

Because of the studios' industrial organization and the nature of its product,
Hollywood came to be known as 'the dream factory.' Hollywood ultimately established
itself as the major national exporter of films around the world. By extension,
Hollywood has come to describe MAINSTREAM cinematic tendencies generally and a
particular style known as CLASSIC NARRATIVE CINEMA that emphasises the crisp and
seamless flow of ACTION, STARS and high PRODUCTION VALUES. Hollywood also refers
to the luxurious suburbs around the studios where many of the STARS live lifestyles of
the rich and famous and, less tangibly, to the concept of that glamorous lifestyle itself.

By the 1930s the Hollywood studios had achieved VERTICAL INTEGRATION, controlling DISTRIBUTION and EXHIBITION as well as production. In 1948, however, the US
Supreme Court delivered the PARAMOUNT DECISION requiring the studios to divest
themselves of their exhibition chains. The studios eventually diversified by concen-
trating on the new medium of TELEVISION as well as film production. With the
demise of the STUDIO SYSTEM, the studios also began renting space to independent
productions. In recent years, the studios have become increasingly diversified as they
have been bought by international CONGLOMERATES and have become merely one of
numerous entertainment formats, which in addition to television includes recorded
MUSIC, theme parks, hotels and sports teams. See also BIG 5, LITTLE 3, NEW HOLLY-
WOOD, POVERTY ROW and entries on individual studios.

Further reading: Balio (1976a), Finler (1988), Gabler (1989), Gomery (1986), Kerr
(1986), Litwak (1986), Mordden (1988), Neale & Smith (1998), Schatz (1988), Wyatt
(1994)

Hollywood Ten The collective title given to a group of film industry employees who became the earliest and best known victims of the House Un-American Activities Committee (HUAC) investigations of alleged communist subversion in the film industry. The Committee, set up just before World War II, renewed its activities in the early Cold War days of May 1947 when testimony from the Motion Picture Alliance for the Preservation of American Ideals led to further hearings involving evidence from witnesses (October 1947). Witnesses were 'friendly' or 'unfriendly' according to whether or not they co-operated with the committee. The Hollywood Ten – originally eleven, including playwright Bertolt Brecht, who fled the country before the group were prosecuted – refused co-operation on the grounds that the investigation violated their rights under the First Amendment of the Constitution. The Ten were asked by the Committee the now notorious question 'Are you now, or have you ever been, a member of the Communist Party?' All refused to answer and, after nearly three years of appeals, were jailed for contempt of Congress. The case led indirectly to the BLACKLIST which denied employment to those thought to have left-wing or communist sympathies long after HUAC had ceased its activities. The Hollywood Ten were Alvah Bessie, Herbert Biberman, Lesley Cole, Edward Dmytryk, Ring Lardner, Jr., John Howard Lawson, Albert Maltz, Sam Ornitz, Adrian Scott and Dalton Trumbo.

Homage A direct or indirect reference within a movie or any art work to another work, artist, or style. Homages are usually respectful, affectionate, even playful, acknowledging the influence of the works cited, as in the case of FRENCH NEW WAVE DIRECTORS such as Jean-Luc Godard and François Truffaut.

Home cinema A high specification home VIDEO (or LASER DISC or DVD) system designed to produce viewing conditions as close to those in a cinema theatre as possible, by use of WIDESCREEN television and SURROUND SOUND DOLBY stereo sound. Curiously, as theatres have shrunk in size, so home viewing has expanded.

Home movies Amateur films or movies made primarily for home or family consumption – the movie equivalent of still snapshots recording families' and others' private events, holidays, etc., typically, in the past, SHOT silent on 8MM, SUPER 8MM, 9.5mm and sometimes on 16MM, and today generally shot on VIDEO. In recent years, home movies have come to be recognized as an important source of documents on the past – as well as fodder for popular TELEVISION shows – and several film-makers have made creative and telling use of their own family home movies in their work, such as Derek Jarman (*The Last of England*, 1987), Su Friedrich (*Sink or Swim*, 1990) and Michelle Citron (*Daughter Rite*, 1979). The boundaries between home movies and (usually EXPERIMENTAL) films proper becomes blurred in much work by Stan Brakhage and in, for example, Jarman's *The Garden* (1990), and work by film-makers like Ross McElwee (*Sherman's March*, 1985; *Time Indefinite*, 1992) walk a fine line between home movies and DOCUMENTARY.

Home video Growing out of VIDEO recording in the TELEVISION industry since the 1950s, the 1970s saw a rapid growth in video recording and playback technology, and the programming to feed it, aimed at the home market – and a battle for market dominance between Sony's Beta/Betamax system and Matsushita's VHS system (a battle won by VHS largely on alliances with programme suppliers, though many thought Sony's system was technically superior). Home video allowed for off-air recording and 'timeshift' – allowing home viewers to record a programme and view it at a different TIME (though this feature of home video was probably more attractive in the UK and Europe than in the US, where television programmes were interrupted at frequent intervals by commercials) – and for viewing pre-recorded tapes which could be rented from video stores or bought outright. The MAJOR STUDIOS were initially wary of the possible effects of home video on THEATRICAL DISTRIBUTION – MCA instituted a suit against Sony on the basis of copyright and fears of piracy, since videotapes could be easily copied – and the resulting initial shortage of product helped boost low-budget INDEPENDENT CINEMA production (often HORROR and SEXPLOITATION), until the majors, realizing that in distribution terms home video offered an additional market for both new and old films, began to reassert their power, to virtually dominate the video market. By 1987 video rentals and sales amounted to $7.2 billion, almost twice the revenues from theatrical distribution, and the WALT DISNEY COMPANY, for example, has proved particularly adept at the phased and restricted RE-ISSUE on video of both old and new films. By the mid 1990s, over 80 million US homes had VCRs, with even higher penetration in the UK and Europe, producing a major shift in the way spectators consume films – many more now seeing films on a small screen at home rather than in cinemas – and the demise of many cinemas previously specializing in REPERTORY and second-run films. This change has also meant that film-makers need to have in mind the smaller and squarer screen conditions in which the majority of viewers will watch, working towards a less busy IMAGE and placing more ACTION in the centre of the screen. The success of home video has resulted in a new film RELEASE pattern, beginning with theatrical release – which serve to establish a film's BOX-OFFICE credentials – then PAY-PER-VIEW, video rental (and, now, DVD sales), CABLE transmission, video 'sell-through' (i.e. sale), network television transmission. See also STRAIGHT-TO-VIDEO.

Further reading: Wasko (1994), Belton and Hilmes in Nowell-Smith (1996)

Hood film Recent SUBGENRE of the GANGSTER FILM focusing on inner-city black life. Made by black DIRECTORS, these movies began to appear after the breakthrough commercial and critical success of Spike Lee's *Do the Right Thing* (1989), which explored the way different CHARACTERS cope with ghetto life in a detailed neighbourhood milieu. While Lee's film was rather EXPRESSIONIST in style, the films that followed sought a greater degree of REALISM, recalling such proletarian WARNER BROS.' movies of the 1930s as *Wild Boys of the Road* (dir. William Wellman, 1933). *Boyz N' the Hood* (dir. John Singleton, 1991), *Juice* (dir. Ernest Dickerson, 1992), *Menace II Society* (dir. Allen and Albert Hughes, 1993) and *Dead Presidents* (dir. Hughes Brothers, 1995) all recall classic gangster films in their emphasis on the social causes and consequences of crime, but tie this theme to racial issues as well, often also emphasizing random and graphic VIOLENCE as an indication of how socialized crime has become. See also BLACK CINEMA.

Further reading: Diawara (1993), Guerrero (1993), Reid (1993)

Horror film A film focusing on the supernatural, the mysterious or on graphic VIOLENCE, aiming to frighten or horrify its audience. The horror film has been a consistently popular GENRE in cinema, although it predates film in such forms as

Grand Guignol theatre, the Gothic novel, sixteenth-century woodcuts, and Arthurian romance. Indeed, stories of fear and the unknown are timeless, no doubt beginning around the prehistoric campfire, a tradition invoked at the beginning of *The Fog* (dir. John Carpenter, 1980) as John Houseman dramatically recounts a ghost story to engrossed children on the beach at night. Horror films address both universal and culturally specific fears, dwelling on both timeless themes (death, our own beastly natures) as well as on more topical fears (for example, atomic radiation, environmental pollution). Horror addresses that which is universally taboo or abject (Creed, 1993), but also responds to such specific anxieties as Reaganomics in the 1980s (Grant in Neale & Smith, 1998). Both kinds of fears are addressed by the main categories of horror as Huss and Ross (1972) usefully group them: Gothic Horror, Monster Terror (overlapping here with SCIENCE FICTION) and psychological THRILLER.

Unlike the MUSICAL and the GANGSTER FILM, which had to wait for the development of SOUND, horror movies were an important genre in the era of SILENT CINEMA. Mary Shelley's *Frankenstein* (1818) was filmed as early as 1910, and the first significant CYCLE of horror in the cinema appeared in GERMAN EXPRESSIONIST film, a movement that contained many horror films, beginning with the influential *The Cabinet of Dr. Caligari* (dir. Robert Wiene, 1919) and *Nosferatu, A Symphony of Terror* (dir. F.W. Murnau, 1922) the first adaptation of *Dracula*. In the 1920s, Lon Chaney, known as 'The Man of a Thousand Faces' because of his mastery of make-up, emerged as the first American horror STAR in a SERIES of films made for UNIVERSAL, beginning with his role as Quasimodo in *The Hunchback of Notre Dame* (dir. Wallace Worsley, 1923) and *The Phantom of the Opera* (dir. Rupert Julian, 1925), and then at MGM with DIRECTOR Tod Browning in *The Unholy Three* (1925), *Chimes after Midnight* (1927) and *The Unknown* (1927).

With the arrival of sound, UNIVERSAL returned to the genre with a cycle of films in the 1930s, from *Dracula* (dir. Browning, 1931), *Frankenstein* (dir. James Whale, 1931), and their numerous SEQUELS that carried on through *Abbott and Costello Meet the Mummy* (dir. Charles Lamont) in 1955. The Universal films were heavily influenced by the MISE-EN-SCÈNE of German expressionism; *The Mummy* (1932) was directed by German CINEMATOGRAPHER Karl Freund, who had photographed *Der Golem* (dir. Paul Wegener and Carl Boese, 1920) and *Metropolis* (dir. Fritz Lang, 1926), among others, before emigrating to HOLLYWOOD in 1929. Although the genre was not emphasized by any STUDIO apart from Universal in the 1930s, others did produce the occasional big-budget horror film, such as PARAMOUNT's *Dr. Jekyll and Mr. Hyde* (dir. Rouben Mamoulian, 1932) with Fredric March and RKO's *King Kong* (dir. Merian C. Cooper and Ernest Schoedsack, 1933).

In the 1940s at RKO PRODUCER Val Lewton made a series of nine horror films with several different directors, including *I Walked with a Zombie* (dir. Jacques Tourneur, 1943) and *The Body Snatcher* (dir. Robert Wise, 1945), that share a common approach of atmosphere and suggestion rather than relying on graphic horror. In the 1950s anxieties over the dangers of atomic power moved the genre in the direction of mutated monsters, as it also did the SCIENCE FICTION FILM. At the same time, the youth AUDIENCE emerged as a significant demographic group, and many horror TEENPICS were produced, such as *I Was a Teenage Frankenstein* (dir. Herbert L. Strock, 1957) and *I Was a Teenage Werewolf* (dir. Gene Fowler, Jr., 1957). Some critics have argued that horror films are particularly enjoyed by adolescents because in their awkwardness they can easily empathize with the monsters, who are social outcasts, and because they express in metaphoric form the physical changes that occur with the onset of puberty (Evans in Grant, 1984).

For a decade beginning in the late 1950s HAMMER studios in Britain revitalized the genre by revisiting but updating its traditional Gothic ICONOGRAPHY with a bold use of COLOUR and a decidedly modern dose of sexual content. Beginning with *The Quatermass Xperiment* (dir. Val Guest) in 1955, the studio would go on to turn out a series of films, many with horror STARS Peter Cushing and Christopher Lee, that reinterpreted the classic monsters (*The Curse of Frankenstein*, dir. Terence Fisher, 1957; *Dracula*, dir. Fisher, 1958; *The Mummy*, dir. Fisher, 1959) as well as invent new ones (*The Gorgon*, dir. Fisher, 1964).

Peeping Tom (dir. Michael Powell, 1959) and *Psycho* (dir. Alfred Hitchcock, 1960) reconfigured the genre even more radically by focusing on psychologically disturbed CHARACTERS in mundane contexts rather than supernatural situations in Gothic settings. *Psycho*, adapted from Robert Bloch's novel which in turn was based in part on the real-life exploits of multiple murderer Ed Gein, has proven to be perhaps the most influential horror film ever made. Set in contemporary motel rooms, hardware stores and used car lots, Hitchcock's film imagined the site of horror in the quotidian world of the viewer, showing that horrifying violence was an integral part of middle-CLASS America, repressed beneath its seemingly placid exterior. *Rosemary's Baby* (dir. Roman Polanski, 1968) and *The Exorcist* (dir. William Friedkin, 1973) continued in the same direction, depicting satanism in contemporary New York and Washington, respectively. Big budget productions that were commercial BLOCKBUSTERS, they brought horror more squarely into the MAINSTREAM.

In 1968 came the phenomenal BOX-OFFICE success of George A. Romero's INDE-PENDENT *Night of the Living Dead*, one of the most famous CULT FILMS and the first MIDNIGHT MOVIE. Several directors of the MOVIE BRAT generation were attracted to the genre, particularly Brian de Palma (*Sisters*, 1973; *Carrie*, 1976; *Dressed to Kill*, 1980). Also, as a result of Romero's success with *Night* and his sequel, *Dawn of the Dead* (1978), a cycle of SPLATTER FILMS temporarily dominated the genre. Horror films such as David Cronenberg's *Rabid* (1976), *The Brood* (1979), *Scanners* (1980), *Videodrome* (1982) and *The Fly* (1986), John Carpenter's remake of *The Thing* (1981), and Clive Barker's *Hellraiser* (1988) showed graphic violation and mutilation of the human body. Similarly, after the huge and surprising success of Carpenter's *Halloween* (1978), numerous SLASHER FILMS appeared featuring elaborate serial killings strung together by weak PLOTS. More recently, POSTMODERN horror films such as *In the Mouth of Madness* (dir. Carpenter, 1995) and *Scream* (dir. Wes Craven, 1996) have offered a fresh approach by creating narratives in which not only the audience but also the films' CHARACTERS are aware of the genre's CONVENTIONS.

Robin Wood set the critical agenda for much of the scholarly analysis of horror in a number of essays published in the late 1970s (see Britton, 1979, and Grant, 1984) in which he offered a STRUCTURAL model of horror featuring a fundamental BINARY OPPOSITION of normal and monstrous. Wood argued that the manner in which any given horror narrative resolves this conflict reveals its IDEOLOGY, and that most movies will be conservative, repressing desire and the id within the self and disavowing it by projecting it outward as a monstrous OTHER. Such films as *Night of the Living Dead*, *Martin* (dir. Romero, 1978), *The Texas Chainsaw Massacre* (dir. Tobe Hooper,

1974), *The Hills Have Eyes* (dir. Wes Craven, 1977) and *It's Alive* (dir. Larry Cohen, 1973) reversed the normal/monstrous opposition to critique different aspects of contemporary society such as patriarchy, capitalism, the family and the military.

FEMINIST critics have subsequently shown how horror monsters may be read as projections of masculine desire and anxiety over sexual difference (see Grant, 1996). However, both Williams (1983 in Grant, 1996) and Clover (1992) have been influential in arguing for horror as potentially empowering for women. Some recent horror films such as *The People Under the Stairs* (dir. Craven, 1991), *Candyman* (dir. Bernard Rose, 1992) and *Tales from the Hood* (dir. Rusty Cundieff, 1995), following upon territory explored only occasionally in earlier films such as *I Walked with a Zombie* and *Blacula* (dir. William Crain, 1972), have addressed issues of CLASS in horror, implicit ever since Bram Stoker represented the vampire as a European aristocrat. See also GIALLO.

Further reading: Berenstein (1996), Carroll (1990), Clarens (1968), Cook & Bernink (1999), Crane (1994), Dika (1990), Donald (1989), Eisner (1969), Gelder (1994), Halberstam (1995), Hardy (1986), Hogan (1986), Hutchings (1993), Iaccino (1998), Jancovich (1992), Jancovich (1996), Landy (1991a), Murphy (1992), Newman (1988), Paul (1994), Pirie (1973), Prawer (1980), Siegel (1972), Skal (1993), Telotte (1985), Tudor (1989), Twitchell (1985), Ursini & Silver (1993), Waller (1986), Waller (1987), Williams (1999)

Horse opera See WESTERN.

House nut Film EXHIBITION term for the expenses incurred by a film exhibitor in showing a film. The house nut is then subtracted from the BOX-OFFICE receipts before the percentage due to the film's DISTRIBUTOR is calculated.

House Un-American Activities Committee (HUAC) See also BLACK-LIST, HOLLYWOOD TEN.

Hype Used both as a noun and a verb to describe the activities involved in heavily promoting a film. Because the word comes from 'hyperbole' meaning exaggeration, the term has negative CONNOTATIONS and suggests that a film is being promoted or 'hyped' beyond its real value. The 'hype' surrounding a film's RELEASE can consist of the whole range of modern MARKETING methods and goes well beyond conventional ADVERTISING.

I

IATSE The International Alliance of Theatrical Stage Employees. See UNIONS.

ICM International Creative Management, one of the two most powerful TALENT AGENCIES in the US entertainment industry.

Iconography Familiar symbols in works of art that have cultural meaning beyond the context of the individual movie, painting or performance. The term was adapted to film studies from the work of art critic Irwin Panofsky by Lawrence

Alloway (1971) and others. In film, iconography may refer to particular objects, STARS, archetypal CHARACTERS, specific ACTORS and even the more general look of a particular GENRE, involving LIGHTING, SETS, PROPS and so on.

Iconography provides genres with a visual shorthand for conveying information and meaning succinctly. For example, pinstripe suits, dark shirts and white ties define characters in a GANGSTER FILM as surely as black hats and white hats define hero and villain in the WESTERN. Iconography may also refer to the general *MISE-EN-SCÈNE* of a genre, as in the case of LOW-KEY LIGHTING and Gothic design in the HORROR FILM or the visual EXCESS of the MELODRAMA. Buscombe (1970) defines iconography as a genre's 'outer forms' and argues that it is connected to its thematic concerns, or inner forms, in that iconography affects the kind of themes toward which particular genres gravitate.

While iconography in genre films may have a culturally determined meaning, the interpretation or value attached to icons is hardly fixed. Rather, their REPRESENTA-TION in any given movie is a reflection of its attitude and theme. A crucifix in a HORROR FILM is an icon of Christianity and dominant IDEOLOGY, but the film itself may either critique or endorse that ideology. In the Western, for example, the town and its various components already represent civilization, but each film will have a particular view of it. John Ford expresses a positive view of social harmony in *My Darling Clementine* (1948), with the characters coming together in celebration on the foundation of the new church in the centre of town. By contrast, *McCabe and Mrs. Miller* (dir. Robert Altman, 1971), in which the town springs up around a brothel, suggests that the ties that bind are less spiritual than material. Buscombe clearly shows how Sam Peckinpah depicts a corrupt world through the careful manipulation of the iconography of the western town in the opening SCENE in *Ride the High Country/Guns in the Afternoon* (1962).

Identification That aspect of the experience of a narrative work whereby the spectator or reader becomes involved with a CHARACTER or characters. In the medium of film, there are numerous techniques such as the SUBJECTIVE CAMERA and VOICE-OVER NARRATION for heightening the viewer's sense of 'being in the shoes' of a character. CLASSIC HOLLYWOOD CINEMA is structured largely around identification with heroes.
Further reading: Aumont (1992), Bordwell & Thompson (1997), McArthur (1972)

Identity See IDENTIFICATION, PSYCHOANALYSIS.

Ideology Term originating in early Marxist thought, ideology is seen as almost the same thing as what Marx called 'false consciousness' – the mass of people manipulated into embracing sets of values that only serve the interests of the ruling CLASS. This fundamental idea has been revised and re-emphasised a number of times, notably in the 1970s and 1980s by the French philosopher Louis Althusser, who argued that ideology was held in place by manufacturing consent through agencies such as the mass media and education, seen not as crude manipulation of the powerless by the powerful, but as a more subtle process of socialization of all members of a society. Ideology consists of a set of ideas that unite a significant group within society, or in the case of dominant ideology, the majority of society. The most important workings of ideology are invisible, when ideas become so deep-rooted and ingrained in people's thinking that they are seen as 'common-sense' or 'natural' rather than products of a particular culture's way of thinking about the world.

Perhaps the development of FEMINIST thought best illustrates both how ideology remains hidden and how it is capable of change over time. In the nineteenth century it was beyond question that child-care and all domestic labour was the responsibility of women and that all positions of real power in a society would be held by men. Now, although Western society still has strong patriarchal roots, such ideas are only tenable at the margins of mainstream thought.

Film can be said to be part of the workings of ideology in that it contributes to the naturalizing of certain values, beliefs and REPRESENTATIONS of social groups. The world-wide dominance of American MAINSTREAM cinema can be said to have important implications for the maintenance of Western capitalist ideology. Perhaps more importantly, mainstream or REALIST cinema tends to hide the means by which it is made in favour of the impression that we simply watch events happen naturally, akin to the working of ideology itself in that the audience is denied a sense that it is watching one particular, highly constructed, vision of the world, one governed by a particular ideological vision. It is part of the function of film CRITICISM and analysis to read films in such a way that their ideological positions and contradictions are exposed. See also CLASS, HEGEMONY, MARXISM.
Further reading: Perkins in Gledhill & Williams (2000), Williams (1976)

IDHEC   The Institut des Hautes Etudes Cinématographiques, French film school. See FEMIS.

ILM   Industrial Light and Magic, the SPECIAL EFFECTS company formed in 1975 by George Lucas for the production of *Star Wars* (dir. George Lucas, 1977), initially headed by John Dykstra. ILM has become the best known and one of the most influential special effects companies worldwide and one of the pioneers of motion control and computer ANIMATION, providing effects for Lucas' s own *Star Wars* series, as well as for films like *Jurassic Park* (dir. Steven Spielberg, 1993).

Image   (1) Broadly, the general visual 'look' of a film. (2) In a mechanical sense, the pictorial reproduction of a photographed SHOT on the film strip. (3) In an aesthetic sense, an individual FRAME from a film, considering all its constituent elements such as the *MISE EN SCÈNE*, CAMERA ANGLE and LIGHTING. (4) In a cultural sense, the ability of an ACTOR or a SCENE to represent a cluster of values or encapsulate an historical moment (for example, the image of Lillian Gish as encapsulating Victorian femininity or the image of Arnold Schwarzenegger's body as embodying MASCULINITY in the Reaganite 1980s). (5) More generally, the meaning or attitude one projects through the CODES of fashion and behaviour.

Imaginary line   See 180° RULE.

IMAX   Abbreviated form of 'maximum IMAGE', a Canadian film PROJECTION system capable of producing projected images far larger than even the biggest available conventional systems, involving passing a 70MM PRINT horizontally through the projector. IMAX auditoria house screens around eight storeys high (the National Museum of Film and Photography in Bradford's is 45 feet high and 62 feet wide) with steeply raked seating to heighten the sense of being in the picture. Films designed for IMAX have been most successful when attempting to re-create such things as the sensation of flight or aspects of the natural world, while the rare attempts at narrative fiction have been too restricted by the technical difficulties of anything more than very short TAKES, so most IMAX screens tend to appear in museums or theme parks rather than conventional cinema environments. See also GAUGE.

Imperfect cinema Idea developed by Cuban film-maker and theorist Julio García Espinosa, closely related to THIRD CINEMA, for revolutionary film-making outside the dominant Western cinema. 'Imperfect cinema can make use of the DOCU-MENTARY or the fictional mode, or both. It can use whatever GENRE, or all genres. It can use cinema as a pluralistic art form or as a specialized form of expression. Imperfect cinema is no longer interested in quality or technique. It can be created equally well with a MITCHELL or with an 8MM camera, in a STUDIO or in a guerrilla camp in the middle of the jungle' (Espinosa in Chanan, 1983, pp. 32–33; also reprinted in Fusco, 1987, and Stam & Miller, 1999). Espinosa, like other Latin American film-makers who became important later, trained in Italy in the early 1950s and come under the influence of Italian NEO-REALISM.

Impressionism Deriving from the movement in French painting of the late nineteenth century, the term describes a group of French film-makers of the 1920s – Germaine Dulac, Jean Epstein, Abel Gance, Marcel L'Herbier and Louis Delluc – whose work can be seen as part of the early struggles to understand what cinema as a medium was capable of, prioritizing attempts to capture pure, subjective moments on screen. As Robert B. Ray puts it, the impressionists foregrounded a dimension of the way that we experience aspects of all movies, 'as intermittent intensities (a face, a landscape, the fall of light across a room) that break free from the sometimes indifferent narratives which contain them' (Hill & Church Gibson, 1998, p. 69). Impressionism's emphasis on the fragmented intensities captured by the camera, unmediated by reconstruction into conventional narrative, was eclipsed by the gradual advance of mass-produced commercial cinema. If MAINSTREAM cinema is about constructing the illusion of seamless reality out of film fragments, impressionism was about using the CAMERA to capture the truly fragmentary nature of experience and leaving it in this raw state.
Further reading: Bordwell & Thompson (1997)

In-camera Term used to denote EDITING and SPECIAL EFFECTS achieved while the film is being SHOT rather than, as is the norm, in POST-PRODUCTION. In-camera editing refers to shooting the film in SEQUENCE with appropriate CUTS or other TRANSI-TIONAL DEVICES, so that when printed the film plays precisely as envisaged in the SCRIPT, without any editing being needed. In-camera effects are special effects made in the CAMERA, rather than in post-production printing or processing, and might refer to FAST, SLOW or REVERSE MOTION, or DOUBLE EXPOSURE (for which the film in the camera would be exposed, then rewound and re-exposed, as in a DISSOLVE) or FADE (for which the APERTURE would be closed down as one shot finished and opened up as the next began). In-camera editing and effects were quite common in SILENT CINEMA and are still quite common in amateur and non-commercial film-making, but would be very rare in commercial film-making today, where such processes are carried out at the OPTICAL printing stage, though some MATTE shots continue to be done in-camera.

Independent cinema   In relation to cinema, 'independent' has several linked but different meanings. In US cinema the first independents were those companies – such as that of William FOX – outside the MOTION PICTURE PATENTS COMPANY (MPPC), which fought the MPPC and, ironically, moved to HOLLYWOOD. Throughout the period of the STUDIO SYSTEM era, independent meant independence from the MAJOR STUDIOS, but what this meant varied. SELZNICK International Pictures, during the 1930s and 1940s, for example, was typical in producing independent features outside the immediate control of the majors but indistinguishable from those of the majors and dependent on them for DISTRIBUTION and EXHIBITION, and sometimes finance. The PARAMOUNT DECISION, designed to encourage independent production, led to many more independent FEATURES during the 1950s, but most remained dependent on the majors, and this situation continues today.

Roger Corman, founder of NEW WORLD PICTURES, argued that 'a true independent is a company that can finance, produce and distribute its own films. Most are partial independents, connected in some way to a major studio. They are independent PRODUCERS but not truly independent companies' (quoted in Hillier, 1993, p. 20). This was certainly the case in the 1980s – a good period for independent production – for companies like Carolco, Castle Rock and Morgan Creek, before they folded or were absorbed by major companies. This situation continued into the 1990s and beyond with small, successful independent companies like MIRAMAX, NEW LINE and Fine Line and October Films. New Line and Fine Line, like Castle Rock, became part of Turner Broadcasting, which in 1996 itself became part of TIME WARNER (merged with, or taken over by, AOL to form AOL Time Warner in 2000). Miramax, which had successfully distributed independent films like *sex, lies and videotape* (dir. Steven Soderbergh, 1989) and *Reservoir Dogs* (dir. Quentin Tarantino, 1991), was taken over by the WALT DISNEY COMPANY by the time of *Pulp Fiction* (dir. Tarantino, 1994), though still committed to independent films.

Independent films of different kinds also exist, outside the aegis of the MOTION PICTURE ASSOCIATION OF AMERICA (MPAA), from features by maverick independents like John Cassavetes in the 1960s and 1970s through to John Sayles, David Lynch and others in the 1980s and 1990s. A film-maker like Spike Lee, with his own production company, tries to balance independence with the financing and distribution only available through the major studios. Though many low budget independent film-makers are independent of necessity and happy to graduate to more dependent conditions but higher budgets, some – like Jim Jarmusch and Jon Jost – continue to do their own work on low budgets (much of the finance coming from outside the US) but in comparative freedom. Many truly independent films are AVANT-GARDE or EXPERIMENTAL, such as STRUCTURAL FILM in the 1960s and 1970s. Film-makers such as Stan Brakhage have enjoyed the description of 'independent American film-maker', even though many of their films depend on grants from various public bodies. See also CHANNEL 4.

Further reading: Cook (1996), Izod (1988), Wyatt and Kleinhans in Lewis (1998), Merritt (2000), Wyatt, Schamus and Lott in Neale & Smith (1998), Nowell-Smith in Nowell-Smith (1996)

Industrial film   A form of DOCUMENTARY made to provide information about a company or industry. Often sponsored by the company that is its subject, they may be PROMOTIONAL FILMS designed to sell or promote the company or industry, or may be intended as in-house training for employees. See also TRAINING FILM.

In-house   In movie production, as in other businesses, an activity performed 'in-house' is undertaken by a UNIT belonging to the STUDIO or company rather than by a specialized unit brought in from outside.

Insert title   See INTERTITLE.

Insert, insert shot   A SHOT, often, but not necessarily, a CLOSE-UP, inserted into a SEQUENCE. In *The Big Heat* (dir. Fritz Lang, 1953), a CHARACTER walking along a street stops to look at a list in his hand; the next shot, an insert, shows what the character is looking at; then the SCENE continues. Later, the character glances off-screen, cueing an insert shot of a clock. Inserts are usually integrated into the TIME and SPACE of a scene, but could show something happening elsewhere. It is in the nature of inserts that they are shot in a different time and place from the main shots of the scene, and inserted at the EDITING stage. See also CUTAWAY.

Institutional Mode of Representation   Term coined by film-maker-theo-retician Noël Burch (1973) to describe the set of CODES and CONVENTIONS that together defined the construction of narrative films and that quickly came to dominate film style after a brief period of so-called 'primitive cinema' at the start of the SILENT CINEMA period. Such techniques as CONTINUITY EDITING work to develop a coherent illusion of TIME and SPACE that moves the spectator through the narrative. Burch argues that the IMR, despite its international entrenchment in the film industry, was not inevitable but a result of numerous historical factors, nor is it the only type of film practice. In recent years the term has been superseded by CLASSIC NARRATIVE CINEMA. See also CINEMA OF ATTRACTIONS.

Instructional film   A form of DOCUMENTARY that has as its purpose the conveying of practical or applied information about a given subject.

Intellectual montage   See DIALECTICAL MONTAGE.

Intercut, intercutting   Normally, an alternative term for PARALLEL EDITING – the cutting between different narrative strands of a film intended to be taken as happening simultaneously. However, intercutting may also refer to cutting between different elements in a film when they have no obvious PLOT relationship (though they may have thematic affinity or contrast), as in, for example, the CZECH NEW WAVE film *Something Different* (dir. Vera Chytilová, 1963), or the Yugoslav film *Innocence Unprotected* (dir. Dusan Makavejev, 1968).

Interior monologue   Literally the words going on inside a CHARACTER'S head, revealed to an AUDIENCE through a CONVENTIONAL device. In the cinema the easiest way to do this is through voice over SHOTS of the character clearly not actually speaking. A moment that makes strange and effective use of the device comes at the end of

Psycho (dir. Alfred Hitchcock, 1960). The device is perhaps distinguished from other uses of voice-over by the visual indication that we are actually hearing the thoughts of the character as they are spoken.

Interior A SHOT or SCENE in an indoor setting, which would be shot inside a STUDIO or on LOCATION. In a SHOOTING SCRIPT, such shots would be marked 'INT.' See also EXTERIOR.

Intertextuality The use of references within one film TEXT to another, explicit or implicit, enabling the film-maker to employ a set of meanings from another text to subtly suggest another dimension to the film. The frequent use of intertextuality is one of the defining qualities of POSTMODERNISM and closely related to BRICOLAGE, which can be seen as a more general recycling of a style. Among the many recent examples of intertextuality is the use of one of the best-known SEQUENCES in SILENT CINEMA – a pram tumbling down the Odessa Steps in Eisenstein's *Battleship Potemkin* (1925) – in *The Untouchables* (dir. Brian de Palma, 1987). In this case the reference is largely a HOMAGE, though there is little doubt that it adds a degree of *gravitas* to the GENRE piece. More extended intertextuality can be seen in the *MISE EN SCÈNE* of *Blade Runner* (dir. Ridley Scott, 1982), which is littered with visual references to *Metropolis* (dir. Fritz Lang, 1926), a similarly dystopian vision of the future of urban existence.

Intertitle Printed words inserted within a film other than in opening or closing CREDITS. Intertitles were common in SILENT FILM to provide narrative information about a story or SCENE, and were largely replaced in the SOUND FILM by the ability of dialogue to convey such information, although intertitles and CAPTIONS are occasionally used in contemporary films, such as *Pulp Fiction* (dir. Quentin Tarantino, 1994).

Invisible editing Another way of describing CONTINUITY EDITING although the notion of the invisibility of the continuity system places a special emphasis on EDITING's contribution to the overall TRANSPARENCY of the CLASSICAL NARRATIVE style. André Bazin puts it well: 'The use of editing can be "invisible"; and this was most frequently the case in the classical pre-war American film. The only purpose of breaking down the SHOTS is to analyse an event according to the physical and dramatic logic of a SCENE. This analysis is rendered imperceptible by its very logicality. The spectator's mind naturally accepts the CAMERA ANGLES that the DIRECTOR offers him because they are justified by the disposition of the ACTION and the shifting of dramatic interest' (Bazin in Graham, 1968, p. 26).

Iris A SHOT showing the gradual appearance of an IMAGE through an expanding circular MASK (iris-in) or the gradual disappearance of the image through a contracting mask (iris-out) either placed in front of the LENS or made with an adjustable diaphragm in the lens barrel. Irises are usually used as a TRANSITIONAL DEVICE to begin or end a SCENE, although they also may focus attention on a particular detail according to its placement in the FRAME or through a pause in its contracting or expanding mask. More common in the SILENT ERA, irises tend to be used today to evoke nostalgia for the period when it was in vogue.

Italian neo-realism See NEO-REALISM.

J

Journal of Film and Video A quarterly publication of the American University Film and Video Association, this film journal is unique in its attempt to balance both academic essays of film CRITICISM with more technical articles involving film production and teaching.

Journal of Popular Film and Television Quarterly film journal, established by the Department of Popular Culture at Bowling Green State University, Ohio, its focus primarily on MAINSTREAM American cinema and TELEVISION, with an emphasis on GENRE, AUTEUR and cultural interpretation.

Jump cut A break or jump in the CONTINUITY of a SHOT or between two shots caused by removing a section of a shot and then SPLICING together what remains of it. The term also refers to the CUTting from one shot to another in such a way as to abruptly change the spatial length between shots. Because of their sense of DISCONTINUITY, jump cuts are commonly used to disorient the viewer by creating a sudden, illogical or mismatched TRANSITION. Once a sign of bad editing because its lack of continuity failed to generate a sense of SUTURE on the part of the SPECTATOR, jump cuts are now accepted as part of the rhetoric of narrative film. In *A bout de souffle* (dir. Jean-Luc Godard, 1959) Michel (Jean-Paul Belmondo) finds a gun in the glove compartment of the car he has stolen as he is being pulled over by a policeman, whom he shoots. The jump cuts in this SCENE express Michel's mental confusion at this moment. *Bonnie and Clyde* (dir. Arthur Penn, 1967), which Godard was originally going to direct, is often cited as one of the first MAINSTREAM films to employ jump cuts.

Jump Cut American film journal focusing on the relations between cinema, IDEOLOGY and politics. The magazine covers MAINSTREAM FILM, but its main emphasis is on DOCUMENTARY, INDEPENDENT and THIRD CINEMA. Published irregularly, *Jump Cut*'s aim of being an alternative journal extends to its own format, which for years was produced on newsprint quality paper.

K

***Kaiju Eiga* (Japanese monster movie)** Influenced by American SCIENCE FICTION movies of the 1950s, such as *The Beast from 20,000 Fathoms* (dir. Eugene Lourie, 1953), the Japanese produced a CYCLE of movies with giant monsters advancing upon and destroying Tokyo, beginning with *Gojira/Godzilla* (dir. Inoshira Honda, 1954). A commercial hit both in Japan and North America, the film has spawned some 15 SEQUELS or SPIN-OFFS. Godzilla, a dinosaur, *Rodan* (dir. Honda, 1956), a giant pterodactyl, and *Mothra* (dir. Honda, 1961), a giant moth, are less frightening than fun – Godzilla and others have been marketed as children's toys – and in such later movies as *Godzilla vs. the Smog Monster* (dir. Yoshimitu Banno, 1972) they are the good guys.

Kammerspielfilm Literally 'chamber talk,' a type of GERMAN EXPRESSIONIST film influenced by the intimate theatre style of Max Reinhardt, which concentrated on psychological drama. According to Eisner (1969, pp. 77–199), *KAMMERSPIELFILMS*, beginning with *Shattered* (dir. Lupu Pick, 1921), sought to eliminate INTERTITLES as much as possible in an effort to convey emotion and CHARACTER through CLOSE-UPS and an intimate visual style.

Key light   The main source of light for the LIGHTING of a SCENE (and for the light reading for exposure of the scene). Normally the key light is positioned in front of, slightly to the side of and slightly above the scene being lit, and is supplemented by other lights. See also FILL LIGHT, LOW-KEY LIGHTING.

Keystone   Film company founded in 1912 by Mack Sennett, known primarily for the SLAPSTICK COMEDIES he produced there. Sennett began his career as an ACTOR in Griffith's BIOGRAPH films and eventually directed for Biograph as well. After leaving Biograph, Sennett initially located in Ft. Lee, New Jersey, but quickly relocated to HOLLYWOOD. Sennett personally directed his films until 1914, after which he acted as a PRODUCER working closely with his DIRECTORS, WRITERS and actors. From 1913 to 1935, Sennett produced for Keystone hundreds of ONE-REELERS and FEATURE FILMS that virtually defined the GENRE of slapstick comedy in such series as the Keystone Kops and Sennett's Bathing Beauties. Chaplin, Buster Keaton and Frank Capra all directed COMEDIES for Keystone, whose roster of STARS also included Harry Langdon, Fatty Arbuckle and W.C. Fields. Though Keystone's comedies were enormously popular through the 1920s, their visual kinetics became out of fashion with the arrival of SOUND, and the studio ceased production in 1935.

Kick light   A small light, usually placed near the CAMERA, designed to pick out and highlight some object, often an ACTOR's eyes. Also known as catchlight, kicker light, cross backlight, eye light. See also LIGHTING.

Kinetoscope, Kinetograph   The Kinetoscope was a 'peepshow' machine, designed for individual viewing of a 50 foot LOOP of film through a slot, usually situated in 'parlors' with banks of Kinetoscopes. The Kinetograph was the first movie photography CAMERA, designed by W.K.L. Dickson for Thomas Edison, and was used to produce the films for the Kinetoscope. The first Kinetoscope was demonstrated in 1893 and the first Kinetoscope parlor opened in New York City in 1894. Edison originally showed little interest in the PROJECTION of films to large AUDIENCES, but the popularity of the Kinetoscope declined rapidly after the LUMIÈRE PROGRAMME had been projected in 1895.
Further reading: Robinson (1996)

Kino Eye   Translated from the Russian as 'cinema eye', the film THEORY of Soviet DOCUMENTARY film-maker Dziga Vertov. Influenced by the movements of CONSTRUCTIVISM and FUTURISM, Vertov believed that the unblinking mechanical eye of the CAMERA could perceive the physical world more fully and more accurately than the human eye, with important implications for the proper and moral use of film, especially in post-revolutionary Russia. Vertov developed his ideas in both polemical manifestos (Vertov, 1984) and in his most important film, *Man with the Movie Camera* (1929), which documents both aspects of daily life in the Soviet Union and the construction of the film itself. See also DZIGA VERTOV GROUP.

Kino Pravda   Russian for 'film truth', *Kino Pravda* was the name of the NEWSREEL produced by Soviet DOCUMENTARY film-maker Dziga Vertov and his KINO-EYE group from 1922–1925 that documented daily life throughout Russia, celebrating the transformation of the country to a communist state.

Kuleshov effect, Kuleshov experiment   Lev Kuleshov was a film theorist and film-maker who taught a workshop in the early 1920s at the Moscow State Film School which formulated ideas about MONTAGE in the Soviet cinema and influenced the work of Vsevolod Pudovkin, Sergei Eisenstein, Kuleshov himself and others. The workshop – partly because it lacked funds for film STOCK – explored EDITING by rearranging SHOTS and SCENES in D.W. Griffith's *Intolerance* (1916), to demonstrate that meaning and emotional effect in film derived not from the content of individual SHOTS but from their juxtaposition, the basis of montage THEORY. The workshop's best known experiment in editing (documented by Pudovkin) involved CLOSE-UP shots of the supposedly expressionless face of the actor Mozhukhin intercut with shots of a bowl of soup, a dead woman in a coffin, and a little girl playing with a toy. It was claimed that AUDIENCES interpreted the actor's expression appropriately in each case, demonstrating the power of editing. See also CREATIVE GEOGRAPHY.
Further reading: Cook (1996), Pudovkin (1970), Thompson & Bordwell (1994)

Kung Fu movie   See MARTIAL ARTS FILM.

L

Langue   In SEMIOTICS, a term coined by linguist Ferdinand de Saussure to distinguish a total language system from individual and idiosyncratic uses of that system (PAROLE). It is through all the individual utterances that the parameters of the langue are defined. In cinema, individual GENRE films are the particular instances of parole that comprise the langue of a given genre; from a larger perspective, the film history constituted of individual narrative films make up the langue of the INSTITUTIONAL MODE OF REPRESENTATION or CLASSIC NARRATIVE CINEMA.

Lap dissolve   Abbreviation of 'overlap dissolve', now generally further abbreviated to DISSOLVE.

Laser disc   Two-sided plastic disc (about the same size as a vinyl LP) from which IMAGES are read by a laser beam – reflecting light from billions of tiny cavities – for transmission on a TELEVISION screen or VIDEO projector. Laser discs offer IMAGE and SOUND quality superior to that of video, making the format a favourite of film purists, especially because it also allows switching between a film and additional material such as a SCENE by scene COMMENTARY. Laser discs are now being supplanted by the DVD format.

Leader   The FOOTAGE attached to the start (and end) of a REEL of a RELEASE PRINT, which allows it to be threaded, or laced up, on the projector without damaging the film proper, and which cues the projectionist to reel changes and the numerical countdown which allows time for FOCUSing. Originally standardized by the ACADEMY OF

MOTION PICTURE ARTS AND SCIENCES (Academy leader), the current universal standard leader was designed by the Society of Motion Picture and Television Engineers (known as SMPTE universal leader).

Legs In film industry parlance, a film RELEASE is said to have 'legs' if it sustains success at the BOX-OFFICE, rather than enjoying initial success but then fading quickly. Jokingly, *Jaws* (dir. Steven Spielberg, 1975), was said to have 'fins'. The term is also used in legitimate theatre, and derives from a general usage, meaning 'to stand up'.

Lens A device, usually made of glass, through which light passes to FOCUS an IMAGE on the strip of CELLULOID inside the CAMERA. A wide variety of lenses are available, each with different aesthetic possibilities in the way a SHOT is seen on the screen. See also ANAMORPHIC LENS, DEEP FOCUS, DEPTH OF FIELD, FISH-EYE LENS, FOCAL LENGTH, SHALLOW FOCUS, VARIABLE FOCUS, WIDE ANGLE, ZOOM.

Lesbian film See GAY AND LESBIAN FILM.

Letterbox Format for showing WIDESCREEN films on TELEVISION (or VIDEO, LASER DISC or DVD) in their original ASPECT RATIO by MASKing the top and bottom of the television screen IMAGE, to produce a long rectangular image shaped like a letterbox.

Lighting The way in which light, whether in a STUDIO or on LOCATION, INTERIOR or EXTERIOR, is organized and controlled for the making of a SHOT or SCENE. Though a shot may be made with AVAILABLE LIGHT, especially in DOCUMENTARY film-making, most shots in commercially made films use some additional lighting from artificial sources. Lighting allows for or enhances a whole range of possibilities for the composition of the film IMAGE. See also ARC LIGHT, BACK LIGHTING, *CHIAROSCURO*, DEEP FOCUS, DEPTH OF FIELD, FILL LIGHT, HIGH KEY LIGHTING, KEY LIGHT, KICK LIGHT, LOW KEY LIGHTING.

Lighting cameraman, lighting camerawoman See CINEMATOGRAPHER.

Line producer The PRODUCER with most direct contact with the daily operation of a film through all the stages of production. Although reporting to an executive producer, the line producer will have much autonomy in controlling the film's finances, hiring of personnel and the administration of whatever stage the film is at. A line producer is therefore likely to be physically present on SET or in POST-PRODUCTION, at least some of the time. A production manager usually reports directly to the line producer.

Linear editing Term used to describe VIDEO editing in which SHOTS from one tape are copied on to a master tape in linear sequence, distinguishing this process from NON-LINEAR EDITING.

Lip sync The synchronization of an ACTOR's lip movements on screen with his or her spoken dialogue on the SOUNDTRACK, sometimes achieved in POST-PRODUCTION with the ACTOR recording dialogue in perfect time with the IMAGES in front of her/him. Needless to say, lip sync's importance is most obvious when it fails to work, with the often amusing SPECTACLE of words and lips working out of time with each other, which often occurs when a film is DUBBED with another language that is very difficult to record in synchronization with the original images.

Little 3 In Hollywood as well as the BIG 5 MAJOR STUDIOS during the STUDIO SYSTEM era from the 1920s–1945s (MGM, PARAMOUNT, RKO, TWENTIETH CENTURY-FOX and WARNER BROS.), which were fully VERTICALLY INTEGRATED – combining production, DISTRIBUTION and EXHIBITION – three other major studios – COLUMBIA, UNITED ARTISTS and UNIVERSAL – were known as the Little 3 because they were not fully vertically integrated, not owning their own theatres. They were included among the major studios because they regularly produced and/or distributed as many FEATURES as the Big 5 studios and had access to the first run theatres owned by the Big 5.
Further reading: Balio (1976a), Gomery (1986), Izod (1988), Maltby (1995), Gomery and Schatz in Nowell-Smith (1996), Thompson & Bordwell (1994)

Live action ACTIONS performed by living people or animals rather than by animated figures. WALT DISNEY's output notably consisted of both live action films and animated films, though live action can be combined with ANIMATION, as in Disney's *Mary Poppins* (dir. Robert Stevenson, 1964) and *Bedknobs and Broomsticks* (dir. Stevenson, 1971), and *Who Framed Roger Rabbit?* (dir. Robert Zemeckis, 1988).

Lobby card US term for the small poster-type photographic cards, displayed in cinema and theatre lobbies as ADVERTISING for either current or future attractions. A popular form of advertising from the period of SILENT CINEMA through to the STUDIO SYSTEM era.

Location A place outside a STUDIO where a film is SHOT. Though generally referring to a 'real' place, most location shooting transforms the location through LIGHTING, various forms of construction, and even landscaping. Since the late 1950s location filming has become the norm for any film requiring a feel of authenticity, though other technical advances have made this easier to simulate. The costs question is now more complex, since film-makers have become increasingly ambitious in their use of locations, which can make location shooting more expensive than studio work. See also LOCATION MANAGER.

Location manager The person responsible for finding LOCATIONS according to the PRODUCER and DIRECTOR'S brief and for managing the smooth running of location shoots, including catering, legal requirements, public relations and security.

Log A document used by all technical departments on a film to record what takes place each day during the making of a film. For example, a CAMERA assistant would record the TAKES taken with all the technical specifications for each SHOT. At the POST PRODUCTION stage, an EDITOR would keep a similar log of decisions taken in the cutting room. In each case the log is essential to creative decision-making at all stages, particularly with very precise technical processes such as NEGATIVE cutting.

Long shot (LS) A SHOT in which the CAMERA is at a great distance from the object(s) being photographed, or a shot in which the subject is seen in its entirety or in small scale, including some surroundings. The long shot may also be conceived in terms of a view that would roughly correspond to an AUDIENCE'S view of the stage within the proscenium arch in live theatre. In the context of the human figure, a standing person would be fully visible in the FRAME. Also called FULL SHOT.

Long take A SHOT of long duration or one that is relatively so in context. The long take is associated with a REALIST aesthetic because it invites a contemplative view, preserves TIME and, along with CAMERA MOVEMENT, SPACE as well. Some long takes, because they require elaborate CHOREOGRAPHY of the CAMERA and the ACTION contained in the FRAME, have become celebrated as examples of PURE CINEMA. The opening shots of Orson Welles's *Touch of Evil* (1958) and John Carpenter's *Halloween* (1978) and the final shot of Michelangelo Antonioni's *The Passenger* (1975) are three notable examples. Long takes also can be used for DISTANCIATION, as in the lengthy SEQUENCE SHOTS by Jean-Luc Godard in such films as *Weekend* (1968) and *Tout va Bien* (co-dir. Jean-Pierre Gorin, 1972).
Further reading: Henderson (1971 in Nichols 1976)

Look See GAZE.

Loop Technical term describing the curve of a strip of film just above and just below the projector gate – through which light is projected through the CELLULOID – which allows the film in PROJECTION to shift between continuous and intermittent movement (similar to the continuous/intermittent movement in the CAMERA). The invention of the loop (or 'Latham loop', after its inventor) solved a major problem for dealing with the repeated pulling; stopping; pulling mechanism in the camera and projector. 'Loop' is also used to describe a strip of film whose beginning and ending are SPLICED together so that it runs continuously, without having to be rethreaded. EDUCATIONAL FILMS are sometimes in loop form, and the idea has been explored by some AVANT-GARDE film-makers: George Landow's *Film in Which There Appear Sprocket Holes, Edge Lettering, Dirt Particles, Etc.* (1966) plays with the loop concept by repetition of the same FOOTAGE. The same meaning of the word loop is applied to a loop of film and audio tape used for DUBBING dialogue for a film: in 'looping', loops of a SCENE and/or of dialogue are played continuously until the ACTORS involved have perfected the required LIP SYNCHronization for recording to take place.

Low angle A SHOT in which the CAMERA is positioned below the object(s) being photographed or below eye level. Because this angle makes the ACTION seem to come toward the camera more quickly and ACTORS appear to loom above us, low angle shots tend to convey CONNOTATIONS of power, strength and control. Low angle shots are typically used to make action SEQUENCES seem more dramatic, as in the climactic chase on the salt flats in *Stagecoach* (1939), where DIRECTOR John Ford abruptly inserts a shot of the thundering horses' hooves taken from a pit below ground level.

Low-budget At one level a self explanatory term, denoting a film made with very little money, but the term is relative: a low-budget film made by a major US studio today could still cost much more than an average film made in the UK. Further, it has taken on different CONNOTATIONS within the film industry at different historical moments. At the height of the HOLLYWOOD STUDIO SYSTEM, low-budget B PICTURES

– denoting deliberately inferior quality – were routinely made as second features for DOUBLE BILLS, but most ART CINEMA films are made on restricted budgets, with different connotations and results. For instance, the lack of major STARS and expensive SPECIAL EFFECTS is often seen as contributing to authenticity and truthfulness.

Low-key lighting A style of lighting that avoids the full illumination of the KEY LIGHT (HIGH-KEY LIGHTING), appearing under or dimly lit, though the overall appearance of darkness and shadow may be contrasted with brighter areas. Low-key lighting is characteristic of THRILLERS and some HORROR movies, and is particularly associated with FILM NOIR, where it often communicates menace and psychological intensity.

Lumière programme Name given to the films shown by Louis and Auguste Lumière at the first public projected screening of moving pictures, Paris, 28 December, 1895 (Thomas Edison having made moving pictures earlier, but not projected them). The short ACTUALITÉS (ACTUALITIES) comprising the programme included single, short SHOTS of SCENES such as workers leaving the Lumière photographic factory in Lyons (*La Sortie des usines Lumière*), a train entering a station (*L'Arrivée d'un train en gare de La Ciotat*), a child being fed (*Le Déjeuner de bébé*), and what many consider the first 'played', or fiction, film (*L'Arroseur arrosé*), a comic scene in a garden involving a water hose. See also CINÉMATOGRAPHE, DOCUMENTARY. Further reading: Gorky in Leyda (1960), Toulet (1995)

M

MacGuffin Term used by Alfred Hitchcock for a PLOT device that seems important but is really only a pretext for creating suspense within a narrative. Hitchcock explained to François Truffaut (Truffaut, 1968, pp. 99–100) that it is something the CHARACTERS consider of great importance – 'the plans, the documents or secrets' – but which really matters little in terms of theme. Hitchcock has cited the uranium in the wine bottles in *Notorious* (1946) and the non-existent Mr. Kaplan in *North by Northwest* (1959) as examples. More recently, *Ronin* (dir. John Frankenheimer, 1998) plays with the idea of the MacGuffin, its entire plot being built around battles between several nefarious groups seeking a briefcase whose contents are never revealed.

Made-for-TV Traditionally, FEATURE films were aimed at the THEATRICAL market; indeed, before TELEVISION, there was no other market. By 1958, all the MAJOR STUDIOS had made deals with television networks for broadcasting pre-1949 features and SHORTS; soon more recent features were leased to television. As the price for recent features rose in the mid 1960s – ABC paid $4 million for screening *The Bridge on the River Kwai* in 1966, though the average was about $400,000 – the networks looked for other sources of material. Studios, led by NBC and MCA/UNIVERSAL, began making made-for-TV movies (and later mini-SERIES), which could often be made for less than the cost of leasing a BLOCKBUSTER film. In 1974, 130 new made-for-TV movies were broadcast, compared with only 118 theatrically-released features.

Originally, there was another motive: US network television converted to COLOUR transmission between 1965 and 1970 and during the mid 1960s HOLLYWOOD production of colour films – largely due to television broadcasting in BLACK-AND-WHITE – fell to less than fifty per cent (rising to 94 per cent by 1970), and made-for-TV movies were produced in colour. Though made-for-TV movies and theatrical movies generally lead very separate lives, there can be some CROSSOVER: Steven Spielberg's first feature, *Duel* (1972), began life as a made-for-TV movie but later enjoyed a successful theatrical RELEASE. The increasing involvement of television companies in film production, especially in Europe, has led to much more movement between small and big screen: Ingmar Bergman's mini-series *Scenes from a Marriage* (1975) and *Fanny and Alexander* (1982) were both released in television and theatrical versions, and the BBC Television film *Persuasion* (dir. Roger Michell, 1995) also enjoyed a successful theatrical release. Further reading: Schulze in Balio (1990), Gomery (1992)

Magic lantern An instrument for projecting glass slide IMAGES on to a screen via a light source (initially a candle) and a LENS, both for home entertainment and for commercial travelling shows. Images were painted on to slides, although in the nineteenth century photographs began to be used. In many ways the forerunner of motion pictures in that they attracted paying AUDIENCES to look at projected images and in that magic lantern shows increasingly simulated movement by the use of SUPERIMPOSED images and sliding panels. Developed in the seventeenth century, magic lanterns were a popular entertainment in Britain in the nineteenth century. A magic lantern is central to a striking SEQUENCE in Ingmar Bergman's *Fanny and Alexander* (1982), and Bergman titled his 1988 autobiography after the device. In *Tarzan* (dir. Kevin Lima and Chris Buck, 1999), Tarzan sees the wonders of the modern world via a magic lantern (and moving pictures via a ZOETROPE). See also PRE-CINEMA. Further reading: Gunning in Gledhill & Williams (2000), Robinson (1966)

Magnetic sound SOUND recorded or played back on magnetic tape, including the magnetic stripe on the film strip that holds the film SOUNDTRACK. Magnetic sound recording replaced OPTICAL SOUND recording because it was cheaper, instantly replayable and better quality. Sound was generally recorded separately from film and then SYNCHRONIZED in the EDITING process. Although RELEASE film PRINTS may have magnetic soundtracks, this is today largely restricted to 70MM prints with stereophonic sound: most cinemas use 35MM prints with optical soundtracks, though this produces lower sound quality.

Mainstream film A commercially-oriented narrative film, typically boasting big STARS and high PRODUCTION VALUES, designed to attract AUDIENCES at the BOX-OFFICE, including contemporary popular MUSIC on the SOUNDTRACK, topical interest in the STORY, or HIGH CONCEPT in packaging and MARKETING. MAINSTREAM FILMS are usually constructed according to the principles of CLASSIC NARRATIVE FILM, such as INVISIBLE EDITING and SUTURE, and engage spectators' IDENTIFICATION with CHARACTERS. Commonly associated with HOLLYWOOD, mainstream film, especially given the contemporary trend toward international CO-PRODUCTIONS, more accurately refers to international cinema, largely because of the dominant influence of American film on so many NATIONAL CINEMAS, and because the classic narrative style has become the universal norm.

Further reading: Bordwell, Staiger & Thompson (1985), Hollows & Jancovich (1995), Wyatt (1994)

Majors, major studios Terms applied to the grouping of film companies comprising the STUDIO SYSTEM in HOLLYWOOD, from the 1920s to the 1950s, and which continue today in a different form. During the studio system era, the majors were the VERTICALLY INTEGRATED BIG 5 (MGM, PARAMOUNT, RKO, TWENTIETH CENTURY-FOX, WARNER BROS.) and the LITTLE 3 (COLUMBIA, UNITED ARTISTS and UNIVERSAL). After the PARAMOUNT DECISION in 1948, the majors ceased to be vertically integrated and became production and DISTRIBUTION companies only. RKO ceased functioning in 1955, but otherwise the majors in the NEW HOLLYWOOD (though often renamed) remain much the same as before: MGM (comprising MGM and United Artists), Paramount, Twentieth Century-Fox, Warner Brothers, Sony Pictures Entertainment (comprising Columbia and TriStar) and Universal. Turner Pictures (comprising Castle Rock and NEW LINE Cinema) was a major until absorbed by Time Warner, but the most significant addition to the majors today is the WALT DISNEY COMPANY and its distribution arm, Buena Vista Pictures. Although the major studios today are responsible for only about half of US releases, they account for as much as 90 per cent of the GROSS US BOX-OFFICE, with similar percentages in Europe and elsewhere.
Further reading: Gomery (1986), Gomery in Nowell-Smith (1996), Gomery and Balio in Neale & Smith (1998), Izod (1988), Lewis (1998), Miller in Miller (1990), Wasko (1994)

Mall cinemas Term applied to purpose-built MULTIPLEX CINEMAS built as part of shopping malls, a major development of EXHIBITION strategies during the 1970s and 1980s, taking over the process of dividing of existing cinemas into several screens which began in the 1960s.
Further reading: Gomery in Miller (1990), Gomery (1992)

Marketing The total strategy used to sell a film, including various forms of ADVERTISING, but embracing other techniques as well. Today market research penetrates all aspects of contemporary life and most large production companies and DISTRIBUTORS employ a permanent small army of researchers to tell them what kinds of films will sell and to detect shifting trends in advance of their competitors. For very large-scale pictures, marketing strategists are a major force from the very beginning, continuing through its making, with focus groups viewing various stages of completion, with the power to radically alter the SCRIPT through their reactions. Once a film is complete, marketing supplements the various forms of conventional advertising (TRAILERS, TELEVISION, radio, press, poster campaigns and the Internet) with other kinds of publicity including getting the film, its STARS and DIRECTOR to appear in as many media as possible through interviews, press profiles and DOCUMENTARIES. The marketing strategist's job is to create an IMAGE for the product as a whole, and where possible tightly monitor and control it.

TIE-INS to other companies and products are now of enormous importance to those marketing both films and the goods associated with them. The launch of *The Phantom Menace* (dir. George Lucas, 1999) produced perhaps the most complete and spectacular range of tie-ins to any film so far: it was possible to purchase a vast array of foodstuffs, toiletries, toys and clothing, most aimed at children, all bearing the film's logo and a picture of one of its CHARACTERS.

Although marketing and advertising are inextricably linked, marketing is more to do with a total strategy that includes extensive research, which informs future strategy. Marketing executives are therefore likely to conceive of their task as circular, with more and more information about public tastes and perceptions feeding into ever more refined marketing campaigns.

Martial Arts film A film in which the main CHARACTERS have some degree of competence in one of the martial arts – karate, kick-boxing, judo, kung fu and so on – and which features the use of that skill, usually in extended fight SCENES featuring elaborate CHOREOGRAPHY that sometimes sacrifices the laws of physics for visual dynamism. The heroes display a disciplined approach that is mental as well as physical, a spiritual and philosophical unity of mind and body. Popular movies from Asian countries, particularly the Japanese SAMURAI FILMS, Chinese swordplay movies and Hong Kong Kung Fu movies (*Fists of Fury*, dir. Lo Wei, 1971, starring Bruce Lee) dominate the GENRE, although by definition the genre includes HOLLYWOOD movies that feature swordplay and boxing, such as *The Mark of Zorro* (dir. Rouben Mamoulian, 1940) and *Rocky* (dir. John G. Avildsen, 1976), respectively, as well as such movies as *The Karate Kid* (dir. John G. Avildsen, 1984) and *The Warriors* (dir. Walter Hill, 1979). The martial arts movie was popularized in the West by Bruce Lee before his death in 1973. In recent years scenes of martial arts combat have been absorbed into many MAINSTREAM ACTION MOVIES.
Further reading: Mintz (1983)

Marxism Philosophical ideas that have some relationship to the writings of the nineteenth-century German philosopher Karl Marx. Whilst Marx's original work was overtly mostly concerned with the economic and political relations between the working and ruling CLASSes under capitalism, his ideas have been interpreted and read in ways which have powerfully influenced the study of culture throughout the twentieth century. The impact of Marxism on film has probably been felt most keenly through its influence on the development of film THEORY (via its impact on literary and cultural theory in general), but some key film-makers have themselves been influenced by Marxist thought, including 1920s Soviet DIRECTORS Sergei Eisenstein, Dziga Vertov, Lev Kuleshov and Vsevolod Pudovkin.

Whilst many earlier Marxist-influenced thinkers expressed optimism about film as a progressive form in itself (see, for example, Benjamin, 1968), most early debates centre on the same aesthetic conflicts that accompanied the rise of MODERNISM in other art forms. The influence of Bertolt BRECHT was central in the early questioning of the progressive credentials of REALISM in a work of art, arguing that even realist work that adopted progressive attitudes encouraged a passive AUDIENCE to indulge in catharsis and naturalized the world as it is, rather than encouraging the desire for change.

Most Marxist thought has seen MAINSTREAM film as reactionary, primarily because of its illusionary properties and the resultant passivity that it induces in its audience. The mainstream realist film hides its means of construction and naturalizes as common-sense its IDEOLOGICAL position and is therefore the opposite of a TEXT designed to encourage people to question the basic structures of the world in which they live. However, there are important historical exceptions to this with, for example, Georg Lukács (see, for example, Selden, 1987) arguing for particular kinds of realism as revealing the truth about the world (see EPIC).

During the post-1970 developments in film theory, Marxist ideas have been more common as components of schools of thought which have revised Marxism, moving away from seeing the economic as the total determinant of the cultural life of a society, and instead seeing art forms as the product of complex forces, one of which is the class relations produced by capitalism. Some of the key influences on film studies – STRUCTURALISM, POST-STRUCTURALISM, PSYCHOANALYTIC theory and FEMINISM – can all be said to have an important relationship to Marxism whilst seeking to refine it in different ways. Chuck Kleinhans maintains that the influence of Marxist thought is today seen most clearly in the area of film studies concerned with economics, such as the global media industry or film finance. Marxism remains a key influence in a wider sense, though, as Kleinhans says, it is today viewed as most effective 'when it combines its analysis of class with an analysis of GENDER, RACE, national, POST-COLONIAL, and other issues raised by progressive social-political movements' (Hill & Church Gibson 1998, p. 111).
Further reading: Hollows *et al.* (2000); Lapsley & Westlake (1988)

Masala film Term used to describe films in the Hindi popular Indian cinema style, characteristically involving a mix of what the West would consider very separate GENRES – song and dance SEQUENCES mixed with broad COMEDY, ACTION, stunts and high MELODRAMA. As Raj Kapoor put it, the Indian spectator 'wants everything rolled up into one' (Thomas, 1985). Masala is Hindi for spices or flavours, and Hindi film-makers thus talk of 'blending the masalas in proper proportions'. See also BOLLYWOOD.

Masculinity As the rise of FEMINIST thought called into question not only older ideas of what it is to be female, but also the notion of an essential female identity, so there has been parallel questioning of the notion of masculinity. Both have been major issues in film studies over the last twenty years.

Whilst feminist film THEORY established the notion that MAINSTREAM cinema was predicated on the male GAZE, it followed that women in film were generally the object at which the spectator was invited to look. By extension, therefore, any passive eroticization of the male form takes on female CONNOTATIONS and leaves the male open to ridicule and, in a heterosexist culture, to risk being seen as homosexual. However, as feminist ideas about representation are changing, and ideas about psychoanalytic theory modified, it is no longer regarded as impossible that the male body can be eroticized for the female spectator. Such changes in the theoretical basis of gender REPRESENTATIONS are perhaps best seen in the context of what Anneke Smelik calls 'the crisis in which the white male heterosexual subject finds himself, a crisis in which his masculinity is fragmented and denaturalized, in which the SIGNIFIERS of "man" and "manly" seem to have lost all their meaning' (in Hill & Church Gibson 1998, p. 141). In an industry so historically dependent on traditional notions of masculinity, such a crisis clearly has profound implications

As Smelik points out, though, a crisis of identity for heterosexual men has been welcomed and celebrated by gay critics, particularly those working in QUEER THEORY. Gay, lesbian and queer theorists have long been reading films 'against the grain' and theirs has probably been the biggest influence on the way that traditional notions of masculinity have ceased to be regarded as normative. The transition from older gay and lesbian arguments around positive IMAGES of non-traditional masculinities to more recent and radical QUEER CINEMA marks the latest stage in what could be described as the drive to confuse and problematize rigid boundaries of GENDER and SEXUALITY. NEW CINEMA that has sought to augment a critical strategy of re-reading older TEXTS by providing diverse and complex explorations of masculinity has come largely from the ART CINEMA and INDEPENDENT sectors with work such as *Edward II* (dir. Derek Jarman, 1991) in the UK, *My Own Private Idaho* (dir. Gus Van Sant, 1992) in the US and *All About My Mother* (dir. Pedro Almodovar, 1999) in Spain.

To date, popular commercial cinema has not been profoundly changed by major shifts in theoretical notions of masculinity, but there have been prominent variations within popular genres associated with deeply entrenched ideas of the masculine. *Unforgiven* (dir. Clint Eastwood, 1992) and *Platoon* (dir. Oliver Stone, 1986) take traditional sites of HOLLYWOOD male heroism, the WESTERN and the WAR FILM, and provide a questioning variation on the male hero. In a totally different vein, *Tootsie* (dir. Sydney Pollack, 1982) and *Mrs Doubtfire* (dir. Chris Columbus, 1993) allow major Hollywood stars – Dustin Hoffman and Robin Williams, respectively – to play almost an entire film in drag.

Further reading: Cohan & Hark (1993), Lehman (1993), Willis in Gledhill & Williams (2000)

Mask An opaque shield placed in front of the projector LENS that blocks out part of the IMAGE to change the ASPECT RATIO of the SCREEN. Also, a shield placed over the CAMERA lens to change the shape of the image. In SILENT CINEMA, masks were frequently used to enhance pictorial composition and focus viewer attention. In SOUND FILM, such shots tend to be motivated by the DIEGESIS as POINT-OF-VIEW shots of characters looking through keyholes or binoculars.

Master shot A SHOT usually taken from a WIDE ANGLE that covers all the action taking place in a scene. This is then edited together with shots either taken simultaneously with the master from different CAMERA ANGLES or shot at different times. The use of a master shot is seen as an essential tool in achieving COVERAGE and CONTINUITY. Master shots are intercut with a variety of mid-shots or CLOSE-UPS with the edits being made on ACTION to achieve the effect of invisibility that is the aim of the CONTINUITY EDITING system.

Match cut See EYELINE MATCH.

Materialist film A sub-type of STRUCTURAL film which foregrounds its material base – CELLULOID, EMULSION, film GRAIN, etc. Peter Gidal discusses the term in his 1976 anthology; examples are *Wavelength* (dir. Michael Snow, 1967), *Rohfilm* (dir. Birgit & Wilhelm Hein, 1968), *Berlin Horse* (dir. Malcolm LeGrice, 1970) and *Film in Which There Appear Sprocket Holes, Edge Lettering, Dirt Particles, Etc.* (dir. George Landow, 1966). Peter Wollen (1982) argues that the materialist approach should be considered a form of 'realism'.

Matte shot SHOT in which part of the FRAME is masked, so that other material can be added later in the unexposed area, originally by exposing different parts of the frame at different times (as with the 'magic' effects in films by Georges Méliès, or the shot of the moving train outside the window at the start of *The Great Train Robbery*, dir. Edwin S. Porter, 1903). Additional material for a shot would now normally be added by OPTICAL printing.

McGuffin See MacGUFFIN.

Meat movie See SPLATTER FILM.

Medium shot (MS) Somewhere between a CLOSE-UP and a LONG SHOT, a SHOT in which the CAMERA is relatively near to the subject or the scale of the object shown is of moderate size. In the context of the human figure, the body is usually shown from the knees or waist up and would fill most of the screen. Sometimes the term is used to refer to a shot in which subject and surroundings are given equal importance visually. Also called MIDSHOT. See also *PLAN AMÉRICAIN*.

Melodrama A somewhat indistinct film GENRE that may refer to WOMEN'S FILMS, movies about familial and domestic tensions, and WEEPIES. Originally the term, deriving from a combination of MUSIC (*melos*) and drama, referred to stage plays that, beginning in the late eighteenth century, used music to emphasize dramatic or particularly emotional moments. More recently the term refers to narratives in any popular form (film, TELEVISION, literature, theatre) that seem contrived or EXCESSIVE in emotion and sentimentality, in which dramatic conflicts and PLOT take precedence over CHARACTER and motivation, and in which there is a clear distinction between good and evil, heroes and villains. Many of D.W. Griffith's SHORT FILMS, as well as some of his later FEATURES such as *Broken Blossoms* (1919) and *Way Down East* (1920) were melodramas, carrying over from the stage such CONVENTIONS as the innocent young woman corrupted by a worldly man. Griffith, along with his CINEMATOGRAPHER G.W. 'Billy' Bitzer, created idealized IMAGES of Victorian womanhood with such STARS as Dorothy and Lillian Gish.

Melodrama tends to reduce history to the emotional problems of individual characters, as in the historical romance. FEMINIST critics have done much work on women's melodramas of the classic STUDIO SYSTEM era, such as *Stella Dallas* (dir. King Vidor, 1937) and *Mildred Pierce* (dir. Michael Curtiz, 1945), analysing how their representations of women are inscribed within domestic space and patriarchal IDEOLOGY. Scholars are drawn to melodrama for they are the only films that regularly feature female protagonists and are often narrated from their POINT OF VIEW. Applying both PSYCHOANALYTIC and MARXIST insights to melodrama as a form, Thomas Elsaesser has argued that melodrama's frequently excessive style is symptomatic of the repressed emotions of the characters, who metaphorically embody contradictions in bourgeois capitalism that spills over into the *MISE EN SCÈNE* (Elsaesser, 1973 in Grant, 1995). Other leftist critics have focused on family melodramas such as *All that Heaven Allows* (dir. Douglas Sirk, 1955), *Bigger Than Life* (dir. Nicholas Ray, 1956) and *Written on the Wind* (dir. Sirk, 1956), showing that the family becomes in melodrama the site of these tensions and contradictions. In the 1970s and 1980s, Rainer Werner Fassbinder, the most prolific DIRECTOR of the NEW GERMAN CINEMA, inspired by the films of Douglas Sirk, made a SERIES of politicized melodramas including *Why Does Herr R. Run Amok?* (1969) and *Ali:*

Fear Eats the Soul (1974, a loose REMAKE of Sirk's *All that Heaven Allows*, 1955). See also GAINSBOROUGH.

Further Reading: Brooks (1979), Byars (1991), Cook & Bernink (1999), Doane (1987), Gehring (1988), Gledhill (1987), Haskell (1973), Kaplan (1992), Landy (1991b), Lang (1989), Mulvey (1989), Petro (1989), Schatz (1981), Vardac (1949)

Merchandising The process of exploiting the title and IMAGES of a film – usually heavily advertised, big-budget films, whether BOX-OFFICE successes or not – in the MARKETING of associated products such as toys, games (including computer games), food and clothing, often aimed at children. A feature of the WALT DISNEY approach to cinema (and other media) since the 1950s, this became a more widespread practice with the advent of BLOCKBUSTERS in the 1970s NEW HOLLYWOOD. *Star Wars* (dir. George Lucas, 1977) and its SEQUELS (and PREQUELS) have been particularly successful at merchandising, to the point at which the films themselves are less important than the massive profits to be realized from ANCILLARY products.

Method, the An approach to performance closely associated with the ACTORS STUDIO and its most prominent DIRECTOR, Lee Strasberg. Its direct influence on screen ACTING was at its height during the late 1940s and 1950s in the work of actors such as Marlon Brando, Rod Steiger and Montgomery Clift, though it can be seen today in the screen performances of actors such as Robert De Niro, Dustin Hoffman and Meryl Streep. The Method was a different approach to creating a CHARACTER, changing the emphasis from outward impersonation to the inner creation of psychological truth. This approach to acting was heavily influenced by the work of Konstantin Stanislavski at the Moscow Arts Theatre in early twentieth century Russia. Although the two approaches have too often been regarded as entirely compatible, the central difference can be summed up by Strasberg's insistence that ACTORS work from their own lived experience to create the psychological states necessary to build a given fictional CHARACTER, whereas Stanislavski's work placed more store on the actor's ability to imagine.

Numerous anecdotes circulate through STAR biographies of the extremes to which certain actors have gone to gain the experience that their approach to the Method suggested they needed to play a particular part, ranging from Dustin Hoffman's sleeping rough on the streets of New York (to the disdain of Laurence Olivier – not a Method disciple) to prepare for key SCENES in *Marathon Man* (dir. John Schlesinger, 1976), to Robert De Niro's legendary weight gain to play the older Jake LaMotta in *Raging Bull* (dir. Martin Scorsese, 1980).

Metteur en scène French word for DIRECTOR (equally in film and theatre, though the term originates in theatre), the person who 'stages' or 'places things/ACTORS on stage'. Although in essence it is a purely descriptive term, it has acquired a somewhat negative connotation in relation to the term AUTEUR or AUTHOR. See also *MISE EN SCÈNE*.

MGM (Metro-Goldwyn-Mayer) The largest of the MAJORS in HOLLYWOOD during the era of the STUDIO SYSTEM. Marcus Loew, owner of a large chain of theatres, bought Metro Pictures Corporation in 1920 and in 1924 also bought Goldwyn Pictures and merged both companies with Louis B. Mayer's production company to form MGM. In the 1930s the STUDIO had more big-name STARS than any other. Among those under contract were Joan Crawford, Greta Garbo, Clark Gable, Spencer Tracy, Judy Garland and Jean Harlow. Directors who worked for the studio included George Cukor, Mervyn LeRoy, Victor Fleming, King Vidor and Vincente Minnelli. With Mayer as head of the studio, a position he was to hold for almost thirty years, and Irving Thalberg, the 'Boy Wonder', as production chief, MGM excelled in turning out lavish films with high PRODUCTION VALUES, as typified by *Grand Hotel* (dir. Edmund Goulding), which won the OSCAR for Best Picture at the 1932 ACADEMY AWARDS. David O. SELZNICK, who began working for MGM as a PRODUCER in 1933, would bring Alfred Hitchcock to Hollywood and produce, among other films, *Gone With the Wind* (dir. Victor Fleming, 1939), one of the studio's most successful movies.

After World War II MGM, like the other studios, suffered as a result of the PARAMOUNT DECISION and the erosion of the AUDIENCE due to the competition of TELEVISION. Other than the string of quality MUSICALS produced by its FREED UNIT, the company had only a few other major hits, including *Ben-Hur* (dir. William Wyler, 1959), *Doctor Zhivago* (dir. David Lean, 1965), and *2001: A Space Odyssey* (dir. Stanley Kubrick, 1968). In 1969 the company was bought by businessman Kirk Kerkorian. MGM moved away from film production and into the hotel business and relinquished its film DISTRIBUTION to UNITED ARTISTS in 1973, which it in turn subsumed in 1981. Since then the company has had several owners, including Atlanta broadcasting MOGUL Ted Turner, who has retained control of the studio's film library. The company still produces films, although without the consistency or quality that once defined it. See also BIG 5.

Further reading: Finler (1988), Fordin (1975), Gomery (1986), Mordden (1988), Schatz (1988)

Mickey-mousing Named after the style of early DISNEY sound CARTOONS, the term refers to the practice of using MUSIC to illustrate ACTION on the screen. As examples, Gorbman (1987) cites the musical rhythm that mimics the walk of Gypo Nolan (Victor McLaglen) in *The Informer* (dir. John Ford, 1935) and the harp glissando accompanying Carmen Sternwood's feigned collapse in *The Big Sleep* (dir. Howard Hawks, 1946). By extension, Mickey-mousing also refers to the practice of using music in a film to enhance the emotional effect of particular scenes, as with the inevitable lush strings in a romantic SCENE.

Microphone (mic, mike) An instrument for transforming the energy from SOUND waves into an electrical signal for recording or transmission. Initially, with the coming of sound to the film industry, microphones were very bulky, restricting ACTOR and CAMERA MOVEMENT, but miniaturization and other technical advances mean that very small microphones can now be worn and/or hidden by actors, and radio microphones have done away with the need for wired links. Directional or unidirectional microphones pick up sound in the direction in which they are aimed – typically to privilege dialogue over other sounds; ultradirectional microphones, sited at the end of long tubes, can pick up sound from a very restricted area; omnidirectional microphones pick up sound from any direction (useful, for example, for AMBIENT SOUND). Typically microphones are suspended over a SCENE being SHOT on a BOOM.

Midnight movie A particular kind of CULT FILM that attained its popularity through the unCONVENTIONal EXHIBITION practice of being screened late at night rather than during prime evening hours. *Night of the Living Dead* (dir. George A. Romero, 1968) was the first movie to attain cult status through repeated midnight showings.
Further reading: Hoberman & Rosenbaum (1983), Mendik & Harper (2000), Telotte (1991)

Midshot See MEDIUM SHOT.

Minimal cinema Loose term, related to minimalism in painting, applied to films in which little that is considered to be CINEMATIC — EDITING, CAMERA MOVE-MENT, for example — is undertaken by the film-makers. Among the best examples are early films by Andy Warhol, like *Sleep*, *Eat* (both 1964), *Empire* (1965) and *Couch* (1966), which employ a FIXED CAMERA and LONG TAKES with minimal ACTION — a kind of return to EARLY CINEMA. The term might also be applied to films like *Wavelength* (dir. Michael Snow, 1967) and *Berlin Horse* (dir. Malcolm LeGrice, 1970), in which very little conventional 'action' (though much else) takes place. Though the term has been applied to ART CINEMA directors like Robert Bresson, this is a rather confusing use. See also MATERIALIST FILM, STRUCTURAL FILM.
Further reading: Peterson (1994), Rees (1999), Sitney (1979)

Miramax American INDEPENDENT production and DISTRIBUTION company founded by brothers Bob and Harvey Weinstein, specializing in promoting independent films from both the USA and abroad whilst remaining financially successful. Among its prominent successes have been *sex, lies and videotape* (dir. Steven Soderbergh, 1989), *Reservoir Dogs* (dir. Quentin Tarantino, 1993), *The Piano* (dir. Jane Campion, 1993) and *Pulp Fiction* (dir. Tarantino, 1994). Miramax was bought by the DISNEY company in 1994 under terms supposedly guaranteeing its ability to act independently.

Mise en scène French term, taken from its usage in theatre, for 'staging' – literally, 'placed on stage' to designate the work done, largely by the DIRECTOR, in realizing in IMAGES the words of the SCRIPT. Bordwell and Thompson (1997) restrict, somewhat confusingly, the elements of *mise en scène* to the PROFILMIC EVENT — what is arranged on SET before shooting — DECOR, COSTUME, disposition of CHARACTERS and aspects of performance, COLOUR, LIGHTING — and make a separate category of the cinematographic qualities of CAMERA ANGLE distance, and CAMERA MOVEMENT. Since these two areas of decision-making are inevitably always in a dynamic relationship, most accounts of *mise en scène* incorporate these cinematographic elements. The term has entered English language film CRITICISM (acquiring some unnecessary hyphens, as *mise-en-scène*) largely because of the young 1950s French film critics, particularly those associated with *CAHIERS DU CINÉMA*, where its use was often not neutral or descriptive. When Antonin Artaud championed the term in the theatre in the 1930s, it was to elevate the role of the theatre director over that of the playwright, and this elevation of the role of the director carried over into the use of the term in French film criticism. Recognizing that many of the HOLLYWOOD directors championed by *Cahiers* critics had little say on the scripts they were assigned within the STUDIO SYSTEM, critical analysis focused on the director's control over what appeared on the screen — achieved through the *mise en scène* — rather than on the script. In many ways, therefore, *mise en scène* describes the work of the director, and *metteur en scène* is the French term for director. However, in a further twist, *Cahiers* critics distinguished between the AUTEUR or author, whose world view would be expressed through the *mise en scène*, and the *metteur en scène*, who lacked the world view or style which would make an *auteur*'s work distinctive and merely SHOT the script in a workmanlike way. Some of these semantic problems can be avoided by not using the term *mise en scène* at all. V.F. Perkins (1972) gives lengthy accounts of decision-making about *mise en scène* using 'direction' and 'director', which is the emphasis of the terms used in most other languages: *regia* (Italian), *regi* (Swedish and German), *direccion* (Spanish). French also uses the term *réalisateur,* stressing the 'realisation' of the script.

Further reading: Cook & Bernink (1999), Hillier (1985), Hillier (1986)

Mise en abîme   IMAGES or ideas recurring within a film which echo the film as a whole, the clearest example being a film being made within a film, when the processes of the film we are watching are played out in ways that comment on the film we are seeing. *Singin' in the Rain* (dir. Stanley Donen and Gene Kelly, 1952) is one of many examples, playing out as drama many of the classical conflicts of cinema – rivalry between STARS, stars versus ACTORS and actors versus STUDIOS – echoing some of the real conflicts involved in the making of *Singin' in the Rain* itself.

Mitchell   Brand name of several very reliable 35mm CAMERA models manufactured by the Mitchell Company. Manufactured for over fifty years, Mitchell cameras were standard equipment in film production. Although no longer produced, many are still in use.

Mix   The act of putting together all the elements involved in a film's final SOUND-TRACK, including dialogue, MUSIC and effects. Each of these can be composed of many different tracks so that the final track can be extremely complex, involving layer upon layer of sound from many different sources. When the audio track is complete, it has to be converted to an OPTICAL SOUND track to run alongside the film, a process usually referred to as DUBBING. Mix is also commonly used as a noun to describe the end product of the sound editing process, as in the 'final mix'.

Mockumentary   A pseudo-DOCUMENTARY; a fictional film that pretends to be, or is a PARODY of, a documentary. *David Holzman's Diary* (dir. Jim McBride, 1968), for example, is a hilariously funny commentary on the CONVENTIONS and IDEOLOGY of DIRECT CINEMA. The film pretends to be a direct cinema autobiography, but in fact is not, while *Forgotten Silver* (dir. Peter Jackson, 1995), a straight-faced account of a fictional New Zealander who is credited with pioneering virtually every important technique in film history, fooled much of that nation when it was first broadcast on national TELEVISION. Jackson's hoax demonstrated how willingly viewers accept the conventions and CODES of documentary as truth, despite the film's sometimes outlandish claims. *This is Spinal Tap* (dir. Rob Reiner, 1984) about a make-believe heavy metal rock band, is perhaps the most well known example.

Modernism   Wide-ranging term for a diverse set of art practices , but also relating to a major tendency in twentieth century political and philosophical thought, modernism incorporates major contradictions. On the one hand, modernism is often associated with a positive and optimistic strain of European philosophy stemming from the Enlightenment and its faith in humans' ability to control and change the world for the better, thus associating modernism with progressive political positions and the pursuit of a world capable of yielding better living conditions for all and a reverence for scientific progress and technology harnessed to relieving human beings from the oppression of the dangerous and repetitive tasks of industrialism. On the other hand, one of the central dramas of modernism has been the terrible price that civilization has paid for technological progress – world wars of mass destruction and the dehumanizing effects of technology. What unites the two strains – and best distinguishes modernism from late twentieth century art and POSTMODERNISM in particular – is a loosely defined belief in the pursuit of 'truth' and the ability of human beings to seek it in a variety of rational ways, one of which is the production of art.

Modernism in art is most clearly distinguished by a concern with form and REFLEXIVITY as shown in the novels of James Joyce or Virginia Woolf, and opposition to the apparent seamlessness of traditional REALISM that writers such as E.M. Forster had inherited from the Victorian tradition. Similarly, in painting, artists such as Picasso and the Cubists reacted against the illusion of three-dimensionality in traditional figurative landscape and portraiture. Modernism and the AVANT-GARDE are therefore closely linked terms, though modernism is a larger, all-embracing movement of which the avant-garde is an important part.

Modernist cinema is part of the tendency in art to explore its own formal qualities, exposing the technological means and the philosophical implications of the act of film-making and spectatorship, including the film-maker's power to look and observe and the VOYEURISTIC position of the film spectator. It also explores film's unique relationship to art's perpetual questioning of its power to represent the real: modernist film is profoundly anti-illusionist. Among the early key landmarks of modernist cinema are the Soviet films of Sergei Eisenstein, Vsevolod Pudovkin and Dziga Vertov, which foregrounded the element of EDITING. Here the film-makers emphasize rather than hide the 'collisions' produced by editing and create meaning – always in the service of progress as opposed to the reactionary nature of CONVENTIONAL realist forms – from MONTAGE rather then CONTINUITY.

Eisenstein's work is one instance of a modernist aesthetic explicitly associated with politics, though some would argue that radicalism in artistic form is in itself political in that it seeks to change the way we see the existing order. This notion underpinned modernism in the work of Jean-Luc Godard and others in France in the mid to late 1960s: Godard called for film-makers to 'make films politically' as opposed to 'make political films', coinciding with the rise of post-1968 film THEORY, which in itself had important roots in modernism. As Lapsley and Westlake put it, 'Colin McArthur spoke for a generation of film theorists when, in calling for a stylised cinema that would provoke a critical stance on the part of its AUDIENCE, he referred to the "pernicious belief (inherent in the realist position) that the world can be understood by contemplating its IMAGE"' (1988, p. 165).

Further reading: Hayward (1996), Smith in Hill & Church Gibson (1998).

Mogul A word derived from a term for an autocratic Far Eastern ruler which has come to be applied to those in positions of great financial power in the film industry (and other industries). Perhaps the term's heyday was the height of HOLLYWOOD STUDIO power: it is often associated with figures like Samuel GOLDWYN, Harry Cohn and Louis B. Mayer, whose exercise of their controlling influence over their respective studios certainly resembled the most autocratic of rulers.

Mondo film An EXPLOITATION FILM presented as a DOCUMENTARY or pseudo-documentary about odd and bizarre events and people around the world. The GENRE is named after *Mondo Cane* (dir. Gualtiero Jacopetti, 1961), the first of such films. By the 1980s mondo movies were emphasising sex and VIOLENCE, as in the notorious *Faces of Death* (dir. Rosilyn T. Scott, 1984), which purports to show a number of deaths onscreen and other bizarre death rituals such as an exclusive restaurant where a monkey is killed at one's table, after which the brain matter is scooped out and eaten. Also referred to as shockumentary.

Money shot Term used in the PORNOGRAPHIC FILM industry for the CLOSE-UP that provides both narrative and sexual climax by showing external ejaculation of the penis. As Williams (1989) points out, money shots are required by the logic of visible REPRESENTATION in the cinema as well as by the male GAZE that dominates cinematic construction. Money shots also provide a sense of narrative CLOSURE in sex SCENES and are the literalization of the phallic power around which such films tend to be organized. Also called 'cum shot.'

Monochrome film Generally used as another way to say BLACK-AND-WHITE FILM, although it can also denote a film in different shades of any single COLOUR.

Monogram American film company, established in 1930, one of the POVERTY ROW smaller STUDIOS that produced LOW-BUDGET films, often B MOVIES, destined for the bottom half of DOUBLE BILLS. Among Monogram's output was the SERIES of Bowery Boys COMEDIES and Charlie Chan MYSTERIES. Allied Artists was created in 1946 as a subsidiary to produce higher quality films. Both companies combined to become ALLIED ARTISTS PICTURES CORPORATION in 1958. FRENCH NEW WAVE DIRECTOR Jean-Luc Godard dedicated his first FEATURE, *A bout de souffle* (1959), to Monogram.

Monster movie See HORROR FILM, KAIJU EIGA (JAPANESE MONSTER MOVIE), SCIENCE FICTION FILM.

Montage From the French word *monter*, meaning 'to assemble,' the term has several meanings in the context of film. (1) a synonym for EDITING or DÉCOUPAGE generally. (2) In HOLLYWOOD cinema, a concentrated SEQUENCE using short SHOTS or such techniques as SUPERIMPOSITIONS, CUTS, JUMP CUTS, WIPES and DISSOLVES in order to create a kaleidoscopic effect to summarize a particular experience or transition in TIME, SPACE or situation (also known as VORKAPICH). Vorkapich montages are also EXPRESSIONIST sequences of intense subjective states of mind, as in Marlowe's drug-induced stupor in *Murder, My Sweet* (dir. Edward Dmytryk, 1944) or the title character's Busby Berkeley fantasy in *The Big Lebowski* (dir. Joel and Ethan Coen, 1998). (3) In European cinema, the process of editing the various shots together into the final film. This emphasis on the designed building of a film contrasts with the trimming for narrative efficiency suggested by the American term 'cutting' and suggests a greater appreciation of film as an artform. (4) THEMATIC MONTAGE or DIALECTICAL MONTAGE (also known as Soviet montage) as developed by Sergei

Eisenstein and others, that is, an arrangement of shots according to principles of collision, even DISCONTINUITY, so as to suggest a concept beyond that contained in the shots individually, as in Eisenstein's INTERCUTting of a preening peacock and details of Kerensky's elaborate uniform to suggest the man's vanity in *October* (1928). (5) Any sequence that creates a particularly noteworthy effect largely as a result of its editing. Thus the murder in the shower in *Psycho* (dir. Alfred Hitchcock, 1960) is a montage sequence (Hitchcock once remarked that his movies were 'little pieces of film glued together') as much as the Odessa Steps sequence in *Battleship Potemkin* (dir. Eisenstein, 1925). See also CONTINUITY EDITING, CROSSCUTTING, INVISIBLE EDITING, PARALLEL ACTION.

Motion Picture Association of America (MPAA) Originally, from 1922, the Motion Picture Producers and Distributors of America (MPPDA), renamed in 1945. The formation of the MPPDA was a response by the MAJOR STUDIOS to scandals like the Fatty Arbuckle case, which threatened the US film industry's IMAGE and to the danger that state and local GOVERNMENT might censor movies. Thus, the MPPDA, which under the leadership of former postmaster general Will Hays was known as the Hays Office, was an attempt to retain CENSORSHIP in the industry's control. Responding to renewed moral challenges and to the coming of SOUND, the MPPDA – guided by Catholics Daniel Lord and Martin Quigley – formulated the Motion Picture Production Code (sometimes known as the HAYS CODE) in 1930. The code was made mandatory in 1934 after pressure from the Catholic Legion of Decency and continuing explicit depictions of SEXUALITY. The Production Code Administration was headed by Catholic Joseph Breen (hence sometimes also known as the BREEN CODE). All major studio films now needed a Production Code seal of approval and fines were levied in cases of non-compliance. The MPPDA offered PRODUCERS advice on what was acceptable at all stages of production, from SCRIPT to FINAL CUT. Detailed rules about the depiction of sexuality and criminality were intended to preserve a wholesome image. Under pressure from STUDIOS faced with declining AUDIENCES and other problems, the Production Code was revised in 1956 and 1966, when it was given a RATING system, itself replaced by the current US advisory rating system in 1968, after which the Code was dropped.

Although the Production Code is the best known aspect of the MPPDA's work, it had a variety of other functions, including the CENTRAL CASTING Bureau and a TITLES Registration Bureau, which arbitrated title disputes. In 1945 the MPPDA became the Motion Picture Association of America (MPAA) and under president Eric Johnston became known as the Johnston Office, which was soon confronted with the aftermath of the PARAMOUNT DECISION, declining audiences, the gradual erosion of the Production Code and the need for expansion abroad – for which the Motion Picture Export Association was founded in 1945. Jack Valenti, head of MPAA and MPEA from 1966 and former aide to President Lyndon Johnson, created an even closer relationship between the industry and government, especially in opening up foreign markets to HOLLYWOOD products, and was responsible for the 1968 rating system. The MPEA and MPAA (whose members include all the current major studios) continue as major forces in the US film industry and in recent years have been particularly active in matters of copyright and piracy, increasingly important with the growth of VIDEO.

Further reading: Black (1994), Leff & Simmons (1990), Maltby (1995), Mast (1982)

Motion Picture Patents Company (MPPC) Name taken by the earliest attempt to establish monopoly control of the movie industry. Formed in 1908 by the nine major film companies of the time – Edison, BIOGRAPH, ESSANAY, Kalem, Lubin, Selig, Vitagraph, plus French companies Pathé and Star-Film and US distributor George Kline – to resolve battles over patents (particularly on Edison's patented PROJECTION equipment) and, effectively, to control film production, DISTRIBUTION and EXHIBITION. The MPCC – or simply 'The Trust' – also entered into an exclusive agreement with Eastman-Kodak for the supply of raw FILM STOCK. It was thus the earliest attempt to effect VERTICAL INTEGRATION in the industry and to stop INDEPENDENT production, distribution and exhibition by law and, when necessary, by physical force. Ironically, the New York based MPPC forced independents to move elsewhere, stimulating the movement of companies to the HOLLYWOOD area of Los Angeles. There they began to produce better and longer FEATURE-length films, overtaking the older MPPC companies and forming the basis of the later STUDIO SYSTEM. Independent producer-distributor-exhibitor William Fox (founder of the company which merged with Twentieth Century in 1935) brought the MPPC to court under the Sherman ANTI-TRUST Act in 1913. The MPPC was declared illegal in 1915, but was already a spent force, overtaken by the independents' move to Hollywood and production of longer films, and most member companies of the MPPC were already, or soon would be, out of business.
Further reading: Cook (1996), Izod (1988), Robinson (1996)

Mountain film Popular CYCLE of German cinema in the 1920s and early 1930s involving a CHARACTER or group of characters striving to climb or conquer a mountain. The physical stamina and determination required to scale mountains, as well as their monumentality and dwarfing of the individual (often shown in breathtaking LOCATION photography), seem to anticipate and suggest a Fascist aesthetic and sensibility. Dr Arnold Franck was the best known DIRECTOR of mountain films, some of which starred Leni Riefenstahl (*The White Hell of Pitz Palu*, co-dir. G.W. Pabst, 1929), who would go on to direct her own mountain film (*The Blue Light*, 1932) before making PROPAGANDA FILMS for the Third Reich (*Triumph of the Will*, 1936).

Movie brats The generation of young American DIRECTORS who rose to prominence in the NEW HOLLYWOOD of the 1970s. The films of Steven Spielberg, George Lucas, Brian de Palma, William Friedkin, Peter Bogdanovich, Francis Ford Coppola, Martin Scorsese and others were very different in style and theme, but tended, as Cawelti (in Grant, 1995) notes, to be revisionist GENRE movies that consciously reworked generic traditions. Several of these directors studied film history as well as film-making in the university context, including Scorsese (New York University), Coppola and Lucas (both UCLA).
Further reading: Pye & Myles (1979)

Movie palace, picture palace As the name implies, the more luxurious – often extremely and exotically so – movie theatres which replaced the NICKELODEONS during the 1910s and 1920s, accompanying the rise of the FEATURE FILM. Unlike STORE THEATRES and nickelodeons, which generally adapted existing buildings, movie palaces were purpose-built, larger and more comfortable – necessary for longer films. Although the biggest movie palaces were in big cities – the first, the

Strand, which opened in New York City in 1914, held almost 3,000, while the Roxy Theatre, also in New York City, opened 1927, held 6,200 – movie palaces were built in most towns and cities in the US and Europe. The 1920s and 1930s are generally considered the age of the movie palace. The large single auditorium continued as the main vehicle for cinema EXHIBITION into the 1960s, although many closed, or were adapted for other uses or demolished, as a result of the steep decline in AUDIENCES that began during the 1950s. From the 1970s, many remaining large cinema were divided into two or more smaller auditoria, or replaced by new MULTIPLEX theatres. See also DRIVE-INS, MALL CINEMAS.
Further reading: Gomery (1992), Robinson (1996)

Movie British film journal founded in 1962, *Movie* is historically important (as its polemically chosen name implied) as the journal which championed US directors such as Howard Hawks, Alfred Hitchcock, Otto Preminger and Samuel Fuller as AUTHORS and insisted on detailed analysis of *MISE EN SCÈNE* (though neither AUTEUR nor *mise en scène* were significant parts of their vocabulary). Though *Movie* was interested in other types of cinema, its main impact was in challenging the orthodoxy of SIGHT AND SOUND and other journals and launching a debate about attitudes to cinema and its critical analysis. Major British film critics associated with *Movie* include V.F. Perkins, Robin Wood and Charles Barr. *Movie* is still published intermittently.

Moviola (or Movieola) Brand name for a versatile EDITING machine, no longer in use, which could handle both IMAGE and SOUNDTRACKS, separately or in SYNC, run at different speeds, backwards and forwards, stop on an individual FRAME, and so on, and operated upright, as opposed to flat-bed machines like the STEENBECK. At one time the Moviola was so widely used that, like the Steenbeck, 'moviola' was used to describe any comparable editing machine.

Multi-media The term can mean any presentation using more than one medium, for example, a live theatre performance that also uses film FOOTAGE, slides and live and recorded SOUND. More commonly it refers to work designed to be run by a computer, recorded on some form of disc, using film footage, TEXT, sound and still IMAGES and which can be run and accessed in a variety of ways by its users. This has important implications for narrative construction since it is possible to offer users choices in the way that PLOT, characterization and other features develop, in short profoundly altering the TEXT/spectator relationship in ways only just beginning to be explored.
Further reading: Friedberg in Gledhill & Williams (2000)

Multiple image See SPLIT SCREEN.

Multiplex A cinema with several screens housed under one roof with a single BOX-OFFICE and often with other services such as MERCHANDISING and restaurants in common. Today the vast majority of films are screened in multiplexes and some credit their improved comfort, convenience and accessibility – they are often housed on out-of-town plots of land with abundant parking – with the resurgence in worldwide cinema attendances in the 1980s and 1990s. There is now a tendency for multiplexes to become bigger with increased emphasis on ancillary leisure facilities, resulting in an increased MARKETING emphasis on the complete cinema-going experience and attempts to reach out beyond traditional youth-orientated AUDIENCES by paying attention to basics like seating comfort and food accessibility. The largest multiplexes are sometimes referred to as megaplexes, especially in the USA. See also DISTRIBUTION, EXHIBITION, MALL CINEMAS.

Multiscreen The PROJECTION of IMAGES on to more than one SCREEN simultaneously. Though this could describe experiments such as Polyvision and 1920s French film-maker Abel Gance's use of triple screens – showing either a continuous image across all three screens, or different images on each screen – and processes like CINERAMA, it is more commonly associated with EXPERIMENTAL work. Malcolm LeGrice, for example, prefers his film *Berlin Horse* (1970) to be shown on two separate but adjacent screens, one showing the original FOUND FOOTAGE, and one showing the transformations brought about by the film-maker.

Music hall See VAUDEVILLE.

Music Music has been an essential part of the cinema almost from its inception. In the days of the NICKELODEON, piano players sat in the pit beneath the screen riffing their way through standard tunes and familiar classical pieces, underscoring the ACTION on the screen. The instrument initially engaged for the musical accompaniment of SILENT FILM was the piano, but it was soon replaced by the theatre organ, equipped with devices to imitate instruments as diverse as a snare drum and a harp. After World War I, it was not uncommon to find a full orchestra replacing the theatre organist. The performance of a musical overture often preceded the film screening, which in turn was accompanied with preselected passages from the popular classics, provided on cue sheets by the STUDIO. As early as 1910, Edison's *Frankenstein* was released with a cue sheet calling for music from such widely different sources as the folk song 'Annie Laurie' and Carl Maria von Weber's opera *Der Freischütz* (1821). D.W. Griffith's *Birth of a Nation* (1915) was one of the first films to feature music composed expressly for it. By the 1920s many major films were distributed with accompanying scores composed specifically for them.

In the 1930s it was standard practice for movies to have original music MIXED into their SOUNDTRACK. HOLLYWOOD studios developed their own music departments with house orchestras, with composers, like ACTORS, SCREENWRITERS and CINEMATOGRAPHERS, signed to exclusive contracts. STUDIOS unable to afford such expenses often resorted to the old practice of recycling the classics. Although soundtracks allowed for the inclusion of music, AMBIENT SOUND, sound effects and dialogue, it was the latter that assumed a privileged position as movies became increasingly focused upon conversation. As a result, the primary function of film music, original rather than borrowed, remained the same as it had been in the silent era: to provide emotional support to the STORY. The use of musical motifs to signify persons, places, things, events and emotions, an idea borrowed from the leitmotif principle of Wagnerian opera, became a CONVENTION of Hollywood film scoring. Indeed, actual Wagnerian leitmotifs have appeared in film scores from *Birth of a Nation* to *Apocalypse Now* (dir. Francis Ford Coppola, 1979). Such film composers as Miklos Rosza, Max Steiner and Alfred Newman excelled in employing the leitmotif style in their scores.

Music in film may also function thematically. In *Bonnie and Clyde* (dir. Arthur Penn, 1967), banjo music by Flatt and Scruggs is heard, like a refrain after every verse in conventional folk ballads, during chases and escapes, functioning as period music, helping to establish the time and place of the story, but also providing ironic COMMENTARY on the VIOLENCE taking place onscreen. As Gorbman (1987, pp. 2–3) notes, music taps deeply in cultural CODES, giving it rich cultural associations and potential meaning, a 'veritable language' that can contribute significantly to a film's overall meaning.

Perhaps the primary aesthetic question facing composers, as well as DIRECTORS, concerns the role of music in the film-making process. Should film music play a secondary role to the narrative and visual content, or should it have a noticeable expressive role of its own? Some composers who have written about the art of film music – Bernard Herrmann, Kurt Weill, Dmitri Tiomkin, Constant Lambert, Maurice Jaubert and Virgil Thomson, among others – argue for the integrity of the music itself even while acknowledging that music must serve a unified function within the entire movie. Certainly, the distinctive vision of many AUTEURS is due in large part to on-going collaboration between director and composer: Alfred Hitchcock and Bernard Herrmann, Federico Fellini and Nino Rota, Peter Greenaway and Michael Nyman are three notable examples.

Popular songs are an important part of film music. Songs originally from Tin Pan Alley and the musical stage were often interpolated into MAINSTREAM films. Two notable examples are 'As Time Goes By', originally written in 1931, which attained its greatest popularity only after its use in *Casablanca* (dir. Michael Curtiz, 1942), and 'Singing in the Rain', written in 1929 and resuscitated in the 1952 FREED UNIT musical *Singin' in the Rain* (dir. Gene Kelly and Stanley Donen). The popular appeal of catchy songs encouraged film-makers to incorporate potential hits into their movies, no matter how inappropriate the context. Thus Paul Newman, Robert Redford and Katharine Ross take time out from the PLOT of *Butch Cassidy and the Sundance Kid* (dir. George Roy Hill, 1969) to cavort on a bicycle to the musical accompaniment of B.J. Thomas singing 'Raindrops Keep Fallin' on My Head'. See also MICKEY-MOUSING, SOUND, SOUND FILM.

Further reading: Kalinak (1992), Prendergast (1977)

Music Video   A visual interpretation, recorded on VIDEO, of a popular piece of MUSIC. Originally designed to assist in the MARKETING of recorded popular music, music videos have become a form in their own right with the potential to sell in large numbers alongside all the other MERCHANDISE generated by the music industry. Probably the single most important outlet for music video is the American TELEVISION station MTV, reaching a large, mainly young, global AUDIENCE via CABLE and SATELLITE delivery systems. Arguably, music video has had some impact on audiences' expectations of film form through its use of rapid EDITING, off-beat CAMERA ANGLES and SPECIAL EFFECTS (which themselves have become much PARODIED clichés), often borrowed from AVANT-GARDE film. Whilst many music videos are produced on LOW BUDGETS, production costs can rival those of the expensive advertisements that they often resemble. O'Sullivan (1998, pp. 196–97) cites Michael Jackson's 'Thriller' (1983) video as one of the earliest music videos moving into big budget territory. Music video can have a more direct relationship with a FEATURE FILM when the music itself is part of the film's SOUNDTRACK; it is common for such a video to incorporate extracts from the film, becoming an extended advert for two products at once. Since the 1990s, music video production has become a major source of DIRECTORS in MAINSTREAM film production, as well as a source of income for more experimental film-makers.

Musical A film GENRE that includes any film with singing and/or dancing as an important element. The musical is most often structured around a romantic PLOT or several romances, as in *On the Town* (dir. Gene Kelly and Stanley Donen, 1949) or *Seven Brides for Seven Brothers* (dir. Donen, 1954), although they may also treat romance cynically, as in *Pennies from Heaven* (dir. Herbert Ross, 1981). Dance and song are artistic expressions of love and desire ideally appropriate to the medium of film. The musical, as DIRECTOR Jean-Luc Godard once said, is 'the idealisation of cinema'. As Dyer (1977, in Altman 1981, p. 177) argues, musicals depict a utopian world in which mind and body are united in perfect harmony, where intangible feeling is unproblematically externalized, given form as concrete yet gracious physical ACTION.

With the possible exception of COMEDY, the musical is the only genre that violates the otherwise rigid tenets of CLASSIC NARRATIVE CINEMA. Often the MUSIC accompanying singing STARS typically comes from nowhere, outside the DIEGESIS, and in popular cinema it is only in musicals and comedies where CHARACTERS sometimes address the spectator or CAMERA directly.

Although inspired by VAUDEVILLE, the music hall and musical theatre, the film musical quickly developed into a genre that was unique to the cinematic medium. No stage production could ever hope to achieve the kind of elaborate SPECTACLES displayed in a Busby Berkeley musical, which were never viewed from the POINT-OF-VIEW of the diegetic AUDIENCE in any case but unfolded for a mobile camera. WARNER BROS.'s *The Jazz Singer* (dir. Alan Crosland, 1927) is often cited as the first FEATURE-length SOUND film and the first musical, although it is mostly a SILENT FILM with a few musical SEQUENCES added. But it was an undeniable harbinger of what was shortly to follow. In the 1930s, numerous Broadway composers, including Irving Berlin, Cole Porter, Rodgers and Hart and the Gershwins, searching for steady employment, happily came to work in HOLLYWOOD on the musicals being churned out by the STUDIOS.

While René Clair experimented with the musical form in *Sous les toits de Paris* (*Under the Roofs of Paris*, 1930) and *A nous la liberté* (1931), early Hollywood musicals, beginning with *Broadway Melody* (dir. Harry Beaumont, 1929) featured the backstage FORMULA, or show-within-a-show format, as a narrative pretext for the inclusion of the production numbers. In the CYCLE of Warner Bros. musicals featuring Berkeley's production numbers in the early 1930s, which included *Footlight Parade* (dir. Lloyd Bacon), *Golddiggers of 1933* (dir. Mervyn LeRoy) and *Forty-Second Street* (dir. Bacon) (all 1933), the CHOREOGRAPHY, as well as the plot, were a response to the Depression in that everyone had to pull together and mount the show within the film, and all the chorines had to perform the dance numbers in synchronization. RKO's series of musicals with Fred Astaire and Ginger Rogers provided slim plots, but by the 1950s, often referred to as the genre's 'golden age,' musicals had become integrated – that is, the production numbers functioned to advance the plot and deepen the depiction of individual CHARACTERS – particularly in the musicals produced by the FREED UNIT at MGM, such as *The Pirate* (dir. Vincente Minnelli, 1948), *An*

American in Paris (dir. Minnelli, 1951), *Singin' in the Rain* (dir. Stanley Donen and Gene Kelly, 1952) and *The Bandwagon* (dir. Minnelli, 1953).

The musical began to founder in the 1960s, and the production of musicals in Hollywood dropped drastically. *West Side Story* (dir. Robert Wise, 1961), *My Fair Lady* (dir. George Cukor, 1964) and *The Sound of Music* (dir. Wise, 1965) were big hits, but most of the studios' BLOCKBUSTER musicals, such as *Star!* (dir. Wise, 1968) were huge flops. The misfortunes of the musical during this period can be linked to the widening gap between the kind of music used in the musicals that the studios were producing and the music that an increasing percentage of the movie-going audience was actually listening to – namely, rock 'n' roll (Grant 1986). Unlike most of the traditional musicals at the time, the two Beatles films directed by Richard Lester, *A Hard Day's Night* (1964) and *Help!* (1965), were commercial hits, as was *Woodstock* (dir. Michael Wadleigh, 1970). More recently, the musical has been replaced by MUSIC VIDEOS, the MONTAGE style of which films such as *Flashdance* (dir. Adrian Lyne, 1983) have sought to emulate. See also MASALA FILM.

Further reading: Altman (1987), Babington & Evans (1985), Cook & Bernink (1999), Feuer (1993), Murphy (1992), Schatz (1981)

Mutual Important STUDIO during the era of SILENT CINEMA. D.W. Griffith left BIOGRAPH in 1913 to work for Mutual, already located in HOLLYWOOD, because the company offered him more creative freedom. Charles Chaplin also worked for Mutual, where he made 12 films including *One A.M.* (1916), *The Pawnshop* (1916) and *Easy Street* (1917). In 1915, Mutual merged with KEYSTONE and Reliance to form the important Triangle Film Corporation, for which Griffith, Thomas Ince and Mack Sennett all worked. An INDEPENDENT, The Mutual Film Company did not belong to the monopolistic MPPC (MOTION PICTURE PATENTS CORPORATION).

Mystery film Like the DETECTIVE FILM, the mystery film involves a search for clues in the attempt to solve a crime or stop a series of crimes from continuing, identify the criminal, and explain his motivation. Because most mystery films focus on the CHARACTER who seeks to solve the narrative enigma, usually a detective or PRIVATE EYE, the mystery film is often considered synonymous with the GENRE of the detective film, although there are some mystery films in which the detective is only a minor character, as in *Psycho* (dir. Alfred Hitchcock, 1960). See also CRIME FILM.

Further reading: Cawelti (1976)

Myth Traditionally the term refers to a society's shared STORIES, normally involving Gods and heroes, that explain the nature of the universe and the relation of the individual to it, and that account for a society's rituals, institutions and values. In ancient civilizations myths were transmitted orally and later in writing, but beginning in the twentieth century myths increasingly have been disseminated through the mass media. Theorist Roland Barthes, in his SEMIOTIC analysis of various POPULAR CULTURE artifacts, shows how mythic CONNOTATIONS are conveyed by mundane consumer products (Barthes, 1972). In the context of film, GENRES are often referred to as cultural myths to help explain their reliance on FORMULA, convention and STEREOTYPE. From this perspective, genre movies tend to be read as ritualized endorsements of DOMINANT IDEOLOGY. Thus, the classic WESTERN may be understood as a mythic

endorsement of American individualism, colonialism and racism, while SCIENCE FICTION films of the 1950s as mythic expressions of nuclear anxiety.
Further reading: Grant (1995)

N

Nagra Swiss-made analogue tape recorder, commonly used for recording SOUND in films. Introduced in 1958, it quickly became the preferred tape recorder for DIRECT CINEMA and CINÉMA VÉRITÉ film-makers. As Ellis (1989, p. 219) explains, 'When crystal synchronization was added, there was no longer even the need for a cable between CAMERA and recorder. Around 1960 vacuum tubes, which consumed a lot of energy, were replaced by transistors and the weight of sound recorders was reduced from 200 pounds to 20 pounds.'

Narration A story-telling device involving a VOICE-OVER from one of the CHARACTERS in the film or from an OMNISCIENT NARRATOR. The latter is sometimes used when the film is adapted from a novel and the narration approximates to the voice of the original AUTHOR, commenting on the ACTION or filling in awkward gaps in the narrative. The amount of narration can vary from running intermittently throughout a FEATURE FILM to appearing only at one or two key moments.

Narration is often seen as an inevitable part of DOCUMENTARY film-making, where explanation and COMMENTARY on the visual IMAGES is usually an integral part of the desire to explain or present a complex argument. Even within documentary, though, there are instances where a superimposed narration is clearly intrusive and it is desirable to let the action speak for itself via live recorded sound. Narration can easily become a form of telling an AUDIENCE what to think rather than letting documentary subjects speak for themselves.

It is perhaps even more common to see narration as an intrusion into feature films, and to regard it as a somewhat lazy way of solving narrative problems, a poor alternative to finding subtler ways of showing events, though there are countless examples of narration working as a subtle counterpoint to other narrative devices, as in *Badlands* (dir. Terrence Malick, 1973) where the young Sissy Spacek's innocent but eerily dull voice-over emphasizes the distorted comic-book vision of the world of the two serial-killer characters. Frequently narration is used as a framing device, occurring at the beginning of a film and then either intermittently or not at all until the very end, with the effect of being led into a STORY by an individual, becoming immersed in it, but then being reminded of the perspective that we have been implicitly witnessing at the end of the film, as in *Brief Encounter* (dir. David Lean, 1945).

Narration also refers to the range of strategies used by a film-maker to tell a story and not simply the variations on a single device referred to above. See also CLASSICAL HOLLYWOOD CINEMA.
Further reading: Aumont (1992), Branigan (1984), Branigan (1992), Stam (2000)

Narrative See CLASSICAL HOLLYWOOD CINEMA.

Narrative space This can include not only the actual LOCATIONS shown to us on the screen where ACTION occurs, but also places that are only implied or suggested by the PLOT and which are crucial to the STORY. As Bordwell and Thompson (1997) put it: 'Normally the place of the story action is also that of the plot, but sometimes the plot leads us to infer other locales as part of the story. We never see Roger Thornhill's home [in *North by Northwest,* dir. Alfred Hitchcock, 1959] or the colleges that kicked Kane out [in *Citizen Kane,* dir. Orson Welles, 1941]. Thus the narrative may ask us to imagine spaces and actions that are never shown.' See also SPACE.

Narrative theory The attempt to systemize the principles by which films structure narrative logic and meaning, and to explain the implications, in terms of RECEPTION and IDEOLOGY, of such structures and principles. Several theorists have attempted to provide totalizing theories of narrative structure in the cinema, as in literature, particularly CLASSIC NARRATIVE CINEMA, which has been a particular focus for narrative analysis because of its refined economy of storytelling techniques, the MYTHic dimensions of its GENRE films, and the pervasive influence of HOLLYWOOD on NATIONAL CINEMAS around the world. Bellour, among others, has argued that classic narrative films are patriarchal texts that share a common OEDIPAL TRAJECTORY, reinforcing a traditional notion of gender and sexual difference (Bellour, 1979). From a FORMALIST perspective, Bordwell argues that narrative structure and comprehension involves an engagement of the spectator with the TEXT in a cognitive process consisting of the framing and resolving of hypotheses based on a succession of enigmas (Bordwell, 1985). Christian Metz has analysed cinematic structure from a SEMIOTIC perspective, seeking to identify the 'language' of filmic narration (Metz, 1974), while Branigan (1984, 1992) and Kawin (1977) have theorized narratorial SUBJECTIVITY in film. See also CLOSURE, PLOT.
Further reading: Armes (1976), Bordwell, Staiger & Thompson (1985), Browne (1982), Burch (1973), Chatman (1978), Heath (1981)

Narrator The CHARACTER (or implied character) who delivers a VOICE-OVER narration at various stages of a film. The use of a narrator is particularly common in DOCUMENTARIES, but also widely used in fiction with varying degrees of success. In the latter case the narrator is either a central character in the film or an abstract authorial voice, as in the case of using the device of a writer's original words over visual IMAGES when a SCREENPLAY has been adapted from a work of prose fiction. See also NARRATION.

National cinema At its simplest the term refers to cinema produced within a particular country, though even here there are often problems of definition: a film might have a British setting, DIRECTOR and CAST but major US investment. However, national cinemas have often been promoted on this level alone as a counter to the HEGEMONY of HOLLYWOOD in particular, and the US in general, over world cinema. At various historical moments there have been imperatives promoting both European national cinemas and those of emerging POST-COLONIAL countries, and film studies has often used national labels in ways that distort the reality of identity in a given country. The idea of a national cinema has begun to be seen in more complex and problematic ways: for example, it is now extremely difficult to talk of a British national cinema in the face of recent political changes giving a degree of autonomy to Scotland, Northern Ireland and Wales and, more directly, in the face of emerging distinctive cinemas in those regions.

Equally, it is now more difficult to see other national cinemas as a positive force against world Hollywood domination. The rise of a strong US INDEPENDENT sector, the increase in the number of black and Hispanic directors and the growth of the SUNDANCE and other FESTIVALS aimed at promoting diversity in US cinema has made older definitions based on Hollywood harder to sustain. At the same time, supposedly distinctive national cinemas such as in France have increasingly had to compromise in order to seek a commercial international market. The increasing domination of global MARKETING and multi-national companies, together with the flow of peoples across national boundaries, has also raised profound questions about the status of national identities. Against this, there have been recent efforts to ensure that national film production survives, such as the recent resurgence in British film production. The big question is whether the survival of a production base will mean the survival on film of IMAGES and ideas which represent anything distinctively national.

National Film Archive A major international archive, the British national film ARCHIVE was founded (as was the National Film Library) in 1935 under Ernest Lindgren, as a division of the BRITISH FILM INSTITUTE (BFI). It is now officially the National Film and TELEVISION Archive, with its main offices, record keeping and viewing facilities within the BFI in London and extensive film conservation and storage facilities outside London, particularly at the J. Paul Getty, Jr. Conservation Centre in Berkhamsted, Hertfordshire.

National Film Board of Canada (NFB) GOVERNMENT film bureau created by federal act in 1939 to make DOCUMENTARY films to 'interpret Canada to Canadians and the rest of the world.' The founding director of the NFB was John Grierson, who pioneered government sponsorship of documentary film production at the British EMPIRE MARKETING BOARD and GPO. The Board's initial focus was the production of war PROPAGANDA FILMS, but in the early 1960s both French-Canadian and English-Canadian UNITS were involved in pioneering work in DIRECT CINEMA and CINÉMA VÉRITÉ. While known primarily for the quality of its documentary films, the NFB has also produced many award-winning EXPERIMENTAL FILMS by such film-makers as Norman McLaren and some excellent FEATURES, beginning in English Canada with *Nobody Waved Goodbye* (dir. Don Owen) in 1964 and in Québec with the FRENCH NEW WAVE-inspired *A tout prendre* (dir. Claude Jutra) in 1963. The NFB still produces films today, although its output has been seriously curtailed by funding cutbacks. See also OBSERVATIONAL CINEMA.
Further reading: Evans (1984), Evans (1991), Jones (1981)

National Film Theatre A major REPERTORY CINEMA owned and run by the BRITISH FILM INSTITUTE, sited on the Thames South Bank in London as part of the UK's largest arts complex. The purpose of the National Film Theatre is to make available worldwide non-commercial cinema and screen film classics. Much of the programming is themed, including RETROSPECTIVES of individual DIRECTORS' work, GENRE or NATIONAL CINEMAS, often linked to lectures and master-classes by a range of practitioners.

NATO Not, in this case, the better known North Atlantic Treaty Organisation but the powerful US National Association of Theatre Owners, representing film exhibitors. Its functions include keeping members abreast of developments in the industry and dealing with movie PRODUCERS and DISTRIBUTORS represented by the MOTION PICTURE ASSOCIATION OF AMERICA (MPAA). See also EXHIBITION.

Naturalism Naturalism has its roots in nineteenth century theatre and the novel and is closely related to that era's interest in science, especially Darwinian interest in man's origins or true nature: the naturalist dramatist can be related to the naturalist as someone studying nature by closely observing and recording it. The crucial question is whether by closely observing in this way we can get any closer to the reality of a complex human being; most subsequent MODERNIST and AVANT-GARDE artistic practice has resorted to other means of seeking the 'real'. The insistence of naturalist dramatists that the truth about the world can be better understood by closely observing and re-creating it on a stage or on film has led to the frequent use of the terms REALISM and naturalism as if they meant identical things. However, if realism means something much broader, embracing ways of trying to discover and represent 'the real', naturalism can seen as a more precise and narrowly focused strategy, involving the faithful recreation of the exact conditions of a location, detailed mimetic performances and the AUDIENCE as observer looking through a one-way mirror as if watching a scientific experiment. The influence of naturalism on film has been widespread and diffuse. The MAINSTREAM twentieth century tradition of cinema has been partly based upon ever more sophisticated striving to reproduce the world in ways that will convince an audience that what they are seeing is 'real' or a copy of life.

Naturalism's influence on screen ACTING is a confused line via Konstantin Stanislavski and the METHOD, but the faithful recreation of the minutiae of human behaviour that has become for many the benchmark of great acting owes much to naturalist thinking. More directly, several naturalist fiction classics have been made into FEATURE FILMS, including Theodore Dreiser's American naturalist classic *An American Tragedy*, filmed by Josef von Sternberg in 1931. Ironically, Dreiser saw the film as betraying some of the essential tenets of his naturalist vision in the way it played down the influence of environment upon the tragic actions of the leading characters. Several of Emile Zola's works have also been filmed, most memorably *La Bête humaine* (dir. Jean Renoir, 1938).
Further reading: Williams (1983)

Nature Film A type of DOCUMENTARY film focusing on wildlife, flora or fauna, in its natural habitat. THE NATIONAL FILM BOARD OF CANADA (NFB) was known for its nature films, as was WALT DISNEY in the United States. One of the great AUTEURS of the nature film was Swedish film-maker Arne Sucksdorff (*A Summer's Tale*, 1941). More recently, nature films have been supplanted by television SERIES, a speciality of BBC Television, although occasionally a FEATURE film such as *The Bear* (dir. Jean-Jacques Annaud, 1989), about a bear cub who finds a new protector in a giant Kodiak, or *Microcosmos* (dir. Claude Nuridsany and Marie Perennou, 1996), about the world of insects, has success in the MAINSTREAM market.
Further reading: Mitman (2000)

Negative Strip of film, exposed or printed, in which dark and light areas are reversed (and in COLOUR film, in addition, colours are complementary to those SHOT). Positive PRINTS made from the negative restore dark, light and colours to their

original form. EDITING is done on a positive WORKPRINT; when editing is completed, the negative is cut to precisely match the FINAL CUT. DUPLICATE NEGATIVES (or DUPES) (sometimes called release negatives) are made from a master print of the negative, and RELEASE PRINTS are made from these, the master negative being preserved for making additional dupe negatives or prints.

Negative cost The cost of a completed negative, or the total cost of the production of a film up to the stage of a completed negative, i.e. excluding subsequent costs in making RELEASE PRINTS, publicity, DISTRIBUTION and EXHIBITION.

Negative pickup Deal or contract in which a DISTRIBUTOR 'picks up' a film in the form of a final NEGATIVE, on which all work is complete, after which all that remains is to strike RELEASE PRINTS. The distributor is thus relieved of worries about PRODUCTION or costs, since the sum to be paid for the completed film has been agreed; a film's PRODUCERS can use the agreement to raise funds for production.

Neo-noir Term describing contemporary films made in the manner of FILM NOIR and employing many of that GENRE's stylistic and narrative CONVENTIONS. The first important neo-noir was Roman Polanksi's *Chinatown* (1974), a paranoid THRILLER set in Los Angeles in the 1930s, the city and time particularly associated with film noir. Since Polanski's film there has been a consistent stream of neo-noirs, with DIRECTORS such as John Dahl (*Red Rock West*, 1993; *The Last Seduction*, 1994) particularly associated with the genre. Also, the recent development of the EROTIC THRILLER, popularized by the enormous success of *Fatal Attraction* (dir. Adrian Lyne, 1987), has encouraged the production of neo-noirs.
Further reading: Martin (1997)

Neo-realism Italian film movement, from toward the end of World War II to the mid-1950s, focusing on real social problems and the dailiness of life in both style and content. 'There must be no gap between life and what is on the screen,' declared Cesare Zavattini (1953), neo-realist SCREENWRITER and leading spokesman of the group that included Roberto Rossellini, Vittorio de Sica and Luchino Visconti. Like the fiction of American NATURALIST writers that in part influenced these Italian film-makers, neo-realism was strongly REALIST in its techniques. They were frequently shot on LOCATION – the film that initiated the movement, *Roma, Città Aperta* (*Rome, Open City*, dir. Rossellini, 1945), about the Italian Resistance movement, contained street SCENES showing actual German soldiers – and were shot surreptitiously with FAST FILM STOCK, AVAILABLE LIGHTING, and a mix of non-professional and professional ACTORS. SOUNDTRACKS were generally post-DUBbed. The DOCUMENTARY look of neo-realist films began as an economic necessity, since film-makers lacked access to STUDIO facilities during Mussolini's Fascist regime, but became an aesthetic choice opposed to the slick, artificial look of studio-produced films that, they felt, falsified reality.

Many neo-realist films use LONG TAKES and CAMERA MOVEMENT to preserve, as Bazin (1971) argues, the SPACE and TIME of PROFILMIC events. EDITING is generally unobtrusive and INVISIBLE. In a celebrated SCENE of *Umberto D* (dir. Vittorio de Sica, 1952), the pregnant young housemaid wakes up in the morning, goes down the hall into the kitchen, and in several lengthy SHOTS is shown going through the various mundane ACTIONS of her morning coffee ritual. Narrative construction tends to be loosely PLOTted and lack CLOSURE, as in *Umberto D* where the dispossessed and impoverished Umberto fails to find any solution to his problems.

Several neo-realist film-makers were Marxists, and saw their work as socially responsible examinations of immediate social problems such as poverty and home-lessness, but most neo-realist films were deeply humanist in their vision, celebrating the resiliency of people in enduring hardship with dignity. At the end of *Bicycle Thieves* (dir. de Sica, 1948), despite the son's disillusionment at witnessing his father's failed attempt to steal a bicycle, the boy slips his hand into his father's as they walk away in the crowd into an uncertain future.

Neo-realism had a profound influence on other NATIONAL CINEMAS, including BRITISH NEW WAVE films such as *This Sporting Life* (dir. Tony Richardson, 1963). By the mid 1950s however, the neo-realist movement was at an end, the result of improved economic conditions and pressure from the church and GOVERNMENT to depict more patriotic, that is, positive, IMAGES of Italy. Today the term is used to describe other fiction films that take a stark, unromantic view of their subject, such as *Pixote* (dir. Hector Babenco, 1981), which unflinchingly shows the horrors of life for street kids in Rio de Janiero. See alo *CINECITTÀ*.
Further reading: Armes (1971), Bondanella (1993), Marcus (1986), Overby (1978), Sitney (1995)

New American Cinema   Though the term has been used to describe NEW HOLLYWOOD or INDEPENDENT post-1960s US cinema, its specific reference is the grouping of late 1950s and early 1960s New York film-makers – Shirley Clarke, Lionel Rogosin, Robert Frank, Emile de Antonio and others – gathered around Jonas Mekas and the journal *FILM CULTURE*. It considered official cinema morally and aesthetically corrupt and bankrupt, and supported the LOW-BUDGET independent, often 16MM, cinema emerging in the US and elsewhere (such as the FRENCH NEW WAVE and British FREE CINEMA). The 1959 Independent Film Award went to *Shadows* (dir. John Cassavetes, 1959) – 'a film that doesn't betray life or cinema, whereas HOLLYWOOD films (and we mean Hollywoods all over the world) reach us beautiful and dead' (Mekas in Sitney, 1971, p. 75). As the 1960s progressed, Mekas increasingly favoured more obviously UNDERGROUND films.
Further reading: James (1989)

New Cinema   Sometimes used as a direct translation of '*das neue Kino*' (see NEW GERMAN CINEMA), but also a loose term for any innovative cinema movement, much used during the 1960s to describe the sense of renewal in cinema, following the FRENCH NEW WAVE and new developments in DOCUMENTARY and a sense of crisis in HOLLYWOOD (as well as radical changes in world politics), that combined aesthetic innovation and social CRITICISM. Manifestations of New Cinema included: Brazilian *CINEMA NÔVO* and other developments in Latin American cinema; the CZECH NEW WAVE; Dusan Makavejev's work in Yugoslavia; Nagisa Oshima's work in Japan; NEW AMERICAN CINEMA, CINÉMA VÉRITÉ and DIRECT CINEMA work in documentary.
Further reading: Cameron (1970), Marcorelles (1973), Nowell-Smith (1996)

New German Cinema   Late 1960s to early 1980s German film movement featuring innovative, striking films by a group of young DIRECTORS, including Rainer Werner Fassbinder, Volker Schlöndorff, Wim Wenders, Werner Herzog, Alexander

Kluge, Doris Dörrie, Hans Jürgen Syberberg, Margarethe von Trotta, and Jean-Marie Straub and Danièle Huillet. The movement also produced a number of STARS of ART CINEMA, including Brunzo Ganz, Hannah Schygulla and Klaus Kinski.

As a result of Germany's defeat in World War II, its division by the Allied forces and the dismantling of its national film industry, German cinema was decimated. In reaction, 26 young film-makers, writers and artists in 1962 signed the Oberhausen Manifesto, attacking the established, foreign-controlled film industry and calling for a new indigenous cinema. In 1965 the West German GOVERNMENT established the Kuratorium Junger Deutscher Film (Board of Young German Film) to provide loans for first-time FEATURE FILM directors and in 1966 opened the Berlin Film and TELE-VISION Academy. New work began to appear, and a number of directors – promoting themselves, like the film-makers of the FRENCH NEW WAVE that in part inspired them, as AUTEURS (Kluge's *autorenkino*) – began to achieve international success. In 1980, Schlöndorff's *The Tin Drum* (1979), an ADAPTATION of the novel by Günter Grass, won the OSCAR for Best Foreign Film.

The New German films were widely divergent in style and theme, although Elsaesser suggests that they shared 'a revulsion against the commercial film industry' (1989, p. 25). Many of the films directly examined IDEOLOGY and the nature of the German State. Fassbinder combined MELODRAMA with a BRECHTIAN style and political content in such films as *Why Does Herr R. Run Amok?* (1969), *Ali: Fear Eats the Soul* (1974) – inspired by Douglas Sirk's *All that Heaven Allows* (1955) – and *The Marriage of Maria Braun* (1978), perhaps his most commercially successful film. The New German Cinema also featured lyrical, romantic work, most notably in Herzog's *Aguirre, the Wrath of God* (1973), *The Enigma of Kaspar Hauser* (1974) and *Nosferatu the Vampyre* (1979).

By the early 1980s the New German Cinema had lost much of its impetus, with films unable to find a domestic AUDIENCE and commercial success (to a large extent because of American control of the industry), and directors finding it more difficult to receive funding for overtly political films. Some left to work abroad; the most prolific film-maker, Fassbinder, died early, age 36, in 1982.

Further reading: Corrigan (1994), Franklin (1983), Knight (1992), Philips (1984), Sandford (1980)

New Hollywood Term used, rather loosely, to describe HOLLYWOOD after the STUDIO SYSTEM. Although Hollywood at the start of the twenty-first century bears striking similarities to 1920s–1950s Hollywood, the differences are also striking enough to talk of a 'new' Hollywood. It is difficult to date precisely the end of the studio system, and even more difficult to date the start of New Hollywood. Should it be dated from the 1948 PARAMOUNT DECISION, the beginning of the end of VERTICAL INTEGRATION and the growth of INDEPENDENT PRODUCTION in the 1950s? Or perhaps from the crises and first wave of take-overs of MAJOR STUDIOS in the 1960s? The most accepted current view (following Thomas Schatz, in Collins *et al.*, 1993), is to date New Hollywood from the advent of BLOCKBUSTERS and SATURATION RELEASE (and other MARKETING ploys), exemplified by the first films to take over $100 million at the BOX-OFFICE, *Jaws* (dir. Steven Spielberg, 1975), and *Star Wars* (dir. George Lucas, 1977), which brought the industry back into profitability and ushered in further take-overs and CONGLOMERATION. See also MOVIE BRATS.

Further reading: Balio (1990), Cook (1996), Kramer in Hill & Church Gibson (1998), Hillier (1993), Hollows *et al.* (2000), Izod (1988), Wyatt and Lewis in Lewis (1998),

Litwak (1986), Smith, Maltby, Gomery and Balio in Neale & Smith (1998), Gomery in Nowell-Smith (1996), Pye & Myles (1979), Wasko (1994)

New Line Founded by Robert Shaye in 1967 to distribute foreign films in the USA, New Line became a signficant INDEPENDENT production company as well, largely as a result of its success with *A Nightmare on Elm Street* (dir. Wes Craven, 1984) and its five SEQUELS. In 1991 New Line founded Fine Line Features to produce and distribute quality films, which have included *The Player* (dir. Robert Altman, 1992) and the DOCUMENTARY *Hoop Dreams* (dir. Steve James, Peter Gilbert and Frederick Marx, 1994). The Turner Broadcasting System purchased New Line in 1995, after which Turner merged with TIME WARNER, which in turn merged with AOL.

New Wave See BRITISH NEW WAVE, CZECH NEW WAVE, FRENCH NEW WAVE.

New World Pictures American INDEPENDENT film production and DISTRIBUTION company begun by DIRECTOR and PRODUCER Roger Corman and his brother Gene in 1970. New World initially concentrated on LOW-BUDGET EXPLOITATION FILMS and TEENPICS, beginning with *The Student Nurses* (dir. Stephanie Rothman, 1970), which was followed by four SEQUELS. The company was known for allowing young directors the opportunity to make films. Rothman, Joe Dante, Paul Bartel, Peter Bogdanovich, Jonathan Demme and John Sayles all began their careers at New World or worked there early on. The company also dabbled in the distribution of European art films, among them *Cries and Whispers* (dir. Ingmar Bergman, 1973) and *Amarcord* (dir. Federico Fellini, 1974). Corman sold the company in 1983, shortly after which it went out of business.
Further reading: Corman (1990), Hillier (1993)

Newsreel Form of DOCUMENTARY combining news FOOTAGE, interviews and dramatic reconstructions that appeared in weekly or biweekly instalments of approximately ten minutes in theatres preceding the FEATURE FILMS. Featuring rapid EDITING, a VOICE-OF-GOD NARRATION and MUSIC, newsreels comprised a string of discrete STORIES that tended to focus on the spectacular, often with a blatant editorial bias. The newsreel first appeared in 1906, when *Day by Day* was screened daily in Leicester Square. In 1910 Frenchman Charles Pathé introduced Pathé News in the US, which was so popular that, according to Lewis Jacobs (1979), within two years Hearst, UNIVERSAL, PARAMOUNT and FOX began producing their own newsreels. One of the most famous newsreels was *The March of Time*, produced by Louis de Rochemont for Time-Life from 1935 to 1951, PARODIED in the *News on the March* sequence at the beginning of *Citizen Kane* (dir. Orson Welles, 1941). Newsreels began to fade out in the 1950s as a result of TELEVISION, which offered a visual package of news, whether mundane or monumental, more immediately or even live. Universal News was the last American company to fold (1967), while British Movietone News and Pathé News struggled on into the 1970s. See also KINO PRAVDA.
Further reading: Fielding (1972)

Nickelodeon Early type of cinema theatre, whose original admission was a nickel (5 cents), while odeon is Greek for theatre. The Nickelodeon, the first proper cinema theatre, opened in Pittsburgh, 1905. Like STORE THEATRES, nickelodeons, converted from shops, halls or shopping arcades, showed only films – ONE-REELERS and TWO-REELERS in continuous programmes lasting up to an hour – but tended to be larger, seating about 100 people. By 1906 there were 1000 nickelodeons in the US, and by 1910 10,000, with similar developments in Great Britain and elsewhere. As film programmes grew longer, especially with the introduction of FEATURE FILMS, nickelodeons were in turn replaced by MOVIE PALACES.

Further reading: Gomery (1992), Izod (1988), Mast (1982), Robinson (1996), Thompson & Bordwell (1994)

Nitrate film Until 1951 FILM STOCK used for commercial 35MM film-making used EMULSION on a cellulose nitrate base, which could deterioriate rapidly and was highly flammable, causing frequent fires in cinemas and EDITING rooms and the consequent loss forever of many films. In 1951, SAFETY FILM, with a more stable and much less flammable acetate base, was introduced.

Non-camera film An experimental type of film made without the strip of film passing through a CAMERA, generally by the film-maker painting or scratching straight on to CELLULOID, FRAME-by-frame or ignoring frame lines. In *Colour Box* (dir. Len Lye, 1935) and *Begone Dull Care* (dir. Norman McLaren, 1949) paint is applied to the FILM STOCK; in *Particles in Space* (dir. Lye, 1979) the EMULSION is scratched. Lye referred to his work as 'direct film' – a good description for Stan Brakhage's unique *Mothlight* (1963), which is neither wholly REPRESENTATIONal nor wholly abstract. Natural detritus like leaves, grasses and moth wings were stuck between two strips of transparent tape then printed on to film. Another method of non-camera film-making, used by Man Ray for *Retour à la raison* (1923), involves placing objects on the surface of raw stock and exposing it to light. See also ABSTRACT FILM.

Non-diegetic See DIEGESIS.

Non-fiction film A term sometimes used in preference to DOCUMENTARY film.

Non-linear editing Term used to distinguish VIDEO EDITING done on computer hard disks from LINEAR EDITING. Computer hard disks store data digitized from a video tape in a random order and allow virtually instant access to any part of it. Sophisticated software allows the EDITOR a range of choices and effects.

Non-theatrical See THEATRICAL.

Nouvelle vague See FRENCH NEW WAVE.

Novelization The process of writing and publishing a novel based on a successful film – a reverse of the process of adapting a successful novel into a film – an ANCILLARY activity which has become more popular with the advent of BLOCKBUSTERS and CONGLOMERATES able to more fully exploit BOX-OFFICE success in different media.

Nudie, nudist film See PORNOGRAPHY.

O

Oater Slang and trade term for FORMULA WESTERN during the STUDIO ERA.

Observational cinema Term used to describe DOCUMENTARY film-making in which the CAMERA follows PROFILMIC events as they are happening and seeks to reveal truths about them. ETHNOGRAPHIC FILM, DIRECT CINEMA and CINÉMA VÉRITÉ are all forms of observational cinema, in which the question of whether and to what extent the camera exploits, manipulates or documents its social ACTORS are crucial. Observational films seem relatively truthful in large part because they are not constrained by earlier technological limitations which required more overt manipulation, such as the dramatic reconstruction of events or the use of a VOICE-OF-GOD NARRATOR. NEWSREELS such as *The March of Time* freely combined actuality with dramatized SEQUENCES in a style that Henry Luce, head of Time, called 'fakery in allegiance to the truth.' Similarly, Robert Flaherty interfered with his Inuit subjects in *Nanook of the North* (1922) to dramatize his epic theme of man's relationship with nature: as Flaherty put it, 'One often has to distort a thing in order to catch its true spirit.' The immediacy of observational cinema made such CONVENTIONS seem outmoded.
Further reading: Issari & Paul (1979), Mamber (1974), Marcorelles (1973)

Odeon Chain of British cinemas founded in the 1930s, taken over by the RANK ORGANISATION in 1941. Odeon cinemas were all built on the same lines, to give cinema-goers a sense of comfort and even luxury, with plush interiors and the tower-mounted neon Odeon sign. Odeons survive though smaller theatres are being eclipsed by the MULTIPLEX chains that now dominate British cinema EXHIBITION. See also MOVIE PALACE.

Oedipal trajectory Theoretical term for the PSYCHOANALYTIC and IDEOLOGICAL implications of the dominant pattern of narrative construction in MAINSTREAM cinema, in which the story focuses on a male hero grappling with some form of disequilibrium (the dramatic conflict) and ultimately triumphing by restoring stability as the narrative attains CLOSURE. This pattern, which may be understood as a MYTHic account of Sigmund Freud's notion of the Oedipus crisis or complex in which man struggles to detach himself from the mother and the feminine and achieve a 'normal' heterosexual masculine identity, is pervasive in such GENRES as the WESTERN and the ACTION FILM, while FILM NOIR has been seen by some critics (e.g., Krutnik, 1991) as expressing its failure or at least exposing its IDEOLOGY.
Further reading: Bellour (1979), Penley (1989)

Omnidirectional MC See MICROPHONE.

Omniscience A position in relation to a STORY that suggests total knowledge of the events and their causes and effects. Some accounts refer to a god-like position whereby an AUDIENCE can see everything, whereas the protagonists in the film can only see their particular angle, its opposite being a highly restricted POINT OF VIEW that tells the entire story from one CHARACTER's perspective. In practice, very few films are built around these extremes and instead manipulate the flow of information about what is going on in a variety of ways that suit the style of the film. Bordwell and Thompson (1997) consider *Birth of a Nation* (dir. D.W. Griffith, 1915) an example of near-omniscience, telling its EPIC civil-war tale through so many different points of view. *The Big Sleep* (dir. Howard Hawks, 1946) is the reverse – the legendarily complex plot unfolds through the eyes of Sam Spade (Humphrey Bogart) only and we are led with him on his tortuous journey of investigation.

One-reeler A SHORT FILM, so-called because the standard REEL held approximately 1,000 feet of 35MM film, running about 10–11 minutes for SOUND FILM (24 FRAMES per second) and 15 minutes for SILENT FILM (16–18 frames per second). Most silent films from about 1908–1914 were one-reelers. TWO-REELERS ran for 20–30 minutes during the silent era; even after the FEATURE length film established itself during the 1910s, most silent short films – like Charlie Chaplin's and Buster Keaton's during the 1910s and 1920s – were two-reelers.

Oppositional cinema A cinema that raises questions about conventional cinematic practices, usually also concerned with wider political debates. Oppositional cinema exposes the processes of film-making that MAINSTREAM CINEMA strives to keep hidden such as EDITING, LIGHTING or CAMERA movement. It also often subverts narrative conventions of TIME, SPACE, CONTINUITY and CLOSURE, tending to DISTANCIATION for the spectator rather than IDENTIFICATION. Oppositional film-making is what Jean-Luc Godard meant in calling on film-makers to 'make films politically rather than make political films'. Oppositional films, though often about overtly political subjects, work through the politics of form, rather than representing the world in classic REALIST/NATURALIST forms. See also COUNTER-CINEMA.

Optical An effect achieved by use of an optical printer, which combines the functions of a CAMERA and a projector, rephotographing each FRAME to add or modify IMAGES to an already processed film. DISSOLVES and FADES, for example, can be achieved IN-CAMERA but are generally achieved with the optical printer, and an optical zoom can simulate the effect of a ZOOM created with the camera.

Optical sound Sound can be recorded for playback with IMAGE in several ways: when SOUND film was introduced, the two major methods were sound on disc and optical sound. Sound on disc proved very awkward and the preferred option became optical sound, in which a variable density track running alongside the image registers sound as a series of horizontal stripes, which are converted into sound impulses by the light beam from the sound head as the film passes over it. Although sound today is recorded and edited on MAGNETIC tape – and some cinemas can play magnetic soundtracks – most RELEASE PRINTS still have optical sound tracks.

Option Commonly used business arrangement in which a STUDIO or PRODUCER pays a fee – normally a small percentage of the final price, for the rights to a PROPERTY – a SCREENPLAY, novel or play – for a certain length of time, after which the rights revert to the property's copyright owner, who can then sell them to someone else. The option arrangement allows producers or AGENTS time to put together a PACKAGE without fully committing financially to the property.

Orion Important 1980s American INDEPENDENT PRODUCTION and DISTRIBUTION company that produced several commercially and critically successful films.

Founded in 1978 by five ex-UNITED ARTISTS employees, Orion had its first success with *10* (dir. Blake Edwards. 1979), then produced a varied group of well-known films including *Platoon* (dir. Oliver Stone, 1986), *Robocop* (dir. Paul Verhoeven, 1987) and *Silence of the Lambs* (dir. Jonathan Demme, 1991). The company filed for bankruptcy in 1991, but survives on a smaller scale.

Oscar The popular name for an ACADEMY AWARD, but really the trophy that goes with the award. The gold-plated statuette presented to winners in various categories is said to be named Oscar because an early librarian of the ACADEMY OF MOTION PICTURE ARTS AND SCIENCES, Margaret Herrick, claimed it reminded her of her Uncle Oscar, though there are other versions of the name's origins.

Other Any person or group different from the norm – the Other can be an individual or a group, defined by such factors as RACE, ethnicity or sexual orientation. According to Roland Barthes (1972, p. 151), 'the petit-bourgeois is a man unable to imagine the Other.' Thus, the Other is depicted as unknowable and threatening to bourgeois IDEOLOGY. For PSYCHOANALYTIC criticism, the REPRESENTATION of difference as Other suggests a repression within a CHARACTER in the DIEGESIS or within the film TEXT itself, a denial of the desire for that which is different from the Self projected outwards as a frightening Other. The clearest example of this dynamic is in monsters of the HORROR FILM: Robin Wood lists monstrous OTHERS in his influential study of this GENRE, including women, the proletariat, other cultures, ethnic minorities, alternative ideologies, bisexuality and homosexuality, and even children (Wood, 1986, pp. 73–77).

Outlaw couple film See GANGSTER FILM, ROAD MOVIE.

Out-take, outtake A SHOT which it is decided during the EDITING not to use in a film, because of poor quality, length or responses from a PREVIEW, or because a different solution than envisaged during shooting a SCENE is found during the editing. The term often describes more specifically a shot CUT from the FINAL CUT of a film, and out-take material would be used for assembling of a DIRECTOR'S CUT of a film.

Overage Any expense incurred on a film production which exceeds what was budgeted for.

Overhead shot A SHOT taken from directly above the ACTION, a CAMERA position often used to imply fate or entrapment, as in *M* (1931), in which DIRECTOR Fritz Lang uses numerous overhead shots combined with a geometric *MISE EN SCÈNE* to express the child murderer's vulnerability to both his own uncontrollable impulses and to the society that hunts him down. Sometimes called a BIRD'S-EYE SHOT, Hitchcock used the camera in precisely this way in *The Birds* (1963) when CUTTING from shots of the destruction the birds have caused in the town below to a position above them hovering in the sky, suggesting a God-like detachment. Busby Berkeley used the overhead shot in the production numbers of his MUSICALS to enhance the SPECTATOR's appreciation of the geometrical precision of his CHOREOGRAPHY.

Package Film industry term for a combination of key elements necessary to sell the idea for a production to financial backers; a PRODUCER or agent might assemble a package from an OPTION on a successful novel, while establishing provisional commitment from two or three major STARS and a major DIRECTOR for involvement in the project.

Pan and Scan The process of formatting WIDESCREEN IMAGES for TELEVISION broadcast or VIDEO release by cropping or PANNING across the SCREEN, necessary because the television screen has a smaller ASPECT RATIO (1.33:1) than the cinema screen. As a consequence, some parts of the images are eliminated, and CUTS and/or camera MOVEMENTS added – all unfortunate distortions of the original TEXT. For widescreen films, a more acceptable alternative is LETTERBOXing.

Pan CAMERA MOVEMENT on the CAMERA's vertical axis or horizontal plane (left to right or vice-versa) with the body turning to the right or left on a stationary TRIPOD, a term sometimes used simply to mean that the camera moves to follow the ACTION. A SWISH PAN is when the camera pans so rapidly that the action becomes blurred. In *Weekend* (1967), Jean-Luc Godard pans the camera a full 360° three times, twice to the left and once to the right, to suggest a visual equivalent to the formal construction of the Mozart composition on the SOUNDTRACK. Pan is also a term to describe a negative review of a film.

Pan shot A SHOT made with a PANning CAMERA MOVEMENT.

Panavision 'Filmed in Panavision' in a film's CREDITS generally indicates not a WIDESCREEN system, but use of an ANAMORPHIC LENS made by specialist manufacturer Panavision Inc. to conventionally squeeze a 35MM IMAGE for projection in an ASPECT RATIO of 2.35:1. Panavision also developed other widescreen systems, such as Super Panavision (unsqueezed image on a 65MM NEGATIVE for a projected image of 2.2:1) and Ultra Panavision (squeezed image on 65mm negative for a projected image of 2.7:1 on a 70MM PRINT).
Further reading: Belton (1992)

Panchromatic stock BLACK-AND-WHITE FILM STOCK named for its sensitivity to the full range of COLOURS in the spectrum. Orthochromatic film, sensitive to blue and green but not red, was used extensively during the SILENT FILM period, giving silent films high contrast. Panchromatic film, rendering a wider range of skin tones in shades of grey, came into widespread use in the SOUND FILM period. With a slower FILM SPEED that was less sensitive to light, the APERTURE had to be opened wider and DEPTH OF FIELD, which had characterized much silent film-making – the work of Victor Sjöström and Erich von Stroheim, for example – was lost. 1930s HOLLYWOOD CINEMATOGRAPHY was often characterized by SHALLOW FOCUS; improvements in the EMULSION and film speed of panchromatic film, and in LIGHTING, made possible the DEEP FOCUS camerawork used by Gregg Toland in his work with William Wyler, Orson Welles and others in the late 1930s and 1940s.
Further reading: Comolli and Ogle in Nichols (1985)

Pantheon In popularizing the AUTEUR THEORY, American critic Andrew Sarris used the term Pantheon – literally, a temple or sacred building dedicated to the Gods – to designate those DIRECTORS who had best succeeded in expressing a personal vision in their films. In *The American Cinema* (1968), Sarris's encyclopaedic account of HOLLYWOOD directors, pantheon directors were Charles Chaplin, Robert Flaherty, John Ford, D.W. Griffith, Howard Hawks, Alfred Hitchcock, Buster Keaton, Fritz Lang, Ernst Lubitsch, F.W. Murnau, Max Ophuls, Jean Renoir, Josef von Sternberg and Orson Welles. In the heady days of auteurism other critics were quick to enumerate their own pantheons.

Paradigm Term used in SEMIOTIC analysis to describe the range of choices available before elements are combined SYNTAGMatically to produce meaning. In a sentence, each individual word is selected from a paradigm and then combined into a sentence (the syntagm). The term could refer to the combining of elements during film-making where the film is the total syntagm and the various choices that make up the film TEXT amount to paradigms. Amongst the clearest paradigms of a film are the STARS. The effect of this kind of analysis can be seen clearly (often amusingly) by mentally substituting one ACTOR for another onto a familiar film.

Parallax Because a CAMERA's VIEWFINDER and LENS need to be sited slightly apart, what the viewfinder sees is not framed in precisely the same way as in the LENS: this displacement between viewfinder and lens is called parallax. Most cameras today are REFLEX CAMERAS, whose viewfinders enable the image being shot to be viewed via the camera lens itself.

Parallel action The suggestion of multiple events occurring simultaneously, achieved through CROSS-CUTTING or PARALLEL EDITING.

Parallel editing A form of narrative construction that alternates between two or more lines of ACTION, used to suggest that different actions are occurring simultaneously or are thematically related. Usually restricted to particular SEQUENCES in a film, D.W. Griffith's *Intolerance* (1916) is structured by parallel editing, shuttling between four stories occurring in different TIMEs and places but connected thematically by the idea of intolerance. See also CROSS-CUTTING.

Paramount One of the BIG 5 MAJOR American STUDIOS. Founded in 1914 by W.W. Hodkinson as the first national DISTRIBUTION company in the US, the company was bought shortly thereafter by Adolph Zukor's FAMOUS PLAYERS company, with Jesse L. Lasky and Ernst Lubitsch as heads of production. Paramount emerged as one of the MAJOR STUDIOS during the SILENT FILM era, employing major DIRECTORS such as D.W. Griffith, Cecil B. DeMille and Erich von Stroheim, and STARS such as Mary Pickford, Gloria Swanson and Rudolph Valentino. The company was important in the development of SOUND, with films by Lubitsch and Rouben Mamoulian. Having successfully achieved VERTICAL INTEGRATION, Paramount overextended financially and declared bankruptcy in 1933. Re-organized as Paramount Pictures Corporation, the company re-attained its position of prominence in HOLLYWOOD. The studio was known for its comedies, producing films by Lubitsch, Billy Wilder and Preston Sturges with such stars as Harold Lloyd,

Mae West, W.C. Fields, the Marx Brothers, Bob Hope and Jerry Lewis. Paramount was also renowned for its EPICS by DeMille (*The Greatest Show on Earth*, 1953; *The Ten Commandments*, 1923, 1956) and for the SERIES of films made by Josef von Sternberg starring Marlene Dietrich.

After the decline of the STUDIO SYSTEM – partly the result of the PARAMOUNT DECISION – the company, like other majors, concentrated more on releasing INDEPENDENT productions. In 1966 Paramount was purchased by the CONGLOMERATE Gulf+Western, in turn taken over by VIACOM in 1993. Throughout this period Paramount continued to turn out its share of BLOCKBUSTERS, including *The Godfather* (dir. Francis Ford Coppola, 1971), *Raiders of the Lost Ark* (dir. Steven Spielberg, 1981), *Beverly Hills Cop* (dir. Martin Brest, 1984), *Top Gun* (dir. Tony Scott, 1986) and *Forrest Gump* (dir. Robert Zemeckis, 1994).

Further reading: Eames (1985), Finler (1988), Gomery (1986), Halliwell (1976), Mordden (1988), Schatz (1988)

Paramount decision In 1948 (begun in 1938 but delayed by appeals and World War II), alleging violation of the ANTI-TRUST laws, the US Supreme Court ruled that PARAMOUNT and the four other MAJOR STUDIOS in HOLLYWOOD constituting the BIG 5 be required to divest themselves of their theatre chains – also known as the 'Paramount decrees' and 'divorcement'. In addition, the Big Five and the LITTLE 3 studios had to stop restrictive DISTRIBUTION practices such as BLOCK BOOKING. In 1951, the studios consented, and the VERTICAL INTEGRATION which had been the basis of the STUDIO SYSTEM and the majors' control of the industry ended (or did by 1958, when the final divorcements took place), as did the system of B PICTURES. Despite this, and the equal crisis of drastically reduced AUDIENCES, the majors remained producers and strengthened their position as distributors. The decrees were intended to encourage INDEPENDENT production, which from the 1950s increased dramatically. After various further crises in the 1960s, the major studios reorganized and continued to exercise considerable control over distribution and EXHIBITION. In the *laissez-faire* economic climate of the 1980s Reagan era, several studios re-acquired theatre chains and in the present a form of vertical integration has been re-established through CONGLOMERATION and the studios' power in TELEVISION, CABLE and VIDEO.

Further reading: Balio (1990), Izod (1988), Maltby (1995), Mast (1982), Gomery in Nowell-Smith (1996)

Parody A humorous imitation of another (often serious) work of art, GENRE or style. Once audiences are familiar with the CONVENTIONS of a genre, or a film has been widely successful, it becomes a target for parody. Mel Brooks's films have consistently parodied other genres and films: his *Blazing Saddles* (1974) mocks the WESTERN, *Young Frankenstein* the CYCLE of HORROR FILMS made by UNIVERSAL in the 1930s, and *High Anxiety* (1977) plays with the THRILLERS of Alfred Hitchcock. Brooks's *Spaceballs* (1987) is a parody of George Lucas's *Star Wars* (1977).

Parole See LANGUE.

Pastiche Unlike PARODY or SATIRE, pastiche borrows narrative and stylistic CONVENTIONS and ICONOGRAPHY from other works, usually of the same GENRE.

Pastiched works are said to be an important element of POSTMODERNISM because they are concerned with surface recombination at the expense of generating meaningful themes themselves. *American Graffiti* (dir. George Lucas, 1973) and *Grease* (dir. Randall Kleiser, 1978) are pastiche TEENPICS, while the diner SCENE in Quentin Tarantino's *Pulp Fiction* (1994) is a pastiche of 1950s American POPULAR CULTURE.

Pay or play   HOLLYWOOD contractual term: to enlist the support of an ACTOR (or DIRECTOR or PRODUCER) on a project, it is agreed the person will be paid whether or not s/he is ultimately involved in the project, and whether or not the project is begun or completed. A 'pay *and* play' agreement ensures both payment for a project and that it will be made.

Pay-per-view   CABLE TELEVISION and satellite in the DIGITAL age makes it possible for individual consumers to request (and be billed for), by telephone or computer, home delivery of television programmes such as sporting events or recent films. Cable infrastructure for potential pay-per-view use (1999) covers seventy five percent of the USA and thirty five percent of the UK public. A major development for the future, MAJOR STUDIOS like this system more than cable subscription systems, because it more closely resembles individual theatre admission for a particular film and is more profitable: pay-per-view could bring in as much as $40 million in one night for a BLOCKBUSTER.
Further reading: Fleming in Hill & McLoone (1996), Wasko (1994)

Peplum film   Term to describe Italian EPIC FILMS set in ancient Roman or Biblical times, derived from the Greek *peplos* – a loose-fitting overskirt or outer tunic, also worn by Romans – highlighting the erotic PLEASURE such movies offer in IMAGES of scantily clad men and women. Beginning with *The Last Days of Pompeii* (1908) and *Cabiria* (dir. Giovanni Pastrone, 1914), which achieved international popularity, Italian film has gravitated toward the historical epic. As Italian NEO-REALISM declined in the 1950s, Italy once again began to produce COSTUME epics with revealingly clad musclemen, such as *Ulysses* (dir. Mario Camerini, 1954) and *Hercules* (dir. Pietro Francisci, 1959), with American beefcake ACTORS Kirk Douglas and Steve Reeves, respectively.

Perspective   Though film LENSES can record the illusions of depth and distance on to a flat surface as they are normally experienced by the human eye, different lenses produce different kinds of perspective. A normal lens with a FOCAL LENGTH of 50mm for a 35MM film will produce an effect close to that of a naked human eye, but a wide-angle lens distorts perspective in several ways, most significantly by enlarging objects in the centre of the FRAME and confusing the central rule of perspective that diminished size means something is further away. Long-FOCUS lenses produce similar size distortions and resultant changes in normal perspective. Such effects can be desirable for particular reasons, but if the aim is to create a sense of normality the changed perspective has to be compensated for by altering other compositional variables such as CAMERA ANGLE or position.

PG   Parental Guidance – a key part of the systems of CERTIFICATION or ratings operating in both the UK and the US. PG signals a film is largely suitable for children, but with minor elements that parents may wish to consider before allowing children to see it unsupervised.

Pickup, or pick-up A pickup SHOT is one taken after principal PHOTOGRAPHY on a film has been completed, generally to solve a problem – the perceived necessity to explain something, or to replace a poor shot. To pickup is also to shoot a new TAKE from where a previous one has ended, usually because of some error. 'Pickup' is also another term for NEGATIVE PICKUP.

Picture palace See MOVIE PALACE.

Pin screen, pin board Method of ANIMATION developed by Alexandre Alexeieff in France in the 1930s, using a large pinhole screen in which pins are placed at various adjustable heights, creating shadows generated by LIGHTING from the side. With career-long collaborator Claire Parker, Alexeieff made many short animated films using the pin screen, including *Night on a Bare Mountain* (1933) and *En Passant* (1943), as well as the prologue and epilogue of Orson Welles's *The Trial* (1963).

Pinewood British film STUDIO important in the 1940s and 1950s, but since 1960 functioning as a facility for rental by INDEPENDENT production companies. In its heyday the studio was associated with the CROWN FILM UNIT (during World War II) and the RANK ORGANISATION; among important DIRECTORS who worked at Pinewood were David Lean and the team of Michael Powell and Emeric Pressburger.

Pitch The presentation of the idea for a film to interest a potential financial backer, a key skill for any PRODUCER. Though the face-to-face meeting is the most dramatically interesting moment of any pitch, pitches include detailed paperwork on financial planning and an arresting account of the SCRIPT or total PACKAGE. If a pitch is for a large-budget FEATURE to a big STUDIO, foregrounded elements would be concerned with attracting BOX-OFFICE success, but bids to arts organizations for more EXPERIMENTAL work need to consider distinctiveness and the reasons why it would not attract commercial funding.

Pixel A combination of 'pictures' (pix) and 'element', used since the 1960s to describe the minute dots that comprise the IMAGE on a TELEVISION or VIDEO SCREEN (the more pixels, the higher degree of image resolution, as in HDTV). Film-maker Michael Almereyda used the term 'Pixelvision' to describe his experimental 1992 feature, *Another Girl, Another Planet*, SHOT on the toy Fisher-Price PXL 2000 camera, as is the work of Sadie Benning.

Pixillation Method of ANIMATION using real people or things rather than drawings, making them appear to move in an odd, staccato fashion or move smoothly but in impossible ways. Pixillated motion is created by filming the subject for one or a few FRAMES at a time, stopping the CAMERA, changing the subject's position slightly, filming a few more frames, and so on, or by EDITING out frames within a SHOT. A famous example of pixillation is Norman McLaren's *Neighbours* (1952), in which the ACTORS seem to glide along lawns and whizz like helicopters.

Plan américain French term, translated as 'American SHOT', signifying a TWO SHOT – in which two CHARACTERS occupy the FRAME – from approximately the knees upwards, essentially a MEDIUM SHOT. Called *plan américain* because French critics found the shot very characteristic, in its stability and balance, of the CLASSICAL HOLLYWOOD style of breaking down a SCENE into shots.

Plan séquence French term for SEQUENCE SHOT.

Pleasure A key concept for all cinema, and important in the formulation of FEMI-NIST and PSYCHOANALYTIC THEORY during the 1970s and 1980s. Key feminist debates focused on the question of who was being offered pleasure by most commercial films, with the unambivalent answer – men, or at least the spectator taking up a male perspective. Films are largely structured around the male GAZE, with women as objects of VOYEURISM or SCOPOPHILIA and men featured as the focus for narcissistic IDENTIFICATION. The theoretical underpinning of such ideas comes from Freudian psychology and its contemporary reworkings in modern psychoanalytic theory, particularly by Jacques Lacan. Central to most of this work in relation to film stud-ies is the relationship of cinema to unconscious desire and the workings of the subconscious itself. In Freud's formulation, the desire to see the forbidden and erotic is male-centred and the conditions of cinema SPECTATORSHIP fulfil this perfectly. As feminist CRITICISM developed, it moved from analysing MAINSTREAM CINEMA's exclu-sively male orientation towards an increasingly complex debate about the potential sources of female pleasure in film.

For feminist film-makers the problem has been how to create a cinema that moves away from a an exclusively male set of pleasures. Many early solutions focused on the denial of the pleasures of MAINSTREAM NARRATIVE cinema. Laura Mulvey, whose *Visual Pleasure and Narrative Cinema* (1975) was central to contemporary definitions of pleasure, contributed to such feminist film-making practice with films, including *Riddles of the Sphinx* (1977). Since then there have emerged women filmmakers with similar aims but willing to engage with commercially viable cinema, not only to reach wider AUDIENCES, but in a spirit of questioning earlier ideas about the limited space (and pleasures) that mainstream film allowed female spectators. Jane Campion's work, such as *The Piano* (1993), is an example of attempts to recast the notion of plea-sure in films as anything but masculine in orientation. The battleground over the nature and sources of pleasure in mainstream cinema has been crucial in the contin-uing evolution of film THEORY, particularly when concerned with the role of GENDER. Further reading: Stam & Miller (2000), Hayward (1996)

Plot Bordwell and Thompson (1997) usefully define plot and distinguish between plot and STORY within the NARRATIVE structure of a film: plot is everything presented to us on the screen in the course of a film, including DIEGETIC events located totally in the world of the film, plus non-diegetic material which might include CAPTIONS and dates, MUSIC and TITLES, all of which are part of the film's narrative strategy. Plot could be said to lead us in the direction of the total story. The balance between plot and story is crucial to the narrative film-maker, who may have, at one extreme, a long, complicated story in mind, but choose to reveal it through an austere, minimal plot, leaving an AUDIENCE to assume a great deal and construct much of the story for itself. Alternatively, story and plot may come close to being the same in a film that chooses to spell out every event, including the chain of cause and effect at the heart of the plot.

The concept of plot versus story is also vital to several other features of a film's narrative strategy. In terms of narrative TIME, structures where plot duration is far less than story duration are common, as in a 'day in the life' structure in which a life story may be inferred from a plot covering a single day. Equally a plot set in a single location can suggest a story which takes in many places. Very open endings, with a low degree of CLOSURE, rely heavily on the audience's willingness to accept a story beyond plot and the fact that such a story could take many different pathways. The relationship between plot and story also determines the range and depth of story information we receive: a great sense of mystery can be created if only limited plot information is provided, by being given from the POINT OF VIEW of a single CHARAC-TER for example, while the greatest possible depth in psychological terms is available if a character is given a VOICE-OVER which details motivation, almost in the style of a novel.

As Bordwell and Thompson argue, the dominant attitudes to plot have tended to favour the explicit and unambiguous. The norm of CLASSICAL HOLLYWOOD CINEMA favours the explicable with a high degree of closure and little narrative space that is free of events, whereas other cinemas, such as ART CINEMA, have demonstrated that it is possible to have a plot that is inconclusive and shows time and spaces where little of narrative consequence happens. See also BACK STORY, NARRATIVE SPACE, NARRA-TIVE THEORY, NARRATOR, OMNISCIENCE.

Poetic Realism Term applied to a strand of 1930s French cinema, which achieved BOX-OFFICE success and international prestige. Although not as defined as a GENRE, and crossing over into MELODRAMA, FILM NOIR and REALISM, Poetic Realism 'designates pessimistic urban dramas, usually set in Paris. . . in working CLASS settings, with doomed romantic narratives often tinged with criminality' (Vincendeau 1996, pp. 115–16), combined with an often lyrical or poetic look, set as they often are in shadowy or nocturnal settings. Classic examples, several of which were re-made in HOLLYWOOD, are Marcel Carné's *Quai des Brumes* (1938), *Le Jour se lève* (1939) and *Hôtel du Nord* (1937) and Jean Renoir's *La Bête humaine* (1938). *Pépé le Moko* (dir. Julien Duvivier, 1937), though set in the Algiers Casbah, shares much of their mood and look (as well as their ARCHETYPAL male STAR, Jean Gabin). Some film-makers associated with Poetic Realism - notably Renoir, Jacques Prévert and Duvivier – were also associated with Popular Front Cinema, and the bleak mood of Poetic Realism owes something to the failure of Popular Front politics. Many commentators see Carné's and Prévert's *Les Enfants du paradis* (1945) as the culmi-nation and end of Poetic Realism, but extending the term to Renoir's *La Grande illu-sion* (1937) and *La Règle du jeu* (1939), as some do, damages any specificity it might have. As Vincendeau argues, it is more useful to point to antecedents in the German and French KAMMERSPIELFILM and STREET FILM.
Further reading: Andrew (1995), Cook (1996), Hayward (1993), Thompson & Bordwell (1994), Williams (1992)

Point of view The eyes through which we view the unfolding of the PLOT. The dominant eye in MAINSTREAM film is taken to be an imaginary neutral CAMERA with only the interspersing of the highly SUBJECTIVE viewpoint of individual CHARACTERS. A number of films make shifting points of view – and by implication versions of 'the truth' – one of their central concerns, the most famous being *Citizen Kane* (dir. Orson Welles, 1941). *Peeping Tom* (dir. Michael Powell, 1960), concerning a psychopath who takes pleasure in filming the deaths of his victims whom he kills with a blade that is part of the camera APPARATUS itself, is perhaps even more explicitly about point of view: Powell uses SHOTS of the murderer's point of view as he carries out the sadistic killings, making *Peeping Tom* a deeply disturbing film about VOYEURISM and by extension, cinema itself.

The most commonplace use of point of view is far less dramatic: most filmed conversations are founded on a MIX of shots that take in all the protagonists together with shots from each point of view in turn, so that the viewer gets a sense of involvement in the conversation as a participant. The amount of point of view time that each participant is allowed can be varied and adjusted so that the AUDIENCE can be steered towards greater IDENTIFICATION with one or other of the characters. Though many films are told from a character's narrow perspective, it is very rare for this to be followed through as a consistent visual point of view, as in *The Lady in the Lake* (dir. Robert Montgomery, 1946). See also NARRATION, NARRATOR, SHOT-REVERSE-SHOT.

Further reading: Aumont *et al.* (1992), Bordwell & Thompson (1997)

Points Major participants in a film's production may enter into a contract to receive a flat sum from the film's profits, or to receive an agreed percentage – hence, 'points' – of the film's GROSS or (more likely) net profits. Also known as (either net or gross) profit participation, the practice has increased significantly in the NEW HOLLYWOOD.

Police film, *policier* A film that focuses on those who enforce the law rather than the criminals who break it, featuring protagonists at any level of law enforcement and on any branch or division, squad or precinct. Films focusing on a detective overlap with the DETECTIVE FILM, and if the focus is equally on the lawman and the lawbreaker, as in *The Big Heat* (dir. Fritz Lang, 1953) and *Heat* (dir. Michael Mann, 1995), then the film is also a CRIME FILM or GANGSTER FILM. Police procedural films, since *Detective Story* (dir. William Wyler, 1951), focus on the routine work of law enforcement. Rural cop movies feature sheriffs, often contrasting their ways with their big city counterparts, as in *Coogan's Bluff* (dir. Don Siegel, 1968) and *One False Move* (dir. Carl Franklin, 1992). Some police films pair two STARS as police partners in a BUDDY FILM, whether as COMEDY in *Lethal Weapon* (dir. Richard Donner, 1987) or as existential tragedy in *Seven* (dir. David Fincher, 1995). Regardless of such wide possibilities in the GENRE, most police films tend to focus on conflicts between duty and desire, material temptation and morality, and the comparison or contrast between those who uphold the law and those who violate it.

Politique des auteurs Literally, the 'authors policy', developed in the 1950s, mostly in the French magazine CAHIERS DU CINÉMA, arguing for personal qualities in cinema and for the DIRECTOR as the author, or AUTEUR, of a film. While not a radical idea for European ART CINEMA, it had major implications for the way that commercial cinema, especially HOLLYWOOD, was viewed. The *politique des auteurs* was polemical rather than theoretical, especially when applied to French cinema (which the

Cahiers critics were later to take by storm as the FRENCH NEW WAVE) and to popular film-makers like Alfred Hitchcock and Howard Hawks. The *politique des auteurs* was rather misleadingly modified in translation, by Andrew Sarris, in the 1960s as the 'auteur theory'. See also AUTEUR THEORY/AUTEURISM, AUTHORSHIP.

Further reading: Cook & Bernink (1999), Hillier (1985), Truffaut in Nichols (1976), Stam (2000), Stam & Miller (2000), Thompson & Bordwell (1994)

Popular culture Popular culture is the world around us – social customs, values, beliefs, activities – but also, more specifically, mass-produced culture, which required both the development of the mass media (beginning with the invention of the printing press) to disseminate it, and the rise of the middle CLASS (with time and money) to consume it. Popular culture is sometimes conceived, often pejoratively, as being opposed to high culture; while high culture involves art works of originality of style and thought, artefacts of popular culture are distinguished by FORMULA and cliché. Since much popular culture is mass-produced (the culture industry), popular culture also lacks the authenticity or AURA of folk art. The main theoretical debate about popular culture has focused on whether and, if so, to what extent, it promulgates dominant IDEOLOGY. Is it foisted upon consumers, or is it created in response to AUDIENCE needs, and does it offer some form of cultural empowerment? Adorno (1991) and others associated with the Frankfurt School take the former, more determinist perspective, while Fiske (1989a, 1989b) argues that readers have the ability to negotiate popular culture TEXTS by adopting resistive readings.

The cinema is a major aspect of popular culture, providing much of its ICONOGRAPHY, STARS, folklore, fashion, MUSIC and of course the movies themselves. Almost all popular films are GENRE films, and genres are both influenced by, and an influence on, popular culture; they reflect changing attitudes and values in society at large, as well as shape them. Movies such as *Casablanca* (dir. Michael Curtiz, 1942) provide popular culture with IMAGES that come to serve as cultural MYTHS; others, like *Star Wars* (dir. George Lucas, 1977), also permeate popular culture through MERCHANDISING. Historically, film has its roots in popular culture, beginning as a working-class form of entertainment, a VAUDEVILLE novelty, frowned upon by legitimate stage ACTORS. Many film STUDIOS today are part of media CONGLOMERATES that own other entertainment industries or produce work in other cultural media and forms, and so the movies' relation to popular culture is more intertwined than in the past. Recordings and recording artists, TELEVISION personalities, consumer name brands and direct references to topical events appear much more frequently in films today. See also CULT FILM, HOLLYWOOD, SYNERGY.

Further reading: Hollows *et al.* (2000), Strinati (1995)

Populism The Populist Party was an upstart third US political party that flickered briefly in the late nineteenth century, a coalition of farmers and workers organizations that, to everyone's surprise, captured over fifty seats in both houses of Congress in 1890, but faltered in the 1892 presidential election and faded. Populism survives to describe a grassroots attitude endorsing common sense and rural over urban values – an attitude permeating the IDEOLOGY of MAINSTREAM American cinema, often invoked in popular movies as the essence of democratic capitalism ('the will of the people'). Frank Capra's films often dealt with populist morality in conflict with institutionalized corruption – as in *Mr. Deeds Goes to Town* (1936), *Mr. Smith Goes* to Washington (1939) and *Meet John Doe* (1941), which had a clear appeal to AUDIENCES during the Great Depression.

Pornography Material in any form that graphically depicts or describes sexual and sado-masochistic acts, heterosexual or homosexual, with the intention of titillating and arousing the spectator or reader. Although the definition of pornography and identification of individual works as pornographic have been the subjects of intense debate among scholars, government officials involved in CENSORSHIP, and local communities, it might be argued that works are pornographic when any of the participants are treated abusively or degradingly or when the works seem to have no redeeming social value.

In pornography there is a fundamental distinction between SOFT-CORE and HARD-CORE, the former showing nudity only and the latter explicit sexual action. Initially pornographic film circulated as UNDERGROUND FILM and STAG FILMS, since hard-core representations of sexual acts was prohibited by law in most countries. Beginning in 1933 with *Elysia, Valley of the Nude* (dir. Brian Foy, 1933), NUDIST FILMS, disguised as DOCUMENTARIES about naturalists as a pretext to show images of people naked, allowed for greater sexual content on the screen. MAINSTREAM nudie films began with Russ Meyer's *The Immoral Mr. Teas* in 1959, about a man who gains the ability to see through women's clothes and whose POINT OF VIEW the CAMERA happily shares. Nudie films showed bare breasts and buttocks, and occasionally full frontal nudity, but were replaced in the late 1960s by hard-core FEATURES, one of the first of which was *Mona: The Virgin Nymph* (dir. Bill Osco, 1970), as a result of the US Supreme Court ruling that left the definition of pornography to local communities. Before many municipalities could draft and enact legislation, *Deep Throat* (dir. Gerard Damiano, 1972), one of the most famous pornographic films of all time, was showing in main street cinemas across the country.

In the same year, *Behind the Green Door* (dir. Mitchell Brothers) and *The Devil in Miss Jones* (dir. Damiano), more ambitious productions with higher PRODUCTION VALUES, spurred the development of a more visible industry complete with its own STARs and AUTEURs. Influential critic Susan Sontag (1969) celebrated pornography as an imaginative liberation from the taboos and constraints of bourgeois IDEOLOGY, but by the 1980s most FEMINIST critics were attacking pornography as an expression of patriarchal domination and the sexual objectification of women. Williams (1989) shows how heterosexual pornography tends to privilege the phallus through such CONVENTIONS as the MONEY SHOT. Along with the development of QUEER THEORY, more recent work by Waugh (1996) and others has examined gay pornography. Today many hard-core films are made STRAIGHT-TO-VIDEO and are easily available over the counter in the US, France, The Netherlands and Denmark, but not in the UK or Canada. See GAY AND LESBIAN FILM.
Further reading: Day & Bloom (1988), Di Lauro & Rabkin (1976), Frank (1989), Schaefer (1999), Shipman (1985), Williams (1989)

Positif French film magazine, founded in 1952 shortly after its great rival CAHIERS DU CINÉMA. *Positif* shared some tastes with *Cahiers,* particularly in European cinema, but was distinctively interested in SURREALISM, eroticism, the fantastic and the HORROR FILM, and the anarchic COMEDY of Frank Tashlin and Jerry Lewis. *Positif* was more politically oriented than *Cahiers,* which in the late 1950s and 1960s it attacked for both its CRITICISM and the films made by former *Cahiers* critics who became DIRECTORS of the FRENCH NEW WAVE. *Positif* has remained less well known than *Cahiers*, less because of the quality of its criticism than because it did not produce film-makers to raise its profile.

Positive Film strip on which the developed IMAGES correspond to the LIGHTING values (and with COLOUR FILM, colours) of what was originally photographed – the opposite of NEGATIVE. A positive print – a WORKPRINT, or a PRINT for PROJECTION or RELEASE – is normally made from a negative (but see REVERSAL FILM).

Post theory Term describing 1990s reactions, based in cognitive film theory, to the dominance of theoretical approaches to film in the 1970s and 1980s, particularly those based in PSYCHOANALYSIS, STRUCTURALISM and SEMIOTICS, and MARXISM. David Bordwell and Noël Carroll argue (1996, p. xiii) that 1970s and 1980s attempts at 'Grand Theory' have outrun their usefulness, proposing alternative approaches which would 'pose concrete questions and focus on specific problems'.

Post-colonial theory Broad term describing the varied efforts by both First and Third world academics to theorize the experiences of peoples emerging from colonialism, though even defining what constitutes a post-colonial society is in itself contentious (some writers have included Australia, New Zealand, Canada and even the US whilst most have tacitly agreed that their experience is so radically different from, say, Kenya, Mozambique or India, that there is little point in grouping them together).

Many have also taken issue with the idea of post-colonialism, implying as it does that the impact of colonialism disappears with the hand-over of political control from the imperial power. Ashish Rajadhyaksha recounts how for many in the Third World post-colonial theory is seen as the province of Third World intellectuals working in Western academia, that the post-colonial state is a Western perspective which underplays the remaining conditions of colonialism in many of the countries whose experience it seeks to describe (Hill & Church Gibson, 1998). Post-colonial theory is probably best considered as a collection of new ways of thinking about the colonial experience rather than as something which literally and unproblematically follows it in chronological terms. Cinema was seen as a key tool in the reconstruction of national identities in Africa, Asia and Latin America in the post-colonial period following World War II, and a number of emerging NATIONAL CINEMAS had some form of direct state intervention, with the avowed aim of creating a cinema that would create new state identities both at home and abroad.

Whilst much such work has become well-known in the West and a number of film-makers emerged as part of a tacit Western AUTEURIST canon – Satyajit Ray being a classic example – much post-colonial thinking would regard this first phase of new cinemas as inevitably bound up with Western ideas, particularly in their dependence on a REALIST aesthetic. Having its roots in this phase of development, but in many ways marking a radical departure from it, is the notion of THIRD CINEMA and its call for a radically different cinema.

Contemporary post-colonial thinking is more resistant to notions of Third Worlds and Third Cinemas, arguing that such ideas hide radical differences within societies on both sides of the former colonial divide, resulting in its embrace of the experience of immigrant and diasporic populations, particularly in Europe and the USA, and the resultant questioning of older ideas of nationalism. In the cinema this has found expression in, for example, Stephen Frears's two collaborations with Hanif Kureshi, *My Beautiful Laundrette* (1985) and *Sammy and Rosie Get Laid* (1987), which deal with the experience of Pakistani immigrants in Britain, while BLACK CINEMA has explored such isues in US black culture. See also CINEMA NÔVO. Further reading: Hollows *et al.* (2000), Stam & Shohat in Gledhill & Williams (2000), Stam (2000)

Postmodernism A movement or phase in twentieth-century thought, dating from the 1960s, which represents a break with the assumptions of MODERNISM, but more commonly associated with the intellectual and aesthetic debates and practices that have dominated the 1980s and 1990s. Among the key influential writers on post-modernity are Jean Baudrillard, Jean François Lyotard and Frederic Jameson (see Lechte, 1994). If modernism stems from a fundamental belief in progress and the pursuit of truth, postmodernism is about the absence of such an over-arching concept and is fundamentally anti-essentialist in viewing large-scale attempts to explain the world or provide political and philosophical prescriptions for improving it as vain – often referred to as a rejection of 'grand narratives'. This loss of faith in over-arching belief systems is related to an equivalent loss of individual identity and any striving for new means of expression that can encompass it, resulting in post-modernism's most accessible qualities of PASTICHE, PARODY, and INTERTEXTUAL references in all art forms.

Postmodernism has been seen as a phase in which art forms have largely ceased to have a relationship with any external reality (whose existence is doubted) but instead relate only to each other. It is argued that most art has begun to relate only to other art and is entirely reliant on knowledge of it for it to mean anything to AUDIENCES. Such a phenomenon is made increasingly possible in an age of rapidly proliferating mass media that recycle IMAGES at such a rate that even the very young have available a limitless range of textual referents.

One result of this is what many critics describe as the predominant playfulness of postmodern art forms. Through the endless flow of recycled images, sounds and words emerges a lack of anything approaching reverence for cultural artefacts and an inevitable blurring of distinctions between high and low culture. To take a simple example, sales of recorded classical MUSIC in the UK are currently higher than they have ever been, partly due to changes in technology and lower costs, but partly also because the mass audience experiences a limited range of the music itself through its recycling in advertisements, TITLE music and theme tunes for popular TELEVISION SERIES.

GENRE is a key concept for postmodern film-making. It is mainly through genre that important patterns of recognition take place and that a film can relate to its audience's prior understanding of the medium. Thus Martin Scorsese makes use, not only of the WESTERN in general, but the highly representative late western – *The Searchers* (dir. John Ford, 1956) – in *Taxi Driver* (1976) and highly idiosyncratic use of the MUSICAL in *New York, New York* (1979). But postmodern film does not depend solely on other cinema for its intertextual references. One of the most frequently cited of all postmodern films, *Blue Velvet* (dir. David Lynch, 1986), is at least as dependent on its visual references to Norman Rockwell's paintings of idealized small-town American life as it is on any film or film genre.

Further reading: Brooker (1992), Stam & Shohat in Gledhill & Williams (2000), Hill & Church Gibson (1998), Jameson (1991), Philips in Nelmes (1999), Sharrett (1999), Stam (2000)

Post-production The increasingly complex stage in the production of a film which takes place largely after shooting has been completed, involving EDITING, the addition of TITLES, the creation of SPECIAL EFFECTS and the final SOUNDTRACK including DUBBING and MIXING. See also PRE-PRODUCTION.

Post-structuralism A shift of philosophical emphasis that first gained credibility in the 1970s and which reacts against the systematic, theoretically rigid close analysis of TEXTs offered by STRUCTURALIST analysis and, instead, offers a more pluralistic theoretical approach centred on the role of the constructed self, closely linked to developments in PSYCHOANALYTIC and FEMINIST THEORY. Post-structuralism is most commonly associated with the work of Jacques Derrida and Michel Foucault and the idea of DECONSTRUCTION. Taken to its logical conclusion the process of deconstruction leads to the denial of the existence of a knowable truth and, in the arts, to the destruction of any sense of a quasi-scientific analysis of texts. A principal result of the advance of post-structuralist ideas has been to shift attention away from interpreting texts and revealing their fundamental structures and towards the interaction of text and spectator. This does not, as is sometimes claimed, lead to the idea that a text can logically mean anything that a spectator may say it does: spectators themselves are the products of a number of factors including RACE, GENDER and CLASS and their readings are principally the products of these determinants. See also RECEPTION THEORY.
Further reading: Brunette in Hill & Church Gibson (1998), Stam (2000)

Potboiler A term that comes from the idea of someone producing a film, novel, painting or other cultural artefact to keep the pot boiling – in short, to eat or survive. In practice, the term is often used loosely in a derogatory way to describe what critics feel to be low-grade production with little pretension, but which will please AUDIENCES in sufficient numbers to turn a profit.

Poverty Row Collective name for the small, INDEPENDENT STUDIOS which flourished during the 1930s and 1940s by producing B PICTURES for the lower halves of DOUBLE BILLS whose main, or A, FEATURE was provided by the MAJOR STUDIOS. The best known were REPUBLIC and MONOGRAM, but there were many others, such as Grand National, Producers Releasing Corporation (PRC), Victory and Majestic. Much product took the form of SERIALS and SERIES, such as Monogram's Bowery Boys and Charlie Chan films.
Further reading: Gomery (1986)

Pre-cinema During the nineteenth century there was growing enthusiasm for moving pictures, met in part by MAGIC LANTERNS and optical toys, like the ZOETROPE, which simulated movement. Following the development of still photography in the first half of the century, interest grew in the possibility of movie photography. In the 1870s and 1880s French inventor-physiologist Etienne-Jules Marey developed a CAMERA gun which SHOT twelve still IMAGES per second to record and analyse human

and animal locomotion, while Edward Muybridge found a way to project such photographs with his Zoopraxiscope, using the principles of the movie projector. It was then only a short step away from Thomas Edison's and W.K.L. Dickson's KINE-TOGRAPH and KINETOSCOPE.
Further reading: Bordwell & Thompson (1997), Robinson (1996)

Première The first showing of a film in a particular context. Because the idea is to attract publicity and give a sense of occasion to the film's screening, ways are found to offer a variety of different premières for one film. Whatever their format, premières are part of a film's MARKETING strategy and because they are attended by celebrities they can become vehicles for the promotion of others not connected with the film. See also DISTRIBUTION, EXHIBITION.

Pre-production The phase of film production that follows the securing of financial backing but precedes shooting. This can encompass a wide variety of activities, including detailed work on the SCRIPT, CASTING of ACTORS, engagement of CREWS, finding LOCATIONS and the construction of SETS as well as more basic, detailed logistical planning such as drawing up schedules and arranging catering. This work is generally done under the supervision of a senior PRODUCER with the involvement of the DIRECTOR, ART DIRECTOR or CINEMATOGRAPHER where applicable. See also POST-PRODUCTION.

Prequel A film whose PLOT takes the STORY of an earlier film back in time, as opposed to the more common SEQUEL, which continues the story forwards. In 1999 *The Phantom Menace* (dir. George Lucas) began a process whereby three successive films will form an EPIC-scale prequel to *Star Wars* (dir. Lucas, 1977) which itself has two SEQUELS. An unusual example is *The Godfather II* (dir. Francis Coppola, 1974) which includes both prequel and sequel material to *The Godfather* (dir. Coppola, 1971).

Press book A compilation, usually a large format booklet, of materials for ADVERTISING and promoting a film, sent by the production company to the distributor, consisting mainly of different sizes and formats of posters, STILLS and STAR portraits and background on the film; press books may also suggest strategies for promoting a film locally, such as stunts or competitions. See also DISTRIBUTION, EXHIBITION.

Press kit A package of material prepared by a film's distributor, aimed primarily at newspapers and magazines, to whom it may be sent or made available at press shows – PREVIEWS for press reviewers – though it may also be sent to exhibitors. Press kits normally contain information on the STARS and DIRECTORS, PLOT synopsis and PRODUCTION STILLS, which is one reason why reviews tend to say the same things. Today, press kits are also designed for TELEVISION or radio use and include VIDEO and SOUND CLIPS. See also DISTRIBUTION, EXHIBITION.

Prestige picture A film with a serious subject or theme intended to enhance the reputation of a STUDIO as much or more than turn a profit. *Citizen Kane* (dir. Orson Welles, 1940) is such a film. Sometimes a film not intended by their PRODUCERS as a prestige picture may become one through word-of-mouth and evolving reputation. Many prestige pictures are PROBLEM FILMS focusing on topical issues for the purpose of drawing attention to or exploiting them. Examples include *I Am a Fugitive From a Chain Gang* (dir, Mervyn Leroy, 1932), *Wild Boys of the Road* (dir. William Wellman, 1933) and *The China Syndrome* (dir. James Bridges, 1978), which explore corruption in the American penal system, juvenile delinquency and the dangers of nuclear power plants, respectively.

Preview   General term for any screening which takes place before a film's official RELEASE, for people in the film business, such as exhibitors or the press, or may be for a selected AUDIENCE on whom the film is to tested (after which the film might be re-edited, based on questionnaires filled out by audience members) in which case it might be referred to as a 'sneak' (unpublicized) preview (though this term is also used for a pre-release screening designed to generate word-of-mouth about a film). 'Preview' is sometimes used as an alternative to the term TRAILER.

Primitive cinema, primitive mode of representation   See SILENT CINEMA.

Print   The positive version of a piece of film that has been printed from the NEGATIVE film that has been SHOT. A print is thus able to be screened. The various stages of printing include WORK PRINTS used for EDITING, though much basic editing is now done DIGITALLY. Once the film is complete a master print will be made which is then used for copying to make RELEASE PRINTS. The order 'print it' is given by a DIRECTOR to send a piece of film to the lab for printing when satisfied with the TAKE of a particular shot.

Private eye film   See DETECTIVE FILM.

Privileged moment   In the types of OBSERVATIONAL DOCUMENTARY (DIRECT CINEMA, ETHNOGRAPHIC CINEMA, CINÉMA VÉRITÉ) dating from the 1960s, the term refers to revelatory instances where the CAMERA succeeds in penetrating the surface reality of PROFILMIC events to reveal a deeper truth, usually in the context of character revelation, when the camera seems to pierce the truth behind a person's social façade. The moment when Jason Holiday's public, theatrical self momentarily crumbles, and his tears flow, after hours of being filmed in CLOSE-UP in *Portrait of Jason* (dir. Shirley Clarke, 1967), is a particularly memorable privileged moment.

Problem film   A somewhat dismissive term that describes a film exploring very directly a social problem, generally from a liberal standpoint. In the US there was a remarkable period for this kind of film in the 1930s, when WARNER BROS. in particular made a number of pictures that were in tune with Franklin D. Roosevelt's presidency and the New Deal. Such films were SOCIAL REALIST in style and frequently dealt with contemporary issues of poverty and crime in the context of the Great Depression. Probably the most frequently cited is *I Am a Fugitive from a Chain Gang* (dir. Mervyn Leroy, 1932), though as Cook (1985, pp. 12–13) points out there are interesting elements of the problem film in a variety of GENRE pictures such as the MUSICAL (*Gold Diggers of 1933*, dir. Leroy, 1933). Problem films were also made in the

US during the immediate post-World War II period dealing with, for example, issues of race, such as *Gentleman's Agreement* (dir. Elia Kazan, 1947).
Further reading: Neve (1992)

Process shot General term applied to a SPECIAL EFFECTS shot in which foreground LIVE ACTION is filmed against a background projected onto a screen by REAR PROJECTION. This was a very common practice in the STUDIO SYSTEM era and is still much used, although LOCATION shooting has become more widespread.

Producer The person with prime responsibility for all the financial and administrative dimensions involved in the production of a film, though it is common for producers to become involved in the creative side of the film at certain key points – which can be extremely damaging if the producer's main motivation for creative intervention is financial. The HOLLYWOOD cliché of a producer demanding a change of ending or a STAR to make a film more bankable is the most obvious example. However, particularly in the present climate of mainly INDEPENDENT production, there are many examples of producers who initiate projects and make great artistic and emotional investment in them. In such cases, producers can be closely involved on SCRIPT development, shooting and POST-PRODUCTION as well as the more traditional tasks of raising the money, hiring and firing and securing a DISTRIBUTION deal. The exact nature of the producer's task varies enormously from film to film. Larger budget pictures will generally have an executive producer as well as several producers of varying levels of seniority, including LINE PRODUCERS. The executive producer's main task is to look after the investment of the major backers, while others are more directly involved with the film. On smaller independent films there is more likely to be a single producer, heavily involved in all stages of the work, and probably a close collaborator of the DIRECTOR and the rest of the creative team.

Product placement A MARKETING technique which arranges for real products, or IMAGES of real products, to be included in a film: a leading character might wear a brand of footwear, eat a particular kind of breakfast cereal and so on. Much secrecy and mythology surrounds product placement since any suspicion that a product's appearance is not part of the genuine and necessary fictional world of the film might ruin the effect of the MARKETING strategy.

Production Code Administration See CENSORSHIP, MOTION PICTURE ASSOCIATION OF AMERICA.

Production designer The production designer is responsible for the overall look of a film, especially for the way that settings, SET DESIGN, set decoration and COSTUME come together. The production designer will generally work very closely with the DIRECTOR, and may be responsible for STORYBOARD material. Terminology for this role has changed over time, partly to reflect its importance: during the STUDIO SYSTEM era, production designers were called ART DIRECTORS, and today's art director was known as the set designer; both art directors and set designers would be contracted to the STUDIO. Production designers have also been credited as design consultants. Long-lasting relationships often exist between directors and production designers, such as between director Joseph Losey and production designer Richard

MacDonald during the 1950s and 1960s (on films such as *Time Without Pity*, 1957; *Blind Date*, 1959; *The Damned*, 1962; and *The Servant*, 1963).

Production still A still photograph taken during the production of a film showing a specific piece of ACTION from a SCENE or related material (such as portraits of the ACTORS, the DIRECTOR rehearsing the actors, or looking through the CAMERA VIEWFINDER). Production stills, usually taken by a special stills photographer, are made for publicity and ADVERTISING purposes; stills purporting to be of a scene from the film offer, at best, an approximation of what appears on the screen (whereas a FRAME enlargement takes a FRAME from the PRINT and blows it up). See also BLOW UP.

Production values A rather vague term used to describe the level of 'finish' of a film in terms of things such as SETS, PROPS, COSTUME, LIGHTING and SOUND. 'High' production values are often seen as commensurate with large budgets and the resultant ability to pay attention to detail. The term is often used in relation to period or COSTUME DRAMA where a large part of what the film is seen to offer is its authenticity through the recreation of historical detail.

Profilmic, profilmic event Theoretical term for the physical reality in front of the CAMERA and which is photographed; the 'profilmic event' is an ACTION recorded by the camera. In OBSERVATIONAL DOCUMENTARY (DIRECT CINEMA, ETHNO-GRAPHIC CINEMA, CINÉMA VÉRITÉ) and in REALIST films such as those of the Italian NEO-REALIST movement, film-makers seek to preserve the spatial and temporal integrity of profilmic events as much as possible.

Projection The means by which a series of still IMAGES developed on film are projected on to a screen at a speed which creates the illusion of movement and CONTI-NUITY through the phenomenon of persistence of vision. SILENT FILM era images were projected at 16 FRAMES per second; when SOUND was added the speed became 24 frames per second. Until relatively recently each auditorium in a cinema needed a skilled projectionist to run a programme, mainly because FEATURE FILMS came on more than one standard REEL of film and were shown on two synchronized projectors to avoid breaks in the screening: projectionists were responsible for the complex process of changing reels and threading film on the projector as well as for lighting and music in the auditorium. Most MULTIPLEXES today control projection for a large number of screens from a single automated unit (sometimes referred to as a 'platter system') with sound and light systems in the auditorium controlled by cues on the film itself. Other projection skills being largely superseded by automation include masking the projector's APERTURE for different ASPECT RATIOS. Generally speaking the projectionist's art is dying and cinema chains tend to require the services of computer engineers rather than than the more romantic idea of a projectionist portrayed in films like *Cinema Paradiso* (dir. Giuseppe Tornatore, 1988).

Promotional film A form of DOCUMENTARY intended to promote and publicize a particular business, industry or social issue.

Propaganda Film A film with the intention of persuading viewers to a particular IDEOLOGY or political cause. Like DOCUMENTARY, propaganda films make truth claims about the world, but they often exceed them in the extent of their wilful or unknowing distortion of fact.

Post-revolutionary Russia (see DIALECTICAL MONTAGE) and Great Britain were the first major film-producing countries to realize the potential of the mass medium of cinema for propaganda purposes, and both provided GOVERNMENT sponsorship for films celebrating the virtues of their respective economic and political systems. The documentary films produced by John Grierson in Great Britain for government agencies (see EMPIRE MARKETING BOARD, GENERAL POST OFFICE), such as *Coal Face* (dir. Alberto Cavalcanti, 1936) and *Night Mail* (dir. Basil Wright and Harry Watt, 1936), are as much about the benefits of industrialization in Britain as they are about coal production and the mail train. In the 1930s, as the world geared up for war, some governments seized control of their national film industries, as did the National Socialists in Germany, so that FEATURE FILMS would expound Aryan and anti-Semitic sentiments, as in *Jud Süss* (*The Swiss Jew*, dir. Veit Harlan, 1940) and *Der ewige Jude* (*The Eternal Jew*, dir. Fritz Hippler, 1940). DIRECTOR Leni Riefenstahl was commissioned by Hitler to make both *Triumph des Willens* (*Triumph of the Will*, 1935) and *Olympia* (1938), documentaries about the 1934 Nazi party congress in Nuremberg and the 1936 Berlin Olympic Games, respectively. In the case of the former, the PROFILMIC event, with its militaristic and ritual pomp, was held for the express purpose of making the film: Riefenstahl was provided with multiple CAMERAS and vantage points from which to film. Riefenstahl's films remain of aesthetic interest beyond their immediate propagandistic value because in their very style they manage to express the Fascist ideology that they promote in their content.

In the US the federal government was reluctant to become directly involved in film production, as popular sentiment viewed such involvement as interference in private enterprise. During Roosevelt's New Deal, however, the government did sponsor two exceptional documentaries by Pare Lorentz, *The Plow that Broke the Plains* (1936) and *The River* (1937), dealing with the government's efforts to deal with the dust bowl drought in the Midwest and the establishment of the Tennessee Valley Authority to bring electricity via a series of dams to that region. During World War II the American armed forces produced several films for the war effort, many of them made by HOLLYWOOD directors, including a SERIES of films produced by Frank Capra (see POPULISM) entitled *Why We Fight* (1942–1945) that were required viewing for military inductees.

Every war and intensely politicized period has its propaganda films and other works of POPULAR CULTURE, but contemporary cultural theory and ideological analysis has demonstrated that movies, similar to other art forms, are consistently propagandistic to the extent that they reflect and endorse dominant ideology. This has been the standard view of CLASSIC HOLLYWOOD CINEMA since the 1970s, as established by FEMINIST and MARXIST analyses.

Further reading: Furhammar & Isaksson (1971), Welch (1983)

Prop An abbreviation of PROPERTY, referring to any object on a film SET that can be used and carried by the ACTORS, as opposed to larger items such as furniture which are considered to be part of the set itself, though a piece of furniture integral to a CHARACTER and used as part of the ACTION can also be seen as a prop. Most DIRECTORS and PRODUCTION DESIGNERS use the symbolic power of props in the creation of the *MISE EN SCÈNE*.

Property A more formal term for PROP, but, in a quite different meaning, also used to denote the basis for a film production – a novel, play or SCRIPT, or something less formed, such as a magazine article or a song, but in any case copyright material.

Psychoanalysis The complex set of theoretical ideas originating with the writings of Sigmund Freud and others in the late nineteenth century, reinterpreted by Jacques Lacan and others to become one of the key influences on the development of cultural theory in general, and film THEORY in particular, since the 1970s. Most writers have concerned themselves principally with Freud's investigations into the way that human desires are channelled or suppressed by their knowledge of 'rules': much psychoanalytic writing focuses on early experience of sexual difference and guilt stemming from forbidden desire. Of particular significance to film studies has been Freud's emphasis on a male perspective, resulting in concepts such as 'lack' being applied to the female, whilst the male subconscious is dominated by an obsession with the phallus and fear of castration, real or symbolic.

Some earlier applications of psychoanalysis to film concentrated on the cinematic APPARATUS – the process by which cinema positions and constructs the spectator watching a film. Christian Metz and others drew comparisons between this and Lacan's reading of Freud's 'mirror stage' of child development, when the infant begins to recognize itself as a separate entity and experiences the illusion of being complete. CLASSICAL NARRATIVE cinema was seen as paralleling this through IDENTIFICATION with screen CHARACTERS and its high degree of CLOSURE, connecting strongly to a stage in psychoanalytic development in which the sense of the self is at its most gratifying, but also its most self-deluding. Metz took this further, seeing cinema as providing the kind of gratifications desired by the male child, suffering permanently from the OEDIPAL sense of loss of the mother. As Creed puts it, 'Narrative structures take up this process in the way they construct stories in which the "lost object" (almost always represented by union with a woman) is recovered by the male protagonist' (Hill & Church Gibson, 1998, p. 82).

It is perhaps through FEMINIST FILM THEORY that the influence of psychoanalysis has been most keenly felt, though it has been based upon feminists' critique, rather than adoption, of Lacan and particularly Freud. Laura Mulvey's 1975 essay *Visual Pleasure and Narrative Cinema* (Mulvey 1989) was seminal in challenging the implicit assumption that the cinema spectator was male and driven by essentially Oedipal impulses. For Mulvey and other earlier feminist theorists, cinema was essentially constructed around a pattern of a masculine GAZE, and the objectification of women, were either passive and fetishised into body parts by the use of the CLOSE-UP, or dangerous and therefore usually destroyed in the course of the narrative (see, for example, Kaplan, 1998). Mulvey argued that this was not an inevitable consequence of the male and female subconscious, but a pattern capable of change as women challenged the social norms of patriarchy (and reflections of it in art forms such as cinema).

The strongest CRITICISM of psychoanalytic theory as the dominant influence on post-1970 film studies – part of a wider questioning of 'grand theory' – has come from those seeing it as potentially ahistorical and therefore ignoring profound questions about the social and political forces that shape the cinema AUDIENCE. It is argued that its influence places a dangerously narrow emphasis on all-embracing theories about the workings of the subconscious as opposed to wider external forces

such as CLASS, RACE or age. Psychoanalysis remains a key influence on much theoretical writing about film today, with the difference that it is rarely looked to for such
all-embracing answers to questions about male and female identities and the formation of SUBJECTIVITY. For example, psychoanalysis is an important element in recent
writing on POST-COLONIAL THEORY or QUEER THEORY, but is not necessarily the
dominant influence. See also GENDER, MASCULINITY, POST-STRUCTURALISM.

Further reading: Hayward (1996), Creed in Hill & Church Gibson (1998), Hollows *et
al.* (2000), Metz (1975), Allen in Stam & Miller (2000)

Pull focus See RACK FOCUS.

Pure Cinema Films that refer to their own qualities as cinema rather than
offering themselves as REPRESENTATIONS are sometimes referred to as pure cinema.
In such films, REALISM or illusion tends to be sacrificed for formal and aesthetic
considerations such as *MISE EN SCÈNE*, COLOUR and movement. In René Clair's
Entr'acte (1924), for example, a woman is shown walking up a flight of stairs carrying a heavy bundle of laundry; just before she reaches the top the IMAGE LOOPS back,
making her repeat her steps several times. This plastic manipulation of the image,
rather than the illusion of real SPACE and TIME, expresses the woman's seemingly
interminable toil. Sometimes the term is used to refer to particular films or
SEQUENCES in films that are particularly effective or expressive, again because of
their exploitation of some aspect(s) of the cinematic medium. The Odessa Steps
SEQUENCE in *Battleship Potemkin* (dir. Sergei Eisenstein, 1925) and the shower
murder in *Psycho* (dir. Alfred Hitchcock, 1960) are noteworthy examples of pure
cinema within the context of narrative film. See also EXPERIMENTAL FILM, AVANT-
GARDE FILM.

Q

Queer cinema The term 'queer' has a long history as a term of abuse for,
mainly, male homosexuals. Recent work by gay men and lesbian women has re-
appropriated the term for a wide variety of new and challenging ways of exploring
sexual identity. Queer cinema seeks to move beyond the notion of positive REPRE-
SENTATIONS in GAY AND LESBIAN FILMS and assert and celebrate diversity in all
sexual practices. This has sometimes led to controversy in the gay and lesbian
community because queer cinema has used gay or lesbian CHARACTERS in ways that
are not simply positive, arguing that the movement towards sexual freedom should
by now have progressed beyond needing to hide behind simple positive representations. Whilst some would argue that the idea of a queer aesthetic has been around
for a very long time, a recognizable body of queer cinema films stems from the early
1990s, when a number of films appeared which which went beyond political
correctness in their treatment of sexual identity and seemed to be addressing a non-
straight AUDIENCE. Among the best known of this group are *My Own Private Idaho*
(dir. Gus Van Sant, 1991), *Edward II* (dir. Derek Jarman, 1991), *Young Soul Rebels*
(dir. Isaac Julien, 1991) and *Swoon* (dir. Tom Kalin, 1992). See also FEMINIST FILM
THEORY, GENDER, MASCULINITY.

Further reading: Dyer (1977), Dyer (1990), Waugh (1996)

Queer theory Like makers of QUEER CINEMA, queer theorists seek to go beyond the redefinitions of SEXUALITY offered by GAY AND LESBIAN theorists and seek radical new ways of thinking about all sexual identity. Bisexuality and androgyny are key areas of exploration for the queer theorist as are so-called straight, but non-normative, sexualities. Queer theory at its most radical seeks to break down conventional theoretical notions of what it is to be male or female, seeing sexuality as complex and fluid rather than, say, lesbian, gay or straight. The films of Pedro Almodovar, such as *All About My Mother* (1999), where CHARACTERS' sexual and GENDER identities are constantly about surprise and redefinition, reflect this type of thinking.

Queer theory is not simply about the affirmation of new work, but also about the re-reading of established TEXTS and practices. Gay and lesbian critics have for some time read work 'against the grain' (see, for example, Dyer, 1990) and queer theorists have continued this tradition by finding more problematic and complex points of identification in former straight, gay or lesbian texts. Such readings emphasize openness in texts that were formerly closed in the way they had been read with regard to the possibilities of spectator IDENTIFICATION. As Alexander Doty puts it, Marlene Dietrich and Bette Davis could be said to have queer STAR images, as they have inspired lesbian, gay and bisexual cultural appreciations (Hill & Church Gibson 1998, p. 150). See also MASCULINITY.
Further reading: Erhart in Miller & Stam (1999), Hollows *et al.* (2000)

Quickie A LOW-BUDGET film SHOT very quickly, usually to fulfil a deliberate low-budget slot, for example in the era of the DOUBLE BILL or B PICTURE. The phenomenon belongs mainly to the heyday of the STUDIO SYSTEM and its existence emphasizes the highly industrialized nature of production during this era, when productivity could be increased to meet specific kinds of demand. See also QUOTA QUICKIE, EXPLOITATION FILM.

Quota quickie Term for many films produced in Britain following the 1927 Cinematographic Films Act which required that a steadily rising proportion of films shown in Britain should be made in Britain. When introduced, around 5 per cent of films exhibited in Britain were British; by 1932 the proportion was around 20 per cent, though in reality many quota quickies were produced by American companies setting up in Britain to avoid the tacit restriction on American imports. See also GOVERNMENT AND CINEMA, HEGEMONY.

R

Race A term used loosely in film study, broadly referring to a person's racial origin as defined by particular physical characteristics. The term is frequently used in ways which intersect with forms of ethnic, national and subcultural identities but, as Robyn Wiegman points out, 'Where ethnicity provides the means for differentiations based on culture, language and national origins, race renders the reduction of human differences to innate, biological phenomena, phenomena that circulate culturally as the visible ledger for defining and justifying economic and political hierarchies between white and non-white groups' (Hill & Church Gibson 1998, p. 160). Race is, then, an essentialist category, and has been used in ways that are IDEOLOGICAL: it is one thing to describe someone as possessing Caucasian physical racial characteristics, but quite another to ascribe to them some kind of natural authority. Below, race is explored as a factor primarily in US and British cinema, but see also THIRD CINEMA.

Much effort has been put into re-reading the past to reveal the ideological underpinning of the REPRESENTATION of race in classic film TEXTS. In the US, one of the defining national GENRES, the WESTERN, centres on racial difference and has been crucial to debate about the representation of race in film. The revered western *The Searchers* (dir. John Ford, 1956) deals with the deep-seated racism that informed the characters of the heroes of the west, personified by Ethan Edwards (John Wayne). Although Ford's film offers alternative perspectives to Edwards' homicidal loathing of the Comanche that murdered his family, there is also a strong sense that the film seeks to understand and justify the racism that underpinned the 'civilization' of the west.

Some work on race has centred on STEREOTYPING, the presentation of complex CHARACTERS through a reductive set of supposed racial characteristics. Celebrated HOLLYWOOD films from *Birth of a Nation* (dir. D.W. Griffith, 1915) through *Gone With the Wind* (dir. Victor Fleming, 1939) to *The Deer Hunter* (dir. Michael Cimino, 1978) have been controversial in terms of racial stereotyping. In American film stereotypes have been predominantly associated with African-Americans or, in the case of the Western, with Native Americans. In Britain there have been many examples of Asian stereotypes, reflecting the different British POST-COLONIAL experience: as recently as 1984, *A Passage to India* (dir. David Lean) offered an extreme stereotype in Alec Guiness's portrayal of the Brahmin, Professor Godbole (also a late high-profile example of another of cinema's controversial intersections with race, the CASTING of white ACTORS in leading black roles). Some critics challenge the focus on stereotypes for discussion of race in film, arguing that it distorts the issues and urging wider concentration on the way film language in general reflects racial difference through the use of CAMERA ANGLES, LIGHTING and the allocation of screen time.

As HOLLYWOOD in particular began to deal with race as an issue from the 1940s onwards, it did so primarily from the position of naïve white liberalism. In this vein are films such as *Guess Who's Coming To Dinner* (dir. Stanley Kramer, 1967) and *In the Heat of the Night* (dir. Norman Jewison, 1967), both starring Sidney Poitier, the first black to approach Hollywood STAR status. The comparative success of these films at the American BOX-OFFICE was a key factor behind the production of BLAX-PLOITATION films in the 1970s, which began to appeal to black working CLASS audiences: films such as *Shaft* (dir. Gordon Parks, 1971) and *Sweet Sweetback's Baadasssss Song* (dir. Melvin Van Peebles, 1971) offered black urban Americans (especially males) very different kinds of IDENTIFICATION figures. Since the 1970s there has emerged a generation of black US film-makers, led by Spike Lee, whose films have reached a wider AUDIENCE and whose contribution to debates around race and cinema at a number of levels has been crucial.

Contemporary thought about race in cinema tends to focus on its intersection with other areas of marginalization, and Lee's work has come in for much unfavourable critical attention from feminist and gay critics. In the British INDEPEN-DENT sector the work of, for example Isaac Julien has explored new black identities and their intersection with QUEER CINEMA. See also BLACK FILM, RACE FILM.
Further reading: Miller & Stam (1999), Smith (1997), Willis (1998)

Race film Term used in the American film industry from the SILENT CINEMA through the 1940s to refer to movies made by African-American film-makers specifically for African-American AUDIENCES, many distributed and exhibited in theatres in areas with large black populations, and often imitations of GENRE movies made on LOW BUDGETS. Oscar Micheaux (*Body and Soul*, 1924; *Harlem After Midnight*, 1934) and Spenser Williams (*The Blood of Jesus*, 1941), both black Americans, produced important race films, the former as WRITER, DIRECTOR and PRODUCER of an astonishing 34 pictures. The term may also apply to Yiddish films made over the same period, such as the Polish *Yidl Mitn Fidl* (*Yidl with his Fiddle*, dir. Joseph Green, 1936) and *Amerikaner Schadchen* (*The Marriage Broker*, dir. Edgar G. Ulmer, 1940). See also BLACK CINEMA.
Further reading: Diawara (1993), Pines (1975), Reid (1993)

Rack Focus A change in the DEPTH OF FIELD during a SHOT from either foreground to background or vice-versa. SHALLOW FOCUS is used to draw attention to one FOCAL plane, which is then altered. A CAMERA OPERATOR employs rack focus simply to keep in focus a main CHARACTER or the element of the shot which the DIRECTOR wants to privilege, although the technique also may be used for thematic purposes. In *Getting Straight* (1970) director Richard Rush's frequent use of rack focus works on several levels simultaneously: it expresses the political and emotional distance between the characters, establishes a visual style embodying the psychedelic era in which the film was made and SET, and creates a sense of a shifting world that parallels the social revolution the film predicts in its climax. Also known as pull focus, shift focus.

Rank Organisation One of the most significant companies in British film history: at its height in the 1940s Rank owned the largest share of production, DISTRIBUTION and EXHIBITION facilities in Britain. Rank's assets included PINEWOOD and Denham STUDIOS and the Gaumont chain of cinemas, and it backed some key films including *Henry V* (dir. Laurence Olivier, 1944) and *The Red Shoes* (dir. Michael Powell and Emeric Pressburger, 1948). The company's founder, J. Arthur Rank, a former Methodist preacher, saw film as a potentially evangelistic medium, though mildly jingoistic patriotism is more evident in the films than any religious message. Rank played an important role in the film trade skirmishes with the US in the late 1940s, at one point deciding to show only British films at Rank-owned cinemas – a stunt that did not last long when the public demonstrated clearly that it wanted to see HOLLYWOOD films even if this was deemed unpatriotic. Rank's film activities declined from the late 1950s, though it remained a key player in the British entertainment and leisure industry, and will probably best be remembered in the popular imagination for its trademark logo of the giant gong being struck at the beginning of each of its productions.

Ratings, rating system An agreed system for the rating or CERTIFICATION of films for their public RELEASE. The present certification systems, based on parental guidance and age restrictions, operating in the UK are U, PG, 12, 15 and 18. The US ratings, which are very similar, are G, PG, PG13, R, NC17, X. See also A CERTIFICATE/AA CERTIFICATE, BBFC, CENSORSHIP, G RATING, H CERTIFICATE, PG, U CERTIFICATE, X RATING.

Reaction shot A SHOT, generally a CLOSE-UP, showing the reaction of a CHAR-
ACTER to some ACTION or dialogue in the previous shot.

Realism The term's general use implicitly compares a filmic REPRESENTATION of
something with an external reality: a film is realistic because it accurately reproduces
that part of the 'real' world to which it refers. Much critical energy has been spent
disputing that such an idea has any validity at all. The simplest way to challenge
notions of realism in the cinema is to raise the issue of mediation: any act of pointing a CAMERA involves choice and selection, a version of the world, not the world
itself, as if seen through a window. Moreover it is a world that is framed, lit and
dressed in ways that impose creative choices on an AUDIENCE's impression of external reality.

More complex are the different ways in which late twentieth century thought has
sought to challenge orthodox ideas of the existence of any external reality at all. If
POSTMODERNISM, for instance, sees the world as a complex patterning of TEXTS and
recycled experiences, then there is no 'real' to attempt to capture. If we set aside for a
moment the 'impossibility' of realism there are, as Susan Hayward puts it, two basic
approaches to the many attempts to capture it in the cinema: 'First, seamless realism,
whose IDEOLOGICAL function is to disguise the illusion of realism. Second, aesthetically motivated realism, which attempts to use the camera in a non-manipulative
fashion and considers the purpose of realism in its ability to convey a reading of reality, or several readings even.' (Hayward, 1996, p. 299)

In the first category is the 'classic realist text', from HOLLYWOOD and elsewhere,
with narrative strategies and CONVENTIONS such as the 180°RULE and CONTINUITY
EDITING designed to hide the constructed nature of the world presented. The result,
if successful, is the acceptance by spectators that they are watching a fully formed
reality with its own internal coherence, even if the narrative includes huge jumps in
TIME and place. In the second category is the critically revered version of cinematic
realism that has also at times been attacked for its presentation of an illusion of reality and (often) lack of a politically progressive attitude. (See, for example, the debate
between MacCabe and McArthur, both 1976). Key examples here include late 1940s
and early 1950s Italian NEO-REALISM, late 1950s and early 1960s BRITISH NEW WAVE
films and the SOCIAL REALIST work of British DIRECTOR Ken Loach, spanning three
decades since his first feature, *Kes* (1969). What these have in common is the adoption of film-making strategies designed to minimize the intrusive mediation of
certain cinematic CODES, including CASTING unknown ACTORS, or even non-actors,
and what Loach has called a 'quiet camera' – avoiding ANGLES and CAMERA MOVE-
MENTS that draw attention to themselves, extensive use of LOCATION shooting, avoidance of intrusive LIGHTING techniques, frequent use of LONG TAKES and improvised
SCENES or dialogue.

While such strategies do not change the basic issue of mediated reality, they
declare a kind of independence from the STAR-orientated manipulation of
conventional MAINSTREAM realism. In terms of narrative, too, clear patterns link
much of this work: to varying degrees all seek to present worlds traditionally
ignored by mainstream cinema, usually the urban working CLASS poor; event and
sensation are played down in favour of an accumulation of detail and texture of
the worlds depicted; and a sense of objectivity is cultivated by multiple perspectives within the narratives, though it is in the nature of such work that it often has

an overtly political agenda and debates between perspectives are restricted to a variety of progressive POINTS OF VIEW.

Most film THEORY has rejected realism as a progressive form because of its comforting illusionism and its presentation of a fixed reality rather than alternative ways of seeing (and by extension changing) the world. Aesthetic agendas from Bertolt Brecht to Jean-Luc Godard have demanded art that reveals the means of its own making and foregrounds its fictional nature, but many are still convinced of the possibility of the progressive realist text (if not of the seamless illusions of commercial cinema). In his work on the post-war British film's realist tendency, Hill (1986) asserts that the aesthetic of realism is most usefully dealt with not by referring to any external reality, but by referring only to other works, by seeing realism, or realisms as relative. See also BRECHTIAN, EPIC, DOCUMENTARY, NATURALISM, SOCIAL REALISM, SOCIALIST REALISM. Further reading: Bazin (1971), Williams (1983), Williams in Gledhill & Williams (2000), Stam (2000)

Rear projection A SPECIAL EFFECTS process achieved by PROJECTING (usually moving) IMAGES in a STUDIO on a SCREEN behind ACTORS to simulate LOCATION photography, often used to create the illusion of CHARACTERS in motion, either in a vehicle or on horseback. A common technique during the era of the STUDIO SYSTEM, especially during the 1930s after the introduction of SOUND made filming on location more difficult, rear projected images grew more noticeable after shooting on location became standard practice and fell out of favour. By 1964, the rear projection images of Tippi Hedren riding a horse in *Marnie* (dir. Alfred Hitchcock) seemed patently artificial, although some critics have argued that this effect works in the film as an EXPRESSIONIST projection of the protagonist's traumatized memory. Also referred to as back projection.

Reception theory An overarching term covering the different ways in which film studies has changed emphasis from interest only in the film TEXT and the determinants of its production, to interest in the AUDIENCE and its 'reception' of specific films or the entire experience of cinema. This interest has taken different forms, from investigations into what Hayward (1996, p. 336) has called 'the spectator as psychic phenomenon' to studies of actual groups of spectators in specific contexts. Work in the former category has tended to be entirely theoretical and focused on PSYCHOAN-ALYTIC THEORY. Earlier work did not even consider the GENDER of the spectator (see, for example, Metz, 1975), but most work since the late 1970s, especially FEMINIST FILM THEORY, has focused on how the cinematic APPARATUS positions the spectator specifically in terms of gender (see, for example, Mulvey, 1989). Such work is concerned less with the 'reception' of actual films than with debates about the workings of cinema on the subconscious mind.

Recent work on studies of real audiences and their relationship to specific film texts has been influenced by the cultural studies approach to other mass media, especially TELEVISION, such as Ien Ang's (1985) study of the audience for the American soap opera *Dallas*. Comparable work on film has been interested in the way audiences make sense not only of films, but key phenomena such as STARS (see Stacey, 1994). Interest in film audiences is not new: early writing about audiences tended to see film as an all-powerful conveyor of 'messages'. In addition, the industry has always taken a keen interest in researching the make-up of its audience as part of ADVERTISING and

MARKETING strategies. Modern film studies has shifted emphasis to the notion of the active audience making different kinds of sense of films, though there has remained an implicit awareness of the influential power of film as a medium.
Further reading: Hollows *at al.* (2000), Jenkins in Gledhill & Williams (2000), Stam (2000)

Reel A metal or plastic spool holding film, which allows the film to wind off into the projector; a separate reel takes up the film after it has passed through the projector. But reel is also the measurement of a film's length and running time, as in ONE-REELER.

Reflex camera, reflex viewfinder A reflex viewfinder, via a mirror or prism system, enables the CAMERA OPERATOR to view the SCENE being SHOT precisely, by means of light entering the LENS of the CAMERA. Reflex VIEWFINDERS are to be found on most cameras these days, but this was not always the case, and PARALLAX meant that the viewfinder did not show exactly what was being shot.

Reflexivity 'The capacity for self-reflexion of a medium or language' (Stam 2000, p. 151); in film, the way a film foregrounds its own processes and CONVENTIONS. Reflexive cinema has generally been seen as consciously opposed to MAINSTREAM CINEMA's realistic illusion, which hides processes and conventions from immediate view. Within this broad meaning, very different kinds of film can be said to foreground their own production. Some mainstream films – *Sherlock Junior* (dir. Buster Keaton, 1924), *Hellzapoppin'* (dir. H.C. Potter, 1941), the Bing Crosby-Bob Hope Road films, Woody Allen's films – can be considered reflexive, though all are COMEDIES, militating against any subversion their reflexivity might suggest. Films about film-making – European like *8½* (dir. Federico Fellini, 1963) or *Day For Night* (dir. François Truffaut, 1973), or American like *Singin' In the Rain* (dir. Gene Kelly and Stanley Donen, 1952) or *The Player* (dir. Robert Altman, 1992) – clearly draw attention to some of the processes of film production, even though remaining largely illusionist. Jean-Luc Godard's films consistently foreground and reflect upon conventions of CAMERA MOVEMENT, EDITING, etc. As V.F. Perkins (in Barr, 1969) says, *Vivre sa vie* (1962) offers 'a string of suggestions as to how one might film a conversation', while *Tout va bien* (1972) also reflects on the economic and IDEOLOGICAL conditions necessary for film production. Much MATERIALIST and other STRUCTURAL film-making (such as *Wavelength*, dir. Michael Snow, 1967, or *Berlin Horse*, dir. Malcolm LeGrice, 1970) foregrounds the qualities of CELLULOID such as EMULSION, light sensitivity and GRAIN. The reflexive impulse, so strong in Godard's 1960s and 1970s work, owes much to the revival of BRECHTIAN and Soviet ideas of the 1920s, and films such as *Man With The Movie Camera* (dir. Dziga Vertov, 1929). Such influences imply a political purpose for reflexivity: to foreground what is usually transparent and make the spectator active and aware. The foregrounding in structural film derives more from past developments in modern painting which foregrounded the brushstroke, canvas and paint. See also COUNTER CINEMA, DIALECTICAL MONTAGE, DISTANCIATION.
Further reading: Bordwell (1985)

Re-issue, re-release The release of a film for DISTRIBUTION some time after its first run, the gap between the original and re-release being usually considerable, though some films have been re-released quite quickly in response to, for example, a strong critical showing in another country or an unexpected nomination for an award. The phenomenon is currently growing as techniques for restoring PRINTS become more sophisticated and distributors see market openings for theatrical showings of old classics. The DIRECTOR'S CUT is a variant on the re-issue/release, purporting to offer AUDIENCES a more authentic version – from the DIRECTOR's perspective – than the original release.

Release The initial DISTRIBUTION of a completed film: 'general release' indicates a widespread, e.g. national, release, while 'select release' indicates more restricted DISTRIBUTION. Typical patterns of release in the past involved, first, restricted release in first run cinemas – normally only one per city – before wider release to second and third run cinemas. Such patterns persist but BLOCKBUSTERS today almost always receive SATURATION RELEASE.

Release print A PRINT of a completed film, struck from a DUPE (or RELEASE) NEGATIVE, intended for release to cinemas.

Remake A film very closely based on an earlier version, with contemporary variations ranging from CASTING to more drastic narrative revisions. American FILM NOIR of the 1940s and 1950s, such as *The Big Sleep* (dir. Howard Hawks, 1946) and *The Postman Always Rings Twice* (dir. Tay Garnett, 1946) seem particularly prone to being remade. Recently (1998), Gus Van Sant has given a new twist to the phenomenon by recreating *Psycho* (dir. Alfred Hitchcock, 1960) virtually SHOT for shot, except in COLOUR rather than the original BLACK-AND-WHITE.

Repertory cinema Cinemas with a number of different films in their programme, shown in sequence over a given time period. Such cinemas often specialize in themed programmes like RETROSPECTIVES of DIRECTORS' work or grouped films from a particular GENRE or movement. Repertory cinemas usually offer a broader range of films than more commercial venues, sometimes emphasizing foreign language cinema, with some overlap with ART HOUSES (though most of these now play a single film at a time). The number of repertory cinemas has declined drastically in recent years, even in large cities, and in Britain they generally survive only with the aid of public subsidy, as with the NATIONAL FILM THEATRE and its regional film theatre outposts.

Representation The process by which art forms use their various languages to ascribe meaning to objects, places, people and, most importantly, social groups. The term is most often associated with SEMIOTICS and the complex ways it has sought to make sense of the means by which signs and CODES interact with AUDIENCES to create meaning. All mass media, including cinema, play a crucial role in the way representations circulate, and by extension in their impact on the way a culture sees and treats those things or people being represented. The media do not simply show something in a particular way and an AUDIENCE receives it: theoretical work of the last thirty years has ascribed varying degrees of agency to the audience. However, the media's power to reproduce similar IMAGES and people's increasing reliance on media for information about the world does give it enormous power.

Interest in cinematic representations has often focused on issues of RACE, GENDER, sexuality and CLASS. Much work has focused on textual analysis, involving reading representations and their repetition across a range of films, but there are also questions about the relationship of cinema to social and historical contexts and the many influences of the institutions of cinema itself on the representations that it offers. There have been huge changes in some of the representations traditionally associated with MAINSTREAM cinema: the range of roles in which both women and men are seen is clearly greater now than in the 1950s, though many argue that such changes are superficial and that older male and female representations remain. By contrast, AVANT-GARDE or INDEPENDENT CINEMA is seen as the more likely source of alternative cinematic representations, though by a slow process these eventually impact on the mainstream.

The biggest single shift in debates about representation has been from simply seeking to substitute so-called positive images of a group for negative ones, to addressing issue of representation and its origins in distortion and STEREOTYPING. For this reason, films that are serious about representation as an issue tend to be formally distinctive, presenting identity as highly complex and in constant flux and challenging audiences to see in new ways. Examples of such work can be found in QUEER CINEMA, such as *My Own Private Idaho* (dir. Gus Van Sant, 1991) and *Looking for Langston* (dir. Isaac Julien, 1988), the latter raising new questions about the representation of both blacks and gay men.

Further reading: Andrew (1984), Dyer (1990), Hollows *et al.* (2000)

Republic Small HOLLYWOOD film production company founded in 1935, known primarily for its juvenile SERIALS and FORMULA WESTERNS, some of which featured rising STAR John Wayne. Under studio boss Herbert J. Yates, the STUDIO produced imitative films on quick production schedules, and even its major FEATURES tended to be B MOVIES with relatively poor PRODUCTION VALUES. In the 1930s and 1940s Republic produced a string of 'singing cowboy' WESTERNS with Gene Autry and Roy Rogers, and several musicals with ice skating star Vera Hruba Ralston (Mrs. Yates). The company absorbed several other POVERTY ROW studios, and in the early 1950s, attempting to rise to the status of a MAJOR, produced at least two important films: John Ford's *The Quiet Man* (1952, for which Ford won an OSCAR for Best DIRECTOR) and Nicholas Ray's *Johnny Guitar* (1954). With the decline of the STUDIO SYSTEM and the B MOVIE, Republic made its last movies in 1958.

Further reading: Gomery (1986)

Retake As a verb, 'retake' is to shoot again a SHOT or a SCENE which has just been shot, normally immediately after the previous TAKE and because the first take was unsatisfactory. A SHOT may be retaken many times until the filmmaker is satisfied with it. As a noun, a 'retake' is a shot which has been 'retaken'.

Retrospective A special series of film screenings organized around a theme, such as showcasing the work of a particular DIRECTOR (sometimes an occasion for a career reassessment) or an overview of a GENRE or NATIONAL CINEMA.

Reversal film Film STOCK which, after exposure, is specially processed to produce a POSITIVE print, eliminating the NEGATIVE stage, making it in some cases less expensive to use. Although the first generation IMAGE can be high quality, making further prints, via DUPE negatives, involves loss of quality. Reversal film is often used for 16MM film-making; the original processed STOCK can be edited and screened – the WORKPRINT becoming the show print.

Reverse angle A position taken up by a CAMERA that is the opposite of that used in the previous SHOT. The most common use of this is when filming conversations and using a SHOT-REVERSE SHOT technique when a reverse angle often follows a POINT OF VIEW shot. See also CAMERA ANGLE.

Reverse motion Reverse motion, or reverse ACTION, shows movement in reverse – opposite to the way it was SHOT, achieved either IN-CAMERA or by OPTICAL PRINTING. Often used for comic effect and for stunts (which can be better controlled by staging in reverse for playback in apparently forward motion), reverse motion should be considered as a property of the medium, and one which enables the CAMERA to do what the human eye cannot: in the LUMIÈRE PROGRAMME, *The Demolition of a Wall* is shown in forward movement, then in reverse. Sergei Eisenstein, using the medium's potential to the full, uses reverse motion in both *Strike* (1924) and *October* (1927) while Jean Cocteau uses it for poetic and magical effect in *La Belle et la bête* (1946) and *Orphée* (1950).

RKO Radio Pictures Incorporated American film company created in 1928 when RCA (Radio Corporation of America), with its own patents for recorded SOUND, combined with the Keith, Albee and Orpheum theatre chains (hence Radio-Keith-Orpheum) aiming to introduce its own system for SOUND FILM. As a VERTICALLY INTEGRATED company, RKO became one of HOLLYWOOD's MAJOR STUDIOS, producing some of Hollywood's best films, including *King Kong* (dir. Merian C. Cooper and Ernest Schoedsack, 1933), *The Informer* (dir. John Ford, 1935), *Citizen Kane* (Orson Welles, 1941), *The Magnificent Ambersons* (Welles, 1942) and *It's a Wonderful Life* (dir. Frank Capra, 1946). The studio also produced a SERIES of popular MUSICALS with Fred Astaire and Ginger Rogers in the 1930s, including *The Gay Divorcee* (dir. Mark Sandrich, 1934), *Top Hat* (dir. Sandrich, 1935) and *Swing Time* (dir. George Stevens, 1936), a series of effectively atmospheric HORROR FILMS in the 1940s with PRODUCER Val Lewton, and many fine FILMS NOIRs in the 1950s by DIRECTORS such as Nicholas Ray (*They Live by Night*, 1949; *On Dangerous Ground*, 1952) and Fritz Lang (*While the City Sleeps* and *Beyond a Reasonable Doubt*, both 1956). The studio's biggest hit was the sentimental *The Bells of St. Mary's* (dir. Leo McCarey, 1945). Eccentric industrialist Howard Hughes bought RKO in 1948, after which the STUDIO experienced a period of mismanagement. In 1955 Hughes sold the company to the General Tire and Rubber Company, which in turn sold it two years later to Desi Arnaz and Lucille Ball, who transformed it into Desilu Productions. See also BIG 5.
Further reading: Finler (1988), Gomery (1986), Jewell & Harbin (1982), Mordden (1988), Schatz (1988)

Road Movie Film GENRE characterized by a journey narrative involving one or more CHARACTERS, often with an EPISODIC structure comprised of people and situations encountered *en route*, the physical journey across SPACE reflecting the inner, psychological journeys of the characters, who change and grow as a result of their travelling experiences. *Two for the Road* (dir. Stanley Donen, 1967) shows the stages in a marriage from youthful idealism to middle-aged disillusionment as a SERIES of SCENES in different cars at different times over many years.

Like the CHASE FILM, road movies exploit the kinetic appeal of motion pictures, as in *Vanishing Point* (dir. Richard Sarafian, 1971), where the protagonist's goal is only to keep moving. At the end of *Two-Lane Blacktop* (dir. Monte Hellman, 1971), the road movie's energy seems to ignite the film itself as the IMAGE appears to burn in the projector. The genre is particularly American, emphasizing spatial distance and mobility: the open road betokens an escape, like the frontier in the WESTERN. Being on the road, as celebrated in Jack Kerouac's CULT Beat Generation novel *On the Road* (1957), provides freedom from responsibilities and middle CLASS concerns. Occasionally, though, the journey is a downward descent into doom from which there is no road back, as for the hapless anti-hero of the FILM NOIR classic, *Detour* (Edgar G. Ulmer, 1945).

The vehicle of choice in road movies is the automobile, because of the opportunity it offers to choose the road not taken, but they also are SET on buses (*Get on the Bus*, dir. Spike Lee, 1996), motorcycles (*Easy Rider*, dir. Dennis Hopper, 1969) and carriages (*Stagecoach*, dir. John Ford, 1939). Road movies also tend to overlap with other genres, as *Kalifornia* (dir. Dominic Sena, 1993) does with the serial killer film, *Mad Max* (dir. George Miller, 1979) with both SCIENCE FICTION and the ACTION FILM, *Stagecoach* with the Western and *Butch Cassidy and the Sundance Kid* (dir. George Roy Hill, 1969) with the BUDDY FILM.

Thelma and Louise (dir. Ridley Scott, 1991) subverted the traditionally masculine focus of the genre with its pair of outlaw women, paving the way for other contemporary variations of the genre such as the QUEER *My Own Private Idaho* (Gus Van Sant, 1991), *The Doom Generation* (Gregg Araki, 1995), and the Australian film *The Adventures of Priscilla, Queen of the Desert* (dir. Stephan Elliot, 1994), a COMEDY about three urban gay men travelling through the outback, and the American remake, *To Wong Foo, Thanks for Everything! Julie Newmar* (dir. Beeban Kidron, 1995). Directors from other countries have also made important road movies, including Jean-Luc Godard (*Weekend*, 1967) and Wim Wenders (*Im Lauf der Zeit/Kings of the Road*, 1975), who named his production company after the genre. Further reading: Cohan & Hark (1997), Sargeant & Watson (1999), Williams (1982)

Road show, roadshow Form of film RELEASE in which major films – normally BLOCKBUSTERS – were first released only to a select few theatres, usually in major cities, for separate (rather than continuous) performances, with higher ticket prices and reserved seats (HARD TICKET) giving the overall character of a special event, and some of the prestige of legitimate theatre-going. A long-established DISTRIBUTION-EXHIBITION practice which was used for D.W. Griffith's *Birth of a Nation* (1915), but especially popular in the 1950s and 1960s for big releases such as *The Bridge on the River Kwai* (dir. David Lean, 1957), *Lawrence of Arabia* (dir. Lean, 1962), *Exodus* (dir. Otto Preminger, 1960), and *Cleopatra* (dir. Joseph L. Mankiewicz, 1963). *VARIETY* reported in 1968 that 'Roadshow is the name of the game now being played by the majors. At current count 12 pix are expected to go out on hardticket in the last four months of this year, as compared to only 10 reserved-seaters during the previous 20 months' (quoted by Wyatt in Lewis 1998, p. 66). Roadshowing was part of the strategy, combined with the production of the blockbuster films themselves, for combating falling AUDIENCES, but has been overtaken since the 1970s by SATURATION RELEASE.

Rockumentary So many DOCUMENTARIES have focused on rock musicians that they have acquired their own GENRE designation. At the height of DIRECT CINEMA and CINÉMA VÉRITÉ, particularly in the US, documentary film-makers sought popular musicians as their subjects to secure funding for and wider DISTRIBUTION of their work. The first rockumentary is arguably *Lonely Boy* (dir. Roman Kroiter/Wolf Koenig, 1961), a NATIONAL FILM BOARD OF CANADA film about Canadian pop singer Paul Anka's breakthrough success in the US market. *Woodstock* (dir. Michael Wadleigh, 1970), filmed with a large budget and multiple CAMERAS, was given a wide and successful theatrical RELEASE. Rockumentaries tend to alternate between SCENES of performance onstage and more candid events backstage, an approach so familiar that the GENRE was PARODIED in *This is Spinal Tap* (dir. Rob Reiner, 1984), a MOCKU-MENTARY about a fictional heavy metal rock group.
Further reading: Plantinga in Grant & Sloniowski (1998)

Romantic comedy Form of COMEDY focusing on a heterosexual couple and the humorous misunderstandings in their relationship. Romantic comedy needed synchronized SOUND for the humorous verbal interplay between couples, as well as charismatic and attractive STARS. In the early days of sound Ernst Lubitsch was known for his sophisticated romantic comedies, including *Love Parade* (1929) and *Trouble in Paradise* (1932). The 1930s was the era of SCREWBALL COMEDY, a specific SUBGENRE of romantic comedy, but also a decade that featured other romantic comedies such as the SERIES of MUSICALS starring Fred Astaire and Ginger Rogers and the series of Thin Man DETECTIVE FILMS starring William Powell and Myrna Loy. In the 1950s romantic comedy became more genteel, as in the bedroom farces starring Doris Day and Rock Hudson, such as *Pillow Talk* (dir. Michael Gordon, 1959). In recent years, *When Harry Met Sally* (dir. Rob Reiner, 1989) shows that romantic comedy can still connect with AUDIENCES, but with changing sexual mores. Romantic comedies like *Chasing Amy* (dir. Kevin Smith) and *As Good as it Gets* (dir. James L. Brooks) (both 1997) have expanded the genre's traditional focus on the heterosexual couple.
Further reading: Babington & Evans (1989), Harvey (1987), Henderson (1978), Kendall (1992)

Rostrum camera A specialized CAMERA set up, with the camera held by a platform looking down vertically (at adjustable distances), used primarily for photographing CELS for ANIMATION work or for taking movie FOOTAGE of still pictures.

Rough cut More advanced stage than the ASSEMBLY edit in the EDITING of a film, in which the STORY line is mapped out and the best TAKES cut together with the SOUND by the EDITOR, generally under the supervision of, or in conjunction with, the DIRECTOR, but without any fine cutting. See also FINE CUT.

Runaway Generally a HOLLYWOOD production made outside the US, primarily to take advantage of cheaper costs, a frequent strategy in the 1950s and 1960s, when the

MAJOR STUDIOS were in financial crisis and US labour and other costs were increasing. Advantage could also be taken of tax shelters, European domestic SUBSIDIES, and – important for EPICS – cheaply hired conscript armies. Britain, Italy and Spain were popular for runaway productions. See also *CINECITTÀ*.

Rushes Generic term for the unedited SHOTS which have been made for a film. Normal practice in commercial film and TELEVISION PRODUCTION is that film shot during a day's shooting is made into positive PRINTS, usually with SYNCHRONIZED SOUND on tape, the night after shooting, for viewing and evaluation by the DIRECTOR and others the next day. In this case, the normal industry term would be DAILIES, since viewed on a daily basis, but rushes do not need to be viewed the day after shooting.

S

Safety film Any FILM STOCK of EMULSION bonded on cellulose ACETATE or triacetate or, increasingly, polyester, all of which are of low flammability and burn slowly. Known as safety film because these stocks, introduced in 1951, replaced the extremely flammable, unstable cellulose NITRATE stock.

SAG The Screen Actors Guild. See GUILD.

Samurai film One of the period or COSTUME (*jidai-geki*) GENRES in Japanese cinema focusing on the figure of the samurai warrior. Samurai films gained popularity in Japan after World War II, becoming known in the West primarily through the films of DIRECTOR Akira Kurosawa with Toshiro Mifune, including *Rashomon* (1950), *Yojimbo* (*The Bodyguard*, 1961) and *Sanjuro* (1961). One type of MARTIAL ARTS FILM, samurai films focus on the skills of the samurai, which rely on a strict code of discipline, and have often been compared to WESTERNS; several Westerns have been REMAKES of samurai films – most famously, *The Magnificent Seven* (dir. John Sturges, 1960), based on Kurosawa's *The Seven Samurai* (1954).
Further reading: Desser (1982), Silver (1983)

Sankofa One of several non-profit making film and VIDEO workshops founded in Britain in the 1980s with financial support from CHANNEL 4, which stipulated that workshops be committed to building new AUDIENCES for their work and to community involvement – in Sankofa's case, the London black community. Sankofa also received vital support from the Greater London Council, eager to fund black cultural activity following the inner-city riots in Britain in 1981. The name Sankofa refers to a bird whose head is turned backwards, alluding to the group's intention to offer a reclaimed past to the black community through its reinterpretation on film. Sankofa's best known film is *Passion of Remembrance* (dir. Maureen Blackwood and Isaac Julien, 1986).
Further reading: Hill (1999)

Sartov shot A type of SOFT FOCUS shot named after Hendrick Sartov, a still photographer and CINEMATOGRAPHER who pioneered the style, shooting Lillian Gish in D.W. Griffith's *Broken Blossoms* (1919) and *Way Down East* (1920).

Satellite television Along with CABLE one of the principal new means of transmitting TELEVISION signals for domestic reception that has grown up to challenge conventional terrestrial television. Though satellite technology in various forms has existed since the late 1950s it was only during the late 1980s that it started to be used for direct broadcast to individual domestic receivers. The potential social and political implications of this include the capacity to by-pass the broadcasting regulations of individual countries as a satellite footprint cannot easily be confined within national boundaries. Amongst a number of premium channels offered to satellite television subscribers is usually a film channel offering access to FEATURE FILMS some time in advance of their RELEASE on VIDEO or to terrestrial broadcasters. As the number of satellite channels proliferate the demand for feature films increases rapidly and outside the first run channels there are a number of specialists that offer, for example, back catalogues of film STUDIOS. However, as with cable television, there is strong evidence that the demand for film inevitably produces a vast quantity of cheaply produced inferior products to fill the ever-expanding air time.

Satire A film (or other art work) that mocks or makes fun of something either openly or implicitly. In POSTMODERN film culture, relying so heavily on INTERTEXTUAL reference, the object of the satire is frequently taken from film itself or another art form. Amongst the most explicit screen satires with film as its starting point is *Blazing Saddles* (dir. Mel Brooks, 1974) – mainly a satire on the WESTERN, but also satirizing all studio GENRES with its riotous ending involving a fight between CHARACTERS from several different genre films. Some film satires have looked at a world much wider than the cinema: Mark Joyce (Nelmes, 1999) uses *The Extraordinary Adventures of Mr West in the Land of the Bolsheviks* (dir. Lev Kuleshov, 1924) as an example of film as direct political satire. Amongst contemporary film-makers, Robert Altman has used satire as a key element in several films, including *M*A*S*H* (1970), *Nashville* (1975) and *Prêt-à-Porter* (1994), which use the COMEDY inherent in the fine details of very particular worlds as their main satiric weapon. See also PARODY, PASTICHE.

Saturation release Saturation release, or saturation booking, describes the initial DISTRIBUTION of a film to a very large number of cinemas or screens at the same time – the currently preferred pattern of RELEASE for expensive BLOCKBUSTERS, using ADVERTISING and other promotion on a national scale, especially heavy TELEVISION advertising, simultaneously to generate maximum BOX-OFFICE revenue in the shortest possible time.

Scenario Generally an outline of a SCREENPLAY giving the main details of the narrative and CHARACTERS, but sometimes used – though this would be considered old-fashioned today – to refer to the completed script itself. See also TREATMENT.

Scene A term much used, but hard to define precisely, a scene is a unit of NARRATION in a narrative film, roughly defined as a dramatic unit, or series of ACTIONS or events, which takes place in continuous TIME and SPACE, so that a scene would end with a change of TIME or place or both. Typically, a scene consists of several SHOTS, but it could be a single shot. Though SEQUENCE is also a rather vague term, a sequence would generally be made up of several scenes (but see SEQUENCE SHOT).

Science fiction film One of the fantastic GENRES, along with both HORROR and FANTASY FILMS, science fiction works by extrapolation, hypothesizing possibilities based on the known laws of nature and science, whether in the near – tomorrow – or distant future or on other worlds. But while horror represents the monster as a frightening OTHER, science fiction is potentially more open to difference. Indeed, the genre is often defined as a narrative form that appeals to our 'sense of wonder,' to a heightened awareness and open attitude to new ideas. Such films as *Frankenstein* (dir. James Whale, 1931), *Alien* (dir. Ridley Scott, 1979) and the two versions of *The Thing* (dir. Christian Nyby, 1951; dir. John Carpenter, 1982) have been categorized as both science fiction and horror because they explore science fiction themes but present their alien creatures largely as loathesome and fearful.

Film is an ideal medium for science fiction, since SPACE, TIME and technology – major themes of the genre – are also crucial aspects of the cinema, wherein NARRATION proceeds according to the manipulation of both space and time (see CLASSIC NARRATIVE CINEMA, INVISIBLE EDITING), and the mechanics of photography and PROJECTION are necessary conditions for its display. Also, the cinematic machine, the APPARATUS, like the Constructors in Stanislaw Lem's novel *The Cyberiad* (1967), is a device capable of imagining and building, through SPECIAL EFFECTS, other machines infinitely more sophisticated than itself. The genre lacks the fixed ICONOGRAPHY of the WESTERN or GANGSTER FILM, but the design of rocket ships, space suits or futuristic cityscapes may function metaphorically or expressively in individual science fiction films. Science fiction narratives tend to be organized more around certain premises, the most familiar of which involve time travel, space travel, future societies, alien contact and the impact of new technology. Most science fiction stories are concerned in some way with the relationship between technology and the human.

Some of Georges Méliès's ONE-REELERS such as *Le Voyage dans la lune* (*A Voyage to the Moon*, 1902) contained science fiction themes and IMAGES, but production of science fiction films was sporadic through the first three decades of film history, with only a few films of distinction: *Aelita* (dir. Jakov Protazanov, 1924), a Soviet film about revolution on Mars; Fritz Lang's GERMAN EXPRESSIONIST EPIC *Metropolis* (1926) and his follow-up *Die Frau im Mond* (*Woman in the Moon*, 1928), which had real German rocket scientists as advisors and invented the countdown, later adopted as launch procedure by NASA; and the stentorian *Things to Come* (dir. William Cameron Menzies, 1936), with a script by H.G. Wells based on his own book about a technocratic future. In the 1930s and 1940s science fiction was primarily the stuff of SERIALS such as *Flash Gordon* (dir. Frederick Stephani, 1936), *Buck Rogers* (dir. Ford Beebe and Saul A. Goodkind, 1939) and *The Phantom Empire* (dir. Otto Brower and B. Reeves Eason, 1935), starring singing cowboy Gene Autry.

A boom in science fiction film occurred at the beginning of the 1950s, the result of a convergence of several factors, including the postwar MARKETING of the teen AUDIENCE and the development of TEENPICS; anxiety over the atomic bomb and the Cold War; fear of communism; a rash of well-documented UFO sightings around the globe; and a growing conservatism and conformity within Eisenhower's America. *Destination Moon* (dir. Irving Pichel), produced by George Pal, and *Rocketship X-M* (dir. Kurt Neumann), both 1950, were the first in a wave of SPACE OPERAS that preceded actual space flight by only a few years; in the following year *The Day the Earth Stood Still* (dir. Robert Wise) and *The Thing* initiated a CYCLE of alien invasion movies. The growing blandness of American society was also reflected in such films as *Invasion of the Body Snatchers* (dir. Don Siegel, 1956), in which average Americans are replaced by emotionless duplicates, and *Not of this Earth* (dir. Roger Corman, 1956) in which invading aliens are depicted merely as Men in Grey Flannel Suits. The recent *Independence Day* (dir. Roland Emmerich, 1996), a PASTICHE of 1950s alien invasion movies, demonstrates that we continue to have the same xenophobic anxieties even after the end of the Cold War.

The monster movie dominated the genre in the 1950s, largely as a result of pervasive anxiety over the newly arrived Atomic Age. Following upon the success of *The Beast from 20,000 Fathoms* (dir. Eugene Lourie, 1953), about a prehistoric Rhedosaurus trampling New York City, innumerable creatures slouched and slithered their way across the screen, including giant ants (*Them!*, dir. Gordon Douglas, 1954), crabs (*Attack of the Crab Monsters*, dir. Corman, 1956) and the buzzard-like supersonic bird of *The Giant Claw* (dir. Fred F. Sears, 1957). *Gojira* (*Godzilla*, dir. Inoshira Honda, 1954) initiated a cycle of Japanese KAIJU EIGA, movies featuring dinosaurs and other giant creatures descending upon Tokyo. Even London was threatened in *Behemoth, the Sea Monster* (*The Giant Behemoth*, dir. Lourie, 1959) and *Gorgo* (dir. Lourie, 1961).

Stanley Kubrick combined science fiction with ART CINEMA in the stylish *2001: A Space Odyssey* (1968) and *A Clockwork Orange* (1971), but the BLOCKBUSTER success of George Lucas's *Star Wars* in 1977, and its pervasive MERCHANDISING campaign, along with that of Steven Spielberg's *Close Encounters of the Third Kind* in the same year and *E.T.: The Extra-Terrestrial* in 1982, once again returned the genre to an adolescent audience. At the same time, taking their cue from the continuous ACTION and frantic narrative pace of Lucas's film, many recent science fiction movies, such as *The Terminator* (dir. James Cameron, 1984), *The Running Man* (dir. Paul Michael Glaser, 1987), *Predator* (dir. John McTiernan, 1987) and *Total Recall* (dir. Paul Verhoeven, 1990) have been ACTION MOVIES adorned with futuristic trappings.

The use of special effects constitutes one of the particular PLEASURES of the genre, and this emphasis is itself an enactment of science fiction's thematic concern with technology. Special effects seek to achieve unreality as realistically as possible – to engage 'our belief, not our suspension of disbelief,' as Sobchack puts it (Sobchack, 1988, p. 88). They announce the powers of cinema, envisioning things that we know are only possible, not actual. Because of the genre's emphasis on special effects, science fiction's primary appeal has been the kinetic excitement of ACTION (Grant in Kuhn, 1999). At least one SUBGENRE of science fiction, the apocalyptic film, is founded on the promise of scenes of mass destruction.

Further reading: Cook & Bernink (1999), Hardy (1984), Hunter (1999), Johnson (1972), Kuhn (1990), Kuhn (1999), Landy (1991a), Lucanio (1987), Murphy (1992), Penley (1989), Penley *et al.* (1991), Schelde (1993), Slusser & Rabkin (1985), Telotte (1995)

Scopophilia Literally the pleasure in seeing or looking, a key element in most PSYCHOANALYTIC THEORY as both Sigmund Freud and Jacques Lacan refer to the drive to see as fundamental to infant development. Much FEMINIST FILM THEORY took as its starting point that cinema was constructed around male scopophilia and that the CAMERA operated through a male GAZE looking at women as objects. Many have theorized about cinema's basis in scopophilia and VOYEURISM, with SPECTATORS sitting in the dark watching what are usually 'private moments' being enacted on the screen. Many films made the act of looking and spying an explicit part of their construction, such as *Rear Window* (dir. Alfred Hitchcock, 1954) and *Peeping Tom* (dir. Michael Powell, 1960).

Further reading: Mulvey (1989)

Screen One of the most influential academic film journals, founded in 1960 by the Society for Education in Film and TELEVISION (SEFT) as *Screen Education*, originally funded by the BRITISH FILM INSTITUTE. *Screen's* emphasis has always been on key developments in critical THEORY, particularly related to IDEOLOGY, PSYCHOANALYSIS and SEMIOTICS, and was influential in disseminating such ideas in English-language higher education during the 1970s and 1980s. *Screen* is currently produced at the Drama, Film and Television Department, University of Glasgow.

Screenplay The finished script for a film, containing dialogue and explicit descriptions of significant ACTION. The degree to which screenplays include CAMERA instructions varies markedly: a script with full information about camera work may need little work to be turned into a SHOOTING SCRIPT. If the WRITER is also the DIRECTOR the screenplay is likely to be very explicit about the way each scene will be SHOT.

Screen test The process by which an ACTOR is auditioned on CAMERA – earlier on film, now more usually on VIDEO – to assess his/her general level of talent or suitability for a particular role. The term also refers to the resulting piece of film.

Screenwriter The individual or team member responsible for producing the finished SCREENPLAY for a film. The status and role of screenwriters have changed markedly over time and some writers now enjoy a far greater prominence than in the past. During the heyday of the HOLLYWOOD STUDIO SYSTEM the individual screenwriter was almost entirely anonymous: STUDIOS would generally employ teams of jobbing writers with particular specialities and it was common to have several working on the same film; writers were seen as highly dispensable and vulnerable to quixotic hire and fire policies if unable to deliver to tight deadlines and specifications.

Screenwriters have also tended to be ignored outside the industry by critics and theorists particularly through the dominance of an AUTEURist view of film (although see Corliss, 1974), which ascribes the central creative role to the DIRECTOR, but some WRITER/director partnerships have achieved prominence, such as Martin Scorsese and Paul Schrader on *Taxi Driver* (1976), *Raging Bull* (1980) and *The Last Temptation of Christ* (1988). Many DIRECTORS are also the principal screenwriters on their films, an increasingly common practice in contemporary cinema, particularly in INDEPENDENT CINEMA: Francis Coppola, Woody Allen, Spike Lee and John Sayles are prominent examples of writer/directors in US cinema.

Screwball comedy Comic film GENRE popularized in HOLLYWOOD during the 1930s featuring the flirtatious sparring of a romantic couple, one of whom is typically a professional and the other a zany free spirit. Initiated by Howard Hawks's *Twentieth Century* and Frank Capra's *It Happened One Night* (both 1934), these COMEDIES offered obvious escapist appeal to AUDIENCES during the Great Depression, and have interested film scholars because of their atypically strong female CHARACTERS. The female leads, played by women who were themselves strong presences on the SCREEN such as Carole Lombard and Katharine Hepburn, were self-assured, independent and equal in wit and energy to the charismatic male ACTORS (Cary Grant, James Stewart) with whom they were paired. Films such as *The Awful Truth* (dir. Leo McCarey, 1937), *Bringing Up Baby* (dir. Hawks, 1938), *His Girl Friday* (dir. Hawks, 1940) and *The Philadelphia Story* (dir. George Cukor, 1940) provided a fast narrative pace filled with comic situations and sophisticated verbal humour about relationships, desire and marriage. The genre declined during the urgency of the War years, although they have appeared since infrequently but consistently, from *What's Up, Doc?* (dir. Peter Bogdanovich, 1972) to *Splendor* (dir. Gregg Araki, 1999). Further reading: Babington & Evans (1989), Cavell (1981), Kendall (1990), Schatz (1981), Shumway (1991), Sikov (1989)

Script See SCREENPLAY.

Script development Process by which a film script develops from original idea to finished SCREENPLAY, initiated in various ways depending on the kind of PROPERTY, from the purchase of film rights to a novel for adaptation to commissioning a writer for a TREATMENT of an original idea. Once a detailed treatment is completed, PRODUCERS will seek a first draft of the screenplay, or a SCENE by scene outline of the narrative. Screenplays frequently go through several drafts and revisions in consultation with producers and DIRECTORS – sometimes known as 'development hell' because so many scripts get stuck for long periods, and are often abandoned, at this stage – before reaching the stage of refinement into a final SHOOT-ING SCRIPT, complete with CAMERA directions.

Second feature See B MOVIE.

Second unit See UNIT.

Selznick After periods in production at MGM and RKO during the early 1930s, David Selznick founded Selznick International Pictures to make large budget, prestige productions, in a sense to out-do the MAJOR STUDIOS, as with the company's biggest success, *Gone With the Wind* (dir. Victor Fleming, 1939). Though INDEPEN-DENT, Selznick needed to distribute through the majors – MGM for *Gone With the Wind* and UNITED ARTISTS for Alfred Hitchcock's first American film, *Rebecca* (1940). Selznick later tried to establish his own DISTRIBUTION company, Selznick Releasing, with very limited success.
Further reading: Thomson (1993)

Semiology/Semiotics Terms coined by the Swiss linguistics theorist Ferdinand de Saussure and the American philosopher C.S. Pierce respectively to refer to the study of signs, not widely used until the 1950s when the French philosopher Roland Barthes began to apply them to the analysis of popular culture. Despite differences between Saussure and Pierce, both are concerned with the relationship between language systems, the external reality that they represent and the AUDIENCE or reader. All types of language mediate reality in IDEOLOGICAL ways, especially important with a medium like film which can seem TRANSPARENT. From a semiotic

POINT OF VIEW, all signs are chosen and further choices are made about their combination or use with other signs. Saussure referred to the range of choices of an individual sign as a PARADIGM, and their combination with others as a SYNTAGM – comparatively easy to see in written and spoken language, where the paradigms are the choices available when selecting individual words, which are then combined into sentences. In film the parameters are less exact and the units of meaning less distinct, though one could consider a particular SCENE as a syntagm made up of a number of choices regarding *MISE EN SCENE*, CASTING, CAMERA position and so on.

The two most useful semiotic terms dealing with the relationship of signs to external reality are DENOTATION and CONNOTATION, the former meaning the simplest, literal meaning of a sign, the latter the complex way in which it is read in a particular context. Connotations produce the ideological dimension to most semiotic analysis, and collections of connotations that frequently recur within a given culture are referred to as MYTHS. Myths may be understood as ways in which a culture makes sense of itself, and semiotics is a tool for understanding society's key myths. Semiotics is important to the study of film in providing a systematic way to analyse TEXTS, but also links readings of individual films to the wider ideological process by which meaning is produced in a given culture: imagine the way that films function differently in radically different cultural contexts – strict Muslim versus liberal Western, or pre-apartheid versus post-apartheid South Africa. Looked at in this way, semiotics has had a particularly important effect on the reading of REALIST texts, exposing claims they might make to present a 'natural', unmediated vision of the world and demonstrating their determination by ideologically-bound choices.
Further reading: Lapsley & Westlake (1988), Nowell-Smith in Gledhill & Williams (2000)

Sensurround A novelty SPECIAL EFFECT, developed by UNIVERSAL Studios and first used in *Earthquake* (dir. Mark Robson, 1974), simulating the effect of an earthquake tremor. Needing the installation of several additional speakers, it was confined to a relatively small number of first-run theatres.

Sequel A film (or novel) which continues the STORY and CHARACTERS begun in an earlier film (while a PREQUEL goes back in time). Though some SERIES films might be considered sequels, the sequel phenomenon is particularly characteristic of NEW HOLLYWOOD, since the 1970s, when financially successful films frequently generated sequels, such as *French Connection II* (dir. John Frankenheimer, 1975, following the 1971 original) or *Exorcist II: The Heretic* (dir. John Boorman, 1977, following the 1973 original). Some films, such as *Halloween* (dir. John Carpenter, 1978), *Nightmare on Elm Street* (dir. Wes Craven, 1984) or *Star Trek* (dir. Robert Wise, 1979), have generated many sequels. Sequels arise from the commercial logic which drives GENRE film-making in general – if a film succeeds, make more as much like the original as possible. 'Sequelitis' has been seen as a sign of lack of creativity but sequels such as the *Star Wars* sequels allow maximum profit to be derived from success, using a pre-established AUDIENCE for more systematic exploitation of ANCILLARY markets and MERCHANDISING.

Sequence A SHOT or SERIES of shots, or even SCENES, in a narrative film, not necessarily depicting ACTION in one SPACE and continuous TIME, but constituting a clearly defined segment of the film's overall structure. A TRANSITIONal series of rapidly EDITED shots in CLASSIC NARRATIVE CINEMA is a MONTAGE sequence, while a lengthy dialogue scene shot in LONG TAKES also constitutes a sequence. See also SEQUENCE SHOT.

Sequence shot Though in some senses, simply a LONG TAKE – a single SHOT of long duration, incorporating a signficant amount of STORY information – 'sequence shot' implies edited material which would normally constitute a SCENE or SEQUENCE being covered in a single long take. This could take the form of a static CAMERA using different planes of ACTION in DEEP FOCUS as in Orson Welles' *Citizen Kane* (1941) and *The Magnificent Ambersons* (1942), as well as in William Wyler's *The Little Foxes* (1941) and *The Best Years of Our Lives* (1946). Sometimes a moving camera is utilized, as in Alfred Hitchcock's *Rope* (1948), Jean Renoir's *La Grande illusion* (1937), and *La Règle du jeu* (1939) as well as in Welles' s work, with the camera shifting spectator attention to different facets of a scene within the continuous shot. The sequence shot/long take is an alternative way of organizing a scene and the spectator's POINT OF VIEW from CONTINUITY EDITING or MONTAGE. Since it is more time-consuming and expensive to set up and shoot several separate shots than a single shot, LOW-BUDGET films often use long take sequence shots. *Last Chants for a Slow Dance* (dir. Jon Jost, 1977) consists mostly of very long take sequences, as do Jim Jarmusch's *Stranger Than Paradise* (1984) and *Mystery Train* (1989). The French *plan séquence* is sometimes preferred because critical thinking about sequence shots owes much to French critical writing, particularly André Bazin's work (1967) on Renoir and the 1940s work of Welles and Wyler.

Serial A STORY developed over a SERIES of films rather than completed in one – now virtually extinct in the cinema though thriving on TELEVISION (many British serial dramas being SHOT on film). The serial form belonged mainly to SILENT CINEMA and was a popular format for children's Saturday morning or matinée cinema. Serial titles that have survived in other forms include *Tarzan*, *The Lone Ranger* and *Flash Gordon*, but with the advent of television and cinema programming of single FEATURES, cheap film serials were no longer an economically viable proposition.

Series Whereas SERIALS – historically aimed primarily at juvenile AUDIENCES – told a continuous STORY in successive but separate episodes, a series consisted of FEATURE FILMS complete in themselves but sharing the same CHARACTERS and LOCATIONS. Series were popular in the 1930s and 1940s during the STUDIO SYSTEM era, with series like MGM's Andy Hardy films (starring Mickey Rooney) and Thin Man series (with William Powell and Myrna Loy), PARAMOUNT's Bing Crosby and Bob Hope 'Road' films, Charlie Chan films (with Warner Oland and later Sidney Toler as leads in over 40 1930s and 1940s films, at TWENTIETH CENTURY-FOX, then at MONOGRAM) and Tarzan films (over 40 films at different STUDIOS), and numerous WESTERN series associated with stars like Hopalong Cassidy. Today, PREQUELS and SEQUELS are based on the same commercial logic as the series (and some sequels, such as the three *Airport* films, may be more like series), and series follow the logic of GENRES: if a film is commercially successful, make another one with the same ingredients, but slightly different in story.

Set A place where a film is to be SHOT that is created or constructed as opposed to a LOCATION, which is essentially 'found'. In practice the distinction can be blurred: locations often need to be adapted and are almost always lit in ways that make it a partly constructed setting. Progressively more portable CAMERAS and LIGHTING equipment have resulted in increasingly widespread location shooting whereas in the heyday of the HOLLYWOOD STUDIOS spectacular sets were constructed on BACK LOTS. Although location shooting offers authenticity, studio sets offer control and flexibility – walls can move, COLOURS be adjusted and special allowance made for concealing lighting and SOUND equipment. See also ART DIRECTION, SET DECORATOR.

Set decorator, set dresser The set decorator meets the requirements of the PRODUCTION DESIGNER for furniture, soft furnishings, objects and other PROPS by buying or renting to decorate a STUDIO set or LOCATION. The set decorator is assisted by a leadperson, who is in turn in charge of the set dressing CREW – the swing gang – which gets the set ready, dresses it, and strikes the set after shooting.

Set designer See ART DIRECTOR, PRODUCTION DESIGNER.

Sexploitation A kind of EXPLOITATION film which aims for the sexual arousal of its spectator. Although the term could be applied to any PORNOGRAPHIC FILM, it is often reserved for more soft-core films with a place in the more conventional forms of DISTRIBUTION and EXHIBITION, often showing in regular cinemas (even if at special times) and DRIVE-INS and on CABLE (and even network) TELEVISION. PRODUCER-DIRECTOR Russ Meyer has specialized in sexploitation films, with large-breasted, semi-undressed and often dominant women CHARACTERS (in films like *Faster, Pussycat! Kill! Kill!*, 1965, and *Vixen*, 1968), and Roger Corman's NEW WORLD PICTURES also contributed to the GENRE, with films such as *The Student Nurses* (dir. Stephanie Rothman, 1971) and *Caged Heat* (dir. Jonathan Demme, 1974). Since some critics have mounted arguments for taking both Meyer's and Corman's productions seriously, they may not be typical of the genre.
Further reading: Schaefer (1999).

Sexuality Term referring to a person's sexual orientation (i.e. heterosexual man or woman, gay man, lesbian, bisexual). Recent cinema, particularly the AVANT-GARDE, has played a key role in the changing ways that IMAGES of sexuality circulate. On one level, there are now more films that use and discuss a range of sexualities in various contexts. Though most films are still made from a heterosexual male perspective, those that are not are both increasing and being distributed more widely, albeit predominantly on the ART CINEMA circuit, including for example the films of Derek Jarman (*Edward II*, 1991; *Blue*, 1993) and Pedro Almodovar (*Women on the Edge of a Nervous Breakdown*, 1988; *Tie Me Up, Tie Me Down*, 1990). As Hayward (1996, p. 316) acknowledges, current debates around sexuality are seen less in isolation and more in their intersection with other areas such as RACE, GENDER and CLASS. Hayward gives the telling example of the construction of black male sexuality in MAINSTREAM HOLLYWOOD cinema as evidence that one can no longer talk simply about a dominant male heterosexual perspective: black male sexuality has always been depicted using myths of potency and threat, as something that has to be destroyed (comparable with the construction of sexually active women, such as the FEMME FATALE in FILM NOIR). See also GAY AND LESBIAN CINEMA, FEMINIST FILM THEORY, MASCULINITY.

SFX Common abbreviation for SPECIAL EFFECTS, though it can also stand for SOUND effects.

Shallow focus A style of CINEMATOGRAPHY in which only a narrow area within the film IMAGE is in sharp FOCUS, with the background (and sometimes foreground) out of focus, whereas DEEP FOCUS keeps all planes in equally sharp focus. Deep focus was characteristic of SILENT CINEMA partly because of ORTHOCHROMATIC film STOCK, whose film SPEED easily captured deep focus, whereas the PANCHROMATIC stock used from the mid-1920s had a slower FILM SPEED, making it more difficult, initially, to shoot in deep focus. Shallow focus inevitably results in film-makers implying more clearly, through what is or is not in focus, what the spectator should be looking at.

Shift focus See RACK FOCUS.

Shooting script The final blueprint for shooting a film, consisting of the finished SCREENPLAY with dialogue, ACTION and SCENE descriptions, but also detailed CAMERA instructions, including detailed set-ups for each scene. In practice shooting will often deviate from the shooting script.

Short end Unexposed film remaining in the CAMERA after shooting and too short to use for another SHOT. Over the course of shooting a film, short ends, which can be salvaged and re-used, may add up to quite a lot of unexposed film, and young film-makers have been known to use short ends to make their first films.

Short film Usually defined as a film with a running time of less than 30 minutes, often referred to as a 'short' or 'short subject'. Today short films are often confined to the ART HOUSE or FESTIVAL circuit, though there is some MAINSTREAM acknowledgement through annual ACADEMY (and BAFTA) awards for best LIVE ACTION and ANIMATED short film. In early cinema all films were short, and short films continued as support for features into the 1940s and 1950s in the form of NEWSREELS, TRAVELOGUES and CARTOONS. The short film is also an important way for new talent to develop: many important DIRECTORS began their careers making shorts. Britain, for example, has many short film competitions and SUBSIDY schemes offering small budgets for ideas that pass the selection processes. Some schemes, such as *10x10* and *Tartan Shorts*, both run by the BBC, are sponsored by TELEVISION companies, guaranteeing broadcast even if they fail to secure THEATRICAL DISTRIBUTION (and in a new development, cheaply made short films are much in demand by the Internet). Short films are also the most common form of ART CINEMA where radical formal experimentation takes place. AVANT-GARDE film-makers Andy Warhol, Stan Brakhage and Yoko Ono all made both extremely short (and extremely long) films as part of their explorations of the medium (see Macdonald, 1993).

Shot (1) A continuously exposed strip of film made from a single uninterrupted run of the CAMERA, without a CUT, regardless of CAMERA MOVEMENT, movement of the PROFILMIC subjects or change of FOCUS. (2) The smallest unit out of which SCENES and SEQUENCES are made. American DIRECTOR D.W. Griffith is generally credited as the first to break up the ACTION of a scene for dramatic purposes, and in CLASSICAL HOLLYWOOD CINEMA every shot is designed to move the viewer through the narrative and enhance its emotional affect. (3) A PRINTed and edited TAKE. (4) Action on the screen that appears to be photographed as one continuous run of the camera. In *Rope* (1948), for example, Alfred Hitchcock hid the cuts, required by the REEL size of the camera magazine, so that the entire film looks like one shot, but in fact is not.

Shots are categorized in several ways: a) by their temporal duration, from SUBLIMINAL INSERTS to LONG TAKES; b) by the distance (or perceived distance, as in the ZOOM SHOT) of the camera in relation to the subject photographed, from BIG CLOSE-UP to EXTREME LONG SHOT; c) by the CAMERA ANGLE from which the subject is viewed, ranging from below ground to AERIAL SHOT; d) the movement of the camera, as in DOLLY SHOT, PAN SHOT, TRACKING SHOT or CRANE SHOT; e) the number of CHARACTERS in the frame, as in one-shot or TWO-SHOT; special techniques used, as in MATTE SHOT and DEEP FOCUS shot.

Shots are connected by CUTS or by TRANSITIONal devices such as the DISSOLVE, SUPERIMPOSITION, FADE, and WIPE. See also BEAVER SHOT, CHEAT SHOT, CUTAWAY, DEEP FOCUS, DUTCH ANGLE, EDITING, ESTABLISHING SHOT, INVISIBLE EDITING, LONG SHOT, LOW ANGLE, MASTER SHOT, MEDIUM SHOT, MONEY SHOT, TILT SHOT, POINT OF VIEW, OVERHEAD SHOT, PROCESS SHOT, REACTION SHOT, SARTOV SHOT, SEQUENCE SHOT, SHOT-REVERSE SHOT, STOCK SHOT.

Shot-reverse shot The standard technique for shooting two-way conversations in which SHOTS from one participant's POINT OF VIEW, or over his/her shoulder, are intercut with those from the other's, partly to avoid the tedium of a continuous TWO-SHOT, but also to increase the spectator's IDENTIFICATION with one or both of the participants through CLOSE-UPS of their reactions. The technique is also used to heighten tension around a physical attack on a CHARACTER by cutting back and forth between the attacker's and victim's perspectives. Shot reverse-shot is an integral part of the CONTINUITY system which combines EDITING and CAMERA ANGLES to produce a seamless effect, the standard REALIST method. See also CAMERA MOVEMENT, CONTINUITY EDITING, EDITING, REVERSE ANGLE, SHOT.

Show reel Selection of an individual's work – DIRECTORS, but also ACTORS, ART DIRECTORS, CINEMATOGRAPHERS and SOUND designers – edited together on a single REEL of film that can be sent to prospective employers or PRODUCERS. Today the show reel is most likely to be in VIDEOtape form because of cost and ease of copying and showing. FILM SCHOOL students expend much energy in putting together a strong graduation show reel to kickstart their careers.

Sight gag A humorous bit of business depending on visual rather than verbal effect, strongly associated with COMEDY films from the SILENT FILM era and STARS such as Charlie Chaplin and Buster Keaton, but nonetheless integral to the comic style of SOUND era comics like Jacques Tati and Jerry Lewis.

Sight and Sound General monthly film magazine, founded in 1934, published by the BRITISH FILM INSTITUTE which has absorbed the function of the defunct *Monthly Film Bulletin* to review and give full details of all films released in the UK

Sight and Sound is not associated with any particular position about cinema but engaged in important debates (for example, with *MOVIE*) about AUTEURISM and MISE EN SCÈNE in the late 1950s and 1960s.

Signifier A key term in SEMIOTICS referring to the physical embodiment of the sign, separate from the process by which it comes to mean something to a reader. The words 'John Wayne' on paper are signifiers, which come to mean something when they interact with the reader's cultural experience. For most people in the West above a certain age, the words DENOTE a film STAR probably, dressed in cowboy clothing, but CONNOTING a range of things dependent on GENDER, political allegiance or RACE. There are different types of signifiers: a photograph of John Wayne stands in an altogether different relationship to the individual film star than his name written on paper. A PRODUCTION STILL from Wayne's later work such as *The Shootist* (dir. Don Siegel, 1976) would be likely to produce different CONNOTATIONS than a still from openly jingoistic work such as the pro-Vietnam *The Green Berets* (dir. John Wayne and Ray Kellogg, 1968). A third kind of signifier that, in the right context, could stand for Wayne would be something with a purely symbolic connection to him, such as a cowboy hat or a sheriff's star.
Further reading: Lapsley & Westlake (1988)

Silent cinema General term for the output of cinema worldwide from its origins in the 1890s to 1927 to the first talkie. Whether the beginnings of cinema date from Thomas Edison's early films or from the first projected LUMIÈRE PROGRAMME, in 1895, the silent cinema lasted for roughly a third of cinema's history so far, and this alone makes it important. 'Silent' cinema was not silent: from the start, films were routinely accompanied by MUSIC and SOUND effects, and sometimes by a lecturer (see BENSHI). Later, MUSIC was considered integral to films and dedicated musical scores were often played by full orchestras, and Edison's interest in CINEMATOGRAPHY in the 1890s was partly as accompaniment to his Phonograph. The end date for silent cinema is also problematic: 1927 is the date of the first FEATURE FILM to incorporate synchronized speech – the beginning of the talkies – but not the beginning of 'sound cinema'.

Silent cinema has been viewed differently by different generations of film historians. An orthodox view prevalent from the 1930s to the 1950s held that the art of film developed essentially in the silent period, with its summits in Soviet experiments with MONTAGE and GERMAN EXPRESSIONISM in the 1920s, with the coming of sound a mere addition to an already complete form, resented as inessential and a constraint on the visual. Later thinking about film showed little interest in silent cinema beyond the early work of some AUTEURS: silent film might be of academic interest, as a prelude to the sound film, but little more. Since the 1980s, silent cinema has become increasingly identified as the period in which mainstream CONVENTIONS emerged.

Silent cinema is usually broken up into shorter periods. The term PRIMITIVE CINEMA is often used for the period from early Edison and the Lumière programme to around 1902–3, marked by simple ACTUALITY material and TRICK FILMS (like those of Georges Méliès) and the growing emergence of narrative as the most popular form. Simple narratives like *The Great Train Robbery* (dir. Edwin S. Porter, 1903) or *Le Voyager dans la lune* (*A Trip to the Moon* dir. Méliès, 1902) were constructed with

SCENES consisting of a single SHOT of ACTIONS on a stage as if viewed from the stalls of a theatre – Noël Burch's (1990) primitive mode of representation. A transitional period from 1902 to 1910–12 – the whole period since 1895 is sometimes referred to as early cinema – is marked by more concern with principles of CONTINUITY and narrative progression, as in British producer Cecil Hepworth's *Rescued by Rover* (dir. Lewis Fitzhamon, 1905). D.W. Griffith's ONE-REELERS for BIOGRAPH like *The Lonely Villa* (1909), *The Lonedale Operator* (1911) and *An Unseen Enemy* (1912), showed the beginnings of scene dissection – the breaking up of scenes into different shots (what Gunning, 1991, calls the 'narrator system'). Overall, this shift from THEATRICAL to a more properly CINEMATIC SPACE marks the emergence of CONVENTIONS associated with CLASSICAL HOLLYWOOD CINEMA, distinguished from the primitive by Burch as the INSTITUTIONAL MODE OF REPRESENTATION.

Such an account of early cinema, interpreting the past from the viewpoint of the present, inevitably distorts. Early film-makers were probably less preoccupied with narrative than it implies, as Gunning suggests in his arguments about a CINEMA OF ATTRACTIONS (in Stam & Miller, 2000) and it may also overstate the movement away from cinema's inheritance from nineteenth century theatre, which remained a very powerful influence, in both form and content, in films like *Way Down East* (dir. Griffith, 1920). Certainly, developments in countries like Denmark and Sweden were also very important: early features like Victor Sjöström's *Ingeborg Holm* (1913) make sophisticated use of dramatic staging in DEEP FOCUS, while his later *The Phantom Carriage* (1920) demonstrates mastery of CONTINUITY conventions. It is in part the cementing of MAINSTREAM conventions by about 1920 which gives rise to significant experimentation with film forms in the 1920s – IMPRESSIONISM, DADA, SURREALIST and other work in France, German EXPRESSIONISM and Soviet MONTAGE experiments. The intensity of such experimentation helped the coming of sound – which seemed to herald a return to a more theatrical cinema – to be viewed negatively.

Industrially, the silent period saw the US film industry's first attempt at monopoly control, through the MOTION PICTURE PATENTS COMPANY (MPPC), and the foundation of HOLLYWOOD by INDEPENDENTS like the FOX FILM CORPORATION, who opposed the MPPC and went west to avoid its influence. The pattern of Hollywood production was also well established in this era, with the emphasis on GENRES, in which silent film COMEDY was in many ways pre-eminent. But many developments came from Europe, where feature-length films were made well before the US, and where innovation seemed more encouraged. The luring of leading European DIRECTORS (including Sjöström, Ernst Lubitsch, F.W. Murnau), ACTORS (including Greta Garbo, Emil Jannings) and technicians (including Karl Freund and Karl Struss) to Hollywood in the mid and late 1920s signalled very clearly the US film industry's growing world dominance by the end of the silent period.

After 1927, sound very quickly took over commercial cinema in Hollywood and everywhere else – much faster and more absolutely than anyone predicted. From that point it was extremely rare, to the point of aberration, to choose to be silent, or even a non-talkie. See also CHASE FILM, CHASER, COLUMBIA, ESSANAY, FAMOUS PLAYERS, FIRST NATIONAL, INTERTITLE, KAMMERSPIEL, KEYSTONE, MGM, MUTUAL, PARAMOUNT, SPECIAL EFFECTS, STOP MOTION, TRICK FILM, UNITED ARTISTS, UNIVERSAL, WARNER BROS.

Further reading: Abel (1996), Bordwell, Staiger & Thompson (1985), Bratton, Cook & Gledhill (1994), Cook (1996), Cook & Bernink (1999), Elsaesser (1990), Gomery

(1986), Gomery (1992), Musser (1990), Musser (1991), Nowell-Smith (1996), Robinson (1996), Salt (1993), Stam (2000), Thompson & Bordwell (1994), Toulet (1995), Vardac (1949)

Skinflick A film in which the emphasis is on showing people naked. See also PORNOGRAPHY.

Slapstick comedy A form of COMEDY relying on physical humour, comic VIOLENCE, or knockabout farce, derived from the two pieces of wood clowns would slap together to make a loud noise to accompany the miming of physical blows. Slapstick was the dominant form of comedy, particularly in American film, in the era of SILENT CINEMA, partly because it need not involve verbal humour. Mack Sennett's KEYSTONE Kops comedies and some of the SHORT FILMS of Laurel and Hardy are among the most famous silent slapstick comedies. The frenetic pace of much silent slapstick comedy also suggests that it was a response to the rapidly increasing pace of life in the early part of the century brought about by such inventions as the automobile: in the Keystone Kops comedies, cars feature prominently in the ACTION, in many of the SIGHT GAGS, and are of equal importance to the CHARACTERS, who are themselves tossed about like mechanical objects. Films today occasionally employ slapstick comedy, as in *The Gods Must Be Crazy* (dir. Jamie Uys, 1980) and *Braindead* (*Dead Alive*, dir. Peter Jackson, 1992).
Further reading: Mast (1979)

Slasher movie A CYCLE of the HORROR FILM that began to develop after *Peeping Tom* (dir. Michael Powell) and *Psycho* (dir. Alfred Hitchcock) (both 1960), although it was not until the 1970s that the term was commonly employed. Slashers typically feature psychotic males, frequently masked like Jason Vorhees in *Friday the 13th* (dir. Sean Cunningham, 1980) and its SEQUELS, who set about systematically killing an isolated group of teenagers. Often the killer is motivated by a past sexual trauma activated by the sexual promiscuity of the victims he stalks, a CONVENTION that has led critics to see slasher movies as staunchly conservative in their sexual IDEOLOGY. The slasher film became a popular form of EXPLOITATION FILM particularly after the commercial success of *The Texas Chain Saw Massacre* (dir. Tobe Hooper, 1974) and *Halloween* (dir. John Carpenter, 1978). Perhaps the most recognizable convention of the slasher movie is the use of a HAND-HELD CAMERA to signify the killer's POINT OF VIEW. Yet to what extent this use of the SUBJECTIVE CAMERA encourages a seemingly amoral IDENTIFICATION on the part of the viewer with the murderer rather than his victims is a matter of debate. Clover (1992) argues that these movies feature a 'final girl' who manages to defeat the killer and survive, thereby empowering female spectators. However, slasher films were the main focus of the VIDEO nasties debate in Britain and prompted the passage of the Video Recordings Bill. By the mid 1980s the slasher film was in decline, but recent self-conscious POSTMODERN horror movies such as *Scream* (dir. Wes Craven, 1996) have proved popular. Also referred to as STALKER FILM.
Further reading: Dika (1990)

Sleeper Term applied to a film which does little BOX-OFFICE business, or had been barely noticed on its first RELEASE because of poor DISTRIBUTION, but which, over time, establishes itself as a critical and/or box-office success.

Slice-and-dice film See SPLATTER FILM.

Slow motion ACTION which appears on the screen slower than when filmed – one of the most common and important (and easily achieved) SPECIAL EFFECTS, achieved by filming at faster than the normal 24 FRAMES per second but projecting at normal speed. Action filmed at 36 or 48 frames per second, for example, would appear on screen slower than normal by one third or one half respectively when projected at 24 frames per second. Slow motion, like FAST MOTION and REVERSE MOTION, should be considered as one of the properties of the CAMERA which enables it to do what the human eye cannot – one of the properties of cinema which Dziga Vertov set out to demonstrate in *Man with the Movie Camera* (1929). Slow motion inevitably has the effect of defamiliarizing and/or highlighting a piece of action, often linked to a subjective evocation of the past in memory or to dream, most often producing a poetic or lyrical effect, whether in EXPERIMENTAL FILMS (such as Maya Deren's and Alexander Hammid's *Meshes of the Afternoon*, 1943), European narrative films (Jean Vigo's *Zéro de conduite*, 1933, Nicholas Roeg's *Don't Look Now*, 1973, Jean-Luc Godard's *Sauve qui peut – la vie*, 1980), DOCUMENTARY films (Leni Riefenstahl's *Olympiad*, 1938) or GENRE films (Rouben Mamoulian's *Love Me Tonight*, 1932; Arthur Penn's *Bonnie and Clyde*, 1967; Sam Peckinpah's *The Wild Bunch*, 1969).

Sneak preview See PREVIEW.

Snuff movie Refers to films other.than DOCUMENTARIES that show the actual taking of a human life, supposedly commissioned by rich patrons for their VOYEURIS-TIC PLEASURE. No examples of such films have yet been authenticated, but rumours about them have circulated for many years. The idea of snuff movies informs the PLOTS of several MAINSTREAM movies, such as *Videodrome* (dir. David Cronenberg, 1983) and *8mm* (dir. Joel Schumacher, 1999).

Social realism Loose designation for films (and other kinds of art) which both aspire to verisimilitude via a NATURALISTIC photographic style and to social relevance, often with a political edge, in subject matter. Many films could be so described, but examples are films (and TELEVISION plays and films) by Ken Loach, such as *Cathy Come Home* (1966), *Kes* (1969), *Hidden Agenda* (1990) and *Raining Stones* (1993) or the series of films adapted from US television plays in the 1950s, such as Paddy Chayevsky SCRIPTS directed by Delbert Mann like *Marty* (1955), *Bachelor Party* (1957), *Middle of the Night* (1959) and others such as *Twelve Angry Men* (dir. Sidney Lumet, 1957). The term has also been applied to BRITISH NEW WAVE films in the late 1950s and early 1960s. Italian NEO-REALISM provided one of the chief models for social realism, which should not be confused with the more specific SOCIALIST REALISM.

Socialist Realism The official doctrine for art – all the arts (including literature and painting), not just film – in the Soviet Union from the early 1930s to after Stalin's death in 1953. Socialist Realism was intended to show ordinary people in sympathetic, heroic roles that conformed to Communist IDEOLOGY, with typical CHARACTERS, not in the sense that they were average people, but rather typifying

Communist ideals, with the inevitable tendency to idealization and optimism. Stylistically, Socialist Realism was required to be easily accessible by avoiding formal experimentation. Such requirements, enshrined by the 1934 Soviet Writers' Congress and closely supervised by state officials, did not encourage radical or adventurous art, but it would be wrong to assume, as many do, that interesting films were not made. Although *Chapayev* (dir. Sergei and Georgy Vasiliev, 1934) is generally considered the film that most conforms to Socialist Realism, films like *We From Kronstadt* (dir. Yefim Dzigan, 1936), *Baltic Deputy* (dir. Alexander Zarkhi and Josif Heifits, 1937) and Grigori Kozintsev and Leonid Trauberg's *The Youth of Maxim* (1935) and *The Return of Maxim* (1937) are all interesting within Socialist Realist guidelines. In addition, the GENRE of films about leaders and other pre-Revolutionary and revolutionary figures, produced Mark Donskoi's Maxim Gorky trilogy (1938–40) as well as Sergei Eisenstein's and Dmitri Vasiliev's *Alexander Nevsky* (1938). Donskoi, Kozintsev and Trauberg all continued to make interesting films through World War II, into the 1950s and beyond.

Socialist Realism has been almost universally vilified – primarily because it was associated with Stalinism and spelled the end of 1920s Soviet experimentation in MONTAGE; Eisenstein's *Bezhin Meadow* was aborted, for example, and he remained inactive until *Nevsky*. Like the film-making in Nazi Germany during the same period, it was also seen as blatant PROPAGANDA for an undesirable regime (though some comparison might be made with the 'Dream Factory' of HOLLYWOOD, where films were also generally made to conform to certain ideological and stylistic norms). Socialist Realism cast a long shadow over other Soviet bloc countries after World War II, and influences may be seen in Polish DIRECTOR Andrzej Wajda's *A Generation* (1954), contrasting with his later *Ashes and Diamonds* (1958); the different strands of formal experimentation, NATURALISM and allegory in the 1960s CZECH NEW WAVE must also be seen in part as reactions against Socialist Realism. The real achievements of Soviet cinema (and other arts) during this period remain to be properly revalued. See also FORMALISM.

Further reading: Kenez in Nowell-Smith (1996), Leyda (1960), Thompson & Bordwell (1994)

Soft focus Though soft FOCUS can result accidentally from poor focusing of the CAMERA lens, it usually denotes a deliberate effect in which, while not blurred, the IMAGE is slightly fuzzy or hazy. This effect, usually achieved by a special LENS or FILTER, is often used to connote romantic, nostalgic or even dream-like feelings, and it has often been a CONVENTION – especially during the STUDIO SYSTEM period – to shoot female STARS in soft focus, which tended to flatter their looks. See also SARTOV SHOT.

Soft-core film See PORNOGRAPHY.

Soundies SHORT FILMS of about 3-minutes featuring musicians and vocalists performing jazz numbers used in specially equipped jukeboxes. Soundies, introduced in 1940, lasted about a decade.

Sound, sound cinema Although the period from 1895–1927 has been labelled the SILENT FILM era, sound was almost always a component of film-going and for Thomas Edison, moving pictures were in some ways an afterthought to his phonograph. Many claim that film is a visual medium on the basis that IMAGES came before sound but, in fact, experiments in adding recorded sound to film existed from the start. Experiments intensified during the 1920s, partly because of the backing of powerful US companies like AT&T, RCA and General Electric – all involved in other developments in sound technology – leading to patent wars in both Europe and the USA. Two competing technologies emerged: sound on shellac disc linked to the projector (following Edison), and sound on film (with the SOUNDTRACK incorporated on to the film strip as variable light signals). Although the main STUDIO innovating with sound, WARNER BROS., opted initially for the VITAPHONE sound-on-disc system, this soon proved unreliable in everyday operation, and FOX's sound-on-film system, renamed Movietone, soon proved the preferred option.

Sound was initially used to record VAUDEVILLE acts and add MUSIC and effects to transitional or hybrid films like *Sunrise* (dir. F.W. Murnau, 1927) and *Wings* (dir. William Wellman, 1927), but Warners soon expanded into talkies with SYNCHRONIZED speech. *The Jazz Singer* (dir. Alan Crosland, 1927), the first 'talkie' actually combined silent SEQUENCES with talkie sequences. Its impact had various effects: some already RELEASEd films were recalled to have sound added, typically with synchronized dialogue in the final REEL, such as the British *Kitty* (dir. Victor Saville, 1929). Alfred Hitchcock's *Blackmail* (1929), originally SHOT silent, was considerably re-shot and released as a talkie (then released also as a silent film, for the many cinemas which had not been converted for sound, a process which took some years). Many commentators remained initially unconvinced about the long-term future of the sound film, but the impact of the first talkies was overwhelming and by 1929 opinion was forced to shift, and film-making was irrevocably changed.

The problems and cost of switching to sound tended to put other technical developments of the 1920s such as WIDESCREEN processes and COLOUR on hold. Other 1930s innovations, such as REAR PROJECTION and less noisy LIGHTING, were responses to the problems of sound recording. The coming of sound affected all film-making, including DOCUMENTARY, but problems in recording LOCATION sound remained until the 1950s, when the transistor and other developments began to make synchronized filming and sound recording easier, encouraging new documemtary styles like CINÉMA VÉRITÉ and DIRECT CINEMA. Sound recording, sound effects and sound quality for the commercial cinema have improved over the years with developments such as SURROUND SOUND and DOLBY.

Many experimentally-minded 1920s film-makers opposed the tendency for sound to mean talkie. Eisenstein, Alexandrov and Pudovkin, Soviet DIRECTORS central to MONTAGE experiments, issued a joint manifesto arguing that the talkie would dominate the sound film and that 'sound will destroy the art of montage. Only the use of sound as counterpoint to visual montage offers new possibilities. The first experiments with sound must be directed towards its "noncoincidence" with images' (Braudy and Cohen, 1999). Although early problems in EDITING sound – which necessitated a return to the more theatrical LONG TAKE and static camera enabling dialogue to be recorded without breaks – were soon overcome, and although film-makers like Hitchcock made inventive use of sound in films like *Blackmail* and *Murder* (1930), the fears of the 1920s Soviet film-makers have been largely justified. Athough sound and soundtracks are probably more important in NEW HOLLYWOOD, there are few examples in sound cinema of radical approaches to its use, such as in the work of Jacques Tati.

The sound dimension of cinema has been under-discussed except at crucial times like the coming of sound, but there are signs that its importance is now being more recognized and that the aesthetics of film sound are being explored in more detail. Further reading: Altman (1992), Aumont *et al.* (1992), Bordwell & Thompson (1997), Buscombe and Gomery in Nichols (1985), Chion (1994), Cook (1996), Cook & Bernink (1999), Gomery (1992), Izod (1988), Bordwell in Kerr (1986), Maltby (1995), Neale (1985), Ryall (1993), Sergi in Neale & Smith (1998), Stam (2000), Stam & Miller (2000), Thompson & Bordwell (1994), Weis & Belton (1985)

Sound recordist The sound CREW member responsible for SOUND recording during shooting on SET, sometimes also known as the 'sound man' (or sound person), or sound or floor mixer.

Soundtrack Technically, soundtrack can refer to the channel on which dialogue, MUSIC or effects (or a combination of these) are recorded, as well as to the physical OPTICAL track on the edge of the strip of CELLULOID. Soundtrack may also refer to the commercially available compilation on CD or tape of a film's musical score (and sometimes other sounds). See also FOLEY.

Soviet montage See DIALECTICAL MONTAGE, THEMATIC MONTAGE.

Space opera A SCIENCE FICTION film that features space travel, adventure, and aliens. In the 1930s SERIALS such as *Flash Gordon* and *Buck Rogers* were space operas – as WESTERNS were 'horse operas' – as are the more recent *Battle Beyond the Stars* (dir. Jimmy T. Murakami, 1980) and *The Last Starfighter* (dir. Nick Castle, 1984).

Space Cinema shares with painting a dependence on the organization of space, and shares with MUSIC a dependence on the organization of TIME. At the same time the three-dimensional space we experience in reality is reduced to a two-dimensional simulation. Both because of this, and because the film FRAME carves out only a selected area of space, space is a central element of film and the film experience. At the height of the arguments about the nature of film as an art form, the British journal *SIGHT AND SOUND* argued against *MOVIE* that 'cinema is about the human situation not about "spatial relationships"' (quoted in Hillier 1985, p. 11), but it is very largely through spatial relationships that meanings are made. Generally speaking, space in cinema is organized both to convince us of the credibility of the world represented (though some films, such as those of GERMAN EXPRESSIONISM, seek to evoke a mental world rather than a real world) and to suggest meaning, usually dramatic meaning, by the way CHARACTERS are placed in relation to both SETting and each other.

Except in some extreme cases – such as, perhaps, Stan Brakhage's NON-CAMERA FILM *Mothlight* (1963) or Derek Jarman's *Blue* (1993), which at the level of the IMAGE consists entirely of a blue screen – film cannot help capturing and organizing space in some way. CAMERA MOVEMENT, EDITING and the use of different LENSES allow for a flexible and always changing approach to space in film, though it was not always so: early SILENT CINEMA was characterized by a theatrical conception of space, in which continuous ACTIONS were performed on a stage and viewed from the fourth wall and filmed as if from the stalls. SCENE dissection – the breaking down of scenes into more than one shot – and what we would now call a more properly FILMIC conception of space was not fully established until the 1910s, although much EXPERIMENTAL and COUNTER CINEMA work has returned to the so-called primitive approach to space. Questions about space are central to André Bazin's seminal theses (Bazin in Graham, 1968; Bazin, 1967, Bazin in Williams, 1980) about REALISM in the cinema and the evolution of film language. Bazin argued that the way space is represented in cinema – by editing, whether of the MONTAGE or the INVISIBLE EDITING variety, or by strategies which seek to preserve spatial (and temporal) continuity – had consequences for the relationship of the spectator to the world represented. Bazin argued that the DEEP FOCUS composition in depth and (often) LONG TAKE style in the 1940s work of Orson Welles (*Citizen Kane*, 1941; *The Magnificent Ambersons*, 1942) and William Wyler (*The Little Foxes*, 1941; *The Best Years of Our Lives*, 1946) accorded more freedom and brought the spectator closer to the relationship which he/she enjoyed with reality itself. Because the film frame excludes what is beyond it, off-screen space is an important factor in the way cinema organizes space: off-screen space can be suggested by a character's look off-screen or by character movement towards an off-screen point, and what is suggested about off-screen space can be important dramatically as, for example, framing within the frame to close down space. See also NARRATIVE SPACE.

Further reading: Aumont *et al.* (1992), Bordwell & Thompson (1997)

Spaghetti western A CYCLE of WESTERNS that got their name because a number of them were actually SHOT on LOCATION in Italy, though some used either Yugoslavia or Spain. All three countries had areas with a rugged mountainous terrain that gave a Darwinian emphasis to the GENRE's landscape. The best known of these films are the collaborations between DIRECTOR Sergio Leone and STAR Clint Eastwood on the 'man with no name' trilogy: *A Fistful of Dollars* (1964), *For a Few Dollars More* (1966) and *The Good, the Bad and the Ugly* (1966).

Further reading: Frayling (1981)

Special effects (often abbreviated to SFX). Artificially contrived effects designed to create the illusion of real (or imagined) events, whether through special photographic effects or created, and recorded normally by a CAMERA. In principle, many common effects such as FADES, DISSOLVES and WIPES should be considered special effects, but the term is usually reserved for three main classes of effects: mechanical effects such as simulated explosions, fires, floods, storms; illusion created by so-called 'trick photography' either IN-CAMERA, during shooting, or via the OPTICAL printer, such as GLASS SHOTS, MATTE SHOTS or REAR PROJECTION in which LIVE ACTION is combined with painted backgrounds or miniatures; and, increasingly, the major use of the term, effects achieved on the photographic IMAGE by DIGITAL means, from electronically programmed motion control to computer graphics and ANIMATION which can move CHARACTERS from one background to another, and so on. Historically, special effects have often been associated with FANTASY GENRES, particularly SCIENCE FICTION, and this continues with films like *Jurassic Park* (dir. Steven Spielberg, 1993) and *Terminator 2: Judgment Day* (dir. James Cameron, 1991), although digital effects are increasingly used in spectacular non-fantasy films like *Titanic* (dir. James Cameron, 1998).

Spectacle Often used in reference to EPIC FILMS to describe expensive and elaborate representations of historical events involving large casts and sweeping ACTION. The Babylonian SCENES in *Intolerance* (dir. D.W. Griffith, 1915), filmed on a giant SET, offer an early example of HOLLYWOOD's emphasis on spectacle in terms of massive scale. A spectacular quality can also be found in contemporary films with scenes of elaborate ACTION, often requiring the use of SPECIAL EFFECTS, as in the realistic depiction of dinosaurs in *Jurassic Park* (dir. Steven Spielberg, 1993) and the destruction of Washington in *Independence Day* (dir. Roland Emmerich, 1996). POSTMODERN culture's emphasis on IMAGE and display is sometimes referred to as the 'society of the spectacle,' a phrase coined by French theorist Guy Debord.

Spectatorship See AUDIENCE, RECEPTION THEORY.

Spin-off A general business term for a (usually beneficial) activity arising from some other primary activity (and also the name for a subsidiary company spun-off from a parent company). In the film industry, spin-off generally refers to, for example, a TELEVISION show based on a successful FEATURE FILM, or a feature film based on, say, a CHARACTER from a previously successful film, though the term can also apply to ANCILLARY activities.

Splatter film A SUBGENRE of the HORROR FILM emphasizing graphic VIOLENCE and prosthetic SPECIAL EFFECTS. As McCarty (1984, p. 1) notes, splatter movies differ from other horror films in that they 'aim not to scare their audiences, necessarily, nor to drive them to the edges of their seats in suspense, but to *mortify* them with scenes of explicit gore. In splatter movies, mutilation is indeed the message – many times the only one.' Splatter movies began with the LOW-BUDGET films of Herschel Gordon Lewis (*Blood Feast*, 1963; *2000 Maniacs*, 1964), but George A. Romero, director of *Night of the Living Dead* (1968), brought better PRODUCTION VALUES with *Dawn of the Dead* (1978), featuring special effects by Tom Savini. The success of gory SLASHER FILMS such as the *Nightmare on Elm Street* and *Friday the 13th* SERIES brought splatter into the MAINSTREAM. New Zealand DIRECTOR Peter Jackson took splatter to its apparent limit with the graphic EXCESS and comic tone of *Braindead* (aka *Dead Alive*, 1992). Also called gore film, meat movie and slice-and-dice film.

Splice The join between two strips of film, either during EDITING or to repair broken PRINTS. CELLULOID strips can be spliced either by scraping the EMULSION away from the celluloid base and cementing an overlapping strip on to it (an overlap cement or lap splice) or by making a direct CUT between FRAMES and joining the two strips end to end with transparent tape (a butt splice). Butt splices are faster and commonly used while prints are being edited, but cement splices are more durable and tend to be used on other prints.

Split screen Use of the film FRAME to contain two or more IMAGES at the same time. DIRECTORS have used this device to manipulate the ASPECT RATIO of the cinema SCREEN, to provide multiple perspectives, and to show temporal simultaneity in a narrative. Brian de Palma used split screen images in *Sisters* (1973), where it was particularly appropriate to a story of separated Siamese twins and a theme of the duality of human nature. The DOCUMENTARY *Woodstock* (dir. Michael Wadleigh, 1970) uses split screen to convey both the scale of the concert event and the drug-altered perspectives of many of the participants.

Sprocket, sprocket hole   A sprocket or sprocket wheel consists of a wheel or roller with teeth that engage with the sprocket holes on the edge of the film strip and thereby move the film strip through a CAMERA, projector or printer. Broken or stretched sprocket holes can interfere with the smooth running of a film through a projector.

Spy Film   Film GENRE focusing on espionage and other covert activities. Although it might be considered a SUBGENRE of the CRIME FILM, with the onset of the Cold War the spy film developed its own distinctive CONVENTIONS, invariably featuring men in trenchcoats, shifting loyalties and duplicity in its CHARACTERS, and the explicit clash of national IDEOLOGIES. Alfred Hitchcock combined romance with spies in his THRILLERS *The Thirty-Nine Steps* (1935), *The Lady Vanishes* (1938), *Notorious* (1946) and *North by Northwest* (1959), but with the coming of World War II the spy film became more overtly political. In the 1940s spies tended to be Nazis or Fifth Columnists, as in *All Through the Night* (dir. Vincent Sherman, 1942), which grafts spy elements onto the GANGSTER FILM, and *The House on 92nd Street* (dir. Henry Hathaway, 1945), but in the 1950s Communists became the threat in movies such as *I Was a Communist for the FBI* (dir. Gordon Douglas, 1951), *Woman on Pier 13* (*I Married a Communist*, dir. Robert Stevenson, 1950) and *Pickup on South Street* (dir. Samuel Fuller, 1953). Later spy films such as *The Spy Who Came In from the Cold* (dir. Martin Ritt, 1966) deglamorized the business of spying and questioned the moral value of espionage itself. In 1962, *Dr. No* (dir. Terrence Young) began a series of blatantly escapist spy movies featuring agent James Bond (initially played by Sean Connery) and featuring sequences with elaborate ACTION and exotic hardware, which were quickly the object of PARODY or pale imitation in such movies as *In Like Flint* (dir. Daniel Mann, 1966) and *Man from O.R.G.Y.* (dir. James A. Hill, 1970). Since the collapse of the Soviet Union and the end of the Cold War, the spy film has lost a sense of immediacy and purpose, as is evident in the nostalgic COMEDY *Austin Powers: International Man of Mystery* (dir. Jay Roach, 1997).
Further reading: Landy (1991a), Rubin (1999)

Stag Film   A pornographic film, originally in 8MM or SUPER 8MM and intended for a primarily male AUDIENCE at social functions such as stags and fraternity parties. By the standards of CLASSIC HOLLYWOOD CINEMA, stag films were made cheaply and illegally and had poor PRODUCTION VALUES. Williams (1989) refers to their style as primitive and points out that their insulation within a world of almost wholly male spectators made them particularly misogynist, preventing them, unlike mainstream PORNOGRAPHY, from addressing issues of female PLEASURE. Since the era of the home VCR the stag film has been replaced by VIDEO, which is more easily available as well as more professionally produced. Also known as BLUE MOVIE.
Further reading: Di Lauro & Rabkin (1976)

Stalker film   See SLASHER FILM.

Star A film star is a performer whose presence in a film can assure BOX-OFFICE success and who generates interest in his or her life beyond film roles. Such a simple definition conceals the complexities of a key area of film studies in the last two decades. At one level, stars can be seen as a key element of film language: like GENRE; they provide advance shorthand of what a film is going to be like and thus sell a film to an AUDIENCE. Accordingly, stars are constructed, with varying degrees of their own collusion, so that PRODUCERS have a recognizable and desirable commodity to associate with their product. Whilst stardom itself is a kind of IDEOLOGICAL construct, representative of a culture founded upon aspiration and material consumption, different types of stars can also be seen as reflecting different, evolving societies. Dyer (1979, p. 6) quotes Raymond Durgnat's observation that 'The social history of a nation can be written in terms of its film stars' and Alexander Walker's that 'Stars are the direct or indirect reflection of the needs, drives and dreams of American society.' Despite the obvious dangers of reading the meaning of stars in such a direct way, there seem to be clear connections, at different historical moments, operating both ways between stardom and society. As one of many components of film language, the meaning(s) of stars is best seen in combination with others components. Patrick Philips provides a useful analysis of *New York, New York* (dir. Martin Scorsese, 1977) based on the three intersecting perspectives of genre, star and AUTEUR, seeing the film in terms of Scorsese's auteur trademarks, its particular take on the MUSICAL, and the highly contrasting star personas of Robert De Niro and Liza Minnelli (in Nelmes, 1999, pp. 121–63).

Since the collapse of the STUDIO SYSTEM in the 1950s, stars have been less tied to production companies and have had more control over their public persona, although contemporary stars are usually contracted to AGENTS with a clear sense of their clients' position in the market place. In addition, in today's public consciousness, cinema is no longer the dominant fodder for gossip columns and magazines, which are just as likely to be filled with the private lives of minor TELEVISION personalities and sports stars as film stars. Film stars today are less central to people's lives than they once were and less remote from them, now rarely sold, as in the past, as the embodiments of impossible dreams and fantasies (though they were never exclusively this – ordinariness and day-to-day life problems have always been elements in the construction of all but a few film stars). See also ACTORS, ACTORS STUDIO, METHOD ACTING. Further reading: Dyer (1986), Geraghty in Gledhill & Williams (2000), Gledhill (1991), Hollows *et al.* (2000)

Star system A method of conceiving, making and MARKETING films that focuses primarily on the public identity of their leading performers or STARS. Although the system is generally associated with HOLLYWOOD and the MAJOR STUDIOS, there are many examples of the cinemas of other cultures using stars in this way (see, for example, BOLLYWOOD). Most accounts of the star system see its origins in the period 1910–1920, when the studios moved from marketing films anonymously to putting the names of their contracted stars on the advertising material. Among the earliest acknowledged film stars were Mary Pickford and Charlie Chaplin, who were soon able to command large salaries on the strength of their value to the STUDIOS. Thus, stars began to be seen as a type of product to be owned, refined and adapted according to the perceived tastes of the cinema-going AUDIENCE and the needs of the studios themselves.

As the system developed, it became more ruthless: stars were paid well but were

also treated harshly when deemed no longer useful. The 1930s and 1940s was the heyday of the star system, with imported stars like Marlene Dietrich and Greta Garbo contracted to major American studios, as well as major native stars of the STUDIO SYSTEM era like John Wayne, James Cagney, Clark Gable, Humphrey Bogart, Shirley Temple, Judy Garland, Barbara Stanwyck and Lauren Bacall. Hayward (1996) notes that there was a real shift in the way that male stars were featured on the screen after the coming of SOUND, but little change in the presentation of women. Whereas before sound, most CHARACTERS were presented as 'types', afterwards there was significant development of more complex male heroic roles, while female roles – particularly those for major stars – stayed more firmly in the area of idealized beauty. As FEMINIST FILM THEORY has stressed, female stars were to be looked at, whereas male stars became active human agents (Johnston in Nichols, 1985).

Most accounts suggest that the star system collapsed with the decline of the major studios in the 1950s. This is not to suggest that stars ceased to become important to films, simply that control of them as a commodity became far less concentrated in the hands of the studios so that it is subsequently difficult to refer to anything approaching a 'system'.

The star system was not only a production policy. Maltby (1995, p. 89) places much emphasis on the studios' efforts to create and maintain their stars' public personae, and the widespread circulation of fan magazines: 'The studio system was committed to the deliberate manufacture of stars as a mechanism for selling movie tickets, and as a result generated publicity around the stars' off-screen lives designed to complement and play upon their screen IMAGES'. The star system was as much about the manufacture of stars as about the production of films, and it sold not only films, but every other conceivable product: as well as selling dreams, fantasy and glamour, the star system was capable of selling detergent and soft drinks, a key element in the burgeoning mass consumer market.

Further reading: Dyer (1986, 1998), Gledhill (1991), Hollows *et al.* (2000), Schatz (1988)

Steadicam A device designed to keep a CAMERA steady when a CAMERA OPERA-TOR is using HAND-HELD techniques. The Steadicam holds the camera on an arm that is strapped to the body of the cameraperson and held steady by a sprung mechanism enabling the camera to be moved at speed and over obstacles whilst filming without camera 'shake'. This enables the camera to follow rapid movement in a way that produces a more raw and immediate effect than TRACKING yet allows the camera-person to go where track laying is not possible. One of the earliest recorded uses of the device is in *Bound for Glory* (dir. Hal Ashby, 1976), for which Haskell Wexler won the ACADEMY AWARD for Best CINEMATOGRAPHY.

Steenbeck One of the best known makes of flat-bed EDITING machines, manu-factured in California. Steenbeck machines became so well-known that 'Steenbeck' often referred to any flat-bed editing table (just as 'Hoover' refers to any vacuum cleaner). See aso MOVIOLA.

Stereoscopy, stereographic cinematography See 3-D.

Stereotyping A term used to refer to the kind of characterization that is based on a narrow fixed set of characteristics. This results in the repetition of basic types across a range of films so that the ACTIONS and responses of the CHARACTERS become predictable.

The range of stereotypes that are in widespread circulation shifts over time and are partly reflective of changes in social and political values, though their use in films can also be said to be a contributor to the maintenance of particular values and beliefs. Although there are clearly stereotyped female characters in contemporary cinema, there is far less likely to be the kind of crude 'dumb-blonde' stereotype that was in circulation in the 1950s and depicted by actresses such as the young Marilyn Monroe. Similarly, the cruder kinds of stereotype – say, the gay man or black mammies – have all but disappeared unless used with a kind of POSTMODERN irony. None of this is to imply that social changes in the areas of RACE, GENDER and SEXU-ALITY have swept away negative stereotypes around these issues, but assumptions that these express essential truths (e.g. all gay men are effeminate and have limp wrists) are far less common.

Although stereotypes are part of a MELODRAMATIC tradition as opposed to REAL-ISM, they do tend to be taken as reflective of broader truths. An example here is stereotypes based on perceived national characteristics. Old-fashioned Irish stereo-types were common in British films whereas in other ex-colonial nations the Irish are replaced by a different culture over which power needs to be exerted.

Although the term is now used entirely negatively, there are various kinds of broad SATIRE for which they are essential. Traditions of types as representative of social groupings are firmly rooted in satirical theatre-going back to the Romans, and it is possible to argue that the legitimacy of their use depends on how aware the film is of its characters' stereotypical nature. Stereotypes are at their least acceptable when it seems that a kind of realistic depth is being attempted and failure results in a crude stereotype. If, however, there are clear signals that the use of types is entirely inten-tional and serves a satirical intent, as in the early films of the British 'Carry On' SERIES of films such as *Carry On Nurse* (dir. Gerald Thomas, 1959), then the term is not entirely pejorative.

It must also be said that stereotyping, rather like the repetitions of GENRE produc-tions, can be part of the PLEASURE of certain kinds of films. Predictability combined with minor variations is one of the staple strategies of much commercial film-making. The James Bond series of films that started in 1962 with *Dr No* (dir. Terence Young) does not offer detailed characterization, but rather repetition of characteri--tics that have evolved over time, but from which we draw knowing pleasure in their very predictability. See also ACTOR.

Still See PRODUCTION STILL.

Stock shot, stock footage SHOTS, or footage, of a variety of different kinds (sometimes known as library shots or FOOTAGE) from everyday activities, street SCENES and natural disasters, to NEWSREEL and combat footage, normally filmed originally for newsreel or DOCUMENTARY purposes and now stored in a library specializing in such material for sale or rental for use in new films, usually docu-mentaries but also in fiction films. They may be used *as* stock footage, as film evidence from the past (see ARCHIVAL FOOTAGE) or may be passed off as belonging to the new production (where they are used as an economic alternative to shooting new footage). See also ARCHIVAL FILM/FOOTAGE, FOUND FOOTAGE.

Stock See FILM STOCK.

Stop-motion photography, stop-action A SPECIAL EFFECT used since the days of Georges Méliès, achieved by stopping the CAMERA during a SHOT, adding or removing something in its view, and continuing shooting again. When the FOOTAGE is projected, objects or ACTORS seem to appear or disappear within the FRAME. When a lengthy process is filmed in this manner requiring such stops at regular intervals, the technique is called TIME-LAPSE photography; when applied to single-frame photography to create the illusion of ANIMATION, the process is called PIXILLATION.

Store theatre, store front theatre Early form of cinema theatre for showing films, and the first, makeshift venues devoted entirely to the showing of films in the USA, converted from ordinary shops or stores, taking over from travelling entertainments such as fairs, and from VAUDEVILLE theatres where films featured as part of an otherwise live show. From about 1905, store theatres become known as NICKELODEONS.
Further reading: Robinson (1996)

Story As Bordwell and Thompson (1997, p. 84) put it, 'The set of all the events in the narrative, both the ones explicitly presented and those the viewer infers, comprises the *story*', whereas PLOT is 'everything visibly and audibly present in the film before us'. The term DIEGESIS is often used to describe the world of the story including people, places and objects that we may never see, but which are inferred, while PLOT includes many non-DIEGETIC elements such as SOUNDTRACK MUSIC, or TITLES and CREDITS, from outside the world of the story. A key element of narrative technique is getting the right balance between plot and story, between the explicit and implicit. Some films present a story, much of which is inferred, with the onus very much on the AUDIENCE to construct the total narrative, particularly common in EXPERIMENTAL or AVANT-GARDE film, whereas MAINSTREAM FILM has tended to favour the explicit. See also BACK STORY, NARRATIVE SPACE, NARRATIVE THEORY, NARRATOR, OMNISCIENCE.
Further reading: Chatman (1978)

Storyboard A series of drawings for a film, or part of a film, SHOT by shot, though still photographs might be used instead of drawings and computer generated IMAGES are increasingly common. The ways that productions use storyboards vary according to the working methods of (usually) the DIRECTOR. Whilst some would only use them to work out a complicated SCENE in advance, shot by shot, others might sketch out a whole FEATURE FILM this way. Alfred Hitchcock claimed that, for him, this was the creative part of the process, and that if he had got it right he would hardly need to look through the CAMERA when shooting (see examples of Hitchcock storyboards in Auiler, 1999). As well as drawings, storyboards will also have CAPTIONS indicating dialogue cues and varying amounts of camera instructions.

Straight-to-video Most films (other than very specialized material such as EXPERIMENTAL or PORNOGRAPHY) that appear on VIDEO do so after a THEATRICAL RELEASE, the success of which is a vital factor in establishing the availability and value of a film on video. A film which bypasses theatrical release and goes straight to video release is therefore likely to be one whose distributors calculate that its theatrical BOX-OFFICE prospects are poor. Although this often means that the films have been cheaply made and are of poor quality, the vagaries of film DISTRIBUTION are such that this is not always the case: many titles which do poor business on theatrical release in North America are then released straight to video in Great Britain or other markets, but this is not necessarily a measure of their artistic quality. During the initial video boom in the early 1980s, when material was in short supply, many films were made primarily for the video market.

Street film A CYCLE of GERMAN EXPRESSIONIST cinema that featured narratives involving CHARACTERS who flee the safety and security of their middle-CLASS homes for life in the chaotic bustle of the street. Beginning with *The Street* (*Die Strasse*, dir. Karl Grune, 1923), the group includes such films as *The Joyless Street* (dir. G.W. Pabst, 1925), *Tragedy of the Street* (dir. Bruno Rahn, 1927) and *Asphalt* (dir. Joe May, 1929). Kracauer (1947, pp. 157–60) interprets the street films as an indication of widespread discontent with and anxiety over the Weimar government.
Further reading: Eisner (1969), Elsaesser in Nowell-Smith (1996), Petro (1989)

Structural film Form of EXPERIMENTAL or AVANT-GARDE film that makes the physical nature of the medium of cinema its primary subject matter. According to P. Adams Sitney (1979, pp. 369–70), who is credited with coining the term to describe the work of such film-makers as Michael Snow, Paul Sharits, Tony Conrad, and Bruce Baillie, 'The structural film insists on its shape, and what content it has is minimal and subsidiary to the outline.... Four characteristics of the structural film are a fixed CAMERA position (fixed *FRAME* from the viewer's perspective), the FLICKER effect, LOOP printing (the immediate repetition of SHOTS, exactly and without variation), and rephotography off a screen.' Two well known examples are Conrad's *The Flicker* (1966), which employs film's illusion of movement and the mechanical means of creating it as its subject, and Snow's *Wavelength* (1967), a 45-minute gradual ZOOM in to a picture on a wall. MATERIALIST FILM is a type of structural film.
Further reading: Gidal (1976), Peterson (1994), Rees (1999)

Structuralism A wide-ranging term for a key movement in late twentieth century philosophy, drawing upon influences from disciplines including linguistics, anthropology, literary CRITICISM and PSYCHOANALYSIS. Its impact on film studies was felt most strongly via SEMIOTICS, itself a branch of linguistics, and it was a crucial influence on the development of film THEORY in the late 1960s and 1970s. At its most all-embracing, structuralism attempts 'total' or 'grand' theory – a theoretical system capable of understanding the underlying structures beneath all human activity. It is therefore one of the key positions in the movement of thought away from the individual as an active, knowing agent in his or her own destiny and towards a view of human activity as the product of deep structures underlying social relations.

Structuralism seemed to offer film (as well as literary) criticism the possibility of a scientific approach to criticism, as opposed to the prevailing intuitive, humanist tendency. Generally speaking, early film criticism tended to assume that a TEXT contained fundamental meaning(s) about the world which it was the responsibility of the critic to uncover. Structuralism de-emphasized the relationship between film and reality and instead concentrated on its relationship to underlying structures that govern the production of all meaning.

Particularly influential in the application of structuralism to film was work on narrative and MYTH by Claude Levi-Strauss, Vladimir Propp and Tzvetan Todorov (see Cook, 1985), whose writings influenced film criticism by pointing to underlying commonalities between seemingly very different stories, demystifying the creativity of the apparent author or creator. Will Wright's work on the WESTERN (1975) sought not only to link the underlying GENRE structures to other narrative patterns, but also to assess the contribution of the Western to the ongoing process of myth creation by which a society speaks to itself.

It is possible to see how structuralist ideas could reinforce the idea of the AUTEUR: by seeking out patterns of style or narrative, or both, across a DIRECTOR's films, structuralism could demonstrate the existence of a unique voice. Yet structuralism also has the potential for the elimination of any original authorial voice, all narratives being common to the human condition and our attempts to understand it. Auteur-structuralism therefore became a term for theoretical attempts to combine the two positions, exemplified by Peter Wollen's *Sign and Meaning in the Cinema* (1998), originally published in 1969.

The strongest objection to structuralist analysis has been its neglect of both the AUDIENCE and the socio-economic context of both production and RECEPTION. Whilst structuralism implied that the meaning of a text did not lie in some essential idea, sought by the critic in relation to an external reality, it replaced it with an idea that came to be seen as too rigid: that meaning was purely the product of interrelated structures of SIGNIFIERS. Subsequent theory, loosely grouped under POST-STRUC-TURALISM and POSTMODERNISM, has replaced the centrality of such views with a concern for the spectator's interaction with a text. See also FEMINIST FILM THEORY, POST THEORY, PSYCHOANALYSIS.

Further reading: Cook (1985)

Studio system The loosely defined system of making films in HOLLYWOOD between the 1920–1950s, controlled by the BIG 5 MAJOR STUDIOS – MGM, PARAMOUNT, TWENTIETH CENTURY-FOX, WARNER BROS. and RKO – and the LITTLE 3 – UNITED ARTISTS, COLUMBIA and UNIVERSAL. The principal features of the studio system were geared to the fast, cheap, mass production of FEATURE FILMS to satisfy the enormous demand of the market at home and abroad. Finance and MARKETING were based on the East Coast in New York, where company heads decided how much money would be spent and on what kind of product – categorized primarily in terms of STARS and GENRES – and almost all production was based on the West Coast in Hollywood. Although studios varied somewhat in practice, production was generally organized along factory lines, with every phase of the process undertaken by specialist departments. PRODUCERS, DIRECTORS, SCREENWRITERS, DIRECTORS OF CINEMATOGRAPHY, ART DIRECTORS and EDITORS as well as stars were employed on long-term contracts – though stars, in particular, could be loaned out to other studios – and generally assigned to projects by studio bosses, although directors and others would often be assigned to projects considered appropriate to their talents. Films, especially the less prestigious ones which formed the majority, were made on an assembly line basis, reflecting new approaches to production in other industries like automobiles. Although control of creativity was concentrated in the hands of senior studio executives, some directors, such as Frank

Capra, Josef Von Sternberg, John Ford, Howard Hawks and Alfred Hitchcock, had a degree of freedom over their projects. However, even they often needed to work within the constraints of a studio's dominant style or generic speciality, and most directors were as much functionaries as anyone else. Despite the system, these conditions allowed much good and even great work, and commentators have had to recognize as well the 'genius of the system' (see Schatz, 1988). To varying degrees, other countries with a significant volume of film production, such as Britain, Italy and Japan (and see also BOLLYWOOD) followed similar practices.

The success of the studio system depended on VERTICAL INTEGRATION: studios not only made films, but also controlled DISTRIBUTION and EXHIBITION, with practices such as BLOCK BOOKING virtually guaranteeing an AUDIENCE for their films. Although such a complex, integrated industry was potentially very profitable, costs were also high and during the 1930s economic conditions increased the tendency for STUDIOS to be controlled by financiers or Wall Street. The 1948 PARAMOUNT DECISION – ruling that studios' ownership of production, distribution and exhibition was monopolistic and forcing them to sell off their cinema theatres – was an important factor in ending the dominance of the studio system. However, there were other factors at work: the rapid decline in audience attendance and the rise of TELEVISION in the post-war years meant that the earlier scale of studios' production was no longer sustainable; studio control of star contracts had already been challenged – notably in Olivia de Havilland's successful 1944 challenge against WARNER BROS. – and several stars, such as James Cagney and Edward G. Robinson had already gone freelance (though this was a route only available to major stars); this tendency increased rapidly as INDE-PENDENT production – often by stars – grew after the Paramount decision. As foreign and independent producers entered the market, US producers began to seek cheaper production opportunities abroad (see RUNAWAYS). Though the studio system as such has not survived, most of the studios survived on distribution and by diversifying into television and other media enterprises, often by CONGLOMERATION and SYNERGY, and talent AGENCIES took over some of the roles previously associated with the studios. See also UNIT.

Further reading: Bordwell, Staiger & Thompson (1985), Cook & Bernink (1999), Maltby (1995)

Studios The term most commonly refers to large companies responsible for the production (and sometimes DISTRIBUTION and EXHIBITION) of FEATURE FILMS. Although studios in this sense have existed in a number of film-making countries (e.g. Britain, France and India), it is most commonly used as a term to refer to the large, so-called MAJOR STUDIOS in HOLLYWOOD – including MGM, PARAMOUNT, TWENTIETH CENTURY-FOX, WARNER BROS. and RKO – that dominated the STUDIO SYSTEM, but which have now declined in power and influence since the 1930s and 1940s. More literally, the term refers to the complexes housing large SOUND stages and BACK LOTS, with specialist sound and vision recording and EDITING facilities required to shoot and complete films, along with offices and the physical infrastructure needed for building and making large scale PROPS. The importance of such facilities has declined drastically since the 1950s and the demise of the studio system. Many of the Hollywood-based companies have sold much of their extensive land holdings to realize its real estate asset value. LOCATION shooting is now much more common, though extensive studio facilities still exist in the US and elsewhere – today, as often leased to INDEPENDENT production companies as used by the parent companies themselves.

The most significant change in the direction of major STUDIOS today is their take-over and ownership, since the 1960s, by large multi-national CONGLOMERATES with leisure industry interests that go far beyond feature films. Although the trade name COLUMBIA is still a very significant one in an era where major studios have a reduced, but still powerful role, Columbia is now owned by the Sony Corporation of Japan, part of its global strategy to sell a range of electronic merchandise, MUSIC and computer software. We may be witnessing another studio era, but with less connection to the 'art' of film, and now with studios run as part of a multinational communications strategy in which the production and theatrical distribution of films is only one part. See BIG 5, LITTLE 3, SYNERGY, WALT DISNEY.

Further reading: Bordwell, Staiger & Thompson (1985), Cook & Bernink (1999), Maltby (1995)

Subgenre A smaller but distinct division within a GENRE: for example, the vampire film and zombie film are both subgenres of HORROR, as the backstage MUSICAL is of the musical.

Subject, subjectivity Films tend to privilege the point of view of certain CHARACTERS over others so that they become the subject of the film, with the spectator invited to take part in their subjectivity and take their viewpoint, not only by narrative devices that construct a particular view of events, but also through a pattern of CAMERA behaviour that allows a particular point of view to dominate. Discussion of the spectator' s subjectivity and the role of film in constructing it during the act of watching has been a key concept for recent film studies. Film has been seen as part of Louis Althusser's 'ideological state apparatuses' that construct the subject IDEOLOGICALLY, though most recent work has seen the film-AUDIENCE relationship as more negotiated and open.

PSYCHOANALYTIC THEORY has seen film spectatorship as a metaphorical re-enactment of a key phase in the development of the self: offering us idealized 'complete' IMAGES (at least in most MAINSTREAM CINEMA), it constructs an illusion of completeness which is continually being denied to us by our subconscious. In this sense, the idea of ourselves being constructed as subject by the film becomes one of the cinema's most primitive and fundamental PLEASURES. As Dudley Andrew (in Turner, 1999) puts it: 'Our fascination with films is now thought to be not a fascination with particular characters and intrigues so much as a fascination with the image itself, based on a primal "mirror stage" in our psychic growth. Just as we were, when infants, confronted with the gloriously complete view of ourselves in the mirror, so now we identify with the gloriously complete presentation of a SPECTACLE on the screen.'

However, this would seem to imply an unGENDERed subject, watching and taking narcissistic pleasure from film, and the implicitly male nature of the way most films construct the viewer in relation to their predominantly female objects has been a key subject for debate in FEMINIST FILM THEORY. Much cinema does not simply tap into the VOYEURISM and/or narcissism that are part of the formation of the subject, it taps into a male version of this, ignoring the female. Perhaps, above all, theoretical work on the subject in relation to film has been important in reminding us of the constructed nature of the self and the way that identities rooted in gender, RACE and CLASS are constructed for us.

Further reading: Andrew (1984), Lapsley & Westlake (1988)

Subjective camera The use of the CAMERA to give the impression that the IMAGES seen on the screen represent the (field of) vision or imagination of one of the CHARACTERS, or possibly of the DIRECTOR providing editorial comment. Kawin (1978, p. 7) distinguishes between two kinds of subjective camera: that which shows what characters see and that which shows what they think or think they see. In CLASSIC NARRATIVE CINEMA the subjective camera is usually clearly marked as such, through such EDITING constructions as the EYELINE MATCH or VOICE-OVER NARRATION. Often it is used to render visually physiological states such as dizziness or drunkenness, but *Lady in the Lake* (dir. Robert Montgomery, 1946) is famous for its use of the subjective camera, restricted to the physical POINT OF VIEW of its protagonist, for the entire film. In ART CINEMA films, however, the distinction between subjectivity and the real world is often ambiguous, as in *8½* (dir. Federico Fellini, 1963), which deliberately confuses reality and fantasy for the film's protagonist, who suffers from an overactive imagination.

Subjective shot See SUBJECTIVE CAMERA.

Subliminal A level of communication below that of the conscious mind: we experience something subliminally without, in the usual sense, knowing it – theoretically at the level of the subconscious. Much mythology has grown up around the notion of subliminal messages, related to other powerful media myths such as brainwashing, so much so that subliminal messages in ADVERTISING are illegal in the UK.

Subsidy Money provided for film production from GOVERNMENT funds, usually indirectly through agencies such as the Arts Council or British Screen in the UK. Subsidies can range from relatively small scale subsidy for SHORT FILMS by first-time film-makers to much larger national or pan-national initiatives to protect a whole industry. The extent of subsidy can change enormously according to the social and economic policies of the elected government. In the UK, from 1979–1997 the amount of subsidy was severely reduced, along with other forms of indirect subsidy such as tax concessions, during 18 years of Conservative governments and yet, during this period, some notable film-makers made FEATURE FILMS with some measure of subsidy allocated by British Screen including Terence Davies (*Distant Voices, Still Lives*, 1991) and Mike Leigh (*Life is Sweet*, 1991). Currently, money generated by the British National Lottery is channelled into arts funding, increasing the amount of money available for film funding. Some of this is allocated for short EXPERIMENTAL film, and some for subsidizing medium-scale British films with some hope of commercial success. In all cases, Lottery funding has to be matched by funds raised elsewhere, promoting a subsidized culture of private investment in film production.

In some European countries, notably France, subsidy of film and other 'cultural industries' has traditionally played a vital role in the protection of a national identity against (principally) American cultural HEGEMONY. Of similar importance was the role of government subsidy in supporting THIRD CINEMA in Latin America. See also GATT, POST-COLONIAL THEORY.

Subtitles Words superimposed onto a film which appear at the bottom of the FRAME. Their most common purpose is to translate a film's dialogue from a foreign language, an alternative to the practice of DUBBING a film into the native language which avoids the resultant problems of SYNCHRONIZATION of lip-movement and SOUND. Historically, foreign-language ART CINEMA films have tended to be sub-titled, while foreign-language popular films have tended to be dubbed, though some countries, such as Italy, have tended to dub all films. Sometimes subtitles are used for films that are in the native language, but with a pronounced dialect or accent. Such decisions are often controversial, as with *Kes* (dir. Ken Loach, 1969), raising questions about the hegemonic nature of some kinds of English over others. See also CAPTION.

Sundance The name of both a well-known FESTIVAL for INDEPENDENT film and the institute that sponsors it, founded mainly through the work of Robert Redford, who persuaded elements in the US film industry to invest in the projects. The Sundance Institute, based in Utah, provides training for young film-makers, with classes and workshops by prominent figures from the industry. The festival is now an established part of the international film calendar, attracting a large number of establishment figures on the look-out for fresh talent. In 1996 Redford launched a full-time CABLE TV channel devoted to INDEPENDENT film – the Sundance Channel – an idea later borrowed by Film Four in the UK. Amongst the many films the Sundance Festival has championed are *Slackers* (dir. Richard Linklater, 1991), *Reservoir Dogs* (dir. Quentin Tarantino, 1992) and *The Brothers McMullen* (dir. Edward Burns, 1995).

Super 16mm 16MM negative film with a picture area 40–46 per cent larger than standard 16mm, used to preserve some of the economy and flexibility of shooting on 16mm while intending to BLOW UP the film to 35MM film for THEATRICAL EXHIBITION. Introduced in 1971, Super 16mm has been used by many INDEPENDENT film-makers in the US and Europe (e.g. Robert Altman's *Come Back to The Five and Dime, Jimmy Dean, Jimmy Dean* and Peter Greenaway's *The Draughtsman's Contract*, both 1982).

Super 8mm The narrowest film GAUGE, introduced in 1966 as an advanced version of 8MM film. As with other 'super' configurations (see SUPER 16MM), this format offered an almost 50 per cent larger picture area, by incorporating a single set of SPROCKET HOLES and 74 FRAMES per foot (as opposed to Standard 8mm's 80 frames), which also made it easier to stripe with magnetic tape for SOUND. Like Standard 8mm, Super 8mm was, and remains, largely an amateur gauge, though it has been used by many EXPERIMENTAL FILM-makers (e.g. Derek Jarman). Though still in use, and prized by some film-makers, most amateur film-making now uses VIDEO technology.

Superimposition The placing of two or more IMAGES over each other in the same FRAME or image (often called 'double exposure' when only two images are involved), achieved either IN-CAMERA or, more commonly, by combining images at the printing stage. A common use of double exposure is for a DISSOLVE. In early SILENT CINEMA – for example, the trick films of Georges Méliès – superimposition was often used to create fantasy and illusion, and one of the main uses of superimposition has been to express SUBJECTIVITY, such as the face of a figure on which other images representing thought or memory are superimposed, as in many 1920s French IMPRESSIONIST films. Also during the 1920s, Soviet film-makers like Sergei Eisenstein and Dziga Vertov experimented with superimposition for both dramatic impact and the expression of ideas. See also MONTAGE.

Surrealism An AVANT-GARDE movement in the arts, founded by André Breton in his famous manifesto of 1924, that stressed the irrational and the unconscious, the fantastic and dreamlike. Surrealism was similar to DADAISM, but the surrealists' penchant for incongruous juxtapositions and shock value often had a more political edge, as in the films of Luis Bunuel such as *Un Chien Andalou* (1928, made with artist Salvador Dali), and the shocking DOCUMENTARY *Las Hurdes* (*Land without Bread*, 1932). Cinema's ability to manipulate TIME and SPACE clearly appealed to Surrealist artists, who were interested in exploring a Freudian approach to consciousness, as in *La Coquille et le clergyman* (*The Seashell and the Clergyman*, dir. Germaine Dulac, 1927). The term is now used as an adjective to describe unusual, dreamlike works of art. See also DREAM FILM.
Further reading: Hammond (1991), Kuenzli (1987)

Surround sound Modern stereophonic SOUNDTRACKS incorporate a separate track that comes through speakers at the sides and rear of the theatre, giving spectators the feeling of being in the middle of the screen ACTION. New DIGITAL sound systems incorporate two separate surround SOUND channels, for speakers on the theatre's left and right sides.

Suspense thriller See THRILLER.

Suture A common term in medicine for the stitching of a wound. In film studies it has come to refer to the way that a spectator is 'stitched' into the film TEXT. One of the key ways that CLASSICAL NARRATIVE CINEMA hides its construction and creates the illusion of a 'whole' reality is the system of SHOT-REVERSE-SHOT, which allows the spectator a sense of completeness of vision through a privileged sense of the whole SPACE even when only part is being shown. In the filming of a two-way conversation, the first SHOT creates a potential anxiety in the spectator because the owner of the GAZE is off-screen; the REVERSE SHOT restores the whole by showing that the previously unknown source of the look was really just the second participant in the conversation. Other aspects of CONTINUITY EDITING also contribute to the suturing of the spectator into the illusion. PSYCHOANALYTIC theorists argue for a strong correspondence between the process of suture and the continuous efforts by the subconscious mind to resolve the difficulties of the divided self and regain a unified identity. The experience of cinema, it is argued, temporarily resolves this conflict, though in ways that are endlessly complicated by, among other things, the question of GENDER.
Further reading: Hayward (1996), Lapsley & Westlake (1988)

Swashbuckler A SUBGENRE of the ADVENTURE FILM featuring the glorified ACTION, athletic ability and fighting skill of a heroic figure, derived from the swaggering swordplay of pirate or similar CHARACTERS. *The Black Pirate* (dir. Albert

Parker, 1926) featuring Douglas Fairbanks, and *Captain Blood* (dir. Michael Curtiz, 1935) and *The Adventures of Robin Hood* (dir. Curtiz and William Keighley, 1938), both with Errol Flynn, are typical examples.

Further reading: Richards (1977)

Swish pan   See WHIP PAN, ZIP PAN.

Sync (or synchronized) sound   SOUND which, aligned in both shooting and EDITING, seems to come directly from the IMAGE on the screen. Lack of sync is especially noticeable when ACTORS' lips do not move to match their supposed speech (very common in films which have been dubbed into English from another language), or when an ACTION such as a door closing is not matched precisely by the sound. Sync sound was a problem for early SOUND CINEMA – put to comic effect in *Singin' in the Rain* (dir. Stanley Donen and Gene Kelly, 1952) – and was of crucial importance to developments in DOCUMENTARY film-making in the 1950s and 1960s, when sync-pulse systems helped make it possible to easily record direct sound on LOCATION.

Synedoche   The REPRESENTATION of an object, place or person by part of it, or the reverse where a whole comes to stand for one of its parts. The former is much more common in film – a trademark piece of clothing to stand for a CHARACTER or a landscape to stand for a whole country, as a segment of rocky, barren landscape can stand for the American west (enabling SPAGHETTI WESTERNS to be SHOT in Italy, Spain, and Yugoslavia whilst retaining many of the same values and symbolic meanings as if shot in Monument Valley). See also SEMIOTICS, SIGNIFIER.

Synergy   Synergy is the process by which the combined effects of different elements add up to something greater than the sum of their individual parts. Synergy has been used to describe developments in the media industries in general, and HOLLYWOOD in particular, since the 1980s. Principally this involves the growth of media empire CONGLOMERATES such as TIME WARNER, VIACOM and News Corporation, which absorbed what were earlier film production, DISTRIBUTION and EXHIBITION companies. Time Incorporated's purchase of WARNER Communications in 1990 aligned Time's interests in CABLE TELEVISION and publishing with Warner's film and television production and distribution, cable television (such as HBO) and MUSIC interests. In 1996, Time Warner merged with Turner Broadcasting's own cable and other film and television interests. Warner can thus capitalize on its films by cross-promoting them via music, publishing, cable, MULTI-MEDIA and so on, in a (new) form of VERTICAL INTEGRATION. Similarly, News Corporation combines TWEN-TIETH CENTURY-FOX film and television production and distribution, FOX network television, worldwide cable and SATELLITE TELEVISION interests and publishing, and Viacom combines PARAMOUNT film and television production and distribution, cable channels like MTV and Nickelodeon, television stations, Simon and Schuster publishers and the Blockbuster VIDEO rental chain.

Another form of synergy has also been tried, though with less success. Apparently fired by the failure of its Beta HOME VIDEO (hardware) system to secure agreements for movies (software) in the format, and conscious of similar battles over future new technologies, Japanese electronics manufacturer SONY acquired COLUMBIA PICTURES in 1989 (having previously acquired CBS Records in 1987), in an attempt to exercise some control over software as well as hardware. Shortly after, in 1990, Japanese manufacturing company Matsushita (which pioneered the VHS home video system and owns brands like JVC, Pioneer and Technics) bought UNIVERSAL (MCA/Universal, though later sold to Canadian distillery giant Seagram).

In the 1990s, MAJOR STUDIOS such as WALT DISNEY and Time Warner, recognising the growing importance of telephone lines for carrying programming in the future, have linked up with telephone companies. In January 2000, signalling the shape of synergy to come, the powerful old media company Time Warner and the new media major player internet provider America On Line (AOL) merged to form the $350 billion corporation AOL Time Warner, labelled by the media as 'a perfect marriage' – AOL's 20 million customers securing an AUDIENCE for Time Warner's film, television, music and print media interests. In June 2000 French-based transnational conglomerate Vivendi bid for Seagram and Universal to create the world's second largest media conglomerate, Vivendi Universal. Like AOL Time Warner, Vivendi Universal aims for synergy by combining old and new media – Universal's films, music and television programming (as well as theme parks in Hollywood, Florida and Spain), the European cable television and film production interests of the French Canal+, interests in satellite broadcasting (via a stake in News Corporation's BSkyB) and internet and telephone services. See also CONGLOMERATE, CROSS OWNERSHIP. Further reading: Wasko (1994), Fleming in Hill & McLoone (1996)

Syntagm The combination of a number of separate signs to produce meaning: separate signs are chosen from PARADIGMS and combined together as a syntagm. A sentence can be said to be made up of separate words chosen from paradigms of all possible words, then composed into a sentence, the syntagm, according to the rules of grammar. Film does not have such clear-cut rules as written and spoken language, though certain kinds of cinematic syntagms have at least unwritten rules. CLASSICAL film language's endeavour to create the illusion of seamless reality produces patterns for combining SHOTS that could be said to be syntagms composed of the individual SHOTS themselves. In film though the boundaries are unclear and a single shot could be said to be a syntagm composed of its SETTING, LIGHTING, PROPS, COSTUME, the CASTING of its characters and sound, all of which will have been selected from the relevant paradigms. See also CODES, SEMIOTICS, SIGNIFIER, STRUCTURALISM.

T

Tableau A static grouping of CHARACTERS within the FRAME, almost always with a stylized effect which freezes the flow of ACTION. The tableau – French for 'picture' or 'painting' – was characteristic of nineteenth century stage MELODRAMA, where it would represent in static form a particularly significant narrative moment. This usage was continued into SILENT CINEMA, which was heavily influenced in this and other ways by THEATRICAL traditions. It was still clearly in use in D.W. Griffith's films, such as, for example, in *Way Down East* (1920) in the SCENE in which the Lillian Gish character, whose unwed mother's past has been revealed, is sent out of the house into the snow storm. Though the tableau has dropped from usage in MAINSTREAM FILM, it has often been used to striking anti-NATURALISTIC effects in COUNTER CINEMA films, such as those directed by Jean-Luc Godard (*Weekend*, 1967; *Tout va bien*, 1972) or Rainer Werner Fassbinder (*The Merchant of Four Seasons*, 1971; *Fear Eats the Soul*, 1973), and in ART CINEMA, such as the stylized family tableaux in *Distant Voices, Still Lives* (dir. Terence Davies, 1988).

Tail The end of a REEL or strip of film, the opposite end to the HEAD. Also known as 'tail end'.

Take A single run of film through the CAMERA as it records a SHOT: both the process and the result may be called a 'take'. In commercial film production, several takes of the same shot would normally be made, until a satisfactory take has been achieved (see RETAKE). Each take is numbered and each number is recorded on a CLAPPER BOARD (or slateboard). See also LONG TAKE.

Takeoff See PARODY.

Talent Industry term for either professional performers in general, or those employed on a particular production, used mainly for ACTORS, though it also refers to others involved in a production such as musicians and animals. See AGENT.

Talkie See SILENT CINEMA, SOUND.

Talking head A CLOSE-UP or MEDIUM SHOT showing a person or character talking. In fiction films talking head shots are often considered static, a visually unimaginative way to show dialogue scenes, but in many DOCUMENTARIES they are often viewed as a direct and relatively unmanipulative way of allowing profilmic subjects to speak for themselves.

Tank Also known as 'studio tank': a large container of water housed either within a STUDIO or BACK LOT, used for photographing sea or other water SCENES, using model boats, typically with facilities for shooting scenes under water – hence 'tank shot'.

Tearjerker See WEEPIE.

Teaser See TRAILER.

Technicolor The US Technicolor Motion Pictures Corporation, founded in 1915 by Herbert T. Kalmus and Donald F. Comstock, pioneered the subtractive system of COLOUR FILM, first in a 2-colour system and later in a 3-colour system. Having developed a successful, though complicated and expensive, system using three colour separation NEGATIVES, Technicolor jealously protected its processes, insisting that productions shooting in Technicolour should use Technicolor's own CAMERA OPERATORS, colour consultants and equipment, until forced by ANTI-TRUST decree to release its patents. From the mid 1950s Eastman Kodak's simpler, single negative EASTMAN COLOR colour STOCK began to replace the Technicolor process. After 1955 'Technicolor' only referred to the laboratory process which produced three separately dyed negatives (and high quality colour PRINTS); since 1975 even Technicolor printing laboratories have converted to an Eastman system. Technicolor also developed a WIDESCREEN process, Technirama, producing high quality 35MM images for PROJECTION through a cinemaScope lens (ASPECT RATIO 2.35:1), and Super Technirama 70, using a 70MM film to project a widescreen image (2.2:1), which were in use during the 1950s and 1960s. Further reading: Cook & Bernink (1999), Neale (1985)

Teenpic Films featuring teenage protagonists in narratives focusing on the difficulties in, and responsibilities of, coming of age and specifically addressed to a young AUDIENCE. In western society, after the end of World War II, young people have had increasing leisure time and so have been targeted and developed as a specific demographic group by all aspects of the culture industry. Consequently, youth culture has become distinctly separate from the rest of POPULAR CULTURE. Since the 1950s the majority of movie patrons have been teenagers and young adults, so it was inevitable that films would be made with, and for, teens.

As Doherty (1988) notes, HOLLYWOOD began to concentrate on making films for teenagers just at the time when the industry was experiencing a serious decline in attendance due to the competition of TELEVISION. Many 1950s teenpics were EXPLOITATION FILMS – beach movies and MUSICALS exploiting the new MUSIC of rock n' roll, SCIENCE FICTION and HORROR (as in *I Was a Teenage Frankenstein*, dir. Herbert L. Strock, and *I Was a Teenage Werewolf*, dir. Gene Fowler, Jr., both 1957) and many were B MOVIES exhibited in DRIVE-INS, where the audience was almost entirely teenagers. PRODUCERS such as Samuel Arkoff and Albert Zugsmith and companies such as AMERICAN INTERNATIONAL PICTURES (AIP) became known for catering to the youth audience. The 1980s saw a CYCLE of fresh teenpics, many written and/or directed by John Hughes (*Sixteen Candles*, 1984; *The Breakfast Club*, 1985; *Pretty in Pink*, dir. Howard Deutch, 1986). Lewis (1992) sees the teen film as addressing major issues like alienation, delinquency, rebellion, sex and GENDER, consumption and nostalgia. Both Doherty and Staehling (in McCarthy & Flynn, 1975) trace the evolution of youth REPRESENTATION in teenpics in the early 1960s from, in Staehling's terms, 'wild to mild,' although some movies, such as *Easy Rider* (dir. Dennis Hopper, 1969), reverted to a more counter-cultural perspective later in the decade.

Telecine Derived from 'TELEVISION CINEMATOGRAPHY' – the process by which film is converted into a signal for conversion into television IMAGES via VIDEOtape. Telecine can also convert film images to video for EDITING purposes, since it is still common practice to shoot much material destined for television on film. Film normally gives a better quality image than video, even when converted to video, and editing is now normally done digitally on computers.

Telephoto See FOCAL LENGTH.

Television From its earliest days television was seen as a profound threat by film industries worldwide, and from the 1940s onwards it had an enormous negative impact on cinema attendance. In the US cinema audiences peaked at around 95 million per week in 1946 and fell to around 46.5 million in 1956 (Nelmes, 1999). This decline cannot be attributed solely to television, but should be seen as part of a growing tendency towards home-based leisure pursuits of which television was easily the most significant. Cinema AUDIENCES continued to decline in the US and UK until the early 1980s when there began a steady recovery (though to nothing like the levels of the 1940s). Ironically, this period has coincided not only with the growth of new television services such as CABLE and SATELLITE, but also the introduction of the domestic VIDEO recorder and its related services. The reasons for this are probably related to a transformation of the cinema-going experience to one more closely linked to other leisure activities. Some speculate that the growth of home video and films delivered via cable and satellite may even have increased the profile of FEATURE FILMS as a specific art form and contributed to increasing cinema attendances.

However, there is an alternative view of the relationship between the film and television industries. From quite early on television was seen as a potential market for films but initial rivalry and suspicion prevented commercial arrangements being agreed for some years. The film industry looked to WIDESCREEN and COLOUR to attract audiences. In some ways this was a phoney war, since a number of STUDIOS established television production arms very early in the life of the new medium. By the 1960s, large sums were being spent on the television transmission of FEATURE FILMS, forming an important part of their revenue potential. More recently there has been a growth of a more symbiotic relationship between television and feature films, with television and cable companies involved in film finance deals allowing them privileged access to films after their THEATRICAL RELEASE, and some films made for television gaining theatrical DISTRIBUTION. Major HOLLYWOOD studio CONGLOMERATES today are involved in television as much as in theatrical films.
Further reading: Balio (1990), Hill & McLoone (1996), Hilmes (1990)

Tent pole Industry term for a film which proves, or is hoped will prove, such a BOX-OFFICE success that it can sustain a STUDIO or company over box-office failures. Typical 'tent poles' are films with sure-fire ingredients for success, such as SEQUELS to successful films.

Text A term associated with SEMIOTICS, referring to a 'readable' structure of meanings that is reproducible. A text can therefore be a relatively simple single SIGNIFIER such as a road sign or a highly complex collection of signs and CODES such as a novel or film. Using 'text' to cover such a range of examples emphasizes the 'readability' of even the simplest texts and draws attention to the similarities between them as signifying structures.

Theatrical In the film industry sense of the word, relating to commercial DISTRIBUTION to, and EXHIBITION in, cinema theatres ('theatre' or 'theater' being preferred in the US, and 'cinema' in the UK). Non-theatrical venues (which, before the advent of VIDEO, would normally have shown films in 16MM prints) include schools, colleges, hospitals and other private groups. In an aesthetic sense, 'theatrical' can mean 'of, or in the style of, the (legitimate) theatre', implying that a performance or staging is 'theatrical' rather than filmic or CINEMATIC, and is generally used pejoratively. A linked usage, related to SILENT CINEMA, refers to 'theatrical space' as opposed to 'filmic space'.

Thematic montage A type of EDITING, pioneered by Soviet film-maker Sergei Eisenstein, in which separate SHOTS are linked together not by their literal or narrative CONTINUITY but by symbolic association. Eisenstein and other 1920s

Soviet film-makers were heavily influenced by the KULESHOV EXPERIMENT, demonstrating the fundamental influence of editing on the spectator's interpretation of IMAGES.

Theme music A musical passage or melody played periodically throughout a film, or associated with a particular CHARACTER, place, TIME or event. Bernard Herrmann, for example, provided individual themes for each of the main characters in *Citizen Kane* (dir. Orson Welles, 1941). Based on the Wagnerian leitmotif, theme MUSIC is a major technique for scoring narrative films. A theme song, similarly, is heard more than once in a film and may have the same associations.
Further reading: Gorbman (1987)

Theory Konigsberg (1997) cites Hugo Münsterberg's *The Photoplay: A Psychological Study* (1916) as the first major work of film theory. Like much other early work, one of its major concerns was to establish film's unique nature as an art form, as was also true of two important theorists who were also practitioners, Vsevolod Pudovkin and Sergei Eisenstein, both of whom worked in the Soviet Union during the 1920s and whose major work was around developing a theory of MONTAGE. This in turn established one of the central planks of all theoretical work about the aesthetic properties of film – its relationship to external reality and how far it should aspire to simply 'record' rather than 'construct'.

The explosion in theoretical writing about film from 1950 onwards begins to intersect with theoretical writing from other disciplines. Many earlier debates were generated in France by André Bazin and later the group of young CAHIERS DU CINÉMA critics. Bazin's twin emphases were on the objective recording of reality and the individual DIRECTOR as the principal source of creativity. The latter was taken up by the *Cahiers* group including François Truffaut, Jean-Luc Godard, Claude Chabrol and Eric Rohmer, instigating debate on the status of the AUTEUR in cinema. In the 1960s and early 1970s the main challenges to auteur theory came from STRUCTURALISM and SEMIOTICS, drawing heavily on theoretical work from other disciplines, which sought to explain not only the various means of human communication, but also to extend such ideas to explanations of all features of human society and culture – the so-called total theory, or grand theory. The emphasis here was on the cinematic TEXT's fundamental structures and the relationship of cinematic narratives to other ways that human beings have sought to make sense of the world. Most rigorously, Christian Metz (1974) attempted what amounted to a complete grammar of film. A linked development through the influence of PSYCHOANALYTIC theory, particularly the work of Jacques Lacan, began to bring questions about the cinematic spectator and AUDIENCE into the theoretical equation.

By the late 1970s it was apparent that attempts at total theory were no longer tenable and theory entered the more fragmented phase of POST-STRUCTURALISM, and the notion of DECONSTRUCTION, most closely associated with Jacques Derrida, which was influential in its denial of a single correct reading of a text. This is also the phase that most emphatically rejected the idea of the auteur, which had already been called into question by semiotics and structuralism, and established the notion of the spectator as author of his or her own text. The birth of a significant body of FEMINIST FILM THEORY paralleled the beginnings of post-structuralism, taking inspiration from psychoanalytic work on the way that cinema constructs the spectator and inserting the extra dimension of GENDER difference: if the cinematic experience reproduces phases of child development, including the realization of sexual difference, how can we understand the ways it is experienced differently by men and women? This was among the fundamental questions originally asked by Laura Mulvey (1989) and others. This kind of investigation is also at the root of theoretical work on RACE, on the POST-COLONIAL experience and on SEXUALITY, leading to new perspectives such as QUEER THEORY.

The current state of film theory is defined by pluralism. Not only are there different branches of film theory, but film is also seen as a useful site of study by other disciplines, and there is a sense of fluid exchange between them. Just as POSTMODERNISM has tended to dissolve boundaries between high and low art and to reduce the importance of questions of ultimate meaning outside the interplay of textual SIGNIFIERS, so contemporary film theory has dissolved barriers between approaches and between itself and other disciplines. See also POST THEORY.

Further reading: Andrew (1984), Branston and Nichols in Gledhill & Williams (2000), Hill & Church Gibson (1998), Hollows *et al.* (2000), Lapsley & Westlake (1988), Miller & Stam (1999), Stam (2000)

Third cinema A term associated with cinema of the third world (or developing world), and linked to the idea of a third way – between the capitalist West and the socialist Eastern bloc – as developed by non-aligned nations from the 1950s. The phrase third cinema was coined by Argentine film-makers Fernando Solanas and Octavio Getino in their essay *Towards a Third Cinema* (reprinted in Chanan, 1983; Fusco, 1987; Nichols, 1976; and Stam & Miller, 2000), as an accompaniment to their agit-DOCUMENTARY *La Hora de los hornos* (*The Hour of the Furnaces*, 1966–68). They argue for a 'third cinema' distinct from both the 'first cinema' – HOLLYWOOD and its imitators – and 'second cinema' – like the European ART FILM. Third cinema was to be socially critical and politically active – effectively a guerrilla cinema, deriving inspiration from the writings of Frantz Fanon, and strongly linked with the anti-imperialist struggles which marked the 1960s and 1970s. It would search for appropriately radical aesthetics, from CINÉMA VÉRITÉ to MONTAGE, with DOCUMENTARY in many ways a privileged form, though 'any militant form of expression is valid'. Solanas and Getino declared that 'our time is one of hypothesis rather than of thesis, a time of works in progress – unfinished, unordered, violent works made with the CAMERA in one hand and a rock in the other' (Chanan, p. 24). Such ideas owed a debt to the earlier writings of Fernando Birri and Glauber Rocha (see Chanan, 1983) and films such as those of the Brazilian CINEMA NÔVO movement. Solanas and Getino argued that 'the model of the perfect work of art . . . has served to inhibit the film-maker in dependent countries' (cf. Julio Garcia Espinosa's IMPERFECT CINEMA).

Ideas about third cinema were developed by Teshome Gabriel and applied to the work of Ousmane Sembene and other African film-makers and to Cuban and other cinema. The concept of third cinema was in many ways a product of 1960s anti-colonial struggles and its politicized aesthetics and aesthetic renewal. The very notion of 'third world' is problematic. India's highly developed popular commercial cinema, for example, poses problems for the concept, and third cinema cannot simply be equated with film production in the third world. Although the concept of third cinema is now seen to beg as many questions as it answers, it has provided a useful framework for the discussion of African, Latin American and other cinemas of the developing world, and for 'diasporic cinema' – for example, cinema made by black film-makers of Afro-Caribbean descent in North America and Europe. See also POST-COLONIAL THEORY.

Further reading: Cook & Bernink (1999), Gabriel (1982), Gabriel in Stam & Miller (1999), Pines & Willemen (1989), Shohat & Stam (1994), Stam (2000)

Thriller Loose GENRE term referring to any film that generates suspense and excitement as a major aspect of its narrative. The thriller is really too diverse to be a genre, as suspense also is an important part of such other genres as the HORROR FILM, SLASHER FILM, MYSTERY FILM, SPY FILM, ACTION and ADVENTURE FILMS. As Rubin (1999, p. 4) concludes, the term is more accurately an adjectival description attached to other genres: 'There is possibly no such thing as a pure, freestanding "thriller thriller".' Most stories employ suspense – an anxiety in the spectator or reader about what is to happen next, what will be the fate of a CHARACTER – in order to maintain interest, but thrillers exploit that particular narrative quality. For Rubin (1994, p. 36), it does not matter whether a thriller is a DETECTIVE FILM, spy film, horror film or CRIME FILM; the creation of a successfully thrilling atmosphere depends upon lifting us out of the quotidian world and transporting us 'to a heightened state of suspension – between the mundane and the marvellous.' In this sense they invoke a kind of sadomasochistic pleasure in the way that we identify with the heroes, who invariably experience suffering and undergo various difficulties before triumphing, usually with narrative CLOSURE.

Further reading: Davis (1973), McCarty (1992), Palmer (1978)

Tie-in Any form of cross-promotion in which the publication (or re-publication) of a book, the issue (or re-issue) of a MUSIC CD, the offering of promotional toys with fast food, the sale of toys or clothing, etc. is tied in with the RELEASE of a film, normally with financial remuneration accruing to the film's distributor, although the benefit is usually mutual. See MERCHANDISING.

Tilt shot A tilt shot involves the CAMERA moving up or down along a vertical axis from a fixed camera position (also known as a vertical PAN, as opposed to the normal pan, which moves left or right horizontally from a fixed camera position). A tilt shot may convey a subjective sense of a CHARACTER looking up or down at something or someone or it may follow action. It may also reveal previously unseen information to the spectator, or comment on the ACTION, as when the camera tilts up to a cloud following a character's dive to his death in *Summer Interlude* (dir. Ingmar Bergman, 1950).

Time The control and manipulation of time is one of the fundamental ways in which films are able to tell STORIES that span vastly different periods. Bordwell and Thompson (1997) identify three kinds of time present in feature films: PLOT time – the duration of the events explicitly presented on the screen, STORY time – which also takes in the duration of implied events, and SCREEN time – the running time of the film. Narrative technique balances each of these in order to tell the story in the way that the film requires. Most films have both a plot and story that last much longer than the film's running time. Oft-quoted exceptions are *High Noon* (dir. Fred Zinnemann, 1952), whose plot time almost matches its screen time (though the story can be said to last much longer), and the French film *Cleo from 5 to 7* (dir. Agnès Varda, 1961). A film usually consists of a plot made up of carefully selected segments of story which may simply be presented chronologically, with the gaps covered by some form of temporal ELLIPSIS such as a SHOT suggesting the passing of time, or a CAPTION. Often, though, time is manipulated in more interesting ways, with devices like FLASHBACKS and FLASHFORWARDS or PARALLEL ACTION. Film is generally seen as compressing time because it tells stories that last much longer than screen time, but almost as important is film's ability to expand story time and present events in the plot that last longer than they would in reality – generally used to emphasise an important event, most simply through SLOW MOTION.

Film has the power to rearrange time so that we see events in different perspectives. It is relatively common to begin a film with a glimpse of its ending so that we see events that lead up to the conclusion in a particular light. Bordwell and Thompson discusses such a structure in their analysis of *Citizen Kane* (dir. Orson Welles, 1941), while the radical re-ordering of time over the first two parts of *The Godfather* (dir. Francis Ford Coppola, 1972, 1974) gives us insights and juxtapositions that a simple chronological account could not achieve.

Further reading: Aumont *et al.* (1992)

Time Warner See WARNER BROS.

Time-lapse Time-lapse CINEMATOGRAPHY records some ACTION or process by exposing one FRAME at a time at predetermined intervals (such as once an hour or once a day); when played back at the normal speed of (usually) 24 frames a second, the recorded action appears speeded up. Like some other effects – REVERSE MOTION, SLOW MOTION, etc. – time-lapse cinematography exploits the mechanics of the photographic process to enable us to see things that the human eye cannot, such as lengthy natural processes like flowers opening and closing, eggs hatching and weather changing. Though rarely used in MAINSTREAM FILMS – but see, for example, *Rumble Fish* (dir. Francis Ford Coppola, 1983) – the technique has often been used for scientific and EXPERIMENTAL purposes.

Tinting A process used to create a COLOUR IMAGE on BLACK-AND-WHITE FILM, extensively used during the era of SILENT CINEMA, either by dyeing the base of the print – printing on to an already dyed base – or by hand-tinting. In early cinema, tinting could be used for SPECIAL EFFECTS, such as the explosion in the mail wagon in *The Great Train Robbery* (dir. Edwin S. Porter, 1903). Though tinting stopped being used in commercial film-making after the introduction of COLOUR FILM, AVANT-GARDE film-makers have sometimes returned to tinting and dyeing processes: Malcolm LeGrice's *Berlin Horse* (1970) experiments with different coloured dyes on both POSITIVE and NEGATIVE black and white images and with SUPERIMPOSITION.

Titles Non-DIEGETIC words appearing on the screen during a film. The most obvious function of titles is to carry the CREDITS at the opening and closing of the film. The design of the opening titles – setting the tone of the film – can be particularly elaborate. SUBTITLES translate dialogue into another language; INTERTITLES were used mainly in SILENT CINEMA to provide dialogue and narrative information. Titles are still used in SOUND film to provide information, usually on times and places, and often at the film's start.

Todd-AO A WIDESCREEN process developed for producer Michael Todd by the American Optical (hence 'AO') Company, the first successful 70MM widescreen process. Reacting to the three-CAMERA, three-projector CINERAMA process, Todd reportedly wanted a widescreen process in which 'everything comes out of one hole'. Todd-AO used 65MM film (ASPECT RATIO 2.2:1), with no ANAMORPHIC process, and 70mm prints with six stereophonic SOUNDTRACKS. Cameras ran at 30 FRAMES per second (not the usual 24), necessitating special projectors and posing problems for wide distribution. To cope with this problem, both *Oklahoma!* (dir. Fred Zinnemann, 1955) and *Around the World in Eighty Days* (dir. Michael Anderson, 1956), two very successful films shot in Todd-AO, were also shot in normal 35MM CinemaScope and in 65MM for reduction to 35mm prints. Presentations of films in Todd-AO's original 70mm format tended to be special ROADSHOW presentations. Todd-AO was bought by TWENTIETH CENTURY-FOX and used in 1960s spectaculars like *Doctor Dolittle* (dir. Richard Fleischer, 1967) and *Star!* (dir. Robert Wise, 1968), commercial flops which did little for Todd-AO's reputation.
Further reading: Belton (1992)

Toga film Slang term for historical EPICS set in ancient Greek, Roman and Biblical times. As with PEPLUM FILM, the term highlights the skimpy COSTUMES worn by the ACTORS and the soft-core PLEASURE that these movies provide.

Total cinema According to film theorist André Bazin, total cinema is the Platonic ideal which cinema has sought from the beginning but the realization of which has been unattainable only because of the limitations of technology. In *The Myth of Total Cinema* Bazin argued that from before the days of early SILENT CINEMA, the goal was to achieve 'an integral REALISM, a recreation of the world in its own IMAGE' (Bazin, 1967, p. 21). For Bazin, film history was comprised of a series of technical innovations – SOUND, COLOUR, WIDESCREEN – that brought us closer to that ideal: 'Every new development added to the cinema must, paradoxically, take it nearer and nearer to its origins' (Bazin 1967, p. 21).

Tracking shot Properly speaking, a 'tracking SHOT' describes a form of CAMERA MOVEMENT in which a shot is taken from a camera mounted on a DOLLY running on specially laid tracks. In practice, the term is used to describe any shot in which the camera moves on wheels, whether on tracks or not. Thus a dolly, or dollying, shot may describe exactly the same kind of shot as 'tracking shot', although 'tracking shot' is generally preferred for shots in which the camera follows the movement of a CHARACTER or other subject. A 'forward tracking shot' moves in the same direction as the subject is moving though it may be behind a character or take the character's POINT OF VIEW – while a 'reverse tracking shot' travels backwards looking back at the subject. Tracking shots can also be 'lateral' or 'horizontal', as they move alongside a subject, looking side on, and the camera can 'track in' and 'track out' to emphasize or point out something. 'Tracking shot' is also sometimes interchangeable with 'trucking shot' – which may be reserved for shots from a moving vehicle – and 'travelling shot'.

Trades, trade papers Most countries with film industries have trade papers covering film and entertainment news. This is very highly developed in the US, where the best known trade paper is VARIETY. Other major US trades are the daily *Hollywood Reporter* and the monthly *Box Office*, aimed primarily at exhibitors. In the UK the main trade paper is the weekly *Screen International*, though *Variety* also publishes a European edition. This use of 'trade' is also used in 'trade show', a film screening organized for the trade press and for exhibitors.

Trailer A short film ADVERTISING a forthcoming attraction at a cinema, normally (though not necessarily) a compilation of CLIPS from that film, and normally prepared by the film's distributor. A trailer can also be known as a PREVIEW (the term preferred in the US, while trailer is preferred in the UK), and a shorter trailer advertising a film still some way from RELEASE is known as a teaser. Trailers may also be shown in other cinemas, especially when parts of theatre chains, in which case they may be called crossplugs.

Training film A form of DOCUMENTARY for teaching a particular skill or task.

Trance film Term used by P. Adams Sitney (1979) to characterize the work of EXPERIMENTAL film-makers like Maya Deren, Kenneth Anger and Stan Brakhage, to distinguish it from 1920s SURREALIST work such as *Un Chien Andalou* (dir. Luis Bunuel & Salvador Dali, 1929). For Sitney, trance films involve (usually) a single protagonist (normally the film-maker) involved in a (usually sexual) quest for identity, and evoke a DREAM state. *Meshes of the Afternoon* (dir. Deren & Alexander Hammid, 1943), *At Land* (dir. Deren, 1944) and *Fireworks* (dir. Anger, 1947) exemplify the form.

Transition, transitional device (1) Any technique used to provide a BRIDGE from one SCENE to another, including the WHIP PAN, FADE, DISSOLVE, SUPERIMPOSITION and WIPE. In SILENT FILM, the IRIS in and out was also a common transitional technique. (2) The straight CUT also provides a transition between SHOTS, but normally some additional cue, whether in the IMAGE or on the SOUNDTRACK, is necessary for the viewer to understand the change in TIME and/or SPACE. (3) The use of a CUTAWAY, particularly in DOCUMENTARY film, to avoid a JUMP CUT when material has been edited out of a shot.

Transparency Transparency has come to define a mode of film practice in which the spectator is relatively unaware of the processes and CONVENTIONS at work in a film. The CLASSICAL HOLLYWOOD style, with a coherent DIEGESIS, INVISIBLE EDITING and logical PLOT development, does not invite awareness of its operations, which appear to take place naturally. The viewer of a REFLEXIVE film, by contrast, may be constantly invited to be aware of the conventions and processes at work. Direct address to the audience by a CHARACTER or ACTOR in an otherwise illusionist film would break through the transparency.

Travelling shot See TRACKING SHOT.

Travelogue A form of DOCUMENTARY, usually a SHORT FILM, showing SCENES from unfamiliar, distant or exotic places. Travelogues, usually produced by tourist boards or GOVERNMENTS to promote tourism, often show bland, predictably upbeat views of places. An early form of travelogue were attractions such as *Hale's Tours* in which, starting in 1904, customers entered an auditorium simulating a moving railroad car with projected scenes of far-off places. Peter Jackson uses a travelogue ironically at the beginning of *Heavenly Creatures* (1994) to depict the official, wholesome REPRESENTATION of Christchurch, New Zealand, before delving into the repressed desire and anxieties of its main CHARACTERS. During the STUDIO ERA travelogues were sometimes shown along with CARTOONS and NEWSREELS before the featured DOUBLE BILL.

Treatment   A full account of a film's narrative written in continuous prose, which also gives a strong sense of how the film might look. Treatments are often used to sell an idea to production executives so they need to convey vivid ideas on CHARACTER, ACTION and settings, generally using only small samples of dialogue to give a flavour of the tone of the projected SCREENPLAY. Treatments are sometimes commissioned from writers, but can also be written speculatively to interest a company in an idea.

Trick Film   A film in which the main interest is SPECIAL EFFECTS or other OPTICAL tricks in the IMAGES that violate the physical laws of the real world. The pioneer of the trick film was Georges Méliès, a French film-maker who was a magician before turning to the cinema. His many ONE-REELERS, of which *Le Voyage dans la lune* (*A Trip to the Moon*, 1902) is the best known, feature CHARACTERS who seem to appear and disappear in puffs of smoke, an effect achieved through a combination of STOP-MOTION PHOTOGRAPHY and the use of trap doors on the SET. In Great Britain numerous trick films were made by film pioneer George Albert Smith of the BRIGHTON SCHOOL.

Tripod   A three-legged supporting stand for a CAMERA, with adjustable legs to allow for a change of height or to balance the camera, and a mounting plate permitting the camera to PAN or TILT. The very first films used the tripod for the basic purpose of keeping the camera steady, enabling it to dwell on whatever was before it with a fixed, penetrating GAZE. The stabilized, rather than the shaky SHOT, has defined almost every MAINSTREAM FILM since. The tripod brings with it the limitation of making the camera immobile. The camera can pivot on its axes, but remains in a fixed position and the ACTION must come to the camera. In one of the LUMIÈRE PROGRAMME films, *L'Arroseur arrosé* (*Watering the Gardener*, 1895), a boy steps on the gardener's hose so that the water stops flowing, the gardener looks at the nozzle, the boy lifts his foot and the gardener gets sprayed in his face. This SIGHT GAG concludes with the gardener catching the boy, dragging him into the camera's line of vision, and turning him around so that we can see him being spanked.

By 1960 new lightweight 16MM cameras had been developed that could be used with portable tape recorders, technology which allowed film-makers to follow PROFILMIC events as they occurred. Many DOCUMENTARY film-makers, following the lead of French anthropologist/film-maker Jean Rouch, abandoned the tripod in favour of the HAND-HELD camera, as did American EXPERIMENTAL film-makers like Stan Brakhage. The 1960 DREW ASSOCIATES' documentary *Primary*, about the Wisconsin John Kennedy-Hubert Humphrey democratic primary election, for example, features a famous shot in which the camera follows Kennedy as he gets out of a limousine, moves through the crowd, enters and traverses a large hall filled with people, mounts the stage and approaches the MICROPHONE. See DIRECT CINEMA, CINÉMA VÉRITÉ, OBSERVATIONAL CINEMA.

Trucking shot   See TRACKING SHOT.

Twentieth Century-Fox One of the major STUDIOS in HOLLYWOOD, created in 1935 by the merger of the FOX FILM CORPORATION and Twentieth Century Pictures, founded two years earlier by Joseph M. Schenck and Darryl F. Zanuck. Early on the STUDIO was known for its MUSICALS, but by the late 1940s it was producing a number of PRESTIGE PICTURES by some important American DIRECTORS, including *The Grapes of Wrath* (dir. John Ford, 1941), about the Oklahoma dust bowl migrations of the 1930s, and *Gentleman's Agreement* (dir. Elia Kazan, 1947), about racial prejudice. Despite the fiasco of the $40 million *Cleopatra* (dir. Joseph L. Mankiewicz) in 1962, Twentieth Century-Fox has continued to produce important and popular films over the decades, including *The Sound of Music* (dir. Robert Wise, 1965), *M*A*S*H* (dir. Robert Altman, 1970), and *Home Alone* (dir. Chris Columbus, 1990). In 1985 the company was purchased by Australian media baron Rupert Murdoch and became Fox Corporation, which also owned Fox TELEVISION and Fox Broadcasting, part of media CONGLOMERATE News Corporation. See also BIG 5, SYNERGY.
Further reading: Finler (1988), Gomery (1986), Mordden (1988)

Two shot Literally, a SHOT with two people dominating the FRAME, usually a CLOSE-UP or MEDIUM SHOT – the standard way of showing two people in conversation. In Europe this has often been referred to as the *PLAN AMÉRICAIN*, or American shot, because it was thought to characterize CLASSICAL HOLLYWOOD CINEMA.

Two-reeler See ONE-REELER.

Typage Term used by Soviet film-maker Sergei Eisenstein in his essay *Through Theatre to Cinema* (1949) to describe his approach to CASTING in which, following from the theatrical tradition of *commedia dell'arte* in which ACTORS performed types rather than acted as individual CHARACTERS, roles were filled according to physical qualities that provided the AUDIENCE with ready visual cues about them – in other words, TYPECASTING deliberately employed as an EXPRESSIONIST device.

Typecasting The selection of ACTORS to play a particular role or CHARACTER because of their physical qualities or mannerisms, relying on these visual qualities to fit STEREOTYPES. The term can also refer to the casting of actors or STARS because of the associations AUDIENCES have of them as a result of previous roles and their resulting ICONOGRAPHIC meaning. CHARACTER ACTORS are often typecast for either or both of these reasons. John Wayne's IMAGE as the rugged American individual was created through a series of roles in WESTERNS and WAR FILMS, an image he could also exploit in later movies such as *True Grit* (dir. Henry Hathaway, 1969) and *The Shootist* (dir. Don Siegel, 1976). See also CENTRAL CASTING.

U

U Certificate The British CERTIFICATE awarded by the BRITISH BOARD OF FILM CLASSIFICATION (BBFC) to a film that is seen as suitable for all AUDIENCES including children. It is an abbreviation of 'Universal' and is the equivalent of the American 'G' (General audience) rating. One of the BBFC's principal functions is the protection of children and the awarding of a U-certificate implies a film entirely devoid of controversy as regards explicit VIOLENCE, sexual content or language. See also CERTI-FICATION, RATINGS, X-RATING.

UFA Abbreviation for internationally important German film company Universum Film Aktiengesellschaft. The company was founded in 1917 when several smaller companies merged and the German GOVERNMENT supplied a third of its financial support. With modern STUDIO facilities in Neubabelsberg, near Berlin, UFA assembled a talented group of DIRECTORS (Fritz Lang, Ernst Lubitsch, F.W. Murnau, G.W. Pabst), STARS (Conrad Veidt, Emil Jannings, Werner Krauss, Brigitte Helm) and CINEMATOGRAPHERS (Karl Freund, Fritz Arno Wagner), and was second only to HOLLYWOOD in scope and resources. In 1918, as a result of Germany's defeat in World War I, the company was privatized. In 1919 UFA released *The Cabinet of Dr. Caligari* (dir. Robert Wiene) to international success and launched the Golden Age of GERMAN EXPRESSIONIST cinema, a movement to which it would contribute many significant films, including *Nosferatu* (dir. Murnau, 1922), the first adaptation of Bram Stoker's *Dracula*, and *Der Letzte Mann* (*The Last Laugh*, dir. Murnau, 1924), featuring a remarkably fluid CAMERA by Freund that would obviate the need for INTERTITLES. Erich Pommer ably served as chief of production beginning in 1923, but the company's financial position faltered because of some extremely expensive productions (most notably, Lang's *Metropolis* in 1926) and competition from HOLLYWOOD, which eventually lured away much of its talent. In 1927 Dr. Alfred Hugenberg, a National Socialist, bought a controlling interest in the company and began using its films for PROPAGANDA purposes. UFA was taken over directly by the government in 1937 and ceased production at the end of World War II in 1945.
Further reading: Elsaesser (2000), Kreimeier (1999)

Ultradirectional mic See MICROPHONE.

Underground film An EXPERIMENTAL or AVANT-GARDE FILM that openly rejects the conventions of MAINSTREAM FILM and explores the possibilities of the medium itself. Can also refer to a film that focuses on taboo, shocking or non-commercial subject matter, such as *Flaming Creatures* (dir. Jack Smith, 1962) and *Scorpio Rising* (dir. Kenneth Anger, 1963), both of which are about alternatives to normative hetero-sexuality. The term tends to be associated with American INDEPENDENT and experi-mental film-making in the 1950s and 1960s, for many of these film-makers (e.g., Stan Brakhage, Jordan Belson) had counter-cultural associations with the Beat and hippie subcultures, and to PORNOGRAPHY. See aslo NEW AMERICAN CINEMA.
Further reading: Battcock (1967), Peterson (1994), Rees (1999), Renan (1967), Sitney (1979), Tyler (1970)

Unidirectional mic See MICROPHONE.

Unions While the GUILDS represent the interests of US professional groups such as DIRECTORS, ACTORS and SCREENWRITERS, many craft workers in the movie (and legit-imate theatre) industry – electricians, COSTUME and make-up artists, GRIPS, painters, SCRIPT supervisors, laboratory technicians and projectionists – are represented by the International Alliance of Theatrical Stage Employees (IATSE), which has more than 850 local union branches – 'locals' – in North America (and 20 in HOLLYWOOD). IATSE is affiliated with the AFL-CIO (American Federation of Labor–Congress of Industrial

Organisations, the equivalent of the UK Trades Union Congress, or TUC) and negotiates standard agreements on pay and conditions on behalf of the locals. A 'union film' – almost all films made by major companies – is one on which union (and guild) members are employed and paid agreed rates; a non-union film – including many LOW-BUDGET INDEPENDENT films – may employ non-union workers or pay below union-agreed rates (sometimes with union agreement). For the UK, see ACTT.

Unit General term for the CREW, or team, on a particular film (hence, 'unit manager', etc), but can be used in other ways: a film being mainly SHOT in a STUDIO may have a 'second unit' (sometimes 'LOCATION unit') responsible for shooting SCENES on LOCATION or for ACTION or stunt SEQUENCES. A film may also have specialized groups working on it such as a 'SPECIAL EFFECTS unit'. In the early 1930s STUDIO SYSTEM, the 'unit production' system, in which individual executive PRODUCERS wielded significant power – a system favoured by David O. Selznick and others – was contrasted with the then dominant 'central producer' system epitomized by Irving Thalberg at MGM and Darryl Zanuck at WARNER BROS. (and later FOX), in which the studio's production boss personally supervised all production. Units often built up a group of personnel who worked together from project to project. Well known examples were producer Arthur Freed's FREED UNIT at MGM, specializing in MUSICALS, including those directed by Vincente Minnelli and by Gene Kelly and Stanley Donen in the 1940s and 1950s, and Val Lewton's B MOVIE HORROR unit at RKO, which produced films like Jacques Tourneur's *Cat People* (1942) and *I Walked With a Zombie* (1943).

United Artists (UA) American film company organized in 1919 by Charles Chaplin, Mary Pickford, Douglas Fairbanks and DIRECTOR D.W. Griffith for the purpose of distributing their own films in order to gain artistic control over their works without interference from the STUDIOS, as well as to receive a greater share of BOX-OFFICE profits. Each of the four founding figures produced important work for the company: Fairbanks starred in *The Mark of Zorro* (dir. Fred Niblo, 1920), Pickford in *Pollyanna* (dir. Paul Powell, 1920), Griffith directed *Broken Blossoms* (1919) and *Way Down East* (1920) and Chaplin made *A Woman of Paris* (1923) and *The Gold Rush* (1925), in which he also starred. Under the leadership of Joseph Schenck, United Artists attracted many STARS and directors, including William Wyler, John Ford, King Vidor, and Gloria Swanson. The company released Chaplin's *City Lights* in 1931, *Modern Times* in 1936 and Alexander Korda's *The Private Life of Henry VIII* in 1933, and arranged to distribute Korda's British films in the US, but languished somewhat because it had insufficient films to distribute and owned no EXHIBITION chain in which to show them.

In the 1940s, despite some excellent films including *Stagecoach* (dir. John Ford, 1939), *Rebecca* (dir. Alfred Hitchcock, 1940) – which gave UA its first OSCAR for Best Picture – and *Spellbound* (dir. Hitchcock, 1946), the company suffered from the departure of important producers such as David O. Selznick, Walt Disney, Sam Goldwyn and Walter Wanger. However, the company benefited from the PARAMOUNT DECISION in 1948, filling in the gap created by the decline in production of the MAJOR STUDIOS, distributing some excellent INDEPENDENT productions including *Gun Crazy* (*Deadly is the Female*, dir. Joseph H. Lewis, 1950), *High Noon* (dir. Fred Zinnemann, 1952), *Night of the Hunter* (dir. Charles Laughton, 1955), *Some Like it Hot* (dir. Billy Wilder, 1959) and *West Side Story* (dir. Robert Wise, 1961).

In 1967 United Artists was absorbed by the CONGLOMERATE Transamerica, releasing several successful movies in the following decade, among them *One Flew Over the Cuckoo's Nest* (dir. Milos Forman, 1975), *Rocky* (dir. John G. Avildsen, 1976) and *Annie Hall* (dir. Woody Allen, 1977). However, the company experienced serious financial difficulty with the $40 million flop *Heaven's Gate* (dir. Michael Cimino, 1980). United Artists became part of MGM in 1981, after which it went through a series of mergers and buyouts, although it has continued to RELEASE films, including those in the James Bond SERIES.

Further reading: Balio (1976a), Balio (1976b), Bergan (1986), Finler (1988), Gomery (1986)

Universal American film production company established in 1921 by Carl Laemmle, combining his own Independent Motion Picture Company (IMP) with several other companies. Universal grew from an INDEPENDENT company to become one of the MAJOR STUDIOS in HOLLYWOOD. With its impressive Universal City facility, Universal produced many films through the 1920s featuring such STARS as Rudolph Valentino and Lon Chaney. In the next decade Universal released one of the era's great PRESTIGE PICTURES, *All Quiet on the Western Front* (dir. Lewis Milestone, 1930), but became known for its CYCLE of HORROR FILMS, with their distinctive EXPRESSIONIST style, beginning in 1931 with *Dracula* (dir. Tod Browning) and *Frankenstein* (dir. James Whale). Financial difficulties forced Laemmle out of the company in 1936, but Universal continued producing dependable product featuring such stars as W.C. Fields, Lon Chaney, Jr., Bela Lugosi, Abbott and Costello, Deanna Durbin and, later, Rock Hudson.

In 1946 the company merged with International Pictures to become Universal-International, but reverted to its original name prior to being purchased by Decca Records. During the 1950s Universal released a SERIES of popular MELODRAMAS produced by Ross Hunter and directed by Douglas Sirk, including *Magnificent Obsession* (1954), *All that Heaven Allows* (1955) and the remake of *Imitation of Life* (1959). In 1962 both Universal and Decca became part of MCA (Music Corporation of America) and diversified more heavily into TELEVISION production. Since the 1970s Universal has had a number of BLOCKBUSTER hits, including *Airport* (dir. George Seaton, 1970), *The Sting* (dir. George Roy Hill, 1973), *Jaws* (dir. Steven Spielberg, 1975), *The Deer Hunter* (dir. Michael Cimino, 1978), *E.T.: The Extra-terrestrial* (dir. Spielberg, 1982), *Back to the Future* (dir. Robert Zemeckis, 1985), *Jurassic Park* (dir. Spielberg, 1993) and *Gladiator* (dir. Ridley Scott, 2000). In 1990 MCA/Universal was purchased by the Japanese electronics corporation Matsushita, which sold control to the Canadian Seagram liquor company in 1995. In June 2000 French-based transnational CONGLOMERATE Vivendi – originally based on the privatized French national water company – bid for Seagram, though with the intention to sell off Seagram's liquor interests and create the world's second largest media CONGLOMERATE, Vivendi Universal. Like AOL TIME WARNER, Vivendi Universal aims for SYNERGY by combining old and new media – Universal's films, MUSIC and TELEVISION programming (as well as successful theme parks in Hollywood, Florida and Spain), the European CABLE TELEVISION and film production interests of the French Canal+, interests in SATELLITE broadcasting (via BSkyB) and internet and telephone services.

Further reading: Dick (1999), Finler (1988), Gomery (1986), Mordden (1988), Schatz (1988)

V

Vamp See *FEMME FATALE*.

Variable focus See FOCAL LENGTH.

Variety The best known of the TRADES or trade papers for the US film industry, founded in 1905 and originally mainly concerned with VAUDEVILLE and other kinds of live entertainment. Thus, it was more or less natural that *Variety* should extend its interest to the fast developing film industry, which was at first part of vaudeville and then supplanted it. *Variety* (which also covers TELEVISION and legitimate theatre) includes news of production activities and reports on BOX-OFFICE results, and has developed an often idiosyncratic and colourful language for dealing with films (hence, *Stix Nix Hix Pix*, for a report about rural audiences not taking to films with rural subjects) and an approach to international politics which sees things in industry terms (the fall of communism in Eastern Europe, for example, being discussed in terms of opportunities for Hollywood films). *Variety* is published weekly in New York and daily on weekdays (*Daily Variety*) in Los Angeles (as well as a European edition).

Varifocal lens See ZOOM LENS.

Vaudeville Vaudeville, in the US and MUSIC HALL, in the UK have a significant place in the history of early SILENT CINEMA. Vaudeville acts were used by Thomas Edison for some of the first films and vaudeville and music hall venues, along with travelling funfairs, were the first to offer public film shows. Recording vaudeville and music hall acts on film was an important element in early cinema, with vaudeville and music hall, along with other popular theatre, providing the bulk of performers. Major STARS of US SLAPSTICK silent COMEDY in the 1910s and 1920s, including Charlie Chaplin, Buster Keaton and Laurel and Hardy, joined the film industry after working in vaudeville and music hall, and continued the vaudeville tradition into the SOUND era. Ultimately, of course, the cinema was a major factor in the eventual decline and death of the form.
Further reading: Jenkins (1993), Musser (1990), Musser (1991), Robinson (1996)

Velvet Light Trap, The Scholarly film journal that began as an initiative by graduate students at the University of Wisconsin-Madison in 1971. At first published irregularly, since 1988 the *Velvet Light Trap* has been published by the University of Texas Press twice yearly, editorial duties alternating between students at both academic institutions. The journal's emphasis is on American film and American film history.

Vertical integration Term used to describe the way in which the US movie industry was organized during the STUDIO SYSTEM era (approximately from the late 1920s to the 1950s). The industry divided into three different activities – production, DISTRIBUTION and EXHIBITION – and the MAJOR STUDIOS exerted significant control over each activity. The oligopolistic effects of vertical integration were the target for ANTI-TRUST suits brought by the US GOVERNMENT from the mid

1930s, culminating in the 1948 PARAMOUNT DECISION, which forced the major STUDIOS to sell off their exhibition outlets, or cinema theatres, and to refrain from unfair distribution and exhibition practices, to encourage INDEPENDENT film production. By the late 1950s, the BIG 5 major studios had divested themselves of their exhibition arms, a major factor, though by no means the only one, in the demise of the old style studio system. Some of the majors re-acquired theatres in the more *laissez-faire* 1980s and 1990s and the increasing importance of HOME VIDEO, CABLE and other developments in the ownership of TELEVISION networks has re-asserted vertical integration in a different but equally powerful form. See also CONGLOMERATES.

Further reading: Balio (1976a), Gomery (1986), Izod (1988), Maltby (1995), Thompson & Bordwell (1994)

VHS Video Home System – the HOME VIDEO tape system designed by the Japanese corporation Matsushita, which competed with and defeated Sony's home VIDEO format, Betamax, during the 1980s. See also SYNERGY.

Further reading: Wasko (1994)

Viacom The parent company of PARAMOUNT Communications, whose other interests include Blockbuster Video, MTV and Nickelodeon CABLE channels, the publisher Simon and Schuster and 19 US television stations under the UPN network (and has just bought the CBS television network), making it the fourth largest media CONGLOMERATE in the world (chief executive: Sumner Redstone). See also SYNERGY.

Video System for recording SOUND and IMAGE on to magnetically-coated tape, either for later TELEVISION transmission or for playback on a videocassette or video-tape recorder (VCR or VTR). Television has used video recording, or telerecording, since the 1950s, transforming an industry that initially was broadcast live, but the technology remained both bulky and expensive, as well as often poor in image quality, until the 1970s, which also saw a rapid growth in HOME VIDEO – video recording and playback technology, and the programming to feed it, aimed at the home market.

In commercial film production terms, the inferior image quality of video technology, as compared with 35MM film, has meant that video has functioned as an aid to, rather than a replacement for, film-making, as in VIDEO ASSIST and video EDITING, though developments in video and television technology like HDTV may make video a more viable commercial technology in the future. However, since many more spectators now see films on video at home than in cinemas, film-makers need to have in mind the smaller and squarer screen conditions in which the majority of viewers will watch, which has meant producing a less busy image and placing more ACTION in the centre of the screen.

In addition, video has had an impact on the commercial film industry in economic terms: home video markets have become a crucial part of the profit potential of a film, and a major player in the home video market like Blockbuster was a crucial part of the media CONGLOMERATE deal in which VIACOM took over PARAMOUNT. Video has had a much larger impact on DOCUMENTARY film-making and in amateur film-making, and in HOME MOVIES in particular, camcorders have now almost entirely replaced 8MM and 16MM film, and made possible new GENRES like the 'video diary'. Video has also made market impact via the MUSIC video – SHORT FILMS made to accompany the RELEASE of popular MUSIC titles, and shown, among other places on the MTV CABLE channel – though most music videos are, in fact, shot on film. See also NON-LINEAR EDITING.

Further reading: Wasko (1994), Belton and Hilmes in Nowell-Smith (1996)

Video assist An electronic form of VIEWFINDER that enables a video CAMERA to record while showing the IMAGES on a monitor. Video assist make it easier to see what is being SHOT and make a recording, which can be consulted either immediately or later.

Vietnam movie Films that have been made, principally in the US, dealing with the war in Vietnam itself or with its consequences. As Jackson (1998) points out, the language of Vietnam films is consistent enough for the form to have become a kind of minor GENRE all of its own: 'the choppers, the unseen Vietnamese enemy in the foliage, the "psychedelic rock SOUNDTRACK".' Virtually all the major American Vietnam films were made after the end of the war in 1975, including *The Deer Hunter* (dir. Michael Cimino, 1978), *Apocalypse Now* (dir. Francis Ford Coppola, 1979), *Platoon* (dir. Oliver Stone, 1986) and *Full Metal Jacket* (dir. Stanley Kubrick, 1987), all of which include extensive SEQUENCES set in Vietnam itself, including battle SCENES. The war also inspired a number of films in which it is still the central subject, but which are set away from the conflict, such as *Coming Home* (dir. Hal Ashby, 1978), often referred to as the first MAINSTREAM US film to take an openly liberal, anti-war stance. A third category of Vietnam films is more amorphous: those movies, like *Taxi Driver* (dir. Martin Scorsese, 1976), that use Vietnam as a kind of brooding backdrop to their CHARACTER's lives, but which are never explicit about the connection between the war and the events of the film. See also WAR FILM.

Further reading: Adair (1989), Anderegg (1991), Auster & Quart (1988), Britton (1981), Dittmar & Michaud (1991), Jeffords (1989), Smith (1975), Wood (1986)

Viewfinder A device attached to or integrated into a CAMERA that enables the operator to see the camera's field of vision through the LENS. Today, most cameras have REFLEX VIEWFINDERS, which show the precise field of vision, and which were introduced to solve the PARALLAX problem. Much filming today also uses VIDEO ASSIST as an extension of the viewfinder.

Vigilante film A movie in which private citizens or group of individuals take the law into their own hands. A CYCLE of movies such as *Walking Tall* (dir. Phil Karlson, 1973), *Magnum Force* (dir. Ted Post, 1973) and *Death Wish* (dir. Michael Winner, 1974) began to appear in the 1970s in the US as a rising crime rate and urban decay became major social and political issues. Abel Ferrara's *Ms. 45* (1981) earned CULT FILM status as a female vigilante film that seemed a FEMINIST response to the SLASHER FILM.

Vignette In still photography, a portrait showing only the head, or the head, shoulders and upper part of the torso, and shading off at the edges into indistinct background. In cinema, the term applies to a CLOSE-UP with a similar composition, a technique associated with G.W. 'Billy' Bitzer, who SHOT many of D.W. Griffith's films. A vignette is also a self-contained, expository SCENE used to introduce a CHAR-ACTER in a film. Gallagher (1986, p. 35) argues that the greatness of DIRECTOR John Ford as an AUTEUR is built on such vignettes – shots or SCENES that briefly isolate and caricature the essence of a given character.

Violence The REPRESENTATION of violence in cinema has always generated controversy, usually focusing on the questions of whether showing it on SCREEN glorifies violence or makes it repugnant, and to what extent screen violence influences behaviour. In *Intolerance* (1916), DIRECTOR D.W. Griffith preaches against war. In the film's Babylonian SEQUENCE, we are meant to condemn the invading Persians and decry the fact that religious persecution leads to bloodshed; but we are just as likely to be fascinated by the scale and CHOREOGRAPHY of the battle and impressed by the SPECIAL EFFECTS that allow us to see men being impaled by spears and decapitated by swords as we are to be convinced of the evils of violence.

Violence has been an essential element of film from the beginning. *The Great Train Robbery* (dir. Edwin S. Porter, 1903), the ONE-REELER often said to have initiated the development of CLASSIC HOLLYWOOD CINEMA, contains a great deal of violence given its rather short length and the context of its time. The very first SHOT in the narrative features two black-clad villains who break through a door at a railroad station, brandish pistols, and beat and bind the stationmaster. The gunfire and dynamite explosion were TINTED yellow to add to their visual impact, and the film also ended with a non-DIEGETIC CLOSE-UP of a cowboy pointing and firing his pistol directly at the CAMERA – that is, at the viewer. The shot encapsulates the film's violent appeal and so was sometimes shown at the beginning rather than at the end of the film, engaging the spectator's desire for the SPECTACLE of violent ACTION at the outset. The arrival of SOUND allowed film-makers new opportunities for representing violence. In the early 1930s, the SOUNDTRACKS of GANGSTER FILMS were filled with the screeching of car tyres, rapid-fire dialogue and, above all, the rat-a-tatting of machine guns.

A number of historical factors in the 1960s converged to push films toward more graphic representations of violence. AUDIENCES had grown more accustomed to the visual representation of violence as a result of daily TELEVISION coverage of the war in Vietnam; the rift in American society regarding intervention in Southeast Asia was growing more intense; and the HAYS CODE, along with the classical STUDIO SYSTEM, was crumbling. Arthur Penn's *Bonnie and Clyde* (1967), a much romanticized treatment of the life of two real but rather minor criminals of the 1930s, had the most immediate cultural impact. The film's violence reflects the depth of the time's social tensions as viewers are positioned on the side of the romantic rebels rather than with the retributive representatives of the law. *Bonnie and Clyde* brought a new visceral quality to the depiction of gunshot wounds and their impact on the body, most memorably in the concluding SCENE in which the couple's bodies jerk crazily as they are riddled with bullets.

Sam Peckinpah's *The Wild Bunch* (1969) continued in the graphic manner of *Bonnie and Clyde*, but added the use of exploding 'squibs' to show blood spurting and spraying upon a bullet's entry into the body. Peckinpah expanded the violence to ensemble proportions in the large-scale massacres that frame *The Wild Bunch*, becoming orgies of bloodlust in which spectators are often as much enthralled as appalled. Peckinpah also employed SLOW MOTION and rapid MONTAGE to give the violence a paradoxical balletic grace. At approximately the same time, *Night of the Living Dead* (dir. George A. Romero, 1968) established the recent emphasis of the HORROR FILM on graphic bodily mutilation that has found its extreme in the SPLATTER FILM.

In recent years a new POSTMODERN style of violence has emerged, as exemplified by *Henry: Portrait of a Serial Killer* (dir. John McNaughton, 1990), which achieves its powerful effect, paradoxically, through a flat, minimalist approach. The film throughout is as bland as the drab, blue-collar world in which Henry lives. It treats its gruesome violence with a kitchen-sink neutrality that captures the matter-of-fact manner in which Henry does everything, from buying a pack of cigarettes to brutally murdering another victim. *Henry*'s style seems to embody the 'waning of affect' that Jameson (1991) and others have claimed characterize the postmodern era.

By contrast, Steven Spielberg in *Saving Private Ryan* (1998) wants to restore the full affective power to the cinematic representation of violence that has been lost over the course of film history. In its powerful opening, a depiction of the carnage involved in the D-Day landing at Normandy, the film attempts to present the horrible reality of combat, stripped of the patina of glory that characterizes conventional battles in the WAR FILM. The blood runs so thick it tints the ocean water and the HAND-HELD CAMERA lends a DOCUMENTARY immediacy to the chaos of the battle. But although *Saving Private Ryan* succeeds on the one hand in subverting the war film, in the end it compromises itself by presenting Capt. Miller (Tom Hanks) and Ryan himself as conventional heroes who in the end selflessly fight to the death in a glorious last stand.

Violence in cinema may also be visited upon the spectator by challenging films that thwart viewer expectations. In *Psycho* (dir. Alfred Hitchcock, 1960), the scenes of violence in the film are actually few, and they are in fact more suggestive than graphic. The film's most famous violent SEQUENCE, the murder of Marion Crane in the shower by the mysterious Mrs. Bates, is rendered entirely through the kinetic violence of montage, the knife never actually shown piercing flesh. In addition, the physical location of the murder in a shower initially suggests Marion's moral cleansing, making viewers feel more at ease with this CHARACTER whom they had been encouraged by the film's EDITING to identify with but whose actions thus far have been ethically questionable. In other words, viewers are momentarily made more comfortable only to feel more violated subsequently. The sequence's powerful effect is thus in part achieved as a result of the cruel subversion of viewer expectation, as the STAR is killed off when the film is only half over and spectators are jerked out of their IDENTIFICATION with the apparent protagonist.

Further Reading: Atkins (1976), Fraser (1974), French (1996), Glucksmann (1971), Prince (1998), Sharrett (1999)

Virtual reality The illusion of reality, using three dimensional interactive technology to simulate the spectator/participant's experience of being present at imagined or reconstructed events or places. The impression of participation and interaction is provided by stereophonic SOUND and IMAGE, via a headset with earphones and liquid crystal monitors, with a computer-linked glove to simulate touch. Though virtual reality will in some form prove part of the future of cinema, it is more commonly used at present in military training, engineering, architecture and archaeology. In modified

form, video and computer games – often spin-offs from movies, or sources of future movies – make use of virtual reality technology. *Strange Days* (dir. Kathryn Bigelow, 1995), *The Matrix* (dir. Andy & Larry Wachowski, 1999) and, in part, *Demolition Man* (dir. Marco Brambilla, 1993) all exploit aspects of the idea of virtual reality.
Further reading: Cook & Bernink (1999)

VistaVision A WIDESCREEN process developed for commercial use by PARA-MOUNT in the 1950s as a response to CinemaScope, though no longer used in its original form after the early 1960s, because of the availability of cheaper alternatives (see PANAVISION). Unlike the ANAMORPHIC LENS system used by CinemaScope, VistaVision achieved its widescreen IMAGE (ASPECT RATIO 1.85:1) by running 35MM film horizontally, rather than vertically, through the CAMERA exposing a FRAME twice the normal size, producing a very high quality projected image. Paramount intended that special projectors would also project the films horizontally, but the expense involved meant that in most theatres images were reduced to normal 35mm film and projected in the normal way. Even so, the resulting images were sharper than conventionally shot 35mm images or those achieved with anamorphic lenses. First used in 1954, among the most notable Paramount films shot in VistaVision were *The Ten Commandments* (dir. Cecil B. DeMille, 1956), *Funny Face* (dir. Stanley Donen, 1957), Alfred Hitchcock's *To Catch a Thief* (1955) and *Vertigo* (1958) and *One-Eyed Jacks* (dir. Marlon Brando, 1961). Such was the industry respect for VistaVision that WARNER BROS. borrowed the process for John Ford's *The Searchers* (1956) and Hitchcock used it for *North by Northwest* (1959) at MGM, and Japanese studio Daiei licensed the system as Daieiscope.
Further reading: Belton (1992)

Visual pleasure A phrase most often associated with FEMINIST FILM THEORY, particularly Laura Mulvey's groundbreaking essay (Mulvey, 1989) on the theoretical exclusion of the female spectator from taking visual PLEASURE in MAINSTREAM FILM since it was founded upon a male GAZE. In this formulation cinema was largely built around a pattern of CAMERA ANGLES and EDITING techniques that objectified and fetishised the female body which could then be looked upon by the VOYEURISTIC male spectator. This idea also builds upon developments in PSYCHOANALYTIC theory with the male gaze being linked to subconscious fears of castration and the consequent desire to control the threat of the female. Although Mulvey's ideas are now best seen as a crucial piece of polemic initiating extensive subsequent debate about the availability of visual pleasure for the female spectator, the idea itself is still very important and relevant not only to ideas about the GENDERed spectator, but also to debates about the viewing positions of spectators in relation to, for example, questions of ethnicity, SEXUALITY and disability. See also AUDIENCE, SCOPOPHILIA, SUTURE.

Vitaphone System for synchronizing recorded SOUND with the moving IMAGE developed by WARNER BROS., first used for the 'hybrid' film *Don Juan* (dir. Alan Crosland, 1926) but most famous as the system used for what became known as the first talkie, *The Jazz Singer* (dir. Crosland, 1927). The system used shellac discs sychronized with the film during PROJECTION, but the fragility of the discs and the problems in maintaining synchronization soon led to its abandonment in favour of the OPTICAL sound-on-film system, Movietone, developed by FOX.

Voice-of-God narration The use of a VOICE-OVER in a DOCUMENTARY film that explains and interprets information. The expression usually refers to the typical voice-over used in Griersonian-style documentary because it is normally male, disembodied and OMNISCIENT, as in, for example, *Coal Face* (dir. Alberto Cavalcanti, 1936) and *Night Mail* (dir. Basil Wright and Harry Watt, 1936). More recently some film-makers have rejected the voice-of-God narrator as patriarchal, ethnocentric and manipulative, opting instead for a personal voice-over, as in *Roger and Me* (dir. Michael Moore, 1989), a female voice, as in *The Falls* (dir. Kevin McMahon, 1991), or multiple voices, as in *Surname Viet Given Name Nam* (dir. Trinh T. Minh-ha, 1989).

Voice-over (VO) Non-synchronous COMMENTARY from an off-SCREEN source. The voice may be that of a disembodied NARRATOR, in either a narrative film or DOCUMENTARY, or of a CHARACTER, either in the form of an INTERIOR MONOLOGUE or addressing the spectator directly. The term also refers to a voice on a SOUNDTRACK preceding the appearance on the screen of the SCENE in which the character to whom the voice belongs is speaking the words heard. While many FEATURE FILMS use a voice-over briefly at some point, Terrence Malick is a DIRECTOR who has relied signif-icantly on the first-person voice-over in his films *Badlands* (1973), *Days of Heaven* (1978) and *The Thin Red Line* (1999). Both *Sunset Boulevard* (dir. Billy Wilder, 1950) and *American Beauty* (dir. Sam Mendes, 1999) offer a surprising twist on the tech-nique in that the characters providing the voice-over in these films are already dead.

Vorkapich In CLASSIC NARRATIVE CINEMA, a SEQUENCE using short SHOTS or such techniques as SUPERIMPOSITIONS, CUTS, JUMP CUTS, WIPES and DISSOLVES to create a kaleidoscopic effect summarizing or condensing a particular experience or TRANSITION in TIME, SPACE or situation. Such sequences are named after Slavko Vorkapich, SPECIAL EFFECTS expert who specialized in making them during the STUDIO ERA. Orson Welles in *Citizen Kane* (1941) parodies this type of MONTAGE construction in the SCENE showing Susan Alexander's unsuccessful opera tour, which ends with the dimming of a cue light and the fading wail of the singer's voice on the SOUNDTRACK.

Voyeurism Refers to the act of watching people without their knowledge or permission. The cinema could be said to reproduce this situation with the AUDIENCE, in the dark and invisible, watching the intimate details of people's lives unfold on the screen. Voyeurism has also been seen in more complex ways through the application of PSYCHOANALYTIC theory to film, with the voyeuristic male spectator able to negate his fear of the threat of the female by controlling her through his GAZE. Much film also adopts the related strategy of fetishising the female body – legs, breasts or arti-cles of clothing associated with sexual arousal such as high-heeled shoes. Some crit-ics have debated whether only the male spectator is positioned voyeuristically in relation to film, and there are also different versions of the position of the female spectator (see Mayne, 1993).

Apart from its relevance to studies of the AUDIENCE and RECEPTION THEORY, voyeurism has also featured as the subject matter of several films. Alfred Hitchcock was particularly interested in the voyeuristic dimension of cinema spectatorship and drew attention to it in a number of his films, particularly *Rear Window* (1954) and *Psycho* (1960). *Peeping Tom* (dir. Michael Powell, 1960) is probably the most explicit exploration of the relationship between voyeurism and the cinema. Numerous contemporary films focus on voyeurism, such as *Copycat* (dir. John Amiel, 1995), which also incorporates new voyeuristic practices via computer technology and the Internet. See also FEMINIST FILM THEORY, SCOPOPHILIA.

W

Walt Disney Company Although Walt Disney began making animated films, or CARTOONS, in HOLLYWOOD in 1923 (with Ub Iwerks), the Walt Disney Company established itself most obviously on the basis of both synchronized SOUND – *Steamboat Willie* (1928), featuring Mickey Mouse, and ANIMATION synchronized with MUSIC such as in the *Silly Symphony* films (and, much later, *Fantasia*, dir. Ben Sharpsteen, 1940) – and COLOUR, *Flowers and Trees* (1932) being their first TECHNI- COLOR film. By the mid 1930s, Disney had established itself as an efficient animation STUDIO with international reach, a reputation cemented by the company's successful introduction of FEATURE-length cartoons, first with *Snow White and the Seven Dwarfs* (dir. Disney, 1937), followed by *Pinocchio* (dir. Ben Sharpsteen and Hamilton Luske, 1940) and *Bambi* (dir. David Hand, 1943).

Because of its smallish output, its specialized family entertainment product and its reliance on the majors for DISTRIBUTION, Disney was not considered a MAJOR STUDIO during the 1930s and 1940s, but it is currently one of the most successful studios, typically taking 18–19 per cent of annual North American BOX-OFFICE receipts. Disney's transformation into a major studio was instructive for the survival of the other majors. Disney brand names, for example, were important for MERCHAN- DISING since the 1930s and its policy of cross-promotion – films promoting theme parks (first, Disneyland, in 1955), theme parks promoting TELEVISION shows, televi- sion shows promoting toys and films – was a lesson learned by others. Disney also branched out into LIVE ACTION films and nature DOCUMENTARIES (*The Living Desert*, 1953) and established its own distribution arm, Buena Vista, in 1954, as well as new studio brand names, Touchstone Pictures, and later Hollywood Pictures, for non- 'family entertainment' films, and absorbed formerly INDEPENDENT distributor, Miramax, in 1993. Under chief executive Michael Eisner in the 1980s and 1990s, Disney was also adept at managing new media, buying the ABC television network in 1995, shrewdly recycling its classic films on VIDEO, and producing the first computer-generated animated film, *Toy Story* (dir. John Lasseter, 1995), as well as re- establishing the popularity of feature-length animated films with *Aladdin* (dir. John Musker and Ron Clements, 1992), *The Lion King* (dir. Roger Allers and Rob Minkoff, 1994) and others.

War film A film dealing with warfare, preparations for war or its aftermath, or warfare as a background to or integral part of the ACTION. D.W. Griffith's historical EPIC about the American Civil War period, *The Birth of a Nation* (1915), is a war film that includes all of these possibilities. Films in the GENRE are set primarily on the front lines, at least for part of the narrative, although they take place away from the field of battle, in prisoner-of-war camps or on the home front as well. Many war films are anti-war in intention, such as the World War 1 movies *All Quiet on the Western Front* (dir. Lewis Milestone, 1930) and *Paths of Glory* (dir. Stanley Kubrick, 1957), although many that are made immediately preceding or during armed conflicts are meant for PROPAGANDA purposes, to convince people to support or join a particular cause or to condemn the enemy as an evil OTHER. Anti-war films are faced with an inevitable aesthetic problem that is seen as far back as Griffith's *Intolerance* (1916). Intended as a pacifist film about the need for tolerance, *Intolerance* contains a climactic battle SCENE in the Babylonian STORY that includes graphic IMAGES of soldiers being impaled and decapitated, providing a greater sense of REALISM, but at the same time inevitably making for exciting cinema. Films with anti-war messages typically balance obligatory anti-war speeches by STARS with scenes of battle featuring explosions, rapid EDITING and lots of ACTION.

The pyrotechnics of staged battle scenes provide one of the main PLEASURES of the war film, similar to the importance of SPECIAL EFFECTS in the SCIENCE FICTION FILM. For just this reason, Jean-Luc Godard made his *Les Carabiniers* (*The Riflemen*, 1963) as a deliberately dull war movie wherein warfare offers no interest as a SPEC-TACLE. Other anti-war movies have tried the opposite tactic, making war so grittily realistic that viewers will feel revulsion. Stanley Kubrick showed the grim psychological effects of basic training in *Full Metal Jacket* (1987), while in *Saving Private Ryan* (1998) Steven Spielberg showed the brutal horrors of combat in his depiction of the D-Day landing at Normandy Beach during World War II, emphasized with a HAND-HELD CAMERA and state-of-the-art prosthetic effects, before lapsing back into the conventional romantic IDEOLOGY of guts and glory in the end. Yet another approach was taken by Jean Renoir, whose *La Grande Illusion* (*Grand Illusion*, 1937), appearing on the eve of World War II, is set during World War 1 and depicts both its French and German CHARACTERS with humanist sympathy.

The onset of World War II brought about an intense production of war films of all kinds, from DOCUMENTARIES and TRAINING FILMS to fiction films. HOLLYWOOD produced numerous war movies during and after the War. Such films as *Wake Island* (dir. John Farrow, 1942), *Baatan* (dir. Tay Garnett, 1943), and *Guadalcanal Diary* (dir. Lewis Seiler, 1944), all made during the War, consistently emphasized the message that individuals must put aside their personal problems and desires to work as part of a group, like the well-disciplined flying crew of *Air Force* (dir. Howard Hawks, 1943). In *The Fighting Seabees* (dir. Edward Ludwig, 1944), no less an ICON of rugged individualism than John Wayne has to sacrifice his own ego and life for the greater good. This necessary submergence of the ego in warfare is also the subject of the recent, more philosophical *The Thin Red Line* (dir. Terrence Malick, 1998). After the War, however, a number of films, such as *From Here to Eternity* (dir. Fred Zinnemann, 1953), *Attack!* (dir. Robert Aldrich, 1956) and *The Caine Mutiny* (dir. Edward Dmytryk, 1954), questioned the nature of leadership and internal pressures within the military group.

The social divisiveness around the Vietnam war prevented a similar CYCLE of war movies from developing in the 1960s, but films such as *The Dirty Dozen* (dir. Aldrich, 1967), set in World War II, and *M*A*S*H* (dir. Robert Altman, 1970), set during the Korean War, were clearly influenced by that conflict. The major film about Vietnam made during the War, *The Green Berets* (dir. John Wayne and Ray Kellogg, 1968), was a commercial flop. But after the end of the War, VIETNAM MOVIES developed into a distinct genre, with movies such as *The Deer Hunter* (dir. Michael Cimino, 1978), *Platoon* (dir. Oliver Stone, 1986), *Casualties of War* (dir. Brian de Palma, 1989) and *Born on the Fourth of July* (dir. Stone, 1989). In the tradition of *The Best Years of Our*

Lives (dir. William Wyler, 1946), there have also been a number of films about the problems encountered by Vietnam veterans returning home to public indifference, such as *Coming Home* (dir Hal Ashby, 1978), *Cutter's Way* (dir. Ivan Passer, 1981) and *First Blood* (dir. Ted Kotcheff, 1982).

Further reading: Adair (1989), Anderegg (1991), Auster & Quart (1988), Basinger (1988), Dick (1985), Dittmar & Michaud (1990), Jeffords (1989), Kane (1982), Landy (1991a), Smith (1975), Suid (1978)

Wardour Street A street in London's Soho between Shaftesbury Avenue and Oxford Street, traditionally the centre of the British commercial film industry: 'Wardour Street' signified 'the British film industry'. Although this usage is less common today than in the 1920s–1970s, there is still a concentration of distributors (mostly US-based) and viewing theatres on the street and nearby.

Warner Bros. American film company founded in 1923 by the four Warner brothers (Harry, Albert, Sam and Jack), who all served as chief executives in different capacities. In 1925 the company bought Vitagraph and in 1926 merged with Western Electric to create the VITAPHONE Company to develop a SOUND-on-disc system for synchronizing sound with film. Warner's release of *The Jazz Singer* (dir. Alan Crosland) in 1927, featuring synchronized musical numbers and several dialogue SCENES, revolutionized the film industry and established the company as one of the MAJOR STUDIOS in HOLLYWOOD. By the turn of the decade Warner Bros. had also acquired the Stanley chain of theatres and the FIRST NATIONAL production company.

In the 1930s Warner Bros., in stark contrast to the lavish PRODUCTION VALUES of MGM, made lean, fast-paced films that were more attuned to the concerns of the working CLASS and that more directly reflected the realities of the Great Depression. The studio produced GANGSTER FILMS such as *Little Caesar* (dir. Mervyn LeRoy, 1930) with Edward G. Robinson and *The Public Enemy* (dir. William Wellman, 1931) with James Cagney, and films about contemporary social problems, such as *I Am a Fugitive from a Chain Gang* (dir. LeRoy, 1932), about the Southern penal system, and *Wild Boys of the Road* (dir. Wellman, 1933), about homelessness and itinerant youth. The STUDIO also made a CYCLE of backstage MUSICALS, including *Forty-Second Street* (dir. Lloyd Bacon, 1933), *Footlight Parade* (dir. Bacon, 1933) and *Dames* (dir. Ray Enright, 1934), that featured the distinctive CAMERA style and CHOREOGRAPHY of Busby Berkeley and the talent of such songwriters as Harry Warren and Al Dubin, and developed the GENRE of the BIOPIC with such movies as *The Story of Louis Pasteur* (dir. William Dieterle, 1936) and *The Life of Emile Zola* (dir. Dieterle, 1937).

Warners turned out many now classic films through the 1940s, including *The Maltese Falcon* (dir. John Huston, 1941) and *Casablanca* (dir. Michael Curtiz, 1942). After the PARAMOUNT DECISION in 1948, Warners successfully diversified into TELEVISION production and created a number of hit shows. In 1967 the studio merged with film DISTRIBUTION company Seven Arts to become Warner Brothers-Seven Arts, which was in turn purchased by Kinney National Services in 1969, becoming Warner Communications in 1971. In 1990 the entertainment giant was purchased by Time Inc. which then merged with Turner Broadcasting in 1996, which in turn merged with AOL in January, 2000 to become one of the world's largest entertainment CONGLOMERATES. Throughout this period of growth and transformation Warner Bros. continued to produce commercially successful films, including *Bonnie and*

Clyde (dir. Arthur Penn, 1967), *The Exorcist* (dir. William Friedkin, 1973), *Goodfellas* (dir. Martin Scorsese, 1990), *Unforgiven* (dir. Clint Eastwood, 1992) and *Natural Born Killers* (dir. Oliver Stone, 1994). See also BIG 5.

Further reading: Finler (1988), Gomery (1986), Higham (1976), Hirschhorn (1979), Mordden (1988), Roddick (1983), Schatz (1988)

Weepie A NARRATIVE work that relies on sentiment and emotional manipulation to elicit a strong, usually sad, emotional response from the AUDIENCE. In reference to HOLLYWOOD movies, the term sometimes is used vaguely to refer to MELODRAMA and the WOMAN'S FILM. Also used synonymously with 'tearjerker'.

Western American historian Frederick Jackson Turner claimed in his famous treatise, *The Significance of the Frontier in American History* published in 1894, that the western frontier was the essential influence on the shaping of the distinctive American national character, and French critic André Bazin described the Western as 'the American GENRE par excellence' (Bazin, 1971). The typical Western NARRATIVE, set on the precarious border between civilization and lawlessness, is perfectly suited for dramatizing what John G. Cawelti calls the 'epic moment' of American history (Cawelti, 1985). The genre's master BINARY OPPOSITION of wilderness and civilization has allowed for a richness of interpretation about the nature of American society. The Western commonly deals with the tension between individualism and social responsibility. As in *Shane* (dir. George Stevens, 1953), the Western hero is a tragic figure who often operates by his own moral code which transcends the more pragmatic values of the townsfolk, whom he must protect.

The Western is one of the most elaborately developed of genres. Indeed, the genre's ICONOGRAPHY exceeds the cinema, frequently appearing within other forms of POPULAR CULTURE such as advertising, comic books, and popular MUSIC. The Western's classic representation for distinguishing between heroes and villains as 'white hats vs. black hats' has become a commonplace of daily discourse. While the MUSICAL, for example, has no determining visual iconography and may be set anywhere, in any historical period, the Western is by definition set temporally within the period of the Wild West (approx. 1865–1890) and geographically on the American frontier (broadly, between the Mississippi River and the California coast). Movies that violate these CONVENTIONS of setting in TIME (e.g., contemporary Westerns such as *Lonely are the Brave*, dir. David Miller, 1962) or place (e.g., 'eastern Westerns' such as *Drums Along the Mohawk*, dir. John Ford, 1939) are among the few exceptions. The setting in Westerns is important symbolically as well as literally, for the landscape functions as an objective correlative of the spiritual state of individual CHARACTERS, as in Anthony Mann's Westerns, or of society more generally, as in John Ford's use of Monument Valley.

The Western's roots can be traced back to the very beginning of American literature, in the numerous captivity narratives written during the Colonial period (1620–1776). Many of the genre's elements were established in the five popular Leatherstocking Tales (1823–1841) of American novelist James Fenimore Cooper, the most famous of which is probably *The Last of the Mohicans* (1826), itself the subject of four film adaptations. Both Cawelti and Henry Nash Smith (1950) trace the evolution of the Western from Cooper through the popular dime novels of the later 19th century to cinema. In 1902, the success of Owen Wister's novel *The*

Virginian popularized the heroic REPRESENTATION of the Western hero that became the standard in the movies. Only one year after the publication of *The Virginian*, Edwin S. Porter's *The Great Train Robbery* (1903) appeared, which, in retrospect, may be seen to have been crucial in the Western's transition to the cinema. The Western's emphasis on beautiful natural landscapes and ACTION guaranteed its prominence in the new visual medium, and the genre quickly became a mainstay of American film production. Many of the movie STARS of the silent period were associated exclusively with Westerns, such as Bronco Billy Anderson, William S. Hart, and Tom Mix. Western SERIALS were a staple of HOLLYWOOD production from the silent era through the 1940s, made by such Hollywood STUDIOS as COLUMBIA, UNIVERSAL, and REPUB-LIC. By the 1930s, though, many Westerns were little more than formula B MOVIES featuring singing cowboys such as Gene Autry.

In 1939, John Ford's *Stagecoach* in 1939 brought a new depth to the genre's conventions, and World War II brought the development of the so-called 'adult west-ern' in which psychological themes were emphasized (e.g., *Duel in the Sun*, dir. King Vidor, 1945; *Pursued*, dir. Raoul Walsh, 1947) and social problems explored (e.g., lynching in *The Ox-Bow Incident*, dir. William Wellman, 1943; racial intolerance in *Broken Arrow*, dir. Delmer Daves, 1950). The 1940s and 1950s marked a period of great achievement, with such AUTEURS as Ford, Mann, Howard Hawks, Samuel Fuller, and Budd Boetticher pushing the genre in new directions. With the escalation of social tensions in the 1960s, newer directors such as Robert Altman (*McCabe and Mrs. Miller*, 1971; *Buffalo Bill and the Indians*, 1976) and Arthur Penn (*Little Big Man*, 1970) made Westerns that subverted or deconstructed the genre's mythic appeal. The Italian SPAGHETTI WESTERNS of Sergio Leone and others further stripped the genre of romanticism and sentimentality in their view of the frontier as a ruthless, amoral jungle wherein only the fittest survive.

Because of the genre's centrality in American culture, the Western has accommo-dated a wide range of critical and theoretical approaches. Writers such as Henry Nash Smith (1950) and Richard Slotkin (1992) have examined the Western from a cultural studies perspective, seeing the genre's MYTHS and conventions as essential expres-sions of American cultural values. Cawelti (1985) has examined the Western for its more universal mythic appeal. Will Wright (1975) and Jim Kitses (1969) have applied a STRUCTURALIST approach to the genre, while Philip French (1973) shows how the genre embodies the political tensions informing the time in which individual Westerns were made. More recently, Jane Tompkins (1992) has discussed the Western within the context of FEMINIST CRITICISM, seeing the genre as an expression of masculinist IDEOLOGY.

In recent years the Western has experienced a decided downturn in popularity and production. Only one film-maker, Clint Eastwood, has managed to work in the genre with any consistency. The ideology of the Western now seems for many people uncomfortably imperialist as well as racist, particularly in its treatment of native Americans. However, there are signs of a new revisionism in the Western as groups previously marginalized by the genre seek to appropriate its mythic reso-nance. In the last decade there have been black Westerns (*Posse*, dir. Mario van Peebles, 1993), feminist Westerns (*The Ballad of Little Jo*, dir. Maggie Greenwald, 1993; *The Quick and the Dead*, dir. Sam Raimi, 1995), and Westerns that have sought to critique American culture from a native perspective (*Dead Man*, dir. Jim Jarmusch, 1996). With the overpopulation and decimation of nature that characterized the end of the 20th century, the conventions of the Western have been increasingly imported into the more immediately relevant genre of SCIENCE FICTION. *Outland* (dir. Peter Hyams, 1981) is a remake of *High Noon* (dir. Fred Zinneman, 1952) on a space station, and *Enemy Mine* (dir. Wolfgang Petersen, 1985) a variation of *Broken Arrow*.

Further reading: Buscombe (1988), Buscombe & Pearson (1998), Cameron & Pye (1996), Coyne (1998), Hardy (1991), Kitses & Rickman (1998), Lenihan (1980), Nachbar (1974), Schatz (1981), Warshow (1970)

WGA The Writers Guild of America. See GUILD.

Whip pan See ZIP PAN.

Whodunit See MYSTERY FILM.

Wide angle See FOCAL LENGTH

Widescreen Widescreen denotes an ASPECT RATIO wider than the norm adhered to more or less from film's origins up until the 1950s – the Academy ratio of 1.33: 1 (later the standard ratio for the TELEVISION IMAGE too). As with SOUND and COLOUR, experiments with widescreen processes were undertaken by various companies, including MAJOR STUDIOS like PARAMOUNT, FOX, WARNER BROS and UNITED ARTISTS in the 1920s, but technical problems and the costs of converting both STUDIOS and theatres for sound pushed other innovations like widescreen into the background. In France, director Abel Gance in *Napoléon* (1927) experimented with Polyvision, using three screens side by side, sometimes showing a continuous – and therefore very wide – image, and sometimes different images. Also in France during the 1920s, Henri Chrétien developed an ANAMORPHIC widescreen system, which squeezed a wide image on to normal 35MM film, which was then unsqueezed in projection. Both these approaches were taken up by US major studios in the 1950s, when widescreen formats were a major strategy for differentiating cinema from television (seen as the main cause of the dramatic fall in cinema attendance). CINERAMA, a three-camera and three-screen process based on Polyvision, was introduced successfully in 1952, but was generally reserved for novelty material designed to show off its format; because it was technically difficult to both shoot and project Cinerama, it was not widely taken up. TWENTIETH CENTURY-FOX had much more success with CinemaScope, an anamorphic widescreen process based on Chrétien's system, which initially used a ratio of 2.55: 1 (later 2.35: 1 to accommodate OPTICAL SOUND). The success of the first CinemaScope release, *The Robe* (dir. Henry Koster, 1953), led to widespread copying by other studios and the incorporation of 'scope' into their own brand names (including other countries – Dyaliscope in France, Daeiscope in Japan, for example). PARAMOUNT took a different route to high quality widescreen images (1.85:1) with VISTAVISION. Later widescreen systems using 70MM film included TODD-AO and PANAVISION. Today the most common widescreen ratio is 1.85:1, and widescreen is the norm, even for much TELEVISION material SHOT on film. Widescreen films shown on television are subjected either to a PAN AND SCAN process or, increasingly, shown in a LETTERBOX format.

Initially, widescreen processes were considered mainly appropriate for EPIC subjects, and unsuitable for intimate subjects, though films like *Rebel Without a Cause* (dir. Nicholas Ray, 1955) proved this wrong. Certainly widescreen formats were usually associated with prestige productions. Many critics, like those on SIGHT AND SOUND, opposed the format, but André Bazin and his colleagues on *CAHIERS DU CINÉMA* welcomed it, arguing against film being 'defined by divine right as silent, narrow and black and white' (Jacques Rivette, quoted in Hillier 1985, p. 271). Bazin argued, as with DEEP FOCUS, that widescreen brought the spectator's view closer to that of reality, and Charles Barr (in Mast and Cohen, 1974) and others argued for the extra dimension brought to *MISE EN SCÈNE* by CinemaScope. See also: DYNAMIC FRAME.

Further reading: Belton in Balio (1990), Belton (1992), Cook (1996), Cook & Bernink (1999), Maltby (1995).

Wild sound, wild track Non-SYNC AMBIENT SOUND recorded independently of the IMAGES, either on LOCATION or afterwards, and designed to be added at the EDITING stage to add atmosphere.

Wipe A TRANSITIONal device, usually a line but any geometrical figure which travels across the screen, seeming to 'push off' one IMAGE and replace it with another. The MUSICAL *Flying Down to Rio* (dir. Thornton Freeland, 1933) is famous for the many different kinds of wipes it used. Popular during the 1930s and 1940s, it is less common in films today, which prefer the greater immediacy implied by the straight CUT, and when a more recent film like *Caged Heat* (dir. Jonathan Demme, 1974) makes extensive use of a variety of wipes, the effect is at once archaic and comic.

Woman's film Movies produced by HOLLYWOOD, particularly from the 1930s through the 1950s, featuring female STARS in STORIES about romance, family, and social and domestic issues deemed important to women, and aimed at a primarily female AUDIENCE. These films tended to be MELODRAMAS involving the heroine in acts of emotional sacrifice, as in, for example, *Stella Dallas* (dir. King Vidor, 1937), or suffering, as in *Dark Victory* (dir. Edmund Goulding, 1939). FEMINIST analyses of these films by Doane (1987) and others have shown how they structure female SUBJECTIVITY and work to contain women within patriarchal IDEOLOGY. Haskell (1973, p. 153) addresses this view well when she remarks, 'What more damning comment on the relations between men and women in America than the very notion of something called "the woman's film"?' See also FEMINIST FILM, FEMINIST FILM THEORY, WEEPIE.

Further reading: Aspinall & Murphy (1983), Cook (1998), Doane (1987), Gledhill (1987), Landy (1991a), Landy (1991b).

Workprint The POSITIVE print on which EDITING is done is called a 'workprint'. When the editing is completed, the NEGATIVE is cut to precisely match the FINAL CUT.

Wrap The industry term for the end of shooting on either an entire film or sometimes a particular scene. The command 'it's a wrap' indicates that the person in charge of shooting is satisfied that no more TAKES are necessary and that the CREW can begin to dismantle the equipment set up for the SCENE.

Wrestling movie (le luche movies) A popular GENRE in Mexico from the 1950s through the 1970s. Wrestlers such as El Santo (the Saint) and Blue Demon are shown as superheroes combating villains both human and supernatural.

Writer See SCREENWRITER.

X

X-Rating/certificate Originally an actual CERTIFICATE used by both the BRITISH BOARD OF FILM CLASSIFICATION and the MOTION PICTURE ASSOCIATION OF AMERICA to denote a film only suitable for adult AUDIENCES, originally defined in the UK as anyone over 16 (later 18), and in the US varying from 17 to 18 according to which state the film was being shown in. Although the official CERTIFICATION title has now been replaced in both countries, the term 'X-rated' survives as a journalistic description of a film (or sometimes just a SCENE) that possesses particularly explicit sexual or violent content.

Z

Z movie If the B MOVIE was considered of lower quality than the A FEATURE, then the alphabetical logic implied by the term 'Z movie' (which, unlike A feature and B movie, is more a popular slang term than an industrial one) is that it is of the lowest possible quality and PRODUCTION VALUES. However, in the current climate in which PASTICHE, kitsch and CAMP are often valued by popular AUDIENCES, a director like Ed Wood can become the subject of a HOLLYWOOD BIOPIC (*Ed Wood*, dir. Tim Burton, 1994) while Wood's ultra cheap 1956 film *Plan 9 From Outer Space* can be voted 'The Worst Film of All Time' and become a CULT classic.

Zip pan Also known as FLASH PAN, FLICK PAN, SWISH PAN, WHIP PAN. A PAN or pan shot, in which the CAMERA moves, on a fixed axis, from one subject to another (usually horizontally, but sometimes vertically) so fast that that the area between the beginning and end point of the pan is blurred. For a device with so many names, it is not very common, but as a TRANSITION it is often used to suggest simultaneity or a rapid passage of TIME, as in the MONTAGE of Kane and Emily Norton at the breakfast table in *Citizen Kane* (1941).

Zoetrope The best known of several optical toys, very popular in the nineteenth century, which created the illusion of movement. Like motion pictures, the zoetrope depended on persistence of vision: the viewer looked through slits in a revolving drum at SEQUENCES of still drawings wrapped round the inside of the drum, and they appeared to move. Francis Ford Coppola named his production company (American Zoetrope) after the toy, in homage to the PRE-CINEMA period.

Zoom Lens A LENS capable of shifting from short (WIDE-ANGLE) to long (TELE-PHOTO) FOCAL LENGTHS. Also known as varifocal lens. See also ZOOM SHOT.

Zoom, zoom shot A shot made with the aid of a ZOOM LENS, giving the effect of CAMERA MOVEMENT without the use of a DOLLY or CRANE and with the camera itself remaining stationary. The subject of the IMAGE increases in size (zoom-in) or decreases in size (zoom-out). The most famous instance of a zoom shot occurs in Michael Snow's STRUCTURAL FILM *Wavelength* (1967), which consists of one gradual 45-minute zoom-in to a photograph on a wall.

Further reading: Bordwell & Thompson (1997)

Books cited for further reading

REFERENCES

Abel, Richard (ed) (1996). *Silent Film*, Athlone Press, London.

Adair, Gilbert (1989). *Hollywood's Vietnam: from* The Green Berets *to* Full Metal Jacket, Heinemann, London.

Adorno, Theodore (1991). *The Culture Industry*, Routledge, London and New York.

Allen, Robert C. and Gomery, Douglas (1985). *Film History: Theory and Practice*, Alfred A. Knopf, New York.

Alloway, Lawrence (1971). *Violent America: the Movies 1946–1964*, Museum of Modern Art, New York.

Altman, Rick (ed) (1981). *Genre: The Musical*, Routledge & Kegan Paul, London.

Altman, Rick (1987). *The American Film Musical*, Indiana University Press, Bloomington.

Altman, Rick (ed) (1992). *Sound Theory, Sound Practice*, Routledge, New York & London.

Altman, Rick (1999). *Film/Genre*, British Film Institute, London.

Anderegg, Michael (ed) (1991). *Inventing Vietnam: Film and Television Constructions of the U.S. Vietnam War*, Temple University Press, Philadelphia.

Anderson, Joseph L. and Richie, Donald (1960). *The Japanese Film*, Grove Press, New York.

Andrew, J. Dudley (1976). *The Major Film Theories*, Oxford University Press, London, Oxford & New York.

Andrew, J. Dudley (1984). *Concepts in Film Theory*, Oxford University Press, Oxford & New York.

Andrew, J. Dudley (1995). *Mists of Regret: Culture and Sensibility in Classic French Film*, Princeton University Press, Princeton.

Ang, Ien (1985). *Watching Dallas: Soap Opera and the Melodramatic Imagination* Methuen, London.

Armes, Roy (1971). *Patterns of Realism: A Study of Italian Neo-Realist Cinema*, A.S. Barnes, South Brunswick, NJ.

Armes, Roy (1976). *The Ambiguous Image: Narrative Style in Modern European Cinema*, Secker & Warburg, London.

Aspinall, Sue & Murphy, Robert (eds) (1983). *Gainsborough Melodrama*, British Film Institute, London.

Atkins, Thomas (ed) (1976). *Graphic Violence on the Screen*, Monarch Press, New York.

Astruc, Alexandre (1948). The Birth of a New Avant-Garde: Le Caméra-Stylo. In Graham, Peter (1968) *The New Wave: Critical Landmarks*.

Aumont, Jacques, Bergala, Alain, Marie, Michel & Vernet, Marc (eds) (1992). *Aesthetics of Film*, University of Texas Press, Austin, TX.

Auiler, Dan (ed) (1999). *Hitchcock's Secret Notebooks*, Bloomsbury, London.

Auster, Al & Quart, Leonard (1988). *How the War Was Remembered: Hollywood and Vietnam*, Praeger, New York.

Babington, Bruce and Evans, Peter (1985). *Blue Skies and Silver Linings: Aspects of the Hollywood Musical*, Manchester University Press, Manchester, UK and Dover, NH.

Babington, Bruce and Evans, Peter (1989). *Affairs to Remember: The Hollywood Comedy of the Sexes*, Manchester University Press, Manchester, UK and Dover, NH.

Babington, Bruce and Evans, Peter (1993). *Biblical Epics*, Manchester University Press, Manchester and Dover, NH.

Bakhtin, Mikhail (trans. Iswolsky, Helene) (1968). *Rabelais and his World*, MIT Press, Cambridge, MA.

Balio, Tino (ed) (1976a). *The American Film Industry*, University of Wisconsin Press, Madison.

Balio, Tino (1976b). *United Artists: The Company Built by the Stars*, University of Wisconsin Press, Madison.

Balio, Tino (ed) (1990). *Hollywood in the Age of Television*, Unwin Hyman, Boston, MA.

Barlow, John D. (1987). *German Expressionist Film*, Twayne, Boston.

Barnouw, Erik (1993). *Documentary: A History of the Non-Fiction Film*, (2nd edn.), Oxford University Press, Oxford and New York.

Barr, Charles, *et al.* (1969) *The Films of Jean-Luc Godard*, Studio Vista, London.

Barr, Charles (ed) (1986). *All Our Yesterdays: 90 Years of British Cinema*, British Film Institute, London.

Barr, Charles (1993). *Ealing Studios* (revised edn), Studio Vista, London.

Barsam, Richard Meran (1973). *Nonfiction Film: A Critical History*, Dutton, New York.

Barsam, Richard Meran (ed) (1976). *Nonfiction Film: Theory and Criticism*, Dutton, New York.

Barthes, Roland (1972). *Mythologies,* Hill & Wang, New York.

Barthes, Roland (1973). The Third Meaning (1973). In Barthes, Roland (1977). *Image/Music/Text*.

Barthes, Roland (1975). *The Pleasure of the Text*, Hill & Wang, New York.

Barthes, Roland (1977). *Image/Music/Text*, Hill & Wang, New York.

Basinger, Jeanine (1986). *The World War II Combat Film: Anatomy of a Genre*, Columbia University Press, New York.

Battcock, Gregory (ed) (1967). *The New American Cinema: A Critical Anthology*, Dutton, New York.

Bazin, André (trans. Gray, Hugh) (1967). *What is Cinema? Vol. 1*, University of California Press, Berkeley.

Bazin, André (trans. Gray, Hugh) (1971). *What is Cinema? Vol. 2*, University of California Press, Berkeley.

Bellour, Raymond (1979). Alternation, Segmentation, Hypnosis: Interview with Raymond Bellour (by Bergstrom, Janet), *Camera obscura* Nos. 3–4, 1979.

Belton, John (1992). *Widescreen Cinema*, Harvard University Press, Cambridge, MA and London.

Belton, John (1989). *American Cinema/American Culture*, McGraw-Hill, New York.

Benjamin, Walter (ed. Arendt, Hannah & trans. Zohn, Harry) (1968). *Illuminations*, Schocken Books, New York.

Berenstein, Rhona (1996). *Attack of the Leading Ladies: Gender, Sexuality and Spectatorship in Classic Horror Cinema*, Columbia University Press, New York.

Bergan, Ronald (1986). *The United Artists Story*, Octopus, London.

Bergson, Henri (1900). Laughter. In Sypher, W. (ed.) *Comedy* (1956).

Black, Gregory (1994). *Hollywood Censored: Morality Codes, Catholics and the Movies* (Cambridge University Press, Cambridge and New York).

Bogle, Donald (1973). *Toms, Coons, Mulattoes, Mammies & Bucks*, Viking Press, New York.

Bondanella, Peter (1993). *Italian Cinema: From Neorealism to the Present* (2nd edn), Continuum, New York.

Bordwell, David (1985). *Narration in the Fiction Film*, Wisconsin University Press, Madison WI, and Routledge, London.

Bordwell, David (1993). *The Cinema of Sergei Eisenstein*, Harvard University Press, Cambridge, MA.

Bordwell, David & Carroll, Noël (eds) (1996). *Post Theory: Reconstructing Film Studies*, Wisconsin University Press, Madison.

Bordwell, David & Thompson, Kristin (1997). *Film Art: An Introduction* (5th edn). McGraw-Hill, New York.

Bordwell, David, Staiger, Janet & Thompson, Kristin (1985). *The Classical Hollywood Cinema: Film Style and Mode of Production to 1960*, Columbia University Press, New York and Routledge, London.

Branigan, Edward (1984). *Point of View in the Cinema: A Theory of Narration and Subjectivity in Classical Film*, Mouton, New York.

Branigan, Edward (1992). *Narrative Comprehension and Film*, Routledge, London and New York.

Bratton, Jacky, Cook, Jim and Gledhill, Christine (eds) (1994). *Melodrama*, British Film Institute, London.

Braudy, Leo & Cohen, Marshall (eds) (1999). *Film Theory and Criticism* (5th edn), Oxford University Press, Oxford and New York.

Brecht, Bertolt (ed. & trans. Willett, John) (1964). *Brecht on Theatre*, Hill & Wang, New York.

Britton, Andrew *et al.* (1979) *American Nightmare: Essays on the Horror Film*, Festival of Festivals, Toronto, Canada.

Britton, Andrew (1981). Sideshows: Hollywood in Vietnam, *Movie* 27/28.

Brooker, Peter (ed) (1992). *Modernism/Postmodernism*, Longman, London and New York.

Brooks, Peter (1979). *The Melodramatic Imagination: Balzac, Henry James, Melodrama and the Mode of Excess*, Yale University Press, New Haven.

Browne, Nick (1982). *The Rhetoric of Filmic Narration*, UMI Research Press, Ann Arbour, MI.

Browne, Nick (ed.) (1990). *Cahiers du Cinéma Vol 3, 1969–1972: The Politics of Representation*, Harvard University Press, Cambridge, MA, and Routledge, London.

Browne, Nick (ed) (1998). *Refiguring American Film Genres: History and Theory*, University of California Press, Berkeley and London.

Browne, Nick, Pickowicz, Paul, G., Sobchack, Vivian and Yau, Esther (eds) (1994). *New Chinese Cinemas: Forms, Identities, Politics*, Cambridge University Press, Cambridge and New York.

Burch, Noël (trans. Lane, Helen R.) (1973). *Theory of Film Practice*, Praeger New York/Secker & Warburg, London.

Burch, Noël (1990). *Life to Those Shadows*, British Film Institute, London.

Burns, Elizabeth & Tom (eds) (1973). *Sociology of Literature and Drama*, Penguin, Harmondsworth.

Buscombe, Edward (ed) (1988). *The BFI Companion to the Western*. André Deutsch, London and Atheneum, New York.

Buscombe, Edward & Pearson, Roberta (eds) (1998). *Back in the Saddle Again: New Essays on the Western*, British Film Institute, London.

Buscombe, Edward (1970) The Idea of Genre in the American Cinema, *Screen* Vol. 11 No 2, reprinted *in* Grant, Barry Keith (ed) (1995). *Film Genre Reader II*.

Byars, Jackie (ed). *All that Hollywood Allows: Re-Reading Gender in 1950s Melodrama* Routledge, London and University of North Carolina Press, Chapel Hill, NC.

Cahiers du Cinéma, Editors of, (1972) *Collective Text on* Young Mr Lincoln, *Screen* Vol. 13, No 3, reprinted in SCREEN (1977) and Nichols (1976)

Cameron, Ian (ed) (1970). *Second Wave*, Studio Vista, London.

Cameron, Ian (ed) (1972). *Movie Reader*, Studio Vista, London and Praeger, New York.

Cameron, Ian (ed) (1993). *The Movie Book of Film Noir*, Studio Vista, London, [pub. in US as *The Book of Film Noir*, Continuum, New York].

Cameron, Ian & Pye, Douglas (eds) (1996). *The Movie Book of the Western*, Studio Vista, London [pub. in US as *The Book of Westerns*, Continuum, New York].

Carroll, Noël (1990). *The Philosophy of Horror; Or, Paradoxes of the Heart*, Routledge, London & New York.

Caughie, John (ed) (1981). *Theories of Authorship*, Routledge & Kegan Paul, London & Boston.

Caughie, John, with Rockett, Kevin (eds) (1996). *The Companion to British and Irish Cinema*, Cassell, London.

Cavell, Stanley (1981). *Pursuits of Happiness: The Hollywood Comedy of Remarriage*, Harvard University Press, Cambridge, MA.

Cawelti, John (1976). *Adventure, Mystery and Romance: Formula Stories as Art and Popular Culture*, University of Chicago Press, Chicago.

Cawelti, John (1985). *The Six-Gun Mystique* (revised edn), Popular Press, Bowling Green, OH.

Ceplair, Larry & Englund, Steven (1980). *The Inquisition in Hollywood: Politics in the Film Community 1930–1960*, Anchor Press/Doubleday, Garden City, New York.

Cha, Theresa Hak Kyung (ed) (1981). *Apparatus*, Tanam Press, New York.

Chanan, Michael (ed) (1983). *Twenty-Five Years of the New Latin American Cinema*, British Film Institute/Channel Four Television, London.

Chatman, Seymour (1978). *Story and Discourse: Narrative Structure in Fiction and Film*, Cornell University Press, Ithaca.

Chion, Michel (1994). *Audio-Vision: Sound on Screen*, Columbia University Press, New York & Chichester.

Clarens, Carlos (1968). *An Illustrated History of the Horror Film*, Secker & Warburg, London and Capricorn, New York.

Clarens, Carlos (1980). *Crime Movies: An Illustrated History*, Secker & Warburg, London and Norton, New York.

Clover, Carol (1992). *Men, Women, and Chain Saws: Gender in the Modern Horror Film*, Princeton University Press, Princeton, NJ.

Coates, Paul (1991). *The Gorgon's Gaze: German Cinema, Expressionism and the Image of Horror*, Cambridge University Press, Cambridge & New York.

Cohan, Steve & Hark, Ina Rae (eds) (1993). *Screening the Male: Exploring Masculinities in Hollywood Cinema*, Routledge, London & New York.

Cohan, Steve & Hark, Ina Rae (eds) (1997). *The Road Movie Book*, Routledge, London & New York.

Collins, Jim, Radner, Hilary & Preacher Collins, Ava (eds) (1993). *Film Theory Goes to the Movies*, Routledge, New York & London.

Cook, David A. (1996). *A History of Narrative Film* (3rd edn), W.W. Norton, New York and London.

Cook, Pam (1976). Exploitation Films and Feminism *Screen*, Vol. 17, No. 2.

Cook, Pam (ed) (1985). *The Cinema Book*, British Film Institute, London.

Cook, Pam (ed) (1998). *Gainsborough Pictures*, Cassell, London.

Cook, Pam and Bernink, Mieke (eds) (1999). *The Cinema Book* (2nd edn), British Film Institute, London.

Copjec, Joan (ed) (1993). *Shades of Noir*, Verso, London.

Corliss, Richard (1974). *Talking Pictures: Screenwriters in the American Cinema*. Penguin, Baltimore and New York.

Corman, Roger (1990). *How I Made a Hundred Movies in Hollywood and Never Lost a Dime*, Random House, New York.

Corner, John. *The Art of Record: A Critical Introduction to Documentary*, Manchester University Press, Manchester and New York.

Corrigan, Timothy (1994). *New German Film: The Displaced Image*, Indiana University Press, Bloomington and Indianapolis.

Coyne, Michael (1998). *The Crowded Prairie: American National Identity in the Hollywood Western*, I.B. Taurus, London.

Crane, Jonathan L. (1993). *Terror and Everyday Life: Singular Moments in the History of the Horror Film*, Sage, Thousand Oaks, CA.

Creed, Barbara (1993). *The Monstrous Feminine: Film, Feminism, Psychoanalysis*, Routledge, London and New York.

Cripps, Thomas (1978). *Black Film as Genre*, Indiana University Press, Bloomington & London.

Curran, James & Porter, Vincent (eds) (1983). *British Cinema History*, Weidenfeld & Nicholson, London.

Curtis, David (1971). *Experimental Cinema: A Fifty-Year Evolution*, Dell, New York.

Davis, Brian (1973). *The Thriller: The Suspense Film From 1946*, Studio Vista, London.

Day, Gary & Bloom, Clive (eds) (1988). *Perspectives on Pornography: Sexuality in Film and Literature*, St Martin's Press, New York.

De Lauretis, Teresa and Heath, Stephen (eds) (1980). *The Cinematic Apparatus*, St Martin's Press, New York.

Desser, David (1982). *The Samurai Films of Akira Kurosawa*, UMI Research Press, Ann Arbor, MI.

Diawara, Manthia (ed) (1993). *Black American Cinema*, Routledge, London & New York.

Dick, Bernard F. (1985) *The Star-Spangled Screen: The American World War Two Film*, University of Kentucky Press, Lexington.

Dick, Bernard F. (1999). *City of Dreams: The Making and Remaking of Universal Pictures*, University of Kentucky Press, Lexington.

Dika, Vera (1990). *Games of Terror:* Halloween, Friday the 13th, *and the Films of the Stalker Cycle*, Fairleigh Dickinson University Press, Rutherford, NJ.

Di Lauro, Al & Rabkin (1976) Gerald. *Dirty Movies: An Illustrated History of the Stag Film, 1915–1970*, Chelsea House, New York.

Dittmar, Linda & Michaud, Gene (eds) (1990). *From Hanoi to Hollywood: The Vietnam War in American Film*, Rutgers University Press, New Brunswick, NJ.

Doane, Mary Ann (1987). *The Desire to Desire: The Woman's Film of the 1940s*, Indiana University Press, Bloomington and Indianapolis.

Doherty, Thomas (1988). *Teenagers and Teenpics: The Juvenalization of American Movies in the 1950s*, Unwin Hyman, Boston and London.

Donald, James (ed) (1989). *Fantasy and the Cinema*, British Film Institute, London.

Douchet. Jean (1999). *French New Wave*, Distributed Art Publishers, New York.

Durgnat, Raymond (1972). *The Crazy Mirror: Hollywood Comedy and the American Image*, Delta, New York.

Dyer, Richard (ed) (1977). *Gays and Film*, British Film Institute, London.

Dyer, Richard (1998). *Stars* (2nd edn), British Film Institute, London.

Dyer, Richard (1986). *Heavenly Bodies: Film Stars and Society*, Macmillan, London and St Martin's Press, New York.

Dyer, Richard (1990). *Now You See It: Studies on Lesbian and Gay Film*, Routledge, London & New York.

Dyer, Richard (1992). *Only Entertainment*, Routledge, London & New York.

Dyer, Richard (1993). *The Matter of Images: Essays on Representation*, Routledge, London and New York.

Eames, John Douglas (1985). *The Paramount Story*, Octopus, London.

Eaton, Mick (ed) (1979). *Anthropology – Reality – Cinema: The Films of Jean Rouch*, British Film Institute, London.

Eberwein, Robert T. (1984). *The Dream Screen: A Sleep and a Forgetting*, Princeton University Press, Princeton, NJ.

Eberwein, Robert T. (1998) The Erotic Thriller, *Post Script*, Vol. 17, No 3.

Eco, Umberto (1986) Casablanca: Cult Movies and Intertextual Collage, *SubStance* Vol. 47, No 2.

Eisenstein, Sergei M. (ed. and trans. Leyda, Jay) (1947). *The Film Sense*, Harcourt, Brace, New York.

Eisenstein, Sergei M. (ed. and trans. Leyda, Jay) (1949). *Film Form: Essays in Film Theory*, Harcourt, Brace, New York.

Eisenstein, Sergei M. (trans. & ed. Taylor, Richard) (1988). *Selected Works Vol. 1: Writings 1922–1934*, British Film Institute, London and Indiana University Press, Bloomington.

Eisner, Lotte (1969). *The Haunted Screen: Expressionism in the Cinema and the Influence of Max Reinhardt*, Thames & Hudson, London and University of California Press, Los Angeles, CA, USA.

Elley, Derek (1984). *The Epic Film: Myth and History*, Routledge & Kegan Paul, London.

Ellis, Jack C. (1989). *The Documentary Idea: A Critical History of the English-Language Documentary Film and Video*, Prentice-Hall, Englewood Cliffs, NJ.

Elsaesser, Thomas (1973). Tales of Sound and Fury: Observations on the Melodrama. *Monogram* No. 4 [reprinted in Gledhill (1987) Grant (1995) and Nichols (1985)].

Elsaesser, Thomas (1989). *New German Cinema: A History*, Macmillan, Basingstoke, and, Rutgers University Press, Brunswick, NJ.

Elsaesser, Thomas (ed) (1990). *Early Cinema: Space, Frame, Narrative*, British Film Institute, London.

Elsaesser, Thomas (2000). *Weimar Cinema and After: Germany's Historical Imaginary*, Routledge, London & New York.

Erens, Patricia (ed) (1990). *Issues in Feminist Film Criticism* (Bloomington: Indiana University Press, Bloomington.

Evans, Gary (1984). *John Grierson and the National Film Board: The Politics of Wartime Propaganda*, University of Toronto Press, London and Toronto.

Evans, Gary (1991). *In The National Interest: A Chronicle of the National Film Board of Canada 1949–1989*, University of Toronto Press, Toronto.

Evans, Walter (1975). Monster Movies: A Sexual Theory *in* Grant (1984).

Feuer, Jane (1993). *The Hollywood Musical* (2nd edn), British Film Institute, London and Indiana University Press, Bloomington.

Fielding, Raymond (1972). *The American Newsreel 1911–1967*, University of Oklahoma Press, Norman, OK.

Finler, Joel (1988). *The Hollywood Story*, Octopus, London and Crown, New York.

Fiske, John (1989a). *Reading the Popular*, Unwin Hyman, London & Boston.

Fiske, John (1989b). *Understanding Popular Culture*, Unwin Hyman, London & Boston.

Fordin, Hugh (1975). *The World of Entertainment: The Freed Unit at MGM*, Avon, New York.

Fowkes, Katherine A. (1998). *Giving Up the Ghost: Spirits, Ghosts and Angels in Mainstream Comedy Films*, Wayne State University Press, Detroit.

Frank, Sam (1989). *Sex in the Movies*, Citadel, New York.

Franklin, James (1983). *New German Cinema: From Oberhausen to Hamburg*, Twayne, Boston.

Fraser, John (1974). *Violence in the Arts*, Cambridge University Press, Cambridge & London.

Frayling, Christopher (1981). *Spaghetti Westerns*, Routledge & Kegan Paul, London.

French, Philip (1973). *Westerns*, Secker & Warburg, London and Viking, New York.

French, Karl (ed) (1996). *Screen Violence*, Bloomsbury, London.

French, Philip & French, Karl (1999). *Cult Movies*, Pavilion, London.

Friedman, Lester (ed) (1993). *British Cinema and Thatcherism*, University College London Press, London.

Frye, Northrop (1970). *Anatomy of Criticism: Four Essays*, Atheneum, New York.

Furhammar, Lief & Isaksson, Folke (1971). *Politics and Film*, Studio Vista, London and Praeger, New York.

Fusco, Coco (ed) (1987). *Reviewing Histories: Selections from New Latin American Cinema*, Hallwalls Contemporary Arts Center, Buffalo, NY.

Gabler, Neal (1988). *An Empire of their Own: How the Jews Invented Hollywood*, Crown, New York, and W.H. Allen, London.

Gabriel, Teshome H. (1982). *Third Cinema in the Third World: The Aesthetics of Liberation*, UMI Research Press, Ann Arbor, MI.

Gallagher, Tag (1986). *John Ford: The Man and his Films*, University of California Press, Berkeley & London.

Geduld, Harry M. & Gottesman, Ron (1973). *An Illustrated Glossary of Film Terms*, Holt, Rinehart & Winston, New York & London.

Gehring, Wes D. (ed) (1988). *Handbook of American Film Genres*, Greenwood Press, New York.

Gehring, Wes D. (1996) *American Dark Comedy: Beyond Satire*, Greenwood Press, Westport, CT.

Gelder, Ken (1994). *Reading the Vampire*, Routledge, London & New York.

Gever, Martha, Greyson, John & Parmar, Pratibha (eds) (1993). *Queer Looks: Perspectives on Lesbian and Gay Film and Video*, Routledge, New York & London.

Gibson, Pamela Church & Gibson, Roma (eds) (1993). *Dirty Looks: Women, Pornography, Power*, British Film Institute, London.

Gidal, Peter (ed) (1976). *Structural Film Anthology*, British Film Institute, London.

Gledhill, Christine (ed) (1987). *Home is Where the Heart Is: Studies in Melodrama and the Woman's Film*, British Film Institute, London.

Gledhill, Christine (ed) (1991). *Stardom: Industry of Desire*, Routledge, London & New York.

Gledhill, Christine and Williams, Linda (eds) (2000). *Reinventing Film Studies*, Arnold, London and Arnold and Oxford University Press, New York.

Glucksmann, Andre (1971). *Violence on the Screen*, British Film Institute, London.

Gomery, Douglas (1986). *The Studio System*, St Martin's Press, New York and Macmillan, Basingstoke.

Gomery, Douglas (1992). *Shared Pleasures: A History of Movie Presentation in the United States*, British Film Institute, London.

Gorbman, Claudia (1987). *Unheard Melodies: Narrative Film Music*, Indiana University Press, Bloomington, and British Film Institute, London.

Graham, Peter (1968). *The New Wave: Critical Landmarks*, Secker & Warburg, London and Doubleday, Garden City, NY.

Grant, Barry K. (ed) (1984). *Planks of Reason: Essays on the Horror Film*, Scarecrow Press, Metuchen, NJ.

Grant, Barry K. (1986) The Classic Hollywood Musical and the 'Problem' of Rock n' Roll, *Journal of Popular Film & Television* Vol. 13, No 4.

Grant, Barry K. (ed) (1995). *Film Genre Reader II*, University of Texas Press, Austin.

Grant, Barry K. (ed) (1996). *The Dread of Difference: Gender and the Horror Film*, University of Texas Press, Austin.

Grant, Barry K. (1998) Rich and Strange: The Yuppie Horror Film. In Neale & Smith 1998.

Grant, Barry K. (1999) Reason and the Visible *in* Kuhn 1999.

Grant, Barry K. & Sloniowski, Jeannette (eds) (1998). *Documenting the Documentary: Close Readings of Documentary Film and Video*, Wayne State University Press, Detroit.

Grierson, John (Hardy, F. Forsyth ed) (1976). *Grierson on Documentary* (2nd edn), Faber & Faber, London.

Grimes, Teresa (1986). BBS: Auspicious Beginnings, Open Endings, *Movie* No. 31/32, Winter 1986.

Guerrero, Ed (1993). *Framing Blackness*, Temple University Press, Philadelphia.

Gunning, Tom (1986). The Cinema of Attractions: Early Film, Its Spectator and the Avant-Garde *Wide Angle* Vol. 8, No. 3–4. [Reprinted *in* Elsaesser (1990), Stam & Miller (2000)]

Gunning, Tom (1991). *D.W. Griffith and the Origins of American Narrative Film*, University of Illinois Press, Chicago & Urbana, IL.

Halberstam, Judith (1995). *Skin Shows: Horror and the Technology of Monsters*, Duke University Press, Durham, NC.

Halliwell, Leslie (1976). *Mountain of Dreams: The Golden Years at Paramount*, Stonehill, New York.

Hames, Peter (1985). *The Czechoslovak New Wave*, University of California Press, Berkeley & London.

Hammond, Paul (ed) (1991). *The Shadow and its Shadow: Surrealist Writings on the Cinema*, Polygon, London.

Hardy, Phil (1991). *The Western: The Complete Film Reference* (revised edn), Aurum, London.

Hardy, Phil (1984). *Science Fiction: The Complete Film Reference*, Aurum, London.

Hardy, Phil (1986). *The Encyclopaedia of Horror Films*, Harper & Row, New York.

Harvey, Stephen (1987). *Romantic Comedy in Hollywood from Lubitsch to Sturges*, Alfred A. Knopf, New York.

Haskell, Molly (1973). *From Reverence to Rape: The Treatment of Women in the Movies*, Penguin Books, Baltimore, and New English Library, London.

Hayes, R.M. (1989) *3-D Movies: A History and Filmography of Stereoscopic Cinema* McFarland, Jefferson, NC.

Hayward, Susan (1993). *French National Cinema*, Routledge, London & New York.

Hayward, Susan (1996). *Key Concepts in Cinema Studies*, Routledge, London & New York.

Heath, Stephen (1981). *Questions of Cinema*, Macmillan, London and Indiana University Press, Bloomington.

Heider, Karl (1976). *Ethnographic Film*, University of Texas Press, Austin.

Heinlein, Robert H. (1967) *Tomorrow the Stars*, Berkeley, New York.

Henderson, Brian (1971). Towards a Non-Bourgeois Camera Style. In Nichols 1976.

Henderson, Brian (1978). Romantic Comedy Today: Semi-Tough or Impossible, *Film Quarterly* Vol. 31, No. 4. [Reprinted in Grant (1995)].

Higham, Charles (1976). *Warner Brothers*, Charles Scribner's Sons, New York.

Hill, John (1986). *Sex, Class and Realism: British Cinema 1956–63*, British Film Institute, London.

Hill, John (1999). *British Cinema in the 1980s*, Oxford University Press, Oxford.

Hill, John & Church Gibson, Pamela (eds) (1998). *The Oxford Guide to Film Studies*, Oxford University Press, Oxford and New York.

Hill, John & McLoone, Martin (eds) (1996). *Big Picture, Small Screen: The Relations Between Film and Television*, John Libbey/University of Luton Press, Luton.

Hillier, Jim (ed) (1985). *Cahiers du Cinéma (Volume 1): The 1950s: Neo-Realism, Hollywood, New Wave*, Routledge & Kegan Paul, London and Harvard University Press, Cambridge, MA.

Hillier, Jim (ed) (1986). *Cahiers du Cinéma (Volume 2): The 1960s: New Wave, New Cinema, Re-Evaluating Hollywood*, Routledge & Kegan Paul, London and Harvard University Press, Cambridge, MA.

Hillier, Jim (1993). *The New Hollywood* (Studio Vista, London and Continuum, New York.

Hilmes, Michèle (1990). *Hollywood and Broadcasting: From Radio to Cable*, University of Illinois Press, Urbana.

Hirsch, Foster (1978). *The Hollywood Epic*, Tantivy, London and A.S. Barnes, New York.

Hirsch, Foster (1981). *The Dark Side of the Screen: Film Noir*, Tantivy, London and A.S. Barnes, San Diego.

Hirschhorn, Clive (1979). *The Warner Bros. Story*, Octopus, London.

Hoberman, J. and Rosenbaum, J. (1983). *Midnight Movies*, Harper, New York.

Hogan, D.J. (1986) *Dark Romance: Sex and Death in the Horror Film*, McFarland, Jefferson, NC.

Hollows, Joanne & Jancovich, Mark (eds) (1995). *Approaches to Popular Culture*, Manchester University Press, Manchester & New York.

Hollows, Joanne, Hutchings, Peter and Jancovich, Mark (eds) (2000). *The Film Studies Reader*, Arnold, London and Arnold/Oxford University Press, New York.

Holmlund, Christine (1993). Masculinity as Multiple Masquerade: the 'Mature' Stallone and the Stallone Clone *in* Cohan and Hark (1993).

Horton, Andrew (1991). *Comedy/Cinema/Theory*, University of California Press, Berkeley & London.

Horton, Andrew (1994). *Writing the Character-Centered Screenplay*, University of California Press, Berkeley & London.

Horton, Andrew (2000). *Laughing Out Loud: Writing the Comedy-Centered Screenplay*, University of California Press, Berkeley & London.

Humm, Maggie (1997). *Feminism and Film*, Edinburgh University Press, Edinburgh.

Hunter, I.Q. (ed) (1999). *British Science Fiction Cinema*, Routledge, London & New York.

Huss, Roy & Ross, T.J. (eds) (1972). *Focus on the Horror Film*, Prentice-Hall, Englewood Cliffs, NJ.

Hutchings, Peter (1993). *Hammer and Beyond: The British Horror Film*, Manchester University Press, Manchester & New York.

Iaccino, James F. (1998) *Psychological Reflections on Cinematic Terror: Jungian Archetypes in Horror Films*, Praeger, Westport, CT.

Issari, Mohammed Ali & Paul, Doris A. (1979) *What Is Cinéma Vérité?*, Scarecrow Press, Metuchen NJ.

Izod, John (1988). *Hollywood and the Box Office 1895–1986*, Macmillan, Basingstoke & London.

Jackson, Kevin (1998). *The Language of Cinema*, Carcanet, Manchester.

Jacobs, Lewis (ed) (1979). *The Documentary Tradition* (2nd edn), Norton, New York.

James, David A. (1989) *Allegories of Cinema: American Film in the Sixties*, Princeton University Press, Princeton, NJ.

James, David (ed.) (1992). *To Free the Cinema: Jonas Mekas and the New York Underground*. Princeton University Press, Princeton, NJ.

Jameson, Fredric. *Postmodernism, or, The Cultural Logic of Late Capitalism*, Verso, London and Duke University Press, Durham, NC.

Jancovich, Mark (1992). *Horror*, Batsford, London.

Jancovich, Mark (1996). *Rational Fears: American Horror in the 1950s*, Manchester University Press, Manchester & New York.

Jeffords, Susan (1989). *The Remasculinization of America: Gender and the Vietnam War*, Indiana University Press, Bloomington.

Jeffords, Susan (1994). *Hard Bodies: Hollywood Masculinity in the Reagan Era*, Rutgers University Press, New Brunswick, NJ.

Jenkins III, Henry (1993). *What Made Pistachio Buts? Early Sound Comedy and the Vaudeville Aesthetic*, Columbia University Press, New York.

Jewell, Richard B. & Harbin, Vernon (1982). *The RKO Story*, Arlington House, New Rochelle, NY.

Johnson, Randall & Stam, Robert (eds) (1982). *Brazilian Cinema*, Fairleigh Dickinson University Press, Rutherford, NJ.

Johnson, William (ed) (1972). *Focus on the Science Fiction Film*, Prentice-Hall, Englewood Cliffs, NJ.

Johnston, Claire (1973). *Women's Cinema as Counter Cinema*, Society for Education in Film and Television, London.

Jones, D.B. (1981) *Movies and Memoranda: An Interpretive History of the National Film Board of Canada*, Canadian Film Institute, Ottawa.

Kael, Pauline (1965). *I Lost It At The Movies*, Little Brown, Boston and Jonathan Cape, London.

Kalinak, Kathryn (1992). *Settling the Score: Music and the Classical Hollywood Film*, University of Wisconsin Press, Madison.

Kaminsky, S. (1974). *American Film Genres: Approaches to a Critical Theory of Popular Film*, Pflaum, Dayton, OH.

Kane, Kathryn (1982). *Visions of War: The Hollywood Combat Films of World War Two*, UMI Research Press, Ann Arbor, MI.

Kaplan, E. Ann (1983). *Women and Film: Both Sides of the Camera*, Methuen, New York & London.

Kaplan, E. Ann (1987). *Rocking Around the Clock: Music Television, Postmodernism and Consumer Culture*, Routledge, London & New York.

Kaplan, E. Ann (1992). *Motherhood and Representation: The Mother in Popular Culture and Melodrama*, Routledge, London & New York.

Kaplan, E. Ann (ed) (1998). *Women in Film Noir* (revised edn). British Film Institute, London and Indiana University Press, Bloomington.

Karnick, Kristina Brunovska & Jenkins III, Henry (eds) (1994). *Classical Hollywood Comedy*, Routledge, London & New York.

Karpf, Stephen L. (1973) *The Gangster Film: Emergence, Variation and Decay of a Genre 1930–1940*, Arno Press, New York.

Kawin, Bruce (1978). *Mindscreen: Bergman, Godard and First-Person Film*, Princeton University Press, Princeton, NJ.

Kawin, Bruce (1987). *How Movies Work*, Collier Macmillan, London and Macmillan, New York.

Kendall, Elizabeth (1990). *The Runaway Bride: Hollywood Romantic Comedy of the 1930s*, Knopf, New York.

Kerr, Paul (ed) (1986). *The Hollywood Film Industry*, Routledge & Kegan Paul, London & New York.

Kitses, Jim (1969). *Horizons West*, Secker & Warburg, London.

Kitses, Jim & Rickman, Gregg (eds) (1998). *The Western Reader*, Limelight Editions, New York.

Kleber, Pia & Visser, Colin (eds) (1990). *Re-interpreting Brecht: His Influence on Contemporary Drama and Film*, Cambridge University Press, Cambridge.

Knight, Julia (1992). *Women and the New German Cinema*, Verso, London & New York.

Konigsberg, Ira (1997). *The Complete Film Dictionary* (2nd edn), Bloomsbury, London.

Kracauer, Siegfried (1965). *Theory of Film: The Redemption of Physical Reality*, Oxford University Press, New York.

Kracauer, Siegfried (1947). *From Caligari to Hitler: A Psychological History of the German Film*, Princeton University Press, Princeton, NJ.

Kreimeier, Klaus (1999). *The UFA Story: A History of Germany's Greatest Film Company, 1918–1945*, University of California Press, Berkeley, CA, and London.

Krutnik, Frank (1991). *In a Lonely Street: Film Noir, Genre and Masculinity*, Routledge, London & New York.

Kuenzli, Rudolf E. (ed) (1987). *Dada and Surrealist Film*, Willis, Locker & Owens, New York.

Kuhn, Annette (1994). *Women's Pictures: Feminism and Cinema* (revised edn), Routledge & Kegan Paul, London.

Kuhn, Annette (ed) (1990). *Alien Zone: Cultural Theory and Contemporary Science Fiction Cinema*, Verso, London & New York.

Kuhn, Annette (ed) (1999). *Alien Zone II: The Spaces of Science Fiction Cinema*, Verso, London & New York.

Landy, Marcia (1991a). *British Genres: Cinema and Society 1930–1960*, Princeton University Press, Princeton, NJ.

Landy, Marcia (ed) (1991b). *Imitations of Life*, Wayne State University Press, Detroit.

Lang, Robert (1989). *American Film Melodrama: Griffith, Vidor, Minnelli*, Princeton University Press, Princeton, NJ.

Lapsley, Robert and Westlake, Michael. *Film Theory: An Introduction*, Manchester University Press, Manchester.

Lechte, John (1994). *Fifty Key Contemporary Thinkers*, Routledge, London & New York.

Leff, Leonard J. & Simmons, Jerold L. (1990) *The Dame in the Kimono: Censorship and the Production Code from the 1920s to the 1960s*, Grove Weidenfeld, New York and Weidenfeld & Nicholson, London.

LeGrice, Malcolm (1977). *Abstract Film and Beyond*, MIT Press, Cambridge, Mass. & London.

Lehman, Peter (1993). *Running Scared: Masculinity and the Representation of the Male Body*, Temple University Press, Philadelphia.

Lenihan, John H. (1980) *Showdown: Confronting Modern America in Film*, University of Chicago Press, Chicago.

Lesage, Julia (1984). Feminist Documentary: Aesthetics and Politics. In Waugh 1984.

Lewis, Jon (1992). *The Road to Romance and Ruin: Teen Films and Youth Culture*, Routledge, London & New York.

Lewis, Jon (ed) (1998). *The New American Cinema*, Duke University Press, Durham, NC & London.

Leyda, Jay (1960). *Kino: A History of the Russian and Soviet Film*, George Allen & Unwin, London.

Litwak, Mark (1986). *Reel Power: The Struggle for Influence and Success in the New Hollywood*, William Morrow, New York.

Lovell, Alan & Hillier, Jim (1972). *Studies in Documentary*, London: Secker & Warburg, London and Viking, New York.

Lucanio, Patrick (1987). *Them or Us: Archetypal Interpretations of Fifties Alien Invasion Films*, Indiana University Press, Bloomington & Indianapolis.

Lukács, Georg (1970). *Writer and Critic*, Merlin Press, London.

Lyons, Charles (1999). *The New Censors*, Temple University Press, Philadelphia.

McArthur, Colin (1972). *Underworld USA*, Secker & Warburg, London.

McArthur, Colin (1976). Days of Hope, *Screen* Vol. 16, No. 4.

MacCabe, Colin (1976). Days of Hope: A Response to Colin McArthur, *Screen* Vol. 17, No 1.

MacCann, Richard Dyer (ed) (1966). *Film: A Montage of Theories*, Dutton, New York.

McCarthy, Todd & Flynn, Charles (eds) (1975). *Kings of the Bs: Working Within the Hollywood System*, Dutton, New York.

McCarty, John (1984). *Splatter Movies: Breaking the Last Taboo of the Screen*, St. Martin's Press, New York.

McCarty, John (1992). *Thrillers: Seven Decades of Classic Film Suspense*, Citadel Press, New York.

McCarty, John (1993). *Hollywood's Gangland: The Movies' Love Affair with the Mob*, St. Martin's Press, New York.

Macdonald, Kevin and Cousins, Mark (eds) (1996). *Imagining Reality: The Faber Book of Documentary*, Faber, London & Boston.

MacDonald, Scott (1993). *Avant-Garde Film: Motion Studies*, Cambridge University Press, Cambridge.

Maltby, Richard (with Craven, Ian) (1995). *Hollywood Cinema: An Introduction*, Blackwell, Oxford & Cambridge, MA.

Mamber, Stephen (1974). *Cinema Verite in America: Studies in Uncontrolled Documentary*, MIT Press, Cambridge, MA and London.

Marcorelles, Louis (1973). *Living Cinema: New Directions in Film-Making*, George Allen & Unwin, London.

Marcus, Millicent (1986). *Italian Film in the Light of Neorealism*, Princeton University Press, Princeton, NJ.

Martin, Richard (1997). *Mean Streets and Raging Bulls: The Legacy of Film Noir in Contemporary American Cinema*, Scarecrow Press, Lanham, MD and London.

Mast, Gerald (1979). *The Comic Mind: Comedy and the Movies* (2nd edn), University of Chicago Press, Chicago, IL.

Mast, Gerald (ed) (1982). *The Movies in Our Midst: Documents in the Cultural History of Film In America*, Chicago University Press, Chicago, IL and London.

Mast, Gerald and Cohen, Marshall (eds) (1985). *Film Theory and Criticism: Introductory Readings*, (3rd edn), Oxford University Press, Oxford and New York.

Mathews, Tom Dewe (1997). *Censored!: A History of British Film Censorship*, Chatto and Windus, London.

Mayne, Judith (1993). *Cinema and Spectatorship*, Routledge, London and New York.

Mayne, Judith (1995). *Directed by Dorothy Arzner*, Indiana University Press, Bloomington and Indianapolis.

Maxfield, James F. (1996) *The Fatal Woman: Sources of Male Anxiety in American Film Noir, 1941–1991*, Fairleigh Dickinson University Press, Madison and Teaneck, NJ, USA and Associated University Presses, London.

Mendik, Xavier and Harper, Graeme (eds) (2000). *Unruly Pleasures: the Cult Film and its Critics*, FAB Press, Guildford.

Merritt, Greg (2000). *A History of American Independent Film*, Thunder's Mouth Press, New York.

Metz, Christian (trans. Taylor, Michael) (1974). *Film Language: A Semiotics of the Cinema*, Oxford University Press, Oxford and New York.

Metz, Christian (1975). The Imaginary Signifier, *Screen*, Vol. 16, No. 3.

Metz, Christian (1975). *Psychoanalysis and Cinema: The Imaginary Signifier*, Macmillan, London and New York.

Meyers, Richard (1983). *For One Week Only: The World of Exploitation Films*, New Century, Piscataway, NJ.

Miller, Mark Crispin (ed) (1990). *Seeing Through Movies*, Pantheon, New York.

Miller, Toby & Stam, Robert (1999). *A Companion to Film Theory*, Blackwell, Malden, MA, and Oxford.

Mintz, Marilyn D. (1983) *Martial Arts Films*, Yoseloff, London and A.S. Barnes, New York.

Mitman, Gregg (2000). *Reel Nature: America's Romance with Wildlife on Film*, Harvard University Press, Cambridge, MA.

Modleski, Tania (1988). *The Women Who Knew Too Much: Hitchcock and Feminist Film Theory*, Methuen, London and New York.

Monaco, James (1976). *The New Wave: Truffaut, Godard, Chabrol, Rohmer, Rivette*, Oxford University Press, New York.

Mordden, Ethan (1988). *The Hollywood Studios: House Style in the Golden Age of the Movies*, Knopf, New York.

Mulvey, Laura (1989). Visual Pleasure and Narrative Cinema, *Screen*, Vol. 16, No. 2 [reprinted *in* Mulvey (1989)].

Mulvey, Laura (1989). *Visual and Other Pleasures*, Macmillan, London and Indiana University Press, Bloomington.

Murphy, Robert (1986). *Riff-Raff: British Cinema and the Underworld*. In Barr 1986.

Murphy, Robert (1992). *Sixties British Cinema*, British Film Institute, London.

Musser, Charles (1990). *The Emergence of Cinema: The American Screen to 1907*: The History of American Cinema Vol. 1, Charles Scribner's Sons, New York and University of California Press, London.

Musser, Charles (1991). *Before the Nickelodeon: Edwin S. Porter and the Edison Manufacturing Company*, University of California Press, Berkeley, CA, and London.

Nachbar, Jack (ed) (1974). *Focus on the Western*, Prentice-Hall, Englewood Cliffs, NJ.

Naremore, James (1988). *Acting in the Cinema*, University of California Press, Berkeley, Los Angeles and London.

Naremore, James (1998). *More than Night: Film Noir in its Contexts*, University of California Press, Berkeley & London.

Neale, Steve (1979). The Same Old Story: Stereotypes and Difference, *Screen Education*, Nos. 32–33.

Neale, Steve (1980). *Genre*, British Film Institute, London.

Neale, Steve (1981). Art Cinema as Institution, *Screen* Vol.22, No. 1.

Neale, Steve (1985). *Cinema and Technology: Image, Sound, Colour*, Macmillan, London and Basingstoke.

Neale, Steve (1995). Questions of Genre, *Screen* Vol. 31, No. 1. [Reprinted *in* Grant (1995)].

Neale, Steve (2000). *Genre and Hollywood*, Routledge, London & New York.

Neale, Steve and Krutnik, Frank (eds) (1990). *Popular Film and Television Comedy*, Routledge, London and New York.

Neale, Steve and Smith, Murray (eds) (1998). *Contemporary Hollywood Cinema*, Routledge, London & New York.

Nelmes, Jill (ed) (1999). *An Introduction to Film Studies* (2nd edn), Routledge, London and New York.

Neve, Brian (1992). *Film and Politics in America: A Social Tradition*, Routledge, London.

Newman, Kim (1988). *Nightmare Cinema: A Critical Guide to Contemporary Horror Films*. Harmony Books, New York.

Nichols, Bill (ed) (1976). *Movies and Methods: Volume I*, University of California Press, Berkeley, CA, and London.

Nichols, Bill (ed) (1985). *Movies and Methods: Volume II*, University of California Press, Berkeley, CA, and London.

Nichols, Bill (1991). *Representing Reality: Issues and Concepts in Documentary*, Indiana University Press, Bloomington.

Nowell-Smith, Geoffrey (1973). *Luchino Visconti* (revised edn), Secker & Warburg, London and Viking, New York.

Nowell-Smith, Geoffrey (ed) (1996). *The Oxford History of World Cinema*, Oxford University Press, Oxford and New York.

Nottridge, Rhoda (1992). *Adventure Films*, Crestwood House, New York.

Overby, David (ed) (1978). *Springtime in Italy: A Reader on Neo-Realism*, Talisman, London and Archon Books, Hamden, CT.

Palmer, Jerry (1978). *Thrillers: Genesis and Structure of a Popular Genre*, Edward Arnold, London and St. Martin's Press, New York.

Palmer, Jerry (1988). *The Logic of the Absurd: On Film and Television Comedy*, British Film Institute, London and University of Illinois Press, Chicago, IL.

Palmer, R. Barton (1994). *Hollywood's Dark Cinema: The American Film Noir*, Twayne, New York.

Palmer, R. Barton (1996). *Perspectives on Film Noir*, G.K. Hall, New York.

Paul, William (1994). *Laughing Screaming: Modern Horror and Comedy*, Columbia University Press, New York.

Peary, Danny. *Cult Movies* (1981), Delta, New York and Vermilion, London (1982).

Peary, Danny (1983). *Cult Movies 2*, Delta, New York/Vermilion, London.

Peary, Danny (1989). *Cult Movies 3*, Sidgwick & Jackson, London.

Penley, Constance (1989). *The Future of an Illusion: Film, Feminism and Psychoanalysis*, Routledge, London & New York.

Penley, Constance, Lyon, Elisabeth and Bergstrom, Janet (eds) (1991). *Close Encounters: Film, Feminism and Science Fiction*, University of Minnesota Press, MN.

Peterson, James (1994). *Dreams of Chaos, Visions of Order: Understanding the American Avant-Garde*, Wayne State University Press, Detroit.

Petric, Vlada (ed) (1981). *Film and Dream: An Approach to Bergman*, Redgrave Publishing Co., South Salem, NY.

Petric, Vlada (1987). *Constructivism in Film: The Man with the Movie Camera*, Cambridge University Press, Cambridge, and New York.

Petro, Patrice (1989). *Joyless Streets: Women and Melodramatic Representation in Weimar Germany*, Princeton University Press, Princeton, NJ.

Phillips, Klaus (ed) (1984). *New German Filmmakers*, Ungar, New York.

Pines, Jim (1975). *Blacks in Films*, Studio Vista, London.

Pines, Jim & Willemen, Paul (eds) (1989). *Questions of Third Cinema*, British Film Institute, London.

Pirie, David (1973). *A Heritage of Horror: The English Gothic Cinema 1946–1972*, Gordon Fraser, London and Avon, New York.

Place, J.A. and L.S. Peterson (1974). Some Visual Motifs of Film Noir, *Film Comment* Vol. 10, No. 1 [reprinted *in* Nichols (1976) and Silver & Ursini (1996)].

Prawer, S.S. (1980) *Caligari's Children: The Film as a Tale of Terror*, Oxford University Press, Oxford and New York.

Prendergast, Roy M. (1977), *A Neglected Art: A Critical Study of Music in Films*, New York University Press, New York.

Prince, Stephen (1998). *Savage Cinema: Sam Peckinpah and the Rise of Ultraviolent Movies*, University of Texas Press, Austin.

Pudovkin, V.I. (1970) *Film Technique and Film Acting*, Grove Press, New York, [orig. pub. London: Victor Gollancz, 1929].

Pye, Michael and Linda Myles (1979). *The Movie Brats: How the Film Generation Took Over Hollywood*, Faber, London and Holt, Rinehart & Winston, New York.

Rees, A.L. (1999) *A History of Experimental Film and Video*, British Film Institute, London.

Reid, Mark A. (1993) *Redefining Black Film*, University of California Press, Berkeley, Los Angeles & Oxford.

Renan, Sheldon (1967). *An Introduction to the American Underground Film* (New York: Dutton, New York) [pub. in UK (1968) as *The Underground Film: An Introduction to its Development*, Studio Vista, London].

Renov, Michael (ed) (1993). *Theorizing Documentary*, Routledge, New York.

Richards, Jeffrey (1977). *Swordsmen of the Screen*, Routledge & Kegan Paul, London.

Richie, Donald (1971). *Japanese Cinema*, Doubleday, Garden City, NY.

Robertson, James C. (1989) *The Hidden Cinema: British Film Censorship in Action 1913–1975*, Routledge, London.

Robinson, David (1996). *From Peepshow to Palace: The Birth of American Film*, Columbia University Press, New York & Chichester.

Rohdie, Sam (1992). *Rocco and his Brothers*, British Film Institute, London.

Roddick, Nick (1983). *A New Deal in Entertainment: Warner Brothers in the 1930s*, British Film Institute, London.

Rosen, Phil (ed) (1986). *Narrative, Apparatus, Ideology*, Columbia University Press, New York.

Rosenthal, Alan (ed) (1999). *Why Docudrama?: Fact-Fiction on Film and TV*, Southern Illinois University Press, Carbondale & Edwardsville.

Rosow, Eugene (1978). *Born to Lose*, Oxford University Press, London & New York.

Roud, Richard (ed). (1980), *Cinema: A Critical Dictionary*, Secker & Warburg, London.

Roud, Richard (1983). *A Passion for Films: Henri Langlois and the Cinémathèque Française*, Secker & Warburg, London.

Rubin, Martin (1999). *Thrillers*, Cambridge University Press, Cambridge & New York.

Russo, Vito (1987). *The Celluloid Closet: Homosexuality in The Movies*, Harper & Row, New York.

Ryall, Tom (1993). *Blackmail*, British Film Institute, London.

Ryan, Michael & Kellner, Doug (1988). *Camera Politica: The Politics and Ideology of Contemporary Hollywood Film*, Indiana University Press, Bloomington.

Salt, Barry (1993). *Film Style and Technology: History and Analysis* (2nd edn), Starword, London.

Sandford, John (1980). *The New German Cinema*, Eyre Methuen, London and Da Capo, New York.

Sarris, Andrew (1968). *The American Cinema: Directors and Directions, 1929–1968*, Dutton, New York.

Sargeant, Jack & Watson, Stephanie (ed) (1999). *Lost Highways: An Illustrated History of Road Movies*, Creation Books, London.

Schaefer, Eric (1999). *Bold! Daring! Shocking! True!: A History of Exploitation Films, 1919–1959*, Duke University Press, Durham and London.

Schatz, Thomas (1988). *The Genius of the System: Hollywood Filmmaking in the Studio Era*, Pantheon, New York.

Schatz, Thomas (1981). *Hollywood Genres: Formulas, Filmmaking, and the Studio System*, Random House, New York.

Schelde, Pere (1993). *Androids, Humanoids, and Other Science Fiction Monsters: Science and Soul in Science Fiction Films*, New York University Press, New York.

Screen (1977). *Screen Reader 1*, Society for Education in Film and Television, London.

Seidman, Steve (1994). *Comedian Comedy: A Tradition in Hollywood Film*, G.K. Hall, Boston.

Selden, Ramesh (1987). *A Reader's Guide to Contemporary Literary Theory*, Harvester, Brighton.

Sennett, Ted (1985). *Lunatics and Lovers: The Golden Age of Hollywood Comedy*, Limelight, New York.

Shadoian, Jack (1977). *Dreams and Dead Ends: The American Gangster/Crime Film*, MIT Press, Cambridge, MA.

Sharrett, Christopher (ed) (1999). *Mythologies of Violence in Postmodern Media*, Wayne State University Press, Detroit.

Shipman, David (1985). *Caught in the Act: Sex and Eroticism in the Movies*, Hamish Hamilton, North Pomfret, VT.

Shohat, Ella & Stam, Robert (1994). *Unthinking Eurocentrism: Multiculturalism and the Media*, Routledge, London & New York.

Shumway, David R. (1991). Screwball Comedy: Constructing Romance, Mystifying Marriage. In Grant (1995).

Siegel, Joel E. (1973) *Val Lewton: The Reality of Terror*, Secker & Warburg, London and Viking, New York.

Siegel, Scott & Siegel, Barbara (1994). *American Film Comedy: From Abbott and Costello to Jerry Zucker*, Prentice-Hall, New York.

Sikov, Ed (1989). *Screwball: Hollywood's Madcap Romantic Comedies*, Crown, New York.

Sikov, Ed (1995) *Laughing Hysterically: American Screen Comedy of the 1950s*, Columbia University Press, New York.

Silver, Alain (1983). *The Samurai Film*, Overlook Press, Woodstock, NY.

Silver, Alain & Ursini, James (eds) (1996). *Film Noir Reader*, Limelight, New York.

Sitney, P. Adams (ed) (1971). *Film Culture*, Secker & Warburg, London [orig. pub. as *Film Culture Reader*, Praeger, 1970, New York].

Sitney, P. Adams (1979). *Visionary Film: The American Avant-Garde 1943–1978* (2nd edn), Oxford University Press, New York.

Sitney, P. Adams (1995). *Vital Crises in Italian Cinema: Iconography, Stylistics, Politics*, University of Texas Press, Austin.

Skal, Donald J. (1990). *The Monster Show: A Cultural History of Horror*, Norton, New York.

Slotkin, Richard (1990). The Continuity of Forms: Myth and Genre in Warner Brothers' The Charge of the Light Brigade *Representations*, No. 29.

Slotkin, Richard (1992). *Gunfighter Nation: The Myth of the Frontier in Twentieth-Century America*, Atheneum, New York.

Slusser, George & Rabkin, Eric S. (eds) (1985). *Shadows of the Magic Lamp: Fantasy and Science Fiction in Film*, Southern Illinois University Press, Carbondale.

Smith, Henry Nash (1950). *Virgin Land: The American West as Symbol and Myth*, Vintage, New York.

Smith, Julian (1975). *Looking Away: Hollywood and Vietnam*, Charles Scribner's Sons, New York.

Smith, Valerie (ed) (1997). *Representations of Blackness*, Athlone Press, London.

Sobchack, Vivian (1988). *Screening Space: The American Science Fiction Film*, 2nd edn. Ungar, New York.

Sobchack, Vivian (1995). 'Surge and Splendor': A Phenomenology of the Hollywood Historical Epic. In Grant 1995.

Sontag, Susan (1969). *Styles of Radical Will*, Delta, New York.

Stacey, Jackie (1994). *Star Gazing: Hollywood Cinema and Female Spectatorship*, Routledge, London and New York.

Staehling, Richard (1975). *From Rock Around the Clock to The Trip: The Truth About Teen Movies*. In McCarthy & Flynn 1975.

Staiger, Janet (1997). Hybrid or Inbred: The Purity Hypothesis and Hollywood Genre Theory, *Film Criticism*, Vol. 22, No. 1.

Stam, Robert (1989). *Subversive Pleasures: Bakhtin, Cultural Criticism, and Film*, The Johns Hopkins University Press, Baltimore & London.

Stam, Robert (2000). *Film Theory: An Introduction*, Blackwell, Malden, MA & Oxford.

Stam, Robert & Miller, Toby (eds) (2000). *Film and Theory: An Anthology*, Blackwell, Malden, MA & Oxford.

Strinati, Dominic (1995). *An Introduction to Theories of Popular Culture*, Routledge, London & New York.

Suid, Lawrence (1978). *Guts & Glory: Great American War Movies*, Addison-Wesley, Reading, MA.

Swann, Paul (1989). *The British Documentary Film Movement, 1926–1946* Cambridge University Press, Cambridge & New York.

Sypher, W. (ed) (1956). *Comedy*, Anchor Doubleday, Garden City, NY.

Tasker, Yvonne (1993). *Spectacular Bodies: Gender, Genre and the Action Cinema*, Routledge, London & New York.

Taves, Brian (1993). *The Romance of Adventure: The Genre of Historical Adventure Movies*, University Press of Mississippi, Jackson.

Telotte, J.P. (1985) *Dreams of Darkness: Fantasy and the Films of Val Lewton*, University of Illinois Press, Urbana.

Telotte, J.P. (1989) *Voices in the Dark: The Narrative Patterns of Film Noir*, University of Illinois Press, Urbana.

Telotte, J.P. (ed) (1991). *Beyond All Reason: The Cult Film Experience*, Austin: University of Texas Press, Austin.

Telotte, J.P. (1995) *Replications: A Robotic History of the Science Fiction Film*, University of Illinois Press, Urbana.

Thomas, Rosie (1985). Indian Cinema: Pleasures and Popularity, *Screen* Vol. 26, No. 3–4.

Thompson, Kristin (1986). *The Concept of Cinematic Excess.* In Rosen, 1986.

Thompson, Kristin & Bordwell, David (1994). *Film History: An Introduction,* McGraw-Hill, New York & London.

Thomson, David (1993). *Showman: The Life of David O. Selznick,* Knopf, New York and Andre Deutsch, London.

Thornham, Sue (1997). *Passionate Detachments: An Introduction to Feminist Film Theory,* Arnold, London.

Todorov, Tzvetan (trans. Howard, R.) (1975). *The Fantastic: A Structural Approach to a Literary Genre,* Cornell University Press, Ithaca.

Tompkins, Jane (1992). *West of Everything: The Inner Life of the Western* (Oxford University Press, Oxford & New York.

Toulet, Emmanuelle (1995). *Cinema is 100 Years Old,* Thames & Hudson, London.

Truffaut, François (1967). *Hitchcock,* Simon and Schuster, New York and Secker & Warburg, London.

Tudor, Andrew (1989). *Monsters and Mad Scientists,* Basil Blackwell, Oxford.

Tudor, Andrew (1974). *Theories of Film,* Secker & Warburg, London and Viking, New York.

Turim, Maureen (1989). *Flashbacks in Film: Memory and History,* Routledge, New York and London.

Turner, Graeme (1999). *Film as Social Practice* (3rd edn), Routledge, London.

Tuska, Jon (1978). *The Detective in Hollywood,* Doubleday, New York.

Tuska, Jon (1988). *In Manors and Alleys: A Casebook on the American Detective Film* Greenwood Press, New York.

Twitchell, James B. (1985) *Dreadful Pleasures: An Anatomy of Modern Horror,* Oxford University Press, Oxford & New York.

Tyler, Parker (1970). *Underground Film: A Critical History,* Grove Press, New York.

Ursini, James & Silver, Alain (1993). *The Vampire Film: From Nosferatu to Bram Stoker's Dracula,* Limelight, New York.

Vardac, Nicholas (1949). *Stage to Screen: Theatrical Method from Garrick to Griffith,* Harvard University Press, Cambridge, Mass.

Vertov, Dziga (ed. Michelson, Annette) (1984). *Kino-Eye: The Writings of Dziga Vertov,* University of California Press, Berkeley, CA, and London.

Vincendeau, Ginette (1996). *The Companion to French Cinema,* Cassell/British Film Institute, London.

Waller, Gregory A. (1986). *The Living and the Undead: From Stoker's Dracula to Romero's Dawn of the Dead,* University of Illinois Press, Urbana.

Waller, Gregory A. (ed) (1987). *American Horrors: Essays on the Modern American Horror Film,* University of Illinois Press, Urbana.

Warren, Charles (ed) (1996). *Beyond Document: Essays on Non-Fiction Film,* Wesleyan University Press and University Press of New England, Hanover & London.

Warshow, Robert (1970). *The Immediate Experience,* Atheneum, New York.

Wasko, Janet (1994). *Hollywood in the Information Age,* Polity Press, Cambridge.

Watson, James & Hill, Anne (2000). *A Dictionary of Media and Communication Studies* (5th edn). Arnold, London and New York.

Waugh, Thomas (ed) (1984). *Show Us Life: Toward a History and Aesthetics of the Political Documentary,* Scarecrow Press, Metuchen, NJ, and London.

Waugh, Thomas (1996). *Hard to Imagine: Gay Male Eroticism in Photography and Film from their Beginnings to Stonewall*, Columbia University Press, New York.

Weales, Gerald (1985). *Canned Goods as Caviar: American Film Comedy of the 1930s*, University of Chicago Press, Chicago.

Weis, Elizabeth & Belton, John (eds) (1985). *Film Sound: Theory and Practice*, Columbia University Press, New York.

Welch, David (1983). *Propaganda and the German Cinema 1933–1945*, Clarendon Press, Oxford.

Williams, Alan (1984). Is a Radical Genre Criticism Possible? *Quarterly Review of Film Studies*, Vol. 9, No. 2.

Williams, Alan (1992). *Republic of Images: A History of French Film-Making*, Harvard University Press, Cambridge, Mass. & London.

Williams, Christopher (ed) (1980). *Realism in the Cinema*, Routledge & Kegan Paul, London & Henley.

Williams, Linda (1973). When the Woman Looks *in* Grant (1996).

Williams, Linda (1989). *Hard Core: Power, Pleasure, and the 'Frenzy of the Visible'*, University of California Press, Berkeley and London.

Williams, Linda (1993). Erotic Thrillers and Rude Women, *Sight & Sound* Vol. 3, No. 7.

Williams, Linda Ruth (1993). *Mirrors Without Memories: Truth, History and* The Thin Blue Line, (1993) *in* Grant and Sloniowski (1998).

Williams, Mark (1982). *Road Movies*, Proteus, New York.

Williams, Raymond (1983). *Keywords: A Vocabulary of Culture and Society* (2nd edn), Fontana, London.

Williams, Tony (1999). *Hearths of Darkness: The Family and American Horror Films*, Fairleigh Dickinson University Press, Rutherford, NJ.

Willis, Sharon (1998). *High Contrast: Race and Gender in Contemporary Hollywood Film*, Duke University Press, Durham, NC.

Wilton, Tamsin (ed) (1995). *Immortal, Invisible: Lesbians and the Moving Image*, Routledge, London & New York.

Winokur, Mark (1996). *American Laughter: Immigrants, Ethnicity and 1930s Hollywood Film Comedy*, St. Martin's Press, New York.

Winston, Brian (1995). *Claiming the Real: The Documentary Film Revisited*, British Film Institute, London.

Winston, Brian (1996). *Technologies of Seeing*, British Film Institute, London.

Wollen, Peter (1982). *Readings and Writings: Semiotic Counter-Strategies*, Verso, London.

Wollen, Peter (1998). *Signs and Meaning in the Cinema* (expanded edn), British Film Institute, London.

Wood, Robin (1965). *Hitchcock's Films Revisited*, Columbia University Press, New York.

Wood, Robin (1979). An Introduction to the American Horror Film. In Britton (1979), Grant (1984), Nichols (1985).

Wood, Robin (1986). *Hollywood from Vietnam to Reagan*, Columbia University Press, New York & Guildford.

Wright, Will. *Six Guns and Society: A structural Study of the Western* (University of California Press, Berkeley, 1975).

Wyatt, Justin (1994). *High Concept: Movies and Marketing in Hollywood*, University of Texas Press, Austin.

Yaquinto, Martha (1998). *Pump 'em Full of Lead: A Look at Gangsters on Film*, Twayne, New York.

Youngblood, Gene (1970). *Expanded Cinema*, Studio Vista, London.

Zavattini, Cesare (1953). Some Ideas on the Cinema, *Sight & Sound*, October 1953. [reprinted in MacCann (1996), and cf. Zavattini in Overbey (1978)].